*I dedicate this book to long-suffering Tullia, as well as to Thomas (even though he does not appear to have been suffering).*

Those who are convinced that they can impart form to the lava will be drawn in and have fewer chances to save themselves from the burning stream than the others.

Sonja Margolina, *Die Fesseln der Vergangenheit* [The Chains of the Past] (Frankfurt am Main: Fischer Verlag, 1993), p. 127: "Auch jemand, der glaubt, der Lava eine Form geben zu koennen, wird da hineigezogen and hat weinger Chancen, aus dem brennenden Fluss gerettet zu werden als die uebrigen."

# How Russia Is Not Ruled
*Reflections on Russian Political Development*

The state remains as important to Russia's prospects as ever. This is so not only because, as in any society, an effectively functioning state administration is necessary for a complex economy and legal system to function properly, but because in Russian circumstances the impact of factors of economic geography tends to make costs of production a multiple of what they are throughout the world. These mutually reinforcing factors include the extreme severity of the climate, the immense distances to be covered, the dislocation between (European) population centers and (Siberian) natural resource centers, and the inevitable predominance of relatively costly land transportation over seaborne transportation. As a result, it is questionable whether Russia can exist as a world civilization under predominantly liberal economic circumstances: In a unified liberal global capital market, large-scale private direct capital investment will not be directed to massive, outdoor infrastructure projects typical of state investment in the Soviet period.

Allen C. Lynch is Director of the Center for Russian and East European Studies and Hugh S. and Winifred B. Cumming Memorial Professor of International Affairs at the University of Virginia. He is the author of numerous books, including *The Soviet Study of International Relations* (Cambridge University Press, 1987), which won the 1988 Marshall D. Shulman Award of the American Association for the Advancement of Slavic Studies, and *The Cold War Is Over – Again* (1992). He is also the author of numerous articles on Russian and Slavic studies.

# How Russia Is Not Ruled

*Reflections on Russian Political Development*

ALLEN C. LYNCH

*University of Virginia*

CAMBRIDGE
UNIVERSITY PRESS

PUBLISHED BY THE PRESS SYNDICATE OF THE UNIVERSITY OF CAMBRIDGE
The Pitt Building, Trumpington Street, Cambridge, United Kingdom

CAMBRIDGE UNIVERSITY PRESS
The Edinburgh Building, Cambridge CB2 2RU, UK
40 West 20th Street, New York, NY 10011-4211, USA
477 Williamstown Road, Port Melbourne, VIC 3207, Australia
Ruiz de Alarcón 13, 28014 Madrid, Spain
Dock House, The Waterfront, Cape Town 8001, South Africa

http://www.cambridge.org

First published 2005

Printed in the United States of America

*Typeface* Sabon 10/13 pt.      *System* LATEX 2$_\varepsilon$   [TB]

*A catalog record for this book is available from the British Library.*

*Library of Congress Cataloging in Publication Data*
Lynch, Allen, 1955–
   How Russia is not ruled : reflections on Russian political development/
Allen C. Lynch.
      p.   cm.
   Includes bibliographical references and index.
   ISBN 0-521-84060-0 (hardback : alk. paper) –
ISBN 0-521-54992-2 (pbk. : alk. paper)
      1. Russia (Federation) – Politics and government – 1991–   2. Russia
(Federation) – Social conditions – 1991–   3. Post-communism – Russia (Federation)
I. Title.
JN6695.L95   2005
320.947–dc22        2004019941

ISBN 0 521 84060 0 hardback
ISBN 0 521 54992 2 paperback

# Contents

# Acknowledgments

I acknowledge the following for their kind assistance in helping this book see the light of day: Melvyn Leffler, then Dean of the College of Arts and Sciences of the University of Virginia, for a Sesquicentennial grant that provided leave for writing the first draft in 2001; Karl Kaiser, then Director of the Research Institute of the German Foreign Policy Association, Berlin, as well as his then deputy, Joachim Krause, for commodious and stimulating research and writing facilities in 2001; my Virginia colleague Gordon Stewart, for helping with the teaching and housing arrangements at the Free University of Berlin; Elizabeth and Robert Valkenier, my Virginia Law School colleague Paul B. Stephan III, Hugh Ragsdale, and two anonymous reviewers for Cambridge University Press for their detailed and critical reading of the entire manuscript in draft form; my Virginia colleague Brantly Womack, who made possible a trip to China for the presentation of the findings to Chinese colleagues, as well as Professor Feng Shao-Lei, Director of the Institute for Russian Studies of East China Normal University, Shanghai, for gracious hospitality and collegiality in December 2003; Eugene B. Rumer of the National Defense University and Celeste Wallander of the Center for Strategic and International Studies, for providing the auspices for the presentation of the conclusion in draft form in April 2003; Vladimir Mau, rector of the Russian Institute on the National Economy, as well as my Virginia colleagues Jeffrey Legro and Herman Schwartz for having read the paper on which Chapter 6 is based; the editors of *Europe-Asia Studies* (Glasgow) and *Critiques Internationales* (Paris), which published Chapter 6 in an earlier incarnation; Angelika Volle, editor of *Internationale Politik* (Berlin), for graciously allowing me to try out two parts of the argument in her journal; Hal Saunders of the

Kettering Foundation, for having made possible a series of trips to Russia in connection with Dartmouth Conference meetings; Emmanuelle and Gustav Weber for their friendship, collegiality, and access to the incomparable private Weber collection in Harlaching, Munich; Rachel Vanderhill, my good research assistant; and finally to Lewis Bateman, the very able editor for the social sciences at Cambridge University Press.

Thanks also to Freedom House for permission to use material in Chapter 5 published in *Nations in Transit* (1998) as well as to *Europe-Asia Studies* for permission to use material in Chapter 6 published in the January 2002 issue of that journal.

Friends and colleagues propose; authors dispose.

# Introduction

> Our country is vast and rich but disorder reigns throughout. . . . Come and
> rule us.
>
>              – Delegation from Novgorod to a Scandinavian prince, AD 862.[1]

> Although Russia lacks a tradition of vigorous self-government, it does not
> necessarily follow that it has one of bureaucratic centralism.
>
>              – Richard Pipes[2]

## I. On the Importance of the State in the Russian Setting

A recurrent theme in the discussion of Russian history, fortunately less
frequent in that history itself, is that of "the time of troubles" (*smutnoye
vremya* in Russian). The English translation provides but a pale sense of
what Russians understand by the term: an apparently indefinite period
of profound economic and social crisis in the body politic, characterized
by the collapse of state authority, a crisis magnified by the comparative
weakness of Russia's non-state institutions to fill the gap opened by the
disintegration of rule from above. Unregulated struggles over political succession, secession of outlying territories, civil strife, foreign intervention,
and above all death, on the mass scale, have all been directly associated
with Russia's several times of troubles, both in the popular imagination
and in actual fact. In practice, the infliction of mass death has also been
associated with periods of overweening state authority, as the reigns of

[1] Michel Heller, *Histoire de la Russie et de son empire* [A history of Russia and its empire]
(Paris: Plon, 1997), p. 21.
[2] Richard Pipes, *Russia under the Old Regime*, second edition (London: Penguin Books,
1995), p. 281.

Peter I ("the Great," 1689–1725) and Josif Stalin (ca. 1927–53) demonstrate.[3] Yet arguably it has been the fear of the consequences attending the decomposition of the state rather than its apotheosis as an unresponsive autocratic Leviathan that touches the raw nerve of Russian political culture.[4] Much of this book stands as a meditation on why this should be so.

Russian preoccupation with order, a much more elemental instinct than that conveyed by the old Prussian idea of a well-regulated police state, can be illustrated in a number of ways. Historically, West European and North American terms for "freedom" and "liberty" have often been rendered into Russian by Russians as *stikhiya*, which in fact most closely resembles the English idea of "anarchy" or "random disorder." (Russian President Vladimir Putin apparently agrees with this interpretation.[5]) In 1868, a Russian poet named Aleksei Tolstoy (cousin of the more famous Lev) penned a charming satirical poem about the cycles of Russian political history, entitled, "A History of the Russian State"; throughout the long poem, the refrain, which encapsulates the ultimate fruitlessness of many of these efforts at reform, and recalls the plea of Novgorod to a foreign prince in A.D. 862, is the same: "But there is just no order in the land" (*Poryadka v ney lish' net*).[6] More recently, the Russian Nobel laureate

---

[3] For recent work based on access to the Russian archives, see Anne Applebaum, *Gulag: A History* (New York: Doubleday, 2003); Aleksandr N. Yakovlev, *A Century of Violence in Soviet Russia* (New Haven: Yale University Press, 2002), a translation of *Krestosev* [Sowers of Graves] (Moscow: Vagrius, 1999). See the "chapter," really a book unto itself, by Nicholas Werth in Stephane Courtois, ed., *Le Livre Noir du Communisme* (Paris: Robert Laffont, 1997), pp. 53–379. See also S. M. Samuylov, ed., *Rossiyskaya Tsivilizatsiya: Cherez Ternii k Zvyozdam* [Russian Civilization: From the Depths to the Stars] (Moscow: Veche, 2000), p. 56, on the human costs of Peter I's rule.

[4] For a somewhat different view, with a focus on an alternative culture of "constrained" autocracy, see Nicolai Petro, *The Rebirth of Russian Democracy* (Cambridge, MA: Harvard University Press, 1995).

[5] On September 26, 2003, Russian President Putin made the following spontaneous remarks to a Columbia University student who asked him whether he was "impeding freedom of speech in Russia." Putin replied: "We have never had freedom of speech in Russia, so I can't understand what I'm impeding. At the beginning of the Nineties, we had the onset of a renaissance of freedom. This was also understood in different ways in society, and by the press as well...freedom and freedom of [the] press in particular was understood as a free-for-all, as anarchy and as a striving for destruction at any price and at all costs." Cited in Robert Cottrell, "Putin's Trap," *New York Review of Books*, December 4, 2003, also at www.nybooks.com/archives.

[6] A. K. Tolstoy, *Izbrannoye* [Selected Works] (Moscow: Izdatel'stvo Pravda, 1986), p. 122. A typical stanza reads:

"Poslushayte, rebyata          [Listen up, ye children
Chto vam rassakazhet ded,      To what your old gramps has to say
Zemlya nasha bogata            Our country is rich
Poryadka v ney lish' net."     But there is no order in it.]

Aleksandr Solzhenitsyn has argued that there have been just three "times of trouble" in Russian history: the early 1600s, when a prolonged Russian succession crisis saw a Polish-backed (and Catholic) claimant to the throne and a Polish occupation of Moscow; the Russian Revolution itself, extending from 1917–21, which catalyzed a civil war that proved far more destructive to Russia than did the First World War, whose until then unparalleled brutality triggered the Russian Revolution and the 1990s, following the disintegration of the USSR. In sum, Solzhenitsyn, who can hardly be accused of sympathy for the Soviet regime, assesses the first post-Soviet decade as more threatening to the health and survival of Russians and of the integrity of Russian civilization than the Stalinist terror or the Second World War, each of which claimed the lives of tens of millions of Soviet citizens.

There are sound reasons for taking such an alarmist view of the impact of the 1990s on Russian life and civilization. Consider only that, in the course of the decade, the Russian national economy contracted by about one-half, leaving Russia with a total gross domestic product (GDP) that is now less than one-fourth that of China's, and a per capita GDP that is now being challenged by China's own per capita standard of living (a detailed treatment of those conditions follows later in this introduction and in subsequent chapters). Relatedly, Russia experienced an annual net outflow of precious capital of $20–30 billion per year over the decade, compared to a net annual inflow of foreign direct investment (FDI) into China of $40–50 billion in recent years. Consequently, a net sum of approximately $200–300 billion in erstwhile Russian capital has been invested abroad, a sum that, when combined with the $80–160 billion that Russians are believed to be holding "under the mattress," approaches Russia's annual GDP when calculated in dollar terms and that stands in stark contrast to Russia's domestic investment requirements for the foreseeable future.[7] This starvation of Russia's domestic infrastructure, public as well as private, has had devastating consequences for the country's public health. To take perhaps the most dramatic index, mortality rates, average male life expectancy in Russia, continuing a trend begun in the late-Soviet period, had declined by the mid-1990s to just fifty-eight years; at the turn of the new century, it hovers on the threshold of sixty. Demographers have estimated that the life expectancy of a Russian teenage boy at the beginning

---

[7] Nikolai Shmelyov, "Nekotorye klyuchevye rossiyskiye voprosy, otveta na kotorye poka net" [Some key Russian questions to which there are not yet answers], in IMEMO, ed., *God Planety. 2003* [World Annual. 2003] (Moscow: Ekonomika, 2003), p. 151.

of the twenty-first century is lower than that of his great grandfather as a teenage boy at the turn of the twentieth century. Given an excess of deaths over births on the order of seven hundred thousand to eight hundred thousand per year, the Russian population, in spite of significant in-migration of Russians and non-Russians from other ex-Soviet republics (due to civil strife, ethnic discrimination, and so on), continues to decline, opening up the prospect of a dramatic diminution of Russia's population in coming decades and a corresponding shift in Russia's geopolitical position in the world, especially in respect to China in Asia. By one analysis, by 2050 Russia's population – taking into account birth, death, and immigration rates – could decline to 86.5 million, compared to 144.2 million in early 2002.[8] One could extend this kind of analysis, to a greater or lesser degree, into many other areas, including public health in general, the condition of Russian education, research and development, as well as the security of Russia's "nuclear archipelago," civilian as well as military. (See Chapter 3 for details.)

Contrary to what many in Western Europe and North America have argued (in the process continuing a hoary Western tradition of viewing Russia through the prism of internal Western preoccupations),[9] this tableau of troubles has much less to do with the relative success or failure of Russian "democratization" and/or "marketization" than it does with the profound shock that has been administered to Russia by the failure of the state to function.[10] The decomposition of the Soviet Russian state arguably began with the death of Stalin in 1953; certainly by the middle of the Leonid Brezhnev period, the limits of the Soviet system to function effectively, given the resources available to it, were an open secret among the enlightened elites within the system itself. Mikhail Gorbachev unwittingly made this latent crisis explicit in attempting to

---

[8] *Johnson's Russia List* (hereafter *JRL*), #6318, June 20, 2002, item no. 7, at www.cdi.org.

[9] Martin Malia, *Russia under Western Eyes: From the Bronze Horseman to the Lenin Mausoleum* (Cambridge, MA: Belknap Press of Harvard University Press, 1999).

[10] My argument thus comes closest to that expressed by Steven Kotkin in *Armageddon Averted* (Oxford, UK: Oxford University Press, 2001) than to the otherwise indispensable work of Peter Reddaway and Dmitri Glinsky, *The Tragedy of Russian Reform: Market Bolshevism versus Democracy* (Washington, DC: United States Institute of Peace, 2001). That is, given the implosion of the Soviet-Russian administrative order and the spontaneous seizure of state economic assets by the state officials in charge of them – all of which took place while the USSR still existed – Russia faced highly constrained choices upon the disintegration of the USSR. In the absence of a minimally coherent and competent state structure, it is hard to see how Russian leaders could have forged a viable post-Soviet economic and thus political course in the aftermath of Soviet disintegration.

save the system through far-reaching structural reform. Even before the end of Gorbachev's tenure in office, the immobilization of the Soviet state that Gorbachev had brought about had triggered what Steven Solnick has called a widespread "bank run" on Soviet state institutions.[11] Strategically placed Soviet elites, especially those with access to commodities that could be sold competitively on the world market (oil, gas, gold, diamonds, aluminum, and so on), discovered that they now faced an unprecedented opportunity to convert their administrative control over Soviet economic assets into the equivalent of private ownership; politically, this reinforced the impulse to secession from the Soviet center that was evident in a number of Soviet Union republics, Russia as well as Ukraine, among others. To a significant extent, Russia's post-Soviet political history has focused on providing legal protection for those who managed to acquire personal control of valuable Soviet economic assets, in the process both reflecting and propelling the crisis of the Russian state.

Why is the capacity of the state to govern so important? First, the ability of the state to govern is central to the prospects for building both a meaningful democracy and capitalism in postcommunist circumstances. The experience of the 1990s throughout postcommunist Europe has shown just how important an effective system of state administration is for the course of political and economic reform.[12] Democracy does not emerge spontaneously from the bosom of "civil society," which is in any case weak throughout postcommunist Europe and especially in post-Soviet states such as Russia and Ukraine[13]; nor does a mature and balanced capitalist economic system develop automatically from the interplay of the forces of supply and demand. Without a competent civil service, and the political authority to draft, pass, and then enforce relevant legislation, the state will not be able to perform the legal and macroeconomic functions required to establish what Russians call a "civilized" capitalism. Moreover, since there appears to be a strong historical correlation among democracy, civil society, capitalism, and the rule of law, a state that cannot (or will not) establish the rule of law thereby undermines the chances that an economically and socially healthy capitalism can take root and with it the chances that a strong civil society, whose independence

---

[11] Steven L. Solnick, *Stealing the State: Control and Collapse in Soviet Institutions* (Cambridge, MA: Harvard University Press, 1998).

[12] Allen C. Lynch, "The Crisis of the State in Russia," *International Spectator* (Rome), April–June 1995, pp. 21–34.

[13] Ernest Gellner, *Conditions of Liberty: Civil Society and Its Rivals* (New York: Allen Lane/Penguin Press, 1994).

in the final analysis depends upon defensible property rights, can arise.[14] In the absence of these social and economic preconditions of democratic political development, it is difficult to envisage how a responsive democratic polity might be built. In short, the state matters, even for those who are primarily concerned with the encouragement of a Russian democracy, liberal or social, and/or a Russian capitalism that might serve as an engine for the creation of wealth and the economic development of the country.

Second, and perhaps more obviously, the ability of the Russian state to exercise effective jurisdiction throughout the Russian Federation affects interests of vital importance not only to Russians but to the rest of the world. The question of whether Russia can effectively manage its nuclear power industry – that is, to prevent another Chernobyl or the like – impinges upon countries throughout the Northern Hemisphere. To the extent that the Russian state cannot effectively fund, and thereby control, the agencies of state administration, that state loses a degree of control over its borders as well as its ability to fulfill treaty obligations under international law. Questions about the leakage of Russian ballistic missile technologies to states such as India and the open sale of nuclear power reactors to Iran fall under this category, as do questions about the transit of narcotics from Afghanistan through Russia's new and vulnerable southern borderlands and the emergence of Russian organized crime as a major international phenomenon. (To a significant extent, Putin's acquiescence, even encouragement, of the U.S. invasion of Afghanistan in October 2001 reflected his understanding that the U.S. military would be solving a problem – that is, an aggressive Taliban government alongside a vital Russian sphere of influence – that the Russian military and the Russian state more generally could not.) Then there is the challenge of maintaining effective command and control over Russia's nuclear forces within the context of a general degradation of the country's armed forces. The entire framework of nuclear arms control has shifted, not so much after the end of the cold war as after the collapse of the Soviet state: Whereas during the cold war the primary problem of international security was to insulate nuclear weapons from the international Soviet–American cold war competition, the problem today is rather how to insulate nuclear weapons from the

[14] Alexander J. Motyl, *Dilemmas of Independence: Ukraine After Totalitarianism* (New York: Council on Foreign Relations, 1993), pp. 51–75; for an impressive empirical demonstration, see the work of the Peruvian economist Hernando de Soto, *The Other Path: The Economic Answer to Terrorism* (New York: Harper & Row, 1989).

uncertainties of internal political and administrative order in countries such as Russia that can no longer be presumed a priori to be stable states. In all of these instances, the extent to which Russia can effectively govern itself, under whatever political dispensation, democratic or otherwise, presents itself as an issue of international security.[15]

Finally, the experience of the 1990s in Russia underscores just how tightly bound up Russia's history, Russian civilization, and – as I shall argue in detail later – the prospects for the survival of historical Russia have been with the integrity and capacity of the central Russian state. As noted earlier, "times of trouble" have fortunately been rare and far between in Russian history. The essential trajectory of Russian political history since the emergence of the Principality of Muscovy as the predominant Russian suzerain in the fifteenth and sixteenth centuries, with all of the inevitable ebbs and flows of that process, has been toward the consolidation of autocratic government within an expanding imperial state.[16] Scholars such as Nicolai Petro have pointed to a number of examples, reaching into the distant Russian past, of what he has termed "constrained autocracy," that is, the effort to induce the sovereign to recognize the specific and autonomous social, economic, and political interests of propertied classes, the Church, in later times commercial and professional classes, and so on.[17] Two facts are pertinent in this regard. However well understood the idea of the public representation of corporate interests may have been by the turn of the twentieth century, the idea was resisted tenaciously and ultimately far too successfully by a succession of Russian Tsars, their courts, and their bureaucracies. In the end, the inability of the Russian Imperial political system to assimilate the social and economic forces engendered by Russia's state-directed economic modernization toward the end of the nineteenth century gravely weakened Russia's already questionable capacity to wage modern war of the sort unleashed throughout Europe in August 1914 and rendered the Imperial system fragile under the burden of such a war.[18] The weakness and fragility of Russia's modern classes, and their alienation from established authority, made possible the victory of the Bolsheviks between 1917–20 and the rapid establishment of an autocracy exceeding the imagination of any Tsar. Unconstrained autocratic

---

[15] Ted Hopf, "Managing Soviet Disintegration," *International Security*, summer 1992, pp. 44–75.

[16] Nancy Shields Kollmann, *Kinship and Politics. The Making of the Muscovite Political System, 1345–1547* (Stanford, CA: Stanford University Press, 1987).

[17] Petro, *The Rebirth of Russian Democracy*, p. 48, passim.

[18] This thus corresponds to the framework of analysis set forth in Samuel P. Huntington, *Political Order in Changing Societies* (New Haven, CT: Yale University Press, 1968).

government had thus been the *leitmotif* of Russian political history from the emergence of Muscovy until the Gorbachev period.

This development, while by no means inevitable, was not accidental, either. As we shall see shortly, the expansion of Russia throughout central Eurasia, ultimately to occupy at its zenith one-sixth of the earth's land surface, is inconceivable without a centralized, militarized Russian state.[19] Although the extension of Russian territorial jurisdiction often followed trails blazed by Russian colonists in search of fertile soil, the consolidation of these holdings depended ultimately upon the power of the Russian military. This process of expansion very early brought Russia into conflict with hostile non-Russian and frequently non-Christian peoples. The ability of the Russian state to integrate – through force, inducement, assimilation, and so on – its expanding colonial realm into the "metropolitan" Russian state had the effect of fusing empire and state into one polity, thereby creating an imperial state that was at the same time more formidable and more fragile than the West European overseas empires. The integration of colonies into the state allowed Russia to absorb resources and energies that propelled Russian state development itself. At the same time, this tight integration of state and empire meant that any challenge to the empire was also a challenge to the state, very unlike the case for the West European empires. Defense of empire, which was in fact the basis for Russia's great power status in the wider world, implied in the final analysis defense of the autocracy. This was the great dilemma faced by Russian reformers since the early-nineteenth century and helps explain why the momentum of great reforms tended to dissipate sooner rather than later: The dismantling of Russian autocracy implied the dismantling of Russian empire and with it of Russia's place in the world.[20] In fact, the collapse of Russian autocracy in 1917 and again in 1991 saw the immediate fragmentation of the state along nationalist lines and the collapse of the country's weight in international affairs. The defense of empire and of great power status thus entailed support for a powerful Russian state.

Correspondingly, Russian "national" consciousness did not develop along strictly nationalist lines. First, the state itself tended to reject the

---

[19] See William Fuller, *Strategy and Power in Russia, 1600–1914* (New York: Free Press, 1992); John LeDonne, *The Russian Empire and the World, 1700–1914* (New York: Oxford University Press, 1997).

[20] Adam B. Ulam, *Russia's Failed Revolutions: From the Decembrists to the Dissidents* (New York: Basic Books, 1981); Robert Wesson, *The Russian Dilemma* (New York: Praeger, 1986).

idea of a Russian "nation" after the French model. To include the peasantry in the "nation" would mean bringing the masses into the political system, an alarming idea to any autocracy. Second, the adoption of a true nationalist ideology, that is, one which saw the ideal polity as one in which the boundaries of the state and of the nation were coextensive, would have the effect under Russian circumstances of relinquishing the large non-Russian colonial periphery, as twentieth-century nationalists such as Solzhenitsyn would in fact advocate (at least with respect to the non-Slavic and/or non-Orthodox non-Russians).[21] What we usually think of as Russian national consciousness hence developed as a particular kind of state-imperial consciousness. Nationality in its ethnic form was no barrier to advancement in Tsarist Russia, as the large presence of ethnic Germans in the later Imperial administrations demonstrates. (An aggressive russifying nationalism developed only in the latter part of the nineteenth century.) Service and loyalty to the Tsar and later to the multiethnic Bolshevik Party, in the practical form of the state, not the nation, became the predominant touchstone of Russian political consciousness.

Finally, the Russian state has been central not only to Russia's imperial expansion eastward and southward but to its ability to assert and defend its interests westward, where the interests and power of technologically superior West European states have been engaged.[22] Central to this task was the capacity of the Russian state to embark from time to time on a significant but constrained program of economic development, that is, to borrow enough from Western Europe economically, administratively, and militarily to enable Russia to compete in the West and expand in the East and South, but limit the borrowings to avoid social and political challenges at home to the prerogatives of Russian autocracy. Indeed, in both Tsarist and Soviet times, the state has been central to Russian economic development, largely for military reasons.[23] We shall explore the reasons for this in depth in Chapter 6. Suffice it to say that, for the general reasons given previously, the state has been the major constant in

---

[21] Aleksandr Solzhenitsyn, *Pismo vozhdyam sovetskogo soyuza* [Letter to the Soviet Leaders] (Paris: YMCA-Press, 1973); idem, *Iz Pod Glyb* [From under the Rubble] (Paris: YMCA-Press, 1974). English translations of each were published in the following year, respectively.

[22] Theodore H. von Laue, *Why Lenin? Why Stalin? Why Gorbachev?* (New York: Harper-Collins, 1993).

[23] Barrington Moore, *Social Origins of Dictatorship and Democracy: Lord and Peasant in the Making of the Modern World* (Boston: Beacon Press, 1967), p. 481.

Russian political, economic, and social development for more than five centuries. In this light, Russia's experience in the 1990s – characterized by the simultaneous collapse of a powerful central government and of plausible external threats – may be seen as the testing of a new hypothesis in Russian history: To what extent is the development, if not the survival, of Russia as a civilization dependent upon the existence of a powerful central state?

## II. The Argument of the Book

The historical and functional analysis that we shall employ in this book leads to one overarching conclusion: The strength of the central government remains critically important for Russian political and economic development and even for Russia's prospects as a distinct civilization.[24] Historically, forces connected to Russia's geopolitical situation along the vast Eurasian steppe, as well as its position within the global political-military system and political economy, have worked to establish a structure of state power that has contained an intense fusion of political and economic power, whether under Soviet or Imperial auspices. Moreover, this patrimonial synthesis of polity and economy, while distinctive among European political systems, was on the whole not ineffective. Russia's state-driven pattern of economic development proved able, if often at brutal cost to its own people, not only to avoid the fate of colonization that befell China after the Opium War of 1839–42 but to maintain and even increase its standing as a great European power. This was not only a question of sheer material power but also of successful integration into European international society, as the ratification of both Peter I's and Catherine II's territorial gains by various European "concerts" of power demonstrated.[25] What changed for Russia from the mid-nineteenth century on was the novel challenge posed by industrialization, with its emphasis on efficiency as distinct from mass in the production process, thereby requiring a qualitative change in the relationship of regime to society. By 1913, that regime had not done so badly; it had, after all, presided

---

[24] See Marshall Poe, *The Russian Moment in World History* (Princeton, NJ: Princeton University Press, 2003), reinforcing von Laue, *why Lenin'?*; Robert Wesson, *The Russian Dilemma: A Political and Geopolitical View* (New York: Praeger, 1986). For a contemporary Russian view, see Samuylov, *Rossiyskaya tsivilizatsiya*, pp. 18–118, inter alia (for example, the work of George Vernadsky, etc.).

[25] Malia, *Russia under Western Eyes*, pp. 75–6.

over three decades of the most dynamic (state-directed) industrial growth among the great powers.[26] Yet in a classic Marxist (or Huntingtonian[27]) fashion, the modernization process itself generated new economic and social forces that demanded a political voice that the regime was incapable of integrating in a stable, postpatrimonial equilibrium. At the same time, the pressures of international politics and of Russia's relatively late start on industrialization saw it fall further behind the leading Western states, most dangerously Germany, even as Russian production was growing by leaps and bounds in absolute terms.[28]

Russia's defeat in the First World War highlighted the patrimonial regime's essential inability to master the modernization process – that is, to assimilate enough Western science, technology, and administration to compete effectively as a great power without in the process fracturing the foundation of Russia's autocratic and increasingly multinational polity. Yet Russia was far from alone in this fate: Germany, too, cracked under the strain of world war. Had the great powers of the day been able to manage their international relationships better, perhaps the internal contradictions of Russia's late development would not have proved so fatal to the country and much of the world. In the event, the Bolsheviks, upon their seizure of power in fall 1917, believed that they had the answer to Russia's modernization dilemma: A new state order in Russia would be the spark of a broader European socialist revolution that would forge an alliance between European capital and Soviet power, in the process resolving both Russia's security problems along its vulnerable western frontier and its relative economic backwardness. Eventually, this Russian-European synthesis would render the state itself obsolete, as it withered away in a Marxist fantasy of undifferentiated social harmony. Whatever plausibility such a view had, the failure of European communism by the early 1920s meant that the Soviet state would have to draw mainly from its own resources in order to modernize rapidly enough to sustain the promise of the Revolution as well as to defend the country against a future German and Japanese threat.

In the end, the Soviet regime met the latter promise better than the former. Through unspeakably brutal means, but also (unlike in 1914–17)

---

[26] Samuylov, *Rossiyskaya tsivilizatsiya*, pp. 76–85; Theda Skocpol, *States and Social Revolutions* (Cambridge, UK: Cambridge University Press, 1979), pp. 90–4.

[27] Along the lines of Huntington, *Political Order in Changing Societies* op. cit.

[28] Skocpol, *States and Social Revolutions*; von Laue, *Why Lenin?*

with a meaningful alliance with the Western powers, Stalin's Russia managed to survive that next German onslaught and emerge after 1945 as
the world's second power. For a time many in the outside world, communists and anticommunists alike, believed that Soviet Russia had discovered a powerful new path to modernity, combining political monopoly
with state ownership to propel backward societies into the forefront of
world politics. In retrospect, it is clear that the Soviet state suffered a
fate similar to that of Tsarist Russia. Its political model, while effective
enough in marshaling resources for state power in an extensive phase
of economic development, proved incapable of making the adjustments
necessary to unleash the productive possibilities of intensive, efficiency-
driven economic development. This was especially necessary in a world
system wherein richer states with more flexible political and social systems, as well as some previously impoverished societies (for example,
South Korea), were helping to create an entirely new kind of international
political economy as well as military order.

  The collapse of the Soviet system, a consequence of Gorbachev's in-
advertent destabilization of its foundations, served to discredit centrally
planned economies, if not the idea of socialism itself. For a while, the
Soviet collapse also reinforced the increasingly widespread notion in the
United States and Great Britain that the state itself was the major im-
pediment to economic progress and that its maximal feasible removal
from the economic sphere would guarantee the greatest prosperity for the
greatest number. In practice, the first post-Soviet decade in Russia suggested that the state remained essential to the economic reform process
itself.[29] For without a state that is capable of formulating laws (a legislative function), enforcing them (an administrative function), and regulating
the framework for the economy as a whole (a macroeconomic function),
the market itself could not take root as a fully developed system for allo-
cating productive resources and distributing the fruits of production in a
way that promoted the health of the society as a whole as well as of its individual members. The paradox in Russia is that many of those who have
been calling most loudly for the establishment (or reestablishment) of a
strong state are also those most opposed to capitalism and democracy as
it is understood in Western Europe and North America. Moreover, those
in Western countries who urged Russians most vehemently to dismantle what remained of the Russian state in the hopes of promoting both

[29] Joseph Stiglitz, *Globalization and Its Discontents* (New York: W. W. Norton, 2002),
   pp. 133–194.

capitalism and democracy helped to set in motion a process that by the late 1990s made it virtually impossible to speak of a pro-reform Russian nationalist.[30]

A minimally capable system of public administration and of legitimate political authority was in fact required if only to compensate for the many disabling legacies – economic, social, organizational, psychological – bequeathed by the Soviet system and the process of Soviet disintegration itself to all of the Soviet successor states. Moreover, we shall argue that compelling facts of Russian (and especially Siberian) economic geography tend to make the costs of production in Russia a multiple of what they are almost anywhere else in the world, rendering the application of a liberal model of economic development of questionable relevance to Russian requirements.[31] The state, in short, remains essential to Russia's prospects, even as Russia attempts to establish the foundations of a market economy and a kind of integration into the world capitalist political economy.

Without wishing to prettify things, Russian President Putin appears to have grasped the implications of this situation. Strengthening the state, seemingly as a prerequisite to establishing investor confidence, not sustained democratic accountability, is the apparent object of his consolidation of federal power in the office of the president.[32] Putin has streamlined the personal income tax at a flat 13 percent rate, with an appreciable effect on revenues flowing into the federal coffers. A land law codifying private property rights has now been passed, and in July 2002 the law was extended to cover agricultural land as well. He has visibly supported the establishment of production sharing agreements with foreign firms, applying foreign arbitration to assure external investors of the security of their holdings in Russia, although this has been contested by the parliament, with unsatisfactory legislative outcomes for foreign investors. The

---

[30] Janine Wedel, *Collision and Collusion* (New York: St. Martin's Press, 1998), chapter 5; this evolution is also detailed in William Zimmerman, *The Russian People and Foreign Policy* (Princeton, NJ: Princeton University Press, 2002), pp. 187–215.

[31] Fiona Hill and Clifford Gaddy, *The Siberian Curse* (Washington, DC: Brookings Institution, 2003); Allen C. Lynch, "Dilemmas of Russian Economic Reform: Liberal Economics and Illiberal Geography," *Europe-Asia Studies*, January 2002, pp. 31–49. For a Russian economist's argument along these lines, see A. N. Parshev, *Pochemu Rossiya ne Amerika* [Why Russia is not America] (Moscow: Krymskiy Most, 1999).

[32] Alexander Rahr, "Modernisierung a la Putin: wohin entwickelt sich Russland?" [Modernization à la Putin: Whither Russia] in Gabriele Lueke and Gustav Weber, eds., *So Kommen Sie nach ... Russland: Der Wirstschaftswegweiser fuer den Mittlestand* [Come to Russia: A Guide to the Russian Economy for the Small and Medium Business Person] (Munich: Primeverlag, 2003), pp. 304–12.

Russian government's decision in late 2001 to impose a 150,000-barrel-per-day quarterly cut in oil production reflects Putin's commitment to the assertion – however modest – of the interests of the state over the particular interests of Russia's mainly private energy companies. In a similar vein was his decisive assertion of control over the board of directors of Gazprom, Russia's natural gas monopoly, almost 40 percent state-owned and central to the fiscal and social stability of contemporary Russia. The arrest in fall 2003 of Mikhail Khodorkovsky, CEO of Yukos, Russia's largest private oil company, may also be seen in this light. The crux of the arrest seems less Khodorkovsky's political meddling per se as it does his plans to merge with ExxonMobil and the Russian firm Sibneft: The former would establish Yukos as a private oil giant on the global scale, while the latter would allow Yukos to dominate the future oil pipeline network, especially toward Nakhodka in the Russian Far East, with direct seaborne access to the Pacific Rim economies.[33] That Putin would not tolerate such an accumulation of energy resources beyond the direct influence of the state is comprehensible in light of the fact that in every major oil-exporting country in the world, oil is a state monopoly. Such a position is all the more understandable as the Russian state remains critically dependent upon energy receipts for its fiscal stability; these have typically made up two-fifths or more of the Russian federal government's budget in recent years. That Putin has been able to act so aggressively reflects in part the influence within his administration of those from the least damaged of Soviet-era institutions, that is, the security services that emerged from the shell of the old KGB, Putin's own home institution.[34] (Relatively high world oil prices have also helped shift the balance of political power within Russia in favor of the state, now awash in energy revenues, and against the "oligarchical" economic interests that proved so influential throughout the 1990s.)

In the diplomatic arena, Putin's alignment of Russia with the United States in the war against terror reflects a programmatic commitment, one as profound as that undergirding Gorbachev's "new political thinking," that a fragile Russia cannot advance its most pressing and vital state interests against concerted U.S. opposition and that it would be far preferable

---

[33] Charles A. Kolhaas, "Pipedreams: Khodorkovsky vs. Putin," November 19, 2003, at www.inthenationalinterest.com.

[34] See Amy Knight, *Spies without Cloaks* (Princeton, NJ: Princeton University Press, 1996).

to advance them with positive U.S. support. In this respect, Putin's foreign policy – in spite of Russia's dissent from the United States in the United Nations Security Council over the prospect of war with Iraq – remains essentially within the framework of partnership between Russia and the industrial democracies that had been established by Gorbachev and which, with ups and downs to be sure, was preserved intact throughout the Boris Yeltsin years.[35] This "partnership" reflects the assumption, first, that the vital interests of Russia and the Group of Seven (G-7) states are not at heart incompatible with each other and, second, that a positive compatibility of interests and values exists that can underwrite a relationship that goes beyond merely correct diplomatic ties. Here is just one specific illustration: Apart from the absence of any ideological animus in the contemporary Russian–Western relationship, key groups in the Russian economic elite, especially in the energy and metals sectors – which together account for nearly three-fifths of Russian exports and only a somewhat smaller percentage of the Russian government's budget receipts – require reliable access to Western markets and thus reasonably harmonious relations with the leading industrial democracies, the United States foremost among them. Relatedly, Russia's foreign debt in mid-2003 stood at around $121 billion. Debt servicing in 2003 amounted to nearly $18 billion, or about one-fourth of the federal government's budget. One should not exaggerate the extent of this debt burden, at least so long as world oil prices remain reasonably high; for example, the ratio of Russian debt to GDP is 28 percent, versus 140 percent for a country such as Japan. Yet any hopes that Russia might obtain relief from servicing its Soviet-era debt (about 70 percent of the total) depend on good relations with the leading creditor states.[36]

In this light, it is not surprising that Russia's government under Yeltsin as well as under Putin has understood that few of Russia's pressing interests at home or abroad could be served in the face of the active hostility of the United States and its chief allies. Consequently, the government has carefully preserved its lines of communication with the Western world even as it tacked to an increasingly nationalist wind in Russian domestic politics. In the absence of territorial disputes, ideological conflict, intense

[35] For the evidence in detail, see Allen C. Lynch, "The Realism of Russian Foreign Policy," *Europe-Asia Studies*, vol. 53, no. 1 (January 2001), pp. 7–31.
[36] Arkady Ostrovsky, "Upgrade Puts Russia on Investment Map," *Financial Times*, October 9, 2003, at www.ft.com; Prime-Tass (Moscow), September 5, 2003, and October 8, 2003, at www.amcham.ru.

economic friction, or irreconcilable geopolitical interests, there is no reason to expect that intelligent diplomacy should not be able to maintain a
normal Russian–Western relationship. Russia's vital state interests require
a viable modus operandi with the United States and its G-7 allies. This
presupposes, however, a political force in Russia that is capable of acting
in the interests of the state, if not of society, as distinct from the collection
of offices and persons that comprise it.

## III. The Organization of the Book

The book that follows leads the reader through a structured historical-
political analysis of the problem of Russian governance. To make my
methodological predilections plain, I see political science and political
history as two sides of the same coin. If political science is at heart about
the influence of structures of power upon political behavior, then political history may be conceived as the evolution of those structures through
time. Although academic hiring and promotion patterns work to dissociate them, intellectually, no account of political behavior can aspire to
true understanding without incorporating both. This book, as with my
courses, thus integrates history and political science into a common framework of analysis.

The book opens with an investigation of the particular importance of
the state in Russian historical development and assesses the Russian idea
of the "time of troubles" as a reflection of Russians' preoccupation with
public order amid the trying circumstances of the central Eurasian steppe.
Chapter 1 analyzes certain historical patterns of Russian political development in an effort to specify the key factors shaping the choices faced by
Russia historically and, arguably, in the present day. Chapter 2 evaluates
a series of Soviet-era legacies that shape, in varying degrees, Russia's path
of postcommunist political and economic evolution. Chapter 3 seeks to
determine the extent to which the 1990s in Russia, in light of the tendencies toward administrative decomposition, may be classified as another of
those "times of trouble." Chapter 4 addresses the condition of the contemporary Russian political system, while Chapter 5 examines this issue in the
broader, comparative perspective of the twenty-seven states undergoing
(in varying degrees) postcommunist transformations. Chapter 6 examines the prospects of Russian economic development in light of the political and legal uncertainties that appear so deeply interwoven in the Russian body politic, magnified by the constraints of geography mentioned

previously. The concluding chapter explores the implications of Russia's condition and plausible prospects for Russia's relations with the outside world and that world's interests in respect of postcommunist Russia. We end with a politically provocative but intellectually necessary question: Must Russia recover?

# Historical Patterns of Russian Political Development

View of an American political scientist: "...the sheer size of the government varied directly with the effort devoted to extraction, state making, protection, and, especially, war making but inversely with the commercialization of the economy and the extent of the resource base."[1]

– Charles Tilly

View of a Russian historian: "Autocracy and serfdom were the price the Russian people had to pay for national survival."[2]

– George Vernadsky

## I. The Argument

The purpose of this chapter is to investigate whether the apparent and distinctive tradition of Russian autocracy, under its Tsarist or Soviet guise, is an entirely random phenomenon and, to the extent that it is not, to identify its permissive conditions. We do so admittedly with an eye on the present: How much have the historical and environmental circumstances that have sustained Russian autocracy changed? How susceptible to political intervention are these circumstances? Finally, how might these circumstances be changed or ameliorated by political action by Russians and their foreign partners?

---

[1] Charles Tilly, "War Making and State Making as Organized Crime," in Peter B. Evans et al., eds., *Bringing the State Back In* (Cambridge, MA: Cambridge University Press, 1985), p. 182.

[2] George Vernadsky, "The Mongol Impact on Russia," in Thomas Riha, ed., *Readings in Russian Civilization*, vol. I. (Chicago: University of Chicago Press, 1969), p. 193.

The argument advanced in this chapter may be summarized as follows: Russian political development has been shaped by the same set of factors that influenced the contours of European political development and the evolution of the various European states in particular. Whatever the degree of Asiatic (that is, Mongol) influences on Russian political culture – and they were significant – as Russia emerged from the northern Russian forest zone under the leadership of Muscovy, Russian rulers found themselves increasingly constrained to participate in an international political system dominated by more powerful and technically more advanced European states. The requirements of success in international power politics interacted with the costs of extracting a usable economic surplus from the Russian vastness to frame the consolidation of a patrimonial form of absolutism in Russia itself. This result found the Russian political system far removed from the mainstream of European political development, even compared with such nonpatrimonial absolutisms as Louis XIV's France.[3] Yet Russian patrimonialism – that is, the distinctive integration of power as sovereignty and power as control of wealth (be it land, minerals, or people), emerged in response to the same general set of factors that framed the emergence of national states in Central and Western Europe. Proceeding from Charles Tilly's dictum that if states make war, war nevertheless makes states, the requirements for waging successful war under Russian geopolitical and economic conditions worked against those striving for what Nicolai Petro has termed "constrained autocracy."[4] In effect, the mutually reinforcing influences of what we shall call the "costs of security" and the "costs of production" framed what Tilly has termed a distinctively "Eastern" European pattern of state development, one in which the sovereign is essentially unaccountable to the various estates of society, such as they are. In this light, Russia's stands out among European powers as the "quintessential coercion-based strategy" of state formation, one in which the meager surplus that could be extracted from the soil meant few cities and thus "little space for an autonomous bourgeoisie, hence for the accumulation and concentration of capital outside the state."[5] It is in the intersection of the demands for establishing the

---

[3] For an excellent comparison in detail, see Hugh Ragsdale, *The Russian Tragedy: The Burden of History* (Armonk, NY: M. E. Sharpe, 1996), pp. 29–38.

[4] Nicolai Petro, *The Rebirth of Russian Democracy* (Cambridge, MA: Harvard University Press, 1995); Tilly, "War Making," p. 170.

[5] Charles Tilly, *Coercion, Capital, and European States, AD 990–1992* (Cambridge, MA: Blackwell, 1992), pp. 137–43.

security of the state (against both external and internal encroachers) and the relative poverty of the soil that the contours and evolution of the historical Russian state may best be understood. Considering Russian political development within the matrix of the costs of security and the costs of production helps us to understand both the trajectory of Russian political history and the relation of that history to more general European and global patterns of state formation, as this chapter's discussion illustrates. (It also helps us to come to terms with the caesura represented by the disintegration of the USSR in 1991: The historically overweening central Russian state had collapsed, but under the novel conditions in which, while the costs of production remained high, the costs of security dropped dramatically in a world that seemed to pose few, if any, external threats to the security of the post-Soviet Russian Federation.)

## II. Specification of Terms

Several preliminary cautions are in order. First, it is not the predominance of the state per se that we are seeking to explain as somehow distinctively Russian, but rather the nature of the Russian state order. Powerful states may be expressed through various political dispensations, from autocratic to authoritarian to democratic, as the examples of the contemporary French or Swedish states, which dispose of more than half of their respective country's gross domestic product (GDP), demonstrate. It is the impressive persistence, with ebbs and flows to be sure, of an essentially unaccountable autocratic state from late-medieval times until the 1980s that we seek to understand.

Second, Russia's political order has not always been perceived as distinctive. Martin Malia has convincingly demonstrated that Peter I ("the Great") established Russia as a peer of the European "republic," by which contemporaries meant the republic of Christian monarchs. His successors, through intermarriage and able exploitation of the possibilities offered by the shifting European balance of power, maintained this reputation, so much so that Catherine II (also "the Great"), although expanding Russia's European empire by leaps and bounds, managed to avoid triggering a countervailing coalition of the sort that routinely foiled the efforts of such aspiring hegemons as Louis XIV or Napoleon I. Indeed, in late *ancien régime* France, Voltaire and other *philosophes* routinely invoked Catherine's Russia (or perhaps better, Russia's Catherine) as the solution to the ills that afflicted France. Because of Russia's attachment to this international, Christian monarchical society, the rest of Europe regarded

Russia's territorial gains as far more legitimate than the holdings of the Islamic suzerains of the Ottoman Empire in the Balkans.

Third, many aspects of Russian life were in fact not so far removed from general European practice, especially if we keep in mind prevailing patterns throughout East-Central Europe and the Balkans. A comparison of similarities and differences between Russia and Western Europe in the seventeenth century suggests that the divergence was at that time usually one of degree, even if at times of major degree, than of kind. Consider Table 1, as constructed by the German historian Hans-Heinrich Nolte.

From this picture, one can conclude that the Russia of the early- to mid-seventeenth century, taking into account its several similarities and differences with Europe, nevertheless belonged to Europe, as exemplified by its confessional, intellectual, social, economic, and political characteristics. This fact, as Nolte observes, was decisive for West European opinion, for whom Russia, as a Christian power, was more readily available as an alliance partner than was the Ottoman Empire.[6]

## III. A European Pattern of Political Development

In fact, the idea of Russia as representing a distinctive, un-European form of civilization is as much the construction of modernizing Western intellectuals, and above all the Marxists, as it is the product of developments within Russia itself. It was the French Revolution that set in motion forces that would eventually see the Western image of Russia transmogrify from one of either peer among the Christian powers of Europe (for the rulers of the *anciens régimes*) or example of enlightened monarchy that in a West European context could strike down oppressive ancient ways (for the *philosophes*), to an increasingly prevalent image of Russia as the gendarme of reactionary Europe against republican and later socialist Europe. Russia had changed much less than had Western Europe by the middle of the nineteenth century, and there, for Russia, was the rub. The looming challenge and eventual crisis of the Russian system in the century after Russia's triumph over Napoleon was connected to the threat that economic modernization in the West, in the form of industrialization, posed to Russia's power abroad and stability at home. Russia's defeat, on Russian soil, in the Crimean War in 1856 by an Anglo-French coalition, a

[6] Hans-Heinrich Nolte, *Kleine Geschichte Russlands* [A Short History of Russia] (Stuttgart: Philipp Reclam jun., 1998), pp. 79–80.

TABLE 1. *Similarities and Differences between Russia and Western Europe in the Seventeenth Century*

| Religion | Catholic Europe | Protestant Europe | Russia |
|---|---|---|---|
| Writing plus tradition as sources of teaching | Yes | No | Yes |
| Apostolic succession of the clergy | Yes | No | Yes |
| Celibacy of the clergy | Yes | No | No |
| Primacy of the Pope | Yes | No | No |
| National churches | No | Yes | Yes |

| Science/scholarship | Catholic Europe | Protestant Europe | Russia |
|---|---|---|---|
| Learned monasteries | Yes | Yes | Yes |
| Universities | Yes | Yes | No |
| Publishers | Yes | Yes | Yes |

| Social Structure | Western Europe | Russia |
|---|---|---|
| Freehold | Yes (Except England) | Yes (Votchina) |
| Feudal estate | Yes | Yes (Pomestiye) |
| A court of peers for nobility | Yes | No |
| A separate court for city dwellers | Yes (esp. Germany) | No |
| Same court for all inhabitants | No | Yes |

| Economy | Western Europe | Russia |
|---|---|---|
| Slash and burn agriculture | Seldom | Often |
| Three-field rotation | Usual | Usual only in the central regions |
| Enclosure | In NW Europe | No |
| Multiple trades and professions | Yes | Yes |
| Manufacturing | Yes | Little, mainly foreign |
| Ocean-going travel | Yes | No |

| Political Structure | Continental Europe | Maritime Europe | Russia |
|---|---|---|---|
| Absolutism | Yes | No | Yes ("autocracy") |
| Imperial-estates general | Yes (in France until 1614) | Yes | Yes (until 1653) |
| Provincial/local estates | Yes | Yes | No |

generation after the worth of the Russian system had appeared vindicated in the triumph over Imperial France, triggered a *crise de conscience*. This crisis would see Russia soon (1861 and thereafter) abolish serfdom and institute a series of related social, administrative, and economic reforms designed to enable Russia to maintain its place among the great powers of the day and avoid the kind of colonization that was taking place (and in which the Russians themselves were eagerly taking part) in China after the Opium War (1842).[7]

In effect, the Industrial Revolution, with its emphasis on technologically driven increases in productivity and thus value-added production, was eclipsing the predominant Russian pattern of political-economic development, that is, the appropriation by the state and its immediate servitors of the fruits of extensive production in agriculture and mining.[8] For example, by the mid-eighteenth century, the Russian Urals, with ninety-seven factories, had become one of the world's major iron-producing areas, producing tens of thousands of tons of iron per year.[9] Indeed, in 1750 and even in 1800, Russia was the largest manufacturing power in Europe, producing 5.0 percent and 5.6 percent, respectively, of world manufacturing output, as against 1.9 percent and 4.3 percent, respectively, for the United Kingdom in those years.[10] By the mid-nineteenth century, however, Russian failure to keep pace with British and later French plant modernization – a complex result of costs of transportation, employment of serf labor, and resistance to Western ideas – saw Russia fall from first place to eighth in world iron production in spite of impressive absolute increases in Russian production and economic development, prefiguring a recurrent pattern in the Russian economy throughout the century. Thus, between 1850 and 1890, the number of Russian factories and the workers employed by them tripled; between 1890 and 1913, the number of manufacturing workers doubled again, to a total of 2,600,000; likewise, Russia would produce 8.8 percent of world manufacturing output by 1900 (compared to 5 percent in 1750), yet Russia was relatively much worse off in terms of key international comparisons: The corresponding

---

[7] Theda Skocpol, *States and Social Revolutions* (Cambridge, UK: Cambridge University Press, 1979), p. 85. George L. Yaney, *The Systematization of Russian Government: Social Evolution in the Administration of Imperial Russia, 1711–1905* (Urbana, IL: University of Illinois Press, 1973), pp. 230–49.

[8] Skocpol, *States and Social Revolutions*, p. 83.

[9] See William L. Blackwell, *The Beginnings of Russian Industrialization, 1800–1860* (Princeton, NJ: Princeton University Press, 1968).

[10] Paul Kennedy, *The Rise and Fall of the Great Powers* (New York: Random House, 1987), p. 149.

figure for Great Britain was 18.5 percent, for Germany, 13.2 percent, and for the United States 23.6 percent. By 1914, after decades of feverish expansion, Russian coal production was just 5 percent that of the United States; likewise, after more than two decades of spectacular railroad construction (the railroad net doubling between 1880–90 and increasing by 50 percent again between 1890–7), by 1900 Russia occupied just twentieth place in the world in terms of kilometers of railroad per one million inhabitants.[11] Perhaps most importantly, and tragically, "however fast and considerable the expansion of the Russian railway system since 1860 had been, by 1914 the density of the German system (miles of railroad to square miles of territory) was over ten times that of the Russian."[12]

Yet even here, we should be cautious about ascribing the ultimate Russian failure to adapt successfully to the challenges of modernization as a distinctively Russian phenomenon. What modernization implied at heart was the need for traditional socioeconomic and political orders to respond to the twin and simultaneous challenges of mass economics and mass politics without becoming unglued along the way. Few passed the test. It was, after all, not only the Russian Empire that succumbed to the strain of World War in 1917, but soon thereafter the Austro-Hungarian Empire, the Ottoman Empire, and even that most modern of societies, Imperial Germany, as well, entailing military defeat, territorial dismemberment, and social upheaval. All of these systems – Russia being merely the first – succumbed to the strain of total war, which highlighted in stark relief the incomplete balance that had been achieved in integrating the new social and economic forces of industrial modernity into their respective political orders.[13] Germany failed this test spectacularly in the entire 1914–45 period. Once again, Russia, even into the twentieth century, stands apart mainly by degree rather than by kind.

## IV. Conditions Governing Russian Success

This challenge of industrialization is significant for our purposes because it brings into focus the conditions that sustained Russian power over the centuries and hence the danger that the entire process of modernization

[11] James H. Bater, *The Soviet Scene: A Geographical Perspective* (London: Edward Arnold, 1989), p. 26; Michel Heller, *Histoire de la Russie et de son empire* (Paris: Plon, 1997), p. 842; Mikhail Pokrovskiy, *Russkaya Istoriya* [Russian history] (St. Petersburg: Poligon, 2002), vol. 3, p. 296.

[12] Skocpol, *States and Social Revolutions*, p. 96.

[13] Samuel J. Huntington, *Political Order in Changing Societies* (New Haven, CT: Yale University Press, 1968); Arno Mayer, *The Persistence of the Old Regime: Europe to the Great War* (London: Croom Helm, 1981).

posed for a country in Russia's situation. What was that historical situation? Consider the following.

First, Russia's international standing was closely connected to Russian autocracy. Given the immense spaces of the Central Eurasian steppe and the poverty of Russian agriculture, only a highly centralized and militarized state, one capable of extracting a usable surplus from a population perpetually on the margins of survival, could translate the circumstances of Russian backwardness into colonial expansion in the East and great power status in the West. This is the meaning of the epigram for this chapter, that "[a]utocracy and serfdom were the price the Russian people had to pay for national survival." Without a highly militarized autocracy, it is difficult to see how Russia could have avoided the fate of China and India as colonies of the Western powers. Moreover, until the onset of industrialization, Russia's very backwardness, as exemplified by the absence of well-developed roads, may be considered to have worked in Russia's favor, as seen in Napoleon's plight in 1812. (This backwardness played a role even as late as 1941 in hindering, even if barely, the pace of the Nazi invasion.) As late as 1848–9, Russian troops played a decisive role in shaping European political order, as Russian intervention in June 1849 to suppress the Hungarian republican uprising – at the invitation of the Austrian government – guaranteed the survival of the Austrian Empire and with it of Europe's classical balance of power. Until the onset of the Crimean War, Russia's autocratic system appeared to its defenders to have proved its worth.[14]

Second, the challenge of industrialization to Imperial Russia was magnified inasmuch as such modernization tended to make the predominant Russian economic pattern obsolete. This was not so much a question of urban versus rural development, or even of industrial production per se versus cottage handicraft as it was of intensive versus extensive means of economic development. Indeed, as we have noted, Russia was the world's largest producer of iron in the late-eighteenth century. Likewise, India and China were the world's two richest economies at that time, measured in terms of gross national product (GNP), each producing 24.5 percent and 32.8 percent, respectively, of the world's manufacturing output in 1750. (China's portion would even incease to 33 percent by 1800 before beginning a decline that reached just 6.2 percent of global manufacturing output in 1900.[15]) Yet none of these countries was in a position to organize itself

---

[14] William Fuller, *Strategy and Power in Russia, 1600–1914* (New York: Free Press, 1992), pp. 177–264.

[15] Kennedy, *The Rise and Fall of the Great Powers.*

so as to take advantage of the revolution in economic production triggered by the steam engine and the scientific-industrial revolution in general.

Russian wealth, in a pattern that was to be replicated in the Soviet era, was based on bringing additional resources, or factors of production, from its immense spaces into economic play. The widespread resort of Russian peasants, especially in the non–Black Earth regions of central Russia, to slash and burn techniques of agriculture was tremendously destructive of the soil's fertility but acceptable in the context of Russia's apparently unlimited resource of space. Peasants could always move on, in a stream of colonization that sustained the territorial expansion of the Russian state. If resources appear unlimited, then the laws of marginal economics do not apply, since economics is by definition the study of allocation, production, and distribution under conditions of scarcity. Once those resources become scarce – and particularly if foreign adversaries (themselves with imperial access to cheap raw materials) have mastered novel techniques based on the intensive, that is, more efficient exploitation of existing factors of production – such a system is thrown into crisis.

From this perspective, Russia's immense spaces have constituted a significant burden on the country's ability to govern itself, not to mention to modernize effectively. The early-twentieth-century geopoliticians, such as Sir Halford Mackinder, were thus wrong to project a forthcoming Russian superstate (the "Heartland") by assuming that a German pattern of (relatively compact) industrial modernization – with its focus on a rapid and well-integrated railroad network – could be superimposed on the transcontinental Russian scale.[16] The famous "interior lines" of classical military strategy, while favoring a modernizing German state by allowing it to transfer troops rapidly from east to west and north to south, found the Eurasian Russian state in a perpetual condition of imperial overreach, especially in the face of fast modernizing Western powers, which by the late-nineteenth century would include Japan. Russia would lose not only the Crimean War against industrial Britain and France but the 1904–5 war against industrializing Japan as well, not least because of the impediments that its vast spaces imposed on Russia's ability to project its power. Taken together, the distinctive spatial aspects of Russia's social geography – immense transcontinental space, with enormous distances from and

---

[16] Halford J. Mackinder, "The Geographical Pivot of History," *Geographical Journal*, vol. 23, no. 4 (1904), pp. 421–44. For a discussion of how Russians have reacted to Mackinder's analysis, see Milan Hauner, *What Is Asia to Us? Russia's Asian Heartland Yesterday and Today* (Boston: Unwin Hyman, 1990), pp. 135–50, 156–62, 171–3, 225–37.

between major cities; low population density; the severity and wildness of nature; a vast multiethnic "polyperiphery"; dislocation between the bulk of the population in European Russia versus the bulk of precious resources in Asiatic Russia; as well as the hindrances posed by the south-to-north flow of the main Siberian rivers – together work to create a fundamentally resistant sociogeographical environment for the governance of the Russian polity. This environment rendors Western European models of economic, political and administrative development difficult to apply.[17]

Economically, mid-nineteenth-century Russia, faced with the modernization of England, France, and Germany (and eventually Japan), found itself in a position comparable to that of the legitimist states of continental Europe after the French Revolution. Whereas republican France rapidly multiplied its military power by the political innovation of the *levée en masse*, or mass conscription, the Western powers dramatically increased their power vis-à-vis Russia by the economic (and social) innovation of the Industrial Revolution. Each innovation represented a qualitative leap forward in terms of the capacity of the respective states to organize power for political ends. Each in turn thus also posed grave threats to traditionalist regimes, whose institutions, pointedly aimed at excluding the masses from the public order, were threatened as much by a successful reform from within as they were by a failed reform from without. That is, modernizing reform would tend to undermine the basis of absolutism by encouraging the development of new social and economic forces and their inevitable claim for political representation, whereas, without such a reform, the given state would rapidly be outclassed in the arena of international power politics. Thus, the most powerful state elites repeatedly rejected or attempted to undermine plans for industrial modernization, from the 1830s when such plans were under active discussion until the turn of the twentieth century, as Finance Minister Sergei Witte was constantly fighting a rearguard action against those in the Imperial bureaucracy who saw (correctly) modernization as a mortal threat to the autocratic order.[18] While perceptive observers such as Count Nikolai Karamzin argued that "a carefully run economy yields more riches than do gold mines," Nicholas I's senior officials decided to "quash further

[17] Sergei Medvedev, "Power, Space and Russian Foreign Policy," in Ted Hopf, ed., *Understandings of Russian Foreign Policy* (University Park, PA: Penn State University Press, 1999), pp. 16–19.

[18] Walter M. Pintner, *Russian Economic Policy Under Nicholas I* (Ithaca, NJ: Cornell University Press, 1978); Theodore H. von Laue, *Sergei Witte and the Industrialization of Russia* (New York: Atheneum, 1968).

growth in manufacturing" out of "a fear of the modern: movement of
people, education of the ignorant, introduction of foreign technologies,
loss of control over society owing to erosion of traditional structures."
Nicholas himself thought that workers needed "energetic and paternal
supervision of their morals; without it this mass of people will gradually
be corrupted and eventually turn into a class as miserable as they are dangerous for their master."[19] This "Russian Dilemma," as Robert Wesson
has termed it, concerning the simultaneous necessity and danger of reform, recurs throughout late-Imperial and Soviet Russian history.

Third, this dilemma framed a powerful tension faced by Russian rulers
in the decades after the Napoleonic wars: either to broaden the basis
of legitimacy and accommodate the nation, however conditionally, in the
public order, or to defend the ancient prerogatives of absolutism in a world
in which they appeared increasingly anachronistic. For example, in 1832,
Nicholas I's Minister for Education S. S. Uvarov proposed expanding the
formal basis of the regime's legitimacy to add *narodnost'*, or a sort of nationality principle, to the extant twin pillars of autocracy and orthodoxy.
Nicholas refused, on the entirely sensible grounds that such a principle
implied admitting the masses into the political system and thus that the
population was indeed a subject in its own right and not simply subject
to the imperial prerogative. This unwillingness to grant recognition to
society would persist until 1917 and the regime's downfall, a downfall no
doubt propelled by the too-narrow social and political foundation over
which Russia's economically modernizing state presided. A comparable
dynamic set in for the Bolsheviks once their expectation that a socialist
Europe (and above all Germany) would rescue them from Russia's rural
poverty and international isolation went unfulfilled. And while the initial
results, as in late-Tsarist Russia, seemed to be spectacularly successful,
once the system became complex enough to warrant new forms of social,
economic, and political mobilization and even participation, the resistance
of the established Soviet order to change meant that there was an insufficiently strong socioeconomic and political foundation for Gorbachev's
reforms and, once those reforms failed, that Russia would shatter in ways
comparable to the years following the collapse of the Tsarist regime in
1917.

---

[19] As cited in Don K. Rowney, "Center–Periphery Relations in Historical Perspective: State
Administration in Russia," in Peter J. Stavrakis et al., eds., *Beyond the Monolith: The
Emergence of Regionalism in Post-Soviet Russia* (Washington, DC: Woodrow Wilson Center
Press, 1997), p. 22.

Fourth, this last point brings up the other side of the dilemma. Russia did try to modernize and moreover did so explicitly in response to the message of Russian institutional obsolescence that was implicitly sent by Russia's defeat in the Crimean War. In the decade after 1861, Russia abolished serfdom, created new legal and administrative structures, established elements of local administration, and eventually instituted a program of rapid industrialization.[20] But the reform process in Russia, before 1861 as well as later, always tended to be halfhearted at best and moreover halted before it could be brought to its logical conclusion. The reasons, as Robert Wesson notes, have to with Russia's peculiar political order: Russia was not simply an autocracy but an empire, one moreover that since Catherine II's time had been acquiring ever larger numbers of non-Russian subjects.[21] (Indeed, the census of 1897 – itself an index of Russia's striving toward modernity – indicated that no more than 44 percent and more likely 40 percent of the Empire's subjects were Russian.[22]) In this context, reform presented a twofold danger for the regime: It threatened not simply the autocracy by devolving decision-making power to elements of a civil society, but the empire itself and with it Russia's great power status by devolving authority to an increasingly non-Russian periphery of what was not a nation-state but an imperial state. Many Russian friends of reform would thus eventually abandon the enterprise rather than see reform lead to independence for Poland, Ukraine, and other outlying territories and hence the eclipse of Russia as a great power. Again, the connection between Russian autocracy and Russia's international standing is evident.

Fifth, the great success achieved by Peter I and bequeathed to the more energetic of his successors – that is, the coercive and brutal mobilization of the country's wealth to sustain Russia's claim to international power and rank – was becoming less viable throughout the nineteenth century, in spite of the apparently relentless expansion of Tsarist Russia into southern Turkestan and the Far East. The demonstrated capacity of a unified German Empire as well as Japan to industrialize with astonishing rapidity meant that Russia was no longer facing relatively weak powers on its extensive and often multinational periphery. Russia's defeat in war by Japan in 1905 only underscored a process that had been under way

---

[20] Yaney, *The Systemication of Russian Government*, pp. 230–380.
[21] Robert Wesson, *The Russian Dilemma: A Political and Geopolitical View* (New York: Praeger, 1986).
[22] Richard Pipes, *The Formation of the Soviet Union* (Cambridge, MA: Harvard University Press, 1954), p. 2.

for more than a decade: Faced with the challenge of German and later Japanese power, and unwilling to relinquish its imperial drive, Tsarist Russia, which in spite of decades of impressive industrialization was further behind Germany in this respect than at the outset, was constrained to conclude an alliance with republican France. A Russia so aligned was not only in the politically awkward position of seeming to legitimize its ideological foe but in the militarily dangerous position of having to face the combined might of the Central Powers (Germany, Austria-Hungary, and Ottoman Turkey) along its frontiers without realistic prospects of substantial assistance from its new-found allies. (Throughout the First World War, Turkish resistance prevented the British from penetrating the Black Sea, thereby preventing significant military and economic assistance to an isolated Russia.) Half a century of attempted modernization thus found Imperial Russia more vulnerable ideologically, economically, and militarily than it had been at the outset of the awesome, overwhelming process.

Even so, by mid-1914, Imperial Russia had been growing economically at the fastest rate in the world for several decades (5 percent per year between 1880–1913, and 8 percent per annum for the 1890s), and possessed one of the most creative and dynamic elite cultures in the world. Even in the sphere of international relations, Russia, in spite of the defeat by Japan, was simultaneously feared – by Germans who dreaded the full-scale industrialization of the Russian giant – and valued – by the French and British, who required the Russian counterweight in order to meet the challenge of German power. (Indeed, the British had all but abandoned their imperial rivalry with Russia in Central Asia and concluded a naval alliance with Japan in order to concentrate on the danger posed by growing German naval power.) As noted, the first World War also undermined the Austro-Hungarian, German, and Ottoman empires, brought large parts of the French Army to a near fatal mutiny, and weakened Britain to such an extent that we can trace its decline as a great power and as an empire from this point. Given these strains, it cannot be excluded that some modern Russian political synthesis might eventually have evolved. Thus Russia's path of political-economic development can only be understood in reference to its European as well as its Eurasian circumstances.

Still, it cannot be denied that Russia's path of political-economic and historical development diverged significantly from that of the rest of Europe, even if by degree. Given the remarkable durability of the achievements of Russian statecraft and the rapidity with which the Bolsheviks restored the bulk of that legacy under the most shattering of circumstances, further inquiry into the distinctive aspects of Russian political development seem warranted.

## V. The Distinctiveness of Russia's Patrimonial Absolutism

While absolutism prevailed through the continent of Europe in the sixteenth and seventeenth centuries, from Spain through France and later Prussia to Russia, Russian "autocracy" was nevertheless quite different from continental absolutism.[23] Ironically, although Russia and England would be colonized almost simultaneously in the Middle Ages by two groups of Norman invaders, economic conditions in each country, particularly the relative fertility of the soil, gave rise to two very different feudal traditions, leading eventually in England to the development of constrained monarchy and ultimately of constitutional government, and in Russia to a distinctive form of absolutism that Richard Pipes has termed "patrimonialism."[24] In Western Europe, the combination of political decentralization (with the decline of papal ideological supremacy), the institution of vassalage (implying mutual obligations between crown and lords) and conditional land tenure (that is, the conferral of usufruct contingent upon the fulfillment of mutual obligations) tended to embed over time a contractual aspect to relations between a monarch and his or her subjects. In England, as early as the Magna Charta but not long thereafter even in France and also throughout the German lands, the landed nobility, exploiting the political possibilities made available by the yield of their properties, proved able to secure royal recognition of certain inalienable rights, as a later generation on another continent would term them. Among the most important of these rights was the nonalienability of property without due process in a court of one's peers. By contrast, even before the Mongol conquest, throughout much of Russia (the commercial republic of Novgorod being a key exception), as distinct from the Kievan lands, there was an unusually wide gulf separating those in political authority from society. Unlike in England, where the Normans divided a richer land and soon turned into a native land-owning aristocracy, in Russia the Normans were primarily interested in the transit and extractive possibilities of the Russian lands between Scandinavia and wealthy Byzantium. Consequently, and by contrast to England, Norman rule was much more imposed on the native society and long retained a

---

[23] Skocpol, *States and Social Revolutions*, p. 85; Tilly, "War Making," pp. 172–3.
[24] Richard Pipes, *Russia under the Old Regime* (New York: Scribners, 1974), pp. 27–140.

semicolonial character, reflecting a proprietary manner of exercising authority. Russia's greatest Marxist historian, Mikhail Pokrovskiy, noted in this respect that the limits on royal prerogative already established in England in the thirteenth were still unknown in Russia in the middle of the seventeenth century.[25]

More decisive still, one cannot avoid the shattering effects of the Mongol conquest of Russia between 1237–41 and the two and one-half centuries of Mongol overlordship that followed. Of particular interest is the fact that it was Russian princes, as agents of the Mongol khan, who assumed immediate colonial authority over the Russian (or, more precisely, Eastern Slavic) peasant populations. As in effect viceroys of the distant khan, the Russian princes (the famous Alexander Nevsky among them) exercised essentially extractive functions in relationship to the resident peoples, their duties being almost exclusively restricted to the collection of tribute for the khan (that is, taxing the population), maintenance of order, and security sufficient for the tribute to flow but without any sense of responsibility for the public well-being – a sense that was at the same time developing, however tenuously, throughout continental Europe and England. The long period of Mongol rule, combined with the political-military requirements of later combating that rule (under the auspices of the Muscovite princes), left a distinctive impression on the Russian political culture. As Pipes has characterized it, the Mongol legacy:

- Isolated the princes even further from the population
- Made the princes less conscious of their political responsibilities toward their own peoples (since their exclusive responsibility was toward the imperial authority in Sarai)
- Provided powerful incentives and opportunities for the Russian princes to use their political power to accumulate vast private estates
- Induced the population to regard political authority as by its very nature arbitrary, as the mere threat of calling in the Mongols on the part of the Russian princes was usually enough to preserve the public order and maintain the flow of tribute eastward.[26]

As a result, Russian life, already tenuous by virtue of the country's marginal geographical location and hence poor soil fertility, became terribly brutalized. To the Russian population, the state came to be known

[25] Pokrovskiy, *Russkaya Istoriya*, p. 344.
[26] Pipes, *Russia under the Old Regime*, p. 75.

as essentially arbitrary and violent, taking what it could lay possession of and giving nothing in return, and exacting obedience solely through its superior physical force. The experience of Mongol rule thus set the stage for the peculiar type of political authority, blending native and Mongol elements, which arose in the Principality of Moscow once the Golden Horde began to lose its grip on Russia as the fourteenth century ran its course.[27]

Other models of governance at the time might in principle have served as sources of political development other than the rigidly patrimonial type, which fused political power as sovereignty over territory with economic power as ownership over wealth, including land, resources, and people. Yet it was always improbable that the commercial republic of Novgorod in the Russian northwest, with its conciliar political traditions, could ever have mobilized the kind of martial power needed to defeat the Mongols (as a point of comparison, think of the Italian city states over which Machiavelli despaired).[28] And it was even less probable that the militarily strong Commonwealth of Lithuania-Poland – with its powerful aristocracy and elective monarch – might have served as a unifier of the Eastern Slavs, if only because its Roman Catholicism made it ineligible to be the unifier of Russia's Orthodox lands. It thus turned out that the Mongols were expelled and the Russian lands unified under the auspices of the Principality of Moscow, where, unlike in Kiev, the authority of the princes preceded the settlement of the lands and thereby entailed the foundation of Russian patrimonialism, the distinctive element of Russian absolutism. The unification of Russia by Muscovy would prove as fateful to the country's subsequent development as the unification of Germany by the Prussian Junkers (as opposed to the Frankfurt liberals) proved to be for Germany. Russian statehood under Moscow's tutelage would reflect not relations between sovereigns and subjects, but rather those between lord and servant.

To be sure, the exact extent of the ruler's prerogatives was in practice frequently the object of political contest between the Russian crown and Russian barons, so much so that Ivan IV ("The Terrible") was led to

---

[27] Ibid., p. 57.
[28] For a view that emphasizes the vitality of these perspectives, see Petro, *The Rebirth of Russian Democracy*; S. M. Samuylov, ed., *Rossiyskaya Tsivilizatsiya: Cherez Ternii k Zvyozdam* [Russian Civilization: From the Depths to the Stars] (Moscow: Veche, 2003), pp. 35–47; Charles Tilly and Wim P. Blockmans, eds., *Cities and the Rise of States in Europe, A.D. 1000–1800* (Boulder, CO: Westview Press, 1989), p. 227.

the murderous liquidation of much of the Russian boyar class in order to consolidate his absolutist prerogatives.[29] Nicolai Petro has properly brought our attention to an alternative Russian tradition to absolutism, what he has termed "constrained autocracy," pointing to the existence of the Novgorod *Veche*, the Boyar *Duma*, and the *Zemskiye Sobory* in medieval Russia, and the *Zemstva* (local councils) in late-nineteenth century Russia as evidence of conciliar and corporatist tendencies in Russian political culture. Petro also notes the Eastern Orthodox tradition of *symphonia* as that which should govern relations between crown and Church, each working together but each also sovereign in its own sphere. It is also true that the Russian court and gentry frequently attempted and occasionally succeeded in undoing the efforts of the most aggressively absolutist of Russia's Tsars, such as Peter I, after the death of the monarch (and at times by arranging the death of the monarch, as seems true of Peter III and Paul I). Thus, after Peter I's death in 1725, a series of palace coups, often placing obscure German princes or princesses on the throne (the easier to control them, it would seem), aimed at reversing Peter's abrogation of the customary restraints on royal power, as exemplified by his abolition of respect for heredity in rewarding service to the state (thereby making the gentry immediately dependent on the crown for its standing) or transforming the Church into a simple governmental department. By 1762, these exertions had led to the abolition of mandatory state service by the gentry to the crown and by 1766 to the formation of an elected legislative commission to help Catherine II rule, and eventually led to plans for the decentralization of the state bureaucracy, to allow local gentry to perform police, social welfare, and local governmental functions.[30]

The fact remains that such efforts to constrain royal prerogative were reactionary in character and almost always died on the vine. Too few resources lay in the hands of the Russian gentry compared to those in the hands of an aggressive monarch and a provincial bureaucracy reporting directly to the crown in St. Petersburg. The key point for our purposes is that Russia never developed a genuine institutional and legalized expression of political relations between crown and gentry. Members of the *Sobor*, for instance, were convened by the issuance of personal

---

[29] Nancy Shields Kollmann, *Kinship and Politics: The Making of the Moscovite Political System, 1345–1547* (Stanford, CA: Stanford University Press, 1987), p. 183.
[30] Yaney, *The Systemization of Russian Government*, pp. 68–80.

invitations by the Tsar to those of its constituent members whom he deigned to see. As Pipes concludes:

In sum, the Duma and the Assemblies may best be viewed as expedients necessary to the state until such time as it could afford an adequate bureaucratic apparatus. The Duma provided a link between the crown and the central administration, the Assembly a link between the crown and the provinces. As the bureaucratic apparatus improved, both institutions were quietly dropped.[31]

The essence of the Russian patrimonial system and its distinctiveness from other European monarchies has been summarized by Nancy Shields Kollmann in her study of the origins and emergence of the Muscovite political order from the fourteenth through the sixteenth centuries:

Muscovite political development lacked the sources of feudalism that helped generate demands for representative institutions or privileges by corporate estates in Europe. Muscovy had no vestigial Roman aristocracy, no Germanic kings and tribal elites, no politicized Roman Catholic papacy and church hierarchy. It lacked the legal traditions bequeathed to Europe as a result of Roman occupation and Germanic invasion and developed by secular and ecclesiastical cultural establishments. Muscovy's political development was also influenced by its social situation: as late as the sixteenth century, Muscovy's military, bureaucratic, and urban classes were too small to demand enfranchisement as their counterparts in the West did.[32]

The result was the virtual exclusivity of power of the Russian grand prince and his immediate baronial entourage, with the nonpolitical classes appeased by various social and economic enticements. Yet neither the bureaucracy nor the merchant classes were enfranchised as institutions; nor did the Church obtain decision-making power.[33]

The patrimonial type of absolutism that emerged in Russia around the time of the rise of partially constrained monarchy in England and nonpatrimonial absolutism in France was made possible (as noted) by the hegemony of Muscovy over the Russian lands and reinforced by a variety of circumstances that made Russia's statist patrimonialism especially resilient. These included the support of the Orthodox Church, most dramatically in the fight against Catholic Poland's claimant to the Russian throne during the first time of troubles in the early 1600s; the geopolitical requirements of defending the steppe, requiring a strong militarized state

---

[31] Pipes, *Russia under the Old Regime*, p. 108.
[32] Kollmann, *Kinship and Politics*, p. 3.
[33] Ibid., p. 182.

to consolidate colonial settlement on vast, featureless plains peopled by hostile, well-armed, mainly Islamic-Turkic populations; and the security implications of maintaining and advancing Russian interests in Europe, which demanded a state powerful enough to extract a usable surplus from a generally poor society to wage war against organizationally and technologically superior powers (as was also largely true of militarist Prussia in the eighteenth century). Consequently, the resource requirements demanded in order to sustain such a state, again in a poor and vast space, led the Russian crown to enserf both the peasants and, in a sense, the nobility as well, tying the latter's property and standing to extended service to the crown. The tension between development and tradition is reflected in Catherine II's invitation to foreigners (Mennonites and Hutterites from the German lands and other European minorities) to settle newly conquered steppeland to the east and south rather than risk a challenge to the Russian feudal order that greater mobility for the Russian peasants implied.[34] (Indicatively, Soviet peasants would remain tied to the land by the absence of internal passports, otherwise available to urban residents, which were issued to collective farmers as a class only at the outset of the Brezhnev period in the mid-1960s. Even then, the urban *propiska* [resident permit] system for major cities such as Moscow remained to constrain peasant mobility.)

## VI. The Facts of Life

Given that the Russian peasant was already living on the margins of survival in the trying circumstances of Russia's geographical endowment, the brutalization that this extra effort on behalf of the state implied for Russian living standards can only be imagined.[35] To give several particulars, throughout the eighteenth century, the calorie consumption of Russian peasants was typically at the level of 1,500 calories per day, that is, a semi-starvation level for a laboring man or woman.[36] A century later, Russia's capacity to finance its industrialization program depended critically upon

---

[34] Bater, *The Soviet Scene*, p. 16.

[35] L. V. Milov, "Prirodno-klimaticheskiy faktor i osobennosti rossiyskogo istoricheskogo protsessa" [The natural-climatic factor and particularities of the Russian historical process], *Voprosy Istorii*, no. 4–5 (1992), pp. 37–56. Deaths as a consequence of Peter I's "reforms" have been estimated at as much as 10 percent of the Russian population. Russian government data of 1710 indicated that the number of taxpayers had declined by one-fourth during Peter's reign, at a time when Peter was fanatically trying to raise revenue by all possible means. Samuylov, *Rossiyskaya Tsivilizatsiya*, p. 56.

[36] Milov, "prirodno-klimaticheskiy faktor," p. 49.

the export of grain for gold, grain that was extracted from peasant consumption by artifically low domestic prices for the sale of grain, which proved to be a signal contributory factor to the awful famine of the early 1890s.[37] Likewise, Soviet industrialization in the 1930s was financed largely at the expense of peasant consumption, reducing millions to penury and death.

Although there would be changes in the degree of economic and social mobility and liberty accorded to the nobility (1762), the peasants (1861), and the merchant and industrial classes (the 1880s) in Tsarist Russia, this never extended to the political system, except fitfully in the crisis triggered by Russia's defeat by Japan in 1905. There thus emerged in the second half of the nineteenth century, in a partially modernizing Russia, a fateful tension between the level of social and economic development of the country, on the one hand, and the resistance of the Tsarist system to accommodate these forces politically, on the other. Russia's tradition of patrimonial absolutism, sustained by the combination of desperate poverty and international challenge, thus fatally inhibited Imperial Russia from making the political adaptations that might have coopted a moderate majority of elites around the turn of the twentieth century and thereby have avoided the political polarization and extremism that were characteristic of the Russian political system on the eve of the First World War. Remarkably, a decade after the collapse of Tsarist patrimonialism (however modified in practice), the Soviet leaders set about to create a new type of patrimonial absolutism. This form of absolutism also fused political power as sovereignty over territory with economic power as ownership of land, capital, and in effect people, but under the auspices of the Communist Party rather than Nicholas II as the "landowner of Russia," as Nicholas identified his occupation in the census of 1897.[38] That the party succeeded in doing so suggests that it was building on a foundation that was deeply fixed, literally, in Russian soil.

## VII. Implications

What conclusion may we then draw about historical patterns in Russian political development? First, in the centuries after the defeat of the Mongol

---

[37] Ibid., p. 50.

[38] Ibid., p. 52; see also Merle Fainsod, "Bureaucracy and Modernization: The Russian and Soviet Case," in Joseph LaPalombara, ed., *Bureaucracy and Political Development* (Princeton, NJ: Princeton University Press, 1967), pp. 239–60, on such comparabilities in Tsarist and Soviet political development.

overlordship, Russia developed a political system that was distinctive in the European setting. The system fused two forms of power which in Europe were gradually dissociated from each other, that is, power as sovereignty and power as ownership. Russia's patrimonial form of absolutism developed for three mutually reinforcing reasons: (a) It was possible, due to the skill of the Muscovite princes and the weakness of plausible contenders; (b) what we might call the opportunity costs of likely alternatives were rather high, given the threats posed by powerful Catholic and Islamic neighbors, and later by the more general contest for power and influence in technologically more advanced Europe; and (c) for a long time, the Russian system appeared to work, at no time more convincingly than in the aftermath of Russia's victory over Napoleon, which coincided with the early stages of the Industrial Revolution in the West. So long as the international system was receptive to the application of power based upon the extensive mobilization of resources, for which Russia's regime was well suited, imperial expansion, military victories, and diplomatic peerage in the West all reinforced the standing of Russia's patrimonial system.

This brings us to the second point, which is that Russian economic development internally and the power of the Russian state externally depended upon extensive as opposed to intensive modes of economic production. The poverty of the Russian soil in the non–Black Earth lands could be compensated by slash-and-burn techniques of cultivation in the short term and migration to the apparently endless reserves of marginally arable land in the longer run. A state that could conscript labor for industrial as well as agricultural and military service proved able to extract enough surplus from Russia's narrow margin of survival to become the world's largest producer of iron by the end of the eighteenth century. So long as human labor as distinct from mechanical labor remained the primary cost of production, Russian patrimonialism sufficed to maintain and even extend Russian influence in the world, as the Russian occupations of Berlin in 1762 and Paris in 1814 underscore. As soon as technological development began to change the ratio of human to machine labor in the production process – that is, as the Industrial Revolution placed increasing emphasis on intensive modes of production based on raising factor productivity as opposed to extensive modes based on bringing new sources of production into play – Russia would find itself at a growing disadvantage abroad and increasingly fragile at home. Interestingly, a comparable pattern can be identified in the decomposition of the Soviet system: After an initial stage of industrialization based on exploiting Russia's surplus of population, land, and mineral resources, made possible by a supermobilized communist state, the exhaustion of these relatively easy early gains by the late 1950s placed increasing burdens on a system that proved too centralized to allow the devolution of economic, social, and political authority that a complex, intensive process of economic growth requires. In the end, the Soviet system, as the Tsarist system, imploded in the face of modernity. To date, Russian economic development has been consistent only with a state powerful enough to mobilize Russia's resources on an extensive basis, however inefficiently, at the expense of the living standards of the population as a whole.

Third, Russian reforms have tended to be triggered by evidence of failure in international politics, as is shown by Peter's reforms after initial defeat by Sweden's Charles XII, after Alexander II's defeat in the Crimean War, the promulgation of the first Russian Constitution after Russia's defeat by Japan in 1905, and Gorbachev's reforms in light of Russia's looming defeat in the cold war. Moreover, these reforms, with the remarkable exception of Gorbachev's, proved halting and temporary in their effects, as Russia's ruling elites drew back from the danger that decentralizing reforms posed both for the autocratic system and for the multinational empire, and hence for Russia's standing in the world. There is thus both overlap and tension between the international and social order: Reform is required to strengthen Russia internationally, but too much reform would weaken the Russian Empire, which has been the historical prerequisite of Russia's standing as a great power. This tension between international power politics and internal social dynamics is hardly unique to Russia. Many countries throughout the world, including China from 1842–1949, Japan from 1853–67, and Europe itself from 1914–45 and thereafter in the form of the cold war, struggled with the impact of international power politics upon domestic socioeconomic and political order.

Fourth, and especially in light of the Bolsheviks' rapid restoration of the bulk of the Tsarist Empire and even of its broader international standing by 1922, Tsarist Russia managed these tensions reasonably well. The expansion of the Russian Empire in the centuries following the rise of Muscovy represents a case of imperial expansion that can only be compared in its extent with the British, Roman, and U.S. empires (that is, U.S. dominance across North America).[39] Russia proved able to absorb and even assimilate much of its overland empire into the Russian state in ways that the European overseas empires were never able to do. Russia

[39] See Richard van Alstyne, *The Rising American Empire* (Chicago: Quandrangle, 1965).

proved able to assimilate enough European technology and organization to continue expanding into Asia and maintain its great power status in Europe until, like many other powers, it was overwhelmed by the First World War. On the whole, and unlike Germany between 1890 and 1945, Imperial Russia pursued a strategy of pragmatic opportunism, avoiding direct conflict with the most powerful Western states while invariably striving to ensure that its territorial gains were ratified by the other great powers. In brief, Russian elites proved able to play by the European rules of the game.

Fifth, periodic collapse has invariably been followed by a rapid recovery of the Russian state to the ranks of the great powers, as evidenced by Russia's recovery from the time of troubles in the early 1600s, Peter's forced draft mobilization of Russian resources after early defeat in the Northern Wars with Sweden, Russia's recovery from the humiliation of the Crimean War, Soviet Russia's modernization in the wake of Russia's defeat by Imperial Germany so as to defeat Nazi Germany a generation later, and lastly Soviet Russia's remarkably rapid recovery after the indescribable devastation inflicted by the Nazis during the Second World War. In each of these cases, a powerful central state was in a position to mobilize Russia's marginal wealth for the purposes of state power. In each of these cases extensive modes of economic production predominated, market forces were strictly limited, and Russia could, with maximum effort and strain, catch up to prevailing Western modes of industrial production.

Finally, each of these patterns highlights the centrality of the state in Russia's historical development, politically, economically, and socially. A powerful militarized state was essential to defend and advance the colonization of the vast, featureless, and thus difficult-to-defend steppe. A state powerful enough to extract a surplus from the margins of Russian survival was required if Russia was to defend its sovereignty against technologically and organizationally superior Western powers. More broadly, a strong state was arguably necessary if Russia as a Eurasian civilization were to develop at all. The predominance of mineral extraction over trade certainly facilitated the increase in scope of the Russian state's power, as control over locations is easier for a state to assert than is regulation of flows such as commerce. From an economic point of view, the predominance of the state was reinforced by the lateness of Russian development compared to the West, requiring an accelerated modernization that only the state could trigger, as well as the inevitably higher costs of production entailed by Russia's geographic circumstances. In short, and to anticipate an argument that we shall take up later in the book (see Chapter 6), the poverty of the Russian soil (especially in the historical Russian heart-lands), the severity of the Russian climate, and the vast spaces of transcon-tinental Russia worked to make the costs of Russian production, both agricultural and industrial, a multiple of what they were throughout the Western world. Without an aggressively interventionist state, it is doubtful whether Russia would have been developed at all, except under colonial circumstances (which is to say simply under another state's auspices). How, in the final analysis, could Russia have modernized in time to keep up with the Western-driven dynamic of international power politics? Clearly, what was required was a state that could both protect Russian industry from foreign competition and redistribute resources from sectors that could be milked for hard currency (raw materials and agriculture) to critical sectors such as manufacturing that could never realistically hope to be competitive on global markets but that were essential to the power potential of the state itself.

## VIII. Costs of Security and Costs of Production

If we think about the problem of political development in terms of the relationship between two primary environmental constraints on states and peoples – that is, the costs of providing security and the costs of production – we can understand both the forces shaping Russia's patri-monial association of political power and property and the different paths taken by Russia's European neighbors and overseas states. As Tilly has put it:

...the sheer size of the government varied directly with the effort devoted to extraction, state making, protection, and, especially, war making but inversely with the commercialization of the economy and the extent of the resource base. What is more, the relative bulk of different features of the government varied with the cost/resource ratios of extraction, state making, protection, and war making.[40]

To some extent, this can be framed in terms of the distinction between continental and maritime states, as direct access to the world's oceans fa-cilitates economic gains to be derived from trade and the exploitation of comparative advantage. Continental states also face the challenge of pro-viding comprehensive security along extensive land frontiers, a proposi-tion that is not only costly economically but reinforces the case for a pow-erful centralized state. Few states faced a logistical challenge as daunting as Russia's in securing a vast Eurasian land periphery, just as few European

[40] Tilly, "War Making," p. 182.

states had to strain as fitfully as did Russians in producing an output of food necessary to assure survival, not to mention to develop a surplus sufficient to stimulate the flourishing of commerce, cities, and learning that was under way in Western Europe in the Middle Ages but which in Russia was delayed until the eighteenth and nineteenth centuries.[41] Consequently, expenditures on the army and the navy typically approached 70–90 percent of the Russian government's budget during the reign of Peter I and "continued to absorb the greater part of the tsarist government's funds from then on."[42]

Consider, by contrast, the condition of England/Great Britain, an insular state relieved of the need to field a large standing army. (Indeed, Britain would not institute conscription until the middle of the First World War.) With easy access to the world's oceans and relieved of the need to respond to the ebbs and flows of powerful states on land frontiers, England could afford a minimalist, "night watchman" state that on the continent – in France and Prussia/Germany as well as in Russia – could only be regarded as a reckless luxury. The development in England of prosperous classes dependent on trade helped propel the establishment of a state that would ensure the interests of this class through enforcement of contract, hence law, as well as a civic-based (as opposed to a collectivist) nationalism.[43] Much the same could be said about the United States. By contrast, poorer states such as Russia, whose economies depended on extracting resources from the land, be they grain or minerals, emphasized possession or control by the state and its agents as opposed to the formalization of exchange relationships in which control of goods would remain in the hands of non-state agents. This reached its extreme but by no means untypical form in the widespread use of prisoner labor in Russia in the eighteenth and nineteenth centuries, far outpacing its employment in continental Europe and anticipating the systematic use of slave labor by the Soviet system to absorb the initial costs of production in the virtually inaccessible reaches of Arctic and Siberian Russia.[44] From this perspective, the widely accepted thesis in U.S. academic (and public) circles that democracy induces peace

[41] See Skocpol, *States and Social Revolutions*; Tilly, "War Making." See also Thomas Ertman, *Birth of the Leviathan: Building States and Regimes in Medieval and Early Modern Europe* (Cambridge, UK: Cambridge University Press, 1997), p. 317.
[42] Samuylov, *Rossiyskaya Tsivilizatsiya*, p. 56; Yaney, *The Systemization of Russian Government*, p. 54.
[43] Leah Greenfield, *Nationalism: Five Roads to Modernity* (Cambridge, MA: Harvard University Press, 1992).
[44] Milov, "Prirodno-klimaticheskiy faktor," p. 52.

TABLE 2. *Costs of Production vis-à-vis Costs of Security*

|  | Insular (e.g., England) | Maritime (e.g., France) | Continental (e.g., Prussia) | Eurasian (Russia) |
|---|---|---|---|---|
| Costs of security | Low | Medium-high | High | High |
| Costs of production | Low | Low | High | High |
| Strength of society | High | Medium | Medium | Low |
| Exposure to Western modernization | High and direct | High and direct | Medium and indirect | Low and indirect |
| Nature of the state | Liberal | Centralized | Centralized | Patrimonial |

TABLE 3. *Costs of Production and Security and Regime Type*

| | |
|---|---|
| *High Costs of Both Security &* *Production*: Russia, 18th century Prussia, Ottoman Empire (patrimonialism, militarism) | *High Costs of Security & Low* *Costs of Production*: France (highly centralized state administration) |
| *High Costs of Production & Low* *Costs of Security*: Pre-Meiji Japan, post-Soviet Russia? (traditionalism cum isolation) | *Low Costs of Both Security &* *Production*: England, USA (liberal state dispensation) |

could be turned on its head: Peace, made possible by lower costs of defense typical of insular powers, appears to be a prerequisite of democratic development. These considerations can be represented in a diagram juxtaposing the costs of production to the costs of security, as represented in Table 2.

Another way of conceptualizing the comparison is shown in Table 3, which simply relates the costs of production to the costs of security.

It is this irreducible context of high costs of security combined with high costs of production that has framed the evolution of Russia's patrimonial state over the centuries, including the Soviet period. A simple look at the map is sufficient to convince one of the enormous challenges that Russia's unparalleled land frontiers, especially those along the featureless steppes of central Eurasia, posed for Russia's rulers. Indeed, George Vernadsky attributes the growth and consolidation of Russian absolutism to the perpetual challenge of securing the frontier in the east and south and competing with European powers in the west. The defeat of the Mongols, Vernadsky notes, was an effort that was truly national in scope; yet liberation from Mongol rule did not lead to a relaxation of the Muscovite state or to the restoration of ancient liberties, such as those enjoyed by prosperous and commercial Novgorod and the Russian barons.[45] Rather, Russian society became increasingly regimented from the late-fourteenth century on, reaching its peak in the 1650s with the abolition of the Russian counterpart of the French Estates-General and the consolidation of serfdom. In the face of instability and danger along Russia's vast periphery – from Tatar tribes in the southeast, Lithuania/ Poland in the west, Sweden in the northwest, as well as a series of Mongol/Tatar succession states to the east – arming and waging such wars amounted to a:

... drain on Russian resources, [which] increased rather than decreased after the emancipation. ... In the absence of natural boundaries, the frontier had to be constantly guarded as expansion into the steppe continued, culminating with the conquest of Crimea in 1783 from the Ottoman Empire. The struggle with Europe was no less costly because of the technological and organizational superiority of the West European states. [Thus,] the regimentation of the social classes which started during the Mongol period and was originally based on the Mongol principles of administration, was carried further and completed by the Moscovite government. Autocracy and serfdom [as stated earlier] were the price the Russian people had to pay for national survival.[46]

Less obvious to the outside observer are the implications of Russia's geographical location for the productivity of the Russian economy, and especially its ability to yield a surplus adequate to provide for external security and propel an organic process of socioeconomic modernization. Indeed, a great deal of what appears to be distinctive about Russian civilization comes into focus when we consider this geographical aspect.

Russia's extreme northern location has dictated a very short growing season, from four months in the north (greater Novgorod, Petersburg), to five months in the central regions of the country (Moscow), to about six months further south (Kiev), in contrast to Western Europe, where growing seasons of eight to nine months have been historically typical. As a rule, West Europeans had one and a half to twice the amount of time to plant, grow, and harvest their crops.[47] This short season, combined with the poor fertility of the soil itself, meant that an enormous collective effort was required, both to clear fields and to farm. Moreover, taking into account the days required for preparation of feed for livestock, peasants in Russia's north-central heartland frequently had less

[45] Samuylov, *Rossiyskaya Tsivilizatsiya*, pp. 35–5.
[46] Vernadsky, "The Mongol Impact on Russia," pp. 192–3.
[47] Samuylov, *Rossiyskaya Tsivilizatsiya*, pp. 29–35.

than three and one-half months of actual working time in the fields to prepare the harvest. Under such circumstances, and equipped with the most rudimentary of farm implements, Russian peasants could not work the soil very intensively. Still, they had to work twice as hard as did peasants in medieval Europe (which incidentally benefited from an extended period of global warming at the time) to produce a much smaller harvest. As a rule, Russian agriculture at best was about one-third as productive as agriculture in Central and Western Europe. Indeed, Russian observers envied the agricultural possibilities of such "southern" European countries as England! The absence of a significant grain surplus meant that commerce was underdeveloped, as was urbanization. The peasant in the field faced a vicious cycle: The poverty of the soil reflected lack of fertilizing, but this in turn resulted from an insufficiently developed livestock base, given that there was so little with which to feed the horses, cows, sheep, and so on. To give one striking example, in eighteenth-century England, a field horse typically received 5.7 kilograms of feed per day, while in Russia at the same time such a horse received 2.6 kilograms per day. Consequently, those animals that existed were as a rule poorly fed, hence small and weak. In springtime, horses were literally dropping from hunger. This situation prevailed through the nineteenth century and into the early-twentieth century fundamentally unchanged. The colonization of the so-called Black Earth zone of southern Russia helped, but given periodic droughts, average annual yields were only marginally above those in central Russia. The Russian economic historian Leonid V. Milov has summarized the implications of this situation as follows, in an analysis that fits perfectly within the framework of state formation established by such Western political scientists as Tilly, Wim Blockmans, Thomas Efird, Theda Skocpol, inter alia[48]:

...the unusually low yields, the peasants' limited reserves, and the weak livestock base in the core historical areas of Russia led to Russian society being characterized by relatively low surplus value. This had enormous significance for the establishment of the specific type of state regime in Russia's historical heartland, inducing the ruling class to create harsh levers of state power, aimed at extracting a level of surplus value adequate for the purposes of the state, its ruling class and society as a whole. It is precisely on this basis that the long tradition of Russian autocratic despotism arose, as well as, in the final analysis, Russian serfdom, which in its severity had no counterpart in the world.[49]

[48] Ibid.
[49] Milov, "Prirodno-klimaticheskiy faktor," p. 47.

Russia has faced high costs of production as well as high costs of security throughout its history. The end of the cold war appeared to reduce the costs of Russian security, as traditionally defined, drastically. It remains to be seen whether the costs of production in Russia can be reduced to the point where a genuine market-driven integration with the world capitalist economy is possible, or whether, like Japan under the Togukawa Shogunate, faced with high costs of production and low costs of security, Russia clings to a traditionalist (by Russian standards) conception of the state and engages the outside world beyond the ex-Soviet borders from an essentially isolationist position. How that outcome might come about, and how it might be avoided, is the subject of the analysis that follows.

2

# Soviet Legacies for Post-Soviet Russia

> Since the Thirty Years' War, no people have been more profoundly injured
> and diminished than the Russian people by the successive waves of violence
> brought to them by this past brutal century.
>
> – George Kennan[1]

## I. Introduction

Karl Marx famously observed that while men make history, they do not
usually do so in the manner that they intend. History itself, in the form
of political, economic, social, cultural, and other historical influences or
legacies, decisively shapes the range of public choice realistically available
to leaders and societies. To what extent and how has Russia's distinctive
historical experience in the Soviet period – which lasted for three-fourths
of the twentieth century (compared to twelve years for Nazi Germany) –
shaped the country's postcommunist circumstances and possibilities?

The Soviet Union that emerged from the Russian Revolution developed
a patrimonial society that was both more comprehensive and more intensive than that of Tsarist Russia at least since the freeing of the gentry from
obligatory service to the crown under Catherine the Great. The fusion of
de facto sovereign power in the form of the communists' monopoly of political power with the communist state's monopoly of virtually all forms
of capital in the state-owned economy both reflected and propelled a
level of international hostility that served to justify the Soviet patrimonial
party-state system itself.

---

[1] *New York Review of Books,* August 12, 1999, p. 12.

Because of the searing memory of defeat by Germany in the First World War, reinforced by the Bolsheviks' deeply rooted conviction that the Soviet state could never be truly secure without the conversion of the international system along Soviet lines, the early Soviet leadership perceived an intrinsically hostile international environment, whatever the status of current state-to-state relations with the leading capitalist states. The emergence of truly mortal threats in the form of Japanese militarism after 1931 and of German national socialism after 1933 dramatically increased the costs of security to the young Soviet state, whether they were in the form of the militarization of the first Five-Year Plan projects or the diplomatic efforts to craft an antifascist coalition with the Western capitalist democracies. In short, the costs of establishing security for the fledging Soviet republic, once it became clear that the expected European socialist revolution would not soon materialize, were high and tending to increase over time.

In addition, and somewhat relatedly, the costs of production also remained high. In the absence of large and immediate infusions of international capital, Soviet Russia could not rely upon the organic processes of market forces to produce the economic surplus needed to trigger a pace of industrialization adequate to the defense of the party-state system, at home as well as abroad. By 1927, the very success of the market-oriented New Economic Policy (NEP) was engendering economic and social interests that must inevitably find expression in claims for political representation as against the communist political monopoly, while after 1931 the threat of first Japanese and then German militarism was plainly aimed at reducing, if not eliminating, the power of the Soviet state in the world. Soviet abandonment of the market after 1927 meant that the costs of industrializing the USSR would be huge, with the bulk of the price exacted from the peasantry, who still made up three-fourths of Soviet Russia's population. The requirements of national security, as refracted through Bolshevik ideology and Stalin's requirements for his own political cum personal security, resulted in a hypertrophic centralization and militarization of the Soviet party-state system. Indeed, the consolidation of a Stalinist order in Soviet Russia by the late 1930s can be interpreted as an intensified and more perfect form of patrimonial absolutism than was ever true of Tsarist Russia. Although the great dictator would die in March 1953, the system that he constructed would be bequeathed intact to his several successors. Indeed, in retrospect, Mikhail Gorbachev's tenure in office may be seen as a heroic and ultimately failed attempt to prove the hypothesis that the roots of the Soviet system ran deeper than those of Stalin's legacy. In this respect, the matrix established in the previous chapter – situating political development at the intersection of the costs of security and the costs of production – continued to apply throughout the Soviet period. The collapse of the Soviet order that followed Gorbachev's efforts to uproot what remained of Stalinism in Soviet life – institutionally and psychologically – continues to shape the trajectory of post-Soviet Russian political development to the present day, as subsequent chapters will detail.

## II. The Argument

In this chapter, we shall analyze several types of legacy bequeathed by the Soviet system in its various aspects to its heirs. To anticipate the argument, in the economic sphere, Soviet communism had the effect of isolating the economies where it took root from the world market system, with the effect that, in spite of impressive absolute gains in certain sectors (especially military development, nuclear research, and space exploration), communist economies tended to be more backward relative to their Western counterparts at the end of the communist experience than at the beginning. In the social sphere, the absolute political victory of a totalitarian ideology in an overwhelmingly peasant, poorly institutionalized country meant that the state could dominate society in ways that proved to be beyond the pale even for such a thoroughgoing totalitarian regime as Nazi Germany. Hitler's Germany implanted itself in an urban, highly institutionalized society in which the class structure remained relatively untouched from the beginning to the end of the Nazi period, especially compared to what occurred in the Soviet Union between 1917–39. To this, one must add the cumulative cycles of mass violence inflicted by the Soviet regime (as well as by the Nazis) on two generations of Russians and Soviet citizens (at the outset, not all Russians were ipso facto citizens, by virtue of their class affiliation), which tended to exhaust an already besieged society both physically and spiritually. While much had changed in Soviet society in the post-Stalin decades to make the country superficially more modern, Soviet society could find no organizational expression for the often impressive range of social, economic, and political views that were developing in the 1950s, 1960s, and 1970s.[2]

---

[2] See Allen C. Lynch, *The Soviet Study of International Relations* (Cambridge, UK: Cambridge University Press, 1987, 1989), for a depiction of a range of Soviet views that dissented from official communist party orthodoxy on international affairs but that, until the Gorbachev period, could find no formal, public outlet for their political application.

In the political sphere narrowly conceived (for what was not political in the Soviet Union?), the effective and prolonged monopoly on power exercised by the Communist Party of the Soviet Union meant that, once a Gorbachev challenged that monopoly, no other public institutions were available to step into the breach and absorb the shock to the old order, as happened in more traditional authoritarian states, as in Spain after the death of Franco in 1975. Given that the Soviet constitution itself legitimated ethnically based union republics as the administrative building blocks of the Soviet state, the destabilization of the Soviet Communist Party – in the absence of other, civic-based, all-Soviet public institutions – unleashed forces that would see fifteen nationally defined states replace the Soviet state.[3] Those in control of these new states would thus have a decisive institutional and organizational advantage over the nascent shoots of civil society that were just emerging from the long Soviet frost. Finally, and within this context of Soviet disintegration, because of the spontaneous seizure of the bulk of Soviet state economic assets by those who were also in control or had privileged (and cash-backed) access to those in control of the emerging new national states, the central pattern of post-Soviet political economy had already been established while the Soviet Union still existed. Consequently, Russia's path toward "crony capitalism" and constricted democratic development was largely forged before the post-Soviet Russian political order was itself consolidated.[4] In the final analysis, a weak state structure facing a fragmented and exhausted society and powerful economic cliques burrowing into the state from within – all products of the Soviet era – have fatefully constrained Russia's prospects for political-economic development after communism. In short, too little structure existed in post-Soviet Russia, in both the state and in the society, to give shape effectively to the country's political and

---

[3] See Reneo Lukic and Allen C. Lynch, *Europe from the Balkans to the Urals: The Disintegration of Yugoslavia and the USSR and International Politics* (Oxford, UK: Oxford University Press, 1996), for an application of this framework of analysis to the ethno-federal structures of the USSR and Yugoslavia.

[4] For a comparable argument, see Stephen Holmes' review of Stephen Cohen's *Failed Crusade: America and the Tragedy of Post-Communist Russia* (New York: W. W. Norton, 2000) published in Russian as *Proval Krestovogo Pokhoda S. Sh. A* (Moscow: AIRO-XXE, 2001), in the *London Review of Books*, April 19, 2001. Holmes writes that, in light of the political-economic incentives presented by the tidal wave of Soviet institutional collapse, "Russia's natural resources bear much greater responsibility for the pathological development of post-communist Russia than [do] neoliberal economic models." In other words, the temptation presented to strategically situated Soviet elites to seize Russia's vast mineral wealth tended to work against even the best-laid plans for economic and political reform.

economic course on behalf of public purposes, as distinct from the private purposes of those who proved able to make the Russian state something much less than the sum of its parts. Liberal ideologues (Russian as well as Western) as well as friends of Russia ignored this reality at their peril.[5]

## III. Economic Legacies: Isolation and Relative Backwardness

Consider that in 1913, the last full year of peacetime before the Russian Revolution of 1917, Russia was at approximately the same level as Italy in terms of many indices of modernity, such as life expectancy, infant mortality rates, literacy levels, per capita national income, the relative density of each country's railroad network, and so on. In sum, both Russia and Italy were among the most backward major states in Europe. Today, Italy is ranked among the top five industrial-technological powers in the world, while throughout the 1990s postcommunist Russia was consistently ranked last (forty-ninth out of forty-nine in 1996 and fifty-ninth out of fifty-nine in 1999) among major economies in terms of the international competitiveness of its economic base. In 2002, Russia ranked sixty-fourth out of eighty.[6] In other words, the communist years did much less than is commonly supposed to shorten the gap of modernity between Russia and the West. Moreover, this is not simply a question of Russia failing to improve its relative position vis-à-vis the leading Western powers, while nevertheless achieving absolute gains compared to Russia's previous condition. In some critical areas, such as male life expectancy, the Russian Federation at the end of the 1990s was worse off than was the Russian Empire at the end of the 1890s.[7]

[5] This is my chief disagreement with Peter Reddaway and Dmitry Glinsky, whose *Tragedy of Russia's Reforms: Market Bolshevism against Democracy* (Washington, DC: U.S. Institute of Peace, 2001) remains indispensable reading. While alternative paths of development are imaginable, it is difficult to see how they could have been implemented in light of the sclerotic capacities of the Russian system of public administration. It remains to be said who, specifically, was available and able to implement a coherent and balanced package of economic and political reforms at minimal short-term cost to the population. In reality, both the Russian state and Russian society were too weak for that purpose.

[6] These statistics are according to studies published by the Lausanne-based International Institute for Management Development and the Geneva-based World Economic Forum. See also *Moscow Times*, May 30, 1996, p. 15; Andrey Kostin, "Navstrechu novym vyzovam globalizatsii" [Toward new challenges of globalization], in IMEMO, ed., *God Planety: 2003* [World annual: 2003] (Moscow: Ekomonika, 2003), p. 22.

[7] *Sotsial'noye polozheniye i uroven' zhizni naseleniya Rossii* [The social condition and living standard of the Russian population] (Moscow: Goskomstat, 1997), p. 10.

Marginalization from global economic and technological processes is not unique to Russia. Many European communist countries found themselves much further behind international economic trends at the end of the communist experience compared to just before the onset of communism in the particular countries. The Baltic states in 1940 had about the same per capita national income as did Finland; indeed, consumption of milk and meat at the time in Latvia was on a par with the United States. By the 1980s, Finland's per capita income was about seven times higher than that of the Baltic states, which nevertheless maintained the highest income levels in the USSR. Likewise, Czechoslovakia, which had been selling advanced industrial goods and high-precision tools on the world market at the same prices as German companies in the 1930s and doing nicely in the bargain, had by the 1980s, in the words of its own economists, become a "museum of an industrial country," even though it had the highest standard of living in the communist world.[8]

## IV. Militarization of the Economy

What is unique to Russia is the extent to which its militarized economic structure, an inheritance of the first Five-Year Plans, magnified by the cold war, had so distorted the allocation of resources throughout the country that it is difficult to see how Russia could become integrated on a competitive basis in the global economy – apart from a few natural resource areas such as oil and natural gas – in the foreseeable future. A sense of the strain that the military economy imposed on Russia as a whole may be inferred from the fact that Soviet Russia, which is now believed to have had a gross domestic product (GDP) of at most one-fourth that of the United States by the 1980s, produced a military machine that was fully comparable to, and in some areas superior to, that of the United States.[9] The full burden of military spending on the economy was no doubt hidden from the Soviet leaders themselves by the distortions implicit in the Soviet statistical system. For example, according to Soviet statistics, Soviet national income rose seventeen times between 1913 and 1955. Yet Russian national income in 1913 was one-fifth that of the United

---

[8] For evidence, based on the Czechoslovak Federal Statistical Report on the economy for 1987, see Radio Free Europe Research, *Situation Report: Czechoslovakia/2*, February 15, 1988; *New York Times*, November 17, 1989, p. A15.

[9] Igor Birman, *Ya–Ekonomist* [I am an economist] (Moscow: Vremya, 2001), pp. 366–81; V. D. Andrianov, *Rossiya v mirovoy ekonomike* [Russia in the world economy] (Moscow: Vlados, 1999), pp. 6–7.

States, a fact openly accepted by Soviet statisticians themselves. In effect, if taken literally, these statistics suggested that the USSR should have achieved parity in national income with the United States by 1955, a patent absurdity. Likewise, Soviet Prime Minister Nikolai Tikhonov declared in 1983 that Soviet industrial production, asserted at 30 percent of U.S. production in 1950 (but see the preceding statistics), had been growing at the average annual rate of 8.4 percent between 1951 and 1982, compared to 3.6 percent for the United States. At that rate, the USSR should have surpassed the United States in industrial production in the mid-1970s, and in the worst case should have been 110 percent that of U.S. production by 1982 – again, a patently implausible outcome.[10]

To obtain a more specific sense of the weight of the defense burden on the Soviet economy, consider that between 1979–88, the Soviet Union produced three and one-half as many tanks, four times as many bombers, and twice as many fighter planes as did the United States. In 1988, three years into the Gorbachev reforms, the Soviet Union produced three times as many tanks and twice as many missiles as did all NATO countries, including the United States, combined. Perhaps 70 percent of all industrial employment in the Soviet Union was involved in the defense sector. In other words, military spending in relation to the national economy was at least three times greater in the USSR than in the United States, amounting to between 16–25 percent of Soviet GDP (compared to a U.S. norm of 5–6 percent in the 1970s and 1980s).[11] In the first half of the 1980s, fully 88 percent of industrial investment was allocated to the nonconsumer goods sector, a marked contrast to the Tsarist era, when consumer goods dominated the industrial structure. By contrast, and in consequence, living space per urban inhabitant in the 1980s was just 8.6 square meters, below the sanitary minimum of 9 square meters (or just under 100 square feet, that is, 10 feet by 10 feet) decreed by Lenin in the early 1920s.[12] To give another example of "consumer" poverty, the simple (and unreliable) Zaporozhets car that Russian President Vladimir Putin's mother won in a lottery and gave to him in the mid-1970s cost two years of an average salary to buy (in addition, she would have had to

---

[10] Pierre Lorrain, *La Mysterieuse Ascension de Vladimir Poutine* [The mysterious rise of Vladimir Putin] (Monaco: Editions de Roche, 2000), pp. 195–6.

[11] Vladimir M. Shamberg, *Soviet Defense Industries: History and Implications after the Collapse of the Soviet Union* (USAF Academy, CO: USAF Institute for National Security Studies, June 2000), pp. 50, 52, 55–6, 81.

[12] James Bater, *The Soviet Scene: A Geographical Perspective* (London: Edward Arnold, 1989), p. 226.

have gotten on a lengthy waiting list before actually obtaining the car).[13] In light of these tendencies, Nikita Khrushchev was once heard to say that the Americans built weapons with one hand and conducted business with the other, whereas the USSR was constrained to build weapons with both.[14] Both Khrushchev and his Soviet successors failed to find a way of fully freeing up one of those hands for civilian-oriented economic activity. That fact, too, weighs heavily upon Russia's chances for early economic recovery.

## V. Social Legacies: Fragmentation and Exhaustion

Western Sovietologists have been broadly, if perhaps unfairly, criticized for not anticipating the rapid (and relatively peaceful) collapse of the Soviet Union in late 1991. Yet the same may be said of Soviet and Russian politicians themselves: Until practically the last minute in December 1991, nearly all nationalist leaders – including those in Russia, Ukraine, Belarus, as well as in the Central Asian republics of the Soviet Union – expected a prolonged transitional period in which power would gradually devolve to the constituent national republics through negotiation with the Soviet central government. They did not expect, and were consequently almost completely unprepared for, the rapid disappearance of the Soviet state and thus for the assumption of the responsibilities of governing fully independent states.

   This unpreparedness was compounded by the fact that the sudden disintegration of the Soviet system, based as it was on the virtual monopoly of all public organizations by an integrated communist party-state system of rule, left the Soviet successor states, and their societies, with few of the institutions required to chart a stable post-Soviet political course, democratic or otherwise. Alexander Motyl has argued persuasively that the prospects for the rapid and stable consolidation of capitalist and democratic transformations are closely correlated with both the state's political and administrative capacity to formulate coherent forward-looking policies for the country, and a healthy civil society, which can serve both as a partner with and monitor on the state.[15] Whatever may be said about

---

[13] Lorrain, *La Mysterieuse Ascension de Vladimir Poutine*, p. 122. The Zaporozhets may be considered an inferior version of the old Fiat 500 or Seat 600.

[14] Oleg Grinevsky, *Tysyachya dnei s Nikitim Sergeyevichim* [One thousand days with Nikita Khrushchev] (Moscow: VAGRIUS, 1998), p. 14.

[15] See the chapter by Alexander J. Motyl in Adrian Karatnycky et al., eds., *Nations in Transit* (New York: Freedom House, 1997), pp. 17–22.

the capacity of post-Soviet states to rule, these societies are on the whole extraordinarily weak in terms of organized civic activism, participation in political parties, and ability to hold the government to account, even during the course of elections, which post-Soviet governments have learned to mold in favor of the incumbent. Strike activity – especially coordinated strike activity across enterprises, industrial branches, and regions – has been remarkably low given the magnitude of both income depression (including widespread wage arrears) and the dramatic widening income and wealth inequality that had taken place in Russia in the 1990s.[16] The amazing burst of civic energy that was unleashed by the Gorbachev reforms of the late 1980s fizzled out just as quickly within the first years of Russian independence, no doubt in large part under the pressures of the daily struggle for existence and a rapid disillusionment with the whole political process following the political violence of fall 1993.[17]

Numbers can be deceiving. While more than one hundred thousand Russian nongovernmental organizations apparently existed, at least on paper, by 2001 the press, television broadcasting, and political institutions were almost completely ignoring these civic associations, as the virtual boycott by these agencies of the first National Conference of Non-Governmental Organizations in Moscow in October 2000 showed. As sympathetic an observer as the British political scientist Mary McAuley must still report that the nongovernmental organizational sector in Russia is "fragmented, weak on horizontal links, [and] still dependent on Western funding...."[18]

McAuley's emphasis on the weakness of the horizontal links among nongovernmental organizations in Russia is crucial to understanding the long-term impact of the Soviet experience on Russian society's capacity to participate effectively in public affairs. If any society approached the ideal type of atomization, in which the vertical links between individual and the state supplanted the horizontal ties binding individuals to each other through work, residence, class, social and personal interests, civic associations, and even family, it was the Soviet Union under Stalin from the late 1920s until the dictator's death in March 1953. To be sure,

---

[16] About 90 percent of all strikes in recent years have been called in the educational establishment, to protest low wages and arrears. ITAR-TASS (Moscow), March 16, 2001, in *Johnson's Russia List* (hereafter *JRL*), #5156, March 17, 2001, at www.cdi.org.

[17] Reddaway and Glinsky, *The Tragedy of Russian Reform*, pp. 171–2, 190.

[18] Mary McAuley, "Letter from Moscow. The Big Chill. Civil Society in Russia in a New Political Season," *JRL*, #5156, March 17, 2001. For McAuley's report in full, see www.fordfound.org.

even then, the actual control of the central Soviet state over its subjects was far from complete.

The resistance and even revolts of workers in old established industries to economic Stalinization in the early 1930s is now coming to light from scholars plying the Soviet archives.[19] Peasant resistance to collectivization, a euphemism for state seizure of the farms, was so widespread that Stalin told Winston Churchill that the crisis was as serious as that posed by the Nazi invasion.[20] Careful interviews of refugee and emigré populations after the Second World War showed that, even among those showing support for the broad features of Soviet socialism, there was a considerable range of views about the appropriate place for the state in heavy industry, as distinct from agriculture and the service sector, while there was never broad support for a terroristic dictatorship, which Stalin's Soviet Union had in fact become.[21] And certainly one point on which the post-Stalin Soviet political elites achieved consensus, whatever their view in retrospect of the dictator in his time, was that random terror had to be removed from the system, if only to achieve an acceptable degree of security for their positions and their persons. Thus, in spite of compelling evidence that Stalin had to some extent succeeded in creating a "new Soviet man," especially among the recent peasant migrants in new Soviet industrial cities such as Magnitogorsk, this success should not be considered absolute.[22] The range of economic and political views among the political and intellectual elites, and even among the population at large, was always considerably broader than the image of a monolithic Soviet

---

[19] Jeffrey Rossman, *Worker Resistance under Stalin: Class and Gender in the Textile Mills of the Ivanovo Region, 1928–1932*. Ph.D. dissertation, University of California at Berkeley, Department of History, 1997.

[20] Winston S. Churchill, *The Second World War: The Hinge of Fate* (Boston: Houghton Mifflin, 1950), p. 498.

[21] Donna Bahry, "Rethinking the Social Roots of Perestroika," *Slavic Review*, Fall 1993, pp. 525–39.

[22] Supporting work published by Steven Kotkin (*Magnetic Mountain: Stalinism as a Civilization* [Berkeley, CA: University of California Press, 1995]), Jochen Hellbeck has convincingly portrayed a tendency, based on access to more than three score Stalin-era diaries, that many efforts by sincere communists to come to terms with the arbitrariness and random violence of the Stalin period were themselves framed in Soviet terms, suggesting a kind of "Stalinism from within," as he puts it. This tends to support the controversial interpretation given by Arthur Koestler in his novel, *Darkness at Noon*, although Koestler was wrong in the specific instance of his protagonist Rubashov, based on Nikolai Bukharin: we know now that Bukharin was threatened with the destruction of his entire family if he did not confess to patent falsehoods concerning alleged treasonous activities. Jochen Hellbeck, ed., *Tagebuch aus Moskau, 1931–1939* [Moscow Diary, 1931–1939] (Munich: DTV Dokumente, 1996).

society, whether propagated by Soviet or Western officialdom, would have us believe. By the mid-1980s, research conducted by the Soviet sociologist Tatyana Zaslavskaya clearly identified a pluralism of political and economic views that corresponded to what we might consider the class interest of the individual concerned. Thus, in terms of attitudes to economic reform and political reform, respectively:

- Unskilled manual workers tended to be against both economic and political reform.
- Skilled workers tended to be hesitant about economic reform and in favor of political reform.
- Highly skilled workers and members of the intelligentsia tended to favor both economic and political reform.
- The top political leaders tended to favor both economic and political reform.
- The bulk of the governmental and party bureaucracy tended to be against both economic and political reform.
- Enterprise managers tended to favor economic reform but to oppose political reform.[23]

Yet attitudes and opinions are one thing; the capacity to give public expression to them is quite another. Even committed adherents of Mohandas Gandhi have come to the conclusion that *satyagraha* as a political strategy and as moral philosophy is doomed to fail in a totalitarian setting such as that of Stalin's USSR or Nazi Germany, if only because the central premise of the approach – that is, the opportunity of appealing to the moral conscience of the other – is generally unavailable in a terror state.[24] And while terror as a central political fact would disappear in the Soviet Union after Stalin's death, the institutions that sustained that terror and that the terror itself had sustained remained in place. Thus, while the preceding summary of Soviet attitudes toward reforms reveals a pluralism of views and interests, perhaps enough to sustain a three-party political system, the Communist Party of the Soviet Union maintained an effective monopoly on political power, as well as on all forms of social organization, until March 1990, less than two years before the Soviet collapse and while the spontaneous repartition of wealth and power was already under way.

---

[23] Silviu Brucan, *Social Change in Russia and Eastern Europe: From Party Hacks to Nouveaux Riches* (Westport, CT: Praeger, 1998), p. 41.

[24] See George Orwell's compelling essay on the historical and political relativism of Gandhi's philosophy of *satyagraha*, in George Orwell, *Collected Essays* (London: Secker and Warburg, 1961).

## VI. Social Organization and Political Regime

The success that the Soviet state had in excluding political competitors and preventing society from establishing itself on autonomous grounds may be gauged from a series of comparisons with the situation in Germany under the Nazis. These comparisons are made not in order to belittle Nazi crimes or anathematize the Soviet system; rather they are intended to suggest some of the social differences between a society such as the Soviet Union, in which a totalitarian (and progressive) ideology was imposed upon a poor, mainly peasant, poorly institutionalized society, and a society such as Nazi Germany, in which a totalitarian (and reactionary) ideology was imposed upon a middle-class, urban, highly institutionalized society.

First, the Soviet economy was more militarized in time of peace than was that of Nazi Germany in time of war, at least until 1943, when Albert Speer rationalized the German war economy.[25] Through the 1980s, the proportion of the Soviet economy devoted to civilian consumption was consistently lower than 45 percent; within the industrial sector, consumer goods production accounted for only 25–7 percent of Soviet GDP, a share that had been consistent for decades.[26] Hitler, by contrast, feared that German society would not tolerate the sacrifices demanded by total war. Accordingly, he allowed the continued production of such consumer items as refrigerators and prohibited the mass employment of German women in the war industries. Not only Stalin's Russia but the Western democracies as well had achieved much greater efficiencies of war economy from the outset of the war, if not earlier. Indeed, Western specialists after the war concluded that the terror bombing of cities like Hamburg had the perverse effect of increasing the efficiency of the German war economy, as the raids tended to destroy large swaths of nonmilitary-oriented production; the consequences of the raid allowed the Nazi government to rationalize and concentrate war production in ways that had been impossible to do within an intact German social economy.[27] It was only after Franklin D. Roosevelt and Churchill issued their demand for Germany's unconditional surrender in early 1943 that the Nazi government began to approach its Soviet (and democratic) enemies in totality of military mobilization. By

---

[25] Richard Overy, "Das Reich des Boesen," *Der Spiegel*, no. 26 (June 25, 2001), pp. 172–3; Albert Speer, *Erinnerungen* (Berlin: Propylaeen Verlag, 1969).

[26] Vasiliy Selyunin and Grigoriy Khanin, "Lukavaya tsaifra" [Lies, damn lies, and statistics], *Novyi Mir*, no. 2 (1987), pp. 181–201; Shamberg, *Soviet Defense Industries*, p. 56.

[27] John Kenneth Galbraith, *A Life in Our Times* (Boston: Houghton Mifflin, 1981).

contrast to the United States and Britain, the Soviet Union after the war maintained a militarized structure of production that had in fact been established a decade before the Nazi invasion.

Second, a careful reading of German memoirs makes clear that there was greater space for antiregime discussion and even organization in wartime Nazi Germany than in the Soviet Union until the beginning of the Gorbachev period. The Russian General Andrei Vlasov, captured by the Nazis and later the commander of a Russian division fighting along-side the Wehrmacht, confessed his "amazement to his German friends at how it was still possible in wartime Nazi Germany to undertake personal initiatives and to speak freely among friends."[28] Indeed, those plotting the July 20, 1944, assassination attempt against Hitler were discussing details of the plot openly in their Foreign Ministry offices, even in front of their secretaries, and managed to keep the entire affair, involving hundreds of individuals, secret to the last.[29] Nothing remotely comparable is even conceivable in the peacetime Soviet Union from 1945–85, given the level of Communist Party and secret police penetration of the society, and the deterrent effect of such penetration. Already by 1950, about 10 percent of the East German population had been induced into collaboration of various degrees with the State Security Service (Stasi), surpassing the success of the Gestapo in this respect.[30] By 1989, Stasi penetration of the German Democratic Republic had reached about one-third of all East German adults. Another case involving a remarkable instance of civic activism (of a sort) in wartime Nazi Germany reinforces the point. In the winter and spring of 1941, a collection of German clerics, judges, mayors, and other social elites organized a protest against the Euthanasia program begun by the Nazis, aimed at killing "undesirable" (non-Jewish) Germans – that is, the senile and the mentally retarded – in an attempt to improve the "racial stock" of the Geman nation. In an effort that has no remotely comparable counterpart in the Soviet Union until the Gorbachev period, these elites were able to force the government to cancel the program,

---

[28] Ernst Nolte, *La Guerre Civile Europeene, 1917–1945*, translated from the German by Jean-Marie Argeles (Paris: Editions des Syrtes, 2000), p. 537.

[29] Kurt Finker, Stauffenberg und der 20 Juli 1944 [Stauffenberg and the Conspiracy of July 20, 1944] (Berlin: Union Verlag, 1971); Hans Paar, *Dilettanten gegen Hitler: Offiziere in Widerstand: ihre Worte, ihre Taten* [Amateurs against Hitler: Officers in Resistance, Their Words and Deeds] (Preussisch Oldendorf: K. W. Schultz, 1985); Marie Vassiltchikov, *The Berlin Diaries, 1940–1945* (London: Chatto and Windus, 1985), pp. 129–241, esp. pp. 85, 189–90, 202.

[30] Curt Riess, *The Berlin Story* (New York: Dial Press, 1952), p. 303.

until it was later moved outside of Germany following the invasion of the Soviet Union in June 1941.[31]

Finally, and in striking contrast to post-Nazi Germany, except for a brief period in the late Gorbachev era, there has been virtually no movement in Russian society to bring to account – either politically or legally – those implicated in the mass murders of the Stalin period. Unlike in post-Nazi Germany, which continued with war crimes prosecutions on its own past the end of Allied occupation (the most significant post-Nuremburg trials having taken place in the early- to mid-1960s), not one person connected with these crimes has even been brought to trial, much less convicted, in post-Soviet Russia. And unlike post-1968 West Germany, no social movement in Russia has initiated a public discussion to identify and hold to account those responsible for the crimes of the past and thereby to influence the political culture of the country. Russian intellectuals are virtually silent on this issue. Few appear interested in trying to identify and understand who were, to invoke Daniel Goldhagen's words, Stalin's "willing executioners."[32] Timothy Garton Ash has counted more than 2,400 movements worldwide seeking to establish political and/or legal justice for crimes of mass violence committed in the living past; that count represents virtually every country in the world, save Russia.[33]

This absence of and indeed the widespread resistance to any coming to terms with Russia's violent past itself reflects the fragmentation and exhaustion of Russian society that are partly the result of such violence. Given the scale of the violence and the depth of Communist Party and

---

[31] Eugen Kogon, Hermann Langbein, and Adalbert Rueckerl, *Les Chambres à Gaz: Secret d'Etat* [The gas chambers: A state secret] (Paris: Editions de Minuit, 1984), pp. 48–51.

[32] Goldhagen's remarkable and disturbing book, while flawed in that it fails to account for the astounding assimilation of Jews in pre-1933 Germany (compared to any other society of the time, including France and the United States), seeks to identify the broad pattern of social cooperation required for an effort on the scale of the Holocaust to take place. See *Hitler's Willing Executioners: Ordinary Germans and the Holocaust* (New York: Alfred A. Knopf, 1996). Along these lines, see also Nicholas Werth's compelling contribution to Stephane Courtois, ed., *Le Livre Noir du Communisme* [The Black Book of Communism] (Paris: Robert Laffont, 1997), p. 377.

[33] Henning Ritter, "The Eternal Return," *Frankfurter Allgemeine Zeitung* (English edition), March 13, 2001; Jutta Scherrer, " 'Lasst die Toten ihre Toten begraben.' Warum Russland von den sowjetischen Massenverbrechen nichts wissen will" ["Let the Dead Bury the Dead": Why Russia Does Not Want to Know about Soviet Crimes against Humanity], in Horst Mueller, ed., *Der rote Holocaust und die Deutschen: Die Debatte um das "Schwarzbuch des Kommunismus"* [The Red Holocaust and the Germans: The Debate over the "Black Book of Communism"] (Munich: Piper Verlag, 1999), pp. 80–5.

KGB penetration of Soviet society, an extraordinarily large number of Russians had to be directly complicit in the management and operation of the Gulag system. Relatedly, many, perhaps a majority of Russians were themselves directly or indirectly involved in relations with the Communist Party and the KGB. That in the 1970s a majority of men between the ages of twenty-five and fifty with higher education were Communist Party members is indicative in this respect.[34] Also indicative is that not one ex-dissident has served in a Russian government since the collapse of the Soviet Union, very much unlike the less thoroughly penetrated societies of Poland, Hungary, and even the Czech Republic. As Zbigniew Bzrezinski has observed, there is no one in the current Russian government who could not have been a member of the Soviet government, during or before the Gorbachev regime, had the Soviet Union survived.[35] In addition, one has to note that the second post-Soviet Russian President, Putin, emerged not from the ranks of civil society but from the one organization that had the most to do operationally with its asphyxiation, the KGB. In sum, there are simply too few individuals with either the inclination or the organizational possibilities of calling the perpetrators of mass political murder to account. Ironically, the one organization that is devoted to this task, the remarkable *Memorial'* society, is almost entirely dependent upon foreign (and mainly U.S.) funding for its activities, as we have noted is true of much of the Russian nongovernmental sector. The social as well as the political soil for such activity is simply not receptive in today's Russia.

Objections will certainly arise to the effect that, in the course of more than half a century of industrialization, urbanization, and increasing professionalization of life in the Soviet Union, new social forces emerged that tended to make the Soviet Union of the early 1980s a very different society than it was in the early 1920s. In this light, pressures for reform of the Soviet system had been building up from within for decades before Gorbachev, who was able to give political expression to attitudes and forces that had been developing but were suppressed or distorted by the Soviet political system. To give one example, the phenomenon of political dissidence that emerged in the 1960s was probably inconceivable without the large-scale construction of private apartments undertaken in the

[34] Jerry Hough and Merle Fainsod, *How the Soviet Union Is Governed* (Cambridge, MA: Harvard University Press, 1979).
[35] Kennan Institute Meeting Report, 2001.

Khrushchev era. Without the privacy of discussion that was unavailable in the communal apartments, where the bulk of the urban population still lived through the 1950s, political dissidence could not have developed as a true sociological, as distinct from an individual, phenomenon.[36]

Likewise, there was broad but carefully modulated disagreement with many of the more egregious aspects of the regime among many of those who otherwise faithfully served that regime, a kind of "within system dissidence," as both Georgy Arbatov and Yevgeny Primakov, key foreign policy advisors in the Brezhnev years, have termed it.[37] These elites desired above all to rationalize the Soviet system, to allow a true "professional-ization" of Soviet life, much in the manner that Russia's late-nineteenth century business, legal, intellectual, and cultural elites sought a fuller representation of their corporate interests than in the end proved possible in the traditionalist autocracy of Tsarist Russia.[38] To be sure, the days were gone when Stalin's chief of the secret police, Lavrenty Beria, could draw up a list comparing rewards and punishments, including the death penalty, for Soviet physicists in the event that the first Soviet atomic bomb test should succeed or fail.[39] Yet all too frequently, pro-Soviet intellectuals were confronted with the following kind of situation, witnessed by academician Mstislav Keldysh, at the time president of the Soviet Academy of Scences:

Since Stalin's death, the defense industries had not been threatened by arrests.... But Soviet leaders continued to interfere with the workings of the defense industries.... In the early 1960s, the Director of [Research Institute #1 of the Ministry of Aircraft Industry] was scheduled to report to Nikita Khrushchev about the [prospects] of their work [on nuclear missiles]. A couple of days before the meeting with Khrushchev they were summoned to the office of the Director of the Department of Defense Industries in the apparatus of the Central Committee [of the Communist Party of the Soviet Union]. He asked them what they were going to report to Comrade Khrushchev. They answered that they were researching five different missile projects, would describe them, and single out which one they th[ought] would be the best. The Central Committee official bluntly told them: "No, you will not do that. You will report all your projects as equally promising and watch for Comrade Khrushchev's reaction. When you understand from the

---

[36] Sonja Margolina, *Russland: Die nichtzivile Gesellschaft* [Russia: The Uncivil Society] (Hamburg: Rowohr, 1994).

[37] Georgy Arbatov, *The System* (New York, 1991); Yevgeny Primakov, *Gody v bol'shoi politike* [Years in high politics] (Moscow, 2000).

[38] Harley Balzer, ed., *Russia's Missing Middle Class: The Professions in Russian History* (Armonk, NY: M. E. Sharpe, 1996); Nicolai Petro, *The Rebirth of Russian Democracy* (Cambridge, MA: Harvard University Press, 1995).

[39] David Holloway, *Stalin and the Bomb* (New Haven, CT: Yale University Press, 1994), p. 218

expression on his face that he likes this or that project, you will present this project as the best and most promising."[40]

To counter this medieval tendency of the Soviet system, even in the decades after the death of Stalin, to reduce technical questions to the dimension of court politics, elites such as Arbatov, Primakov, and many others worked, within the limits of political prudence to be sure, to modernize the system. While the space accorded technical expertise would expand in the Brezhnev years, Soviet technical and more broadly intellectual specialists could not truly consider themselves to be professionals, with the wide corporate and individual autonomy that this term, derived from the idea of the "free" professions, implies. At heart, regime intellectuals were hoping that a hypercentralized political economy would give way to a more flexible division of social, economic, and even political labor. In fact, it was no coincidence that large numbers of what we might call the Soviet "white-collar" classes were most enthusiastic in support of Gorbachev's early reform initiatives, as they saw in them the opportunity for those with the technical and other specialized knowledge needed to run a modern society to acquire a legitimate public voice. Moshe Lewin's *The Gorbachev Phenomenon* is the most eloquent expression of this essentially sociological explanation of the advent of the Gorbachev reforms. According to Lewin, by the 1980s, "more than ever, the political organs are responding to the powerful contradictory pressures of domestic social reality as well as to the stresses and demands of international events."[41] Does this not then testify, especially in light of the remarkable outburst of civic activism in Moscow and Leningrad after 1987, to the gathering strength of Soviet social forces?

Because of the specific nature and structure of the Soviet system, things were not what they seemed at first glance. Soviet "professionals" were not truly professionals in the Western sense of that term. Rather, they were servants of the regime that hired them and that maintained a highly effective monopoly on employment and rewards, monetary and otherwise,

---

[40] Shamberg, *Soviet Defense Industries*, pp. 42–3. Considering that a major impetus to Khrushchev's placement of shorter-range missiles in Cuba in the fall of 1962 was the failure of the first-generation Soviet ICBM Program, the consequences of this disregard of professional expertise could have been epochal. Relatedly, Khrushchev apparently did not consult a single Soviet expert on the United States before deciding to ship the missiles to Cuba. On both points, see Graham Allison and Philip Zelikow, *Essence of Decision: Explaining the Cuban Missile Crisis* (New York: Longman, 1999), pp. 92–3, 109.
[41] Moshe Lewin, *The Gorbachev Phenomenon: A Historical Interpretation* (London: Radius, 1988), p. 82.

such as travel abroad. Their jobs, pay, and social status were all dependent
on the state system that many hoped (and some sought) to modernize. As
Gorbachev's foreign policy advisor Andrei Grachev has observed, "Even
the highest officials of the Soviet state remained, in their souls, true pro-
letarians, because they possessed nothing beyond the sum of the goods
and privileges, officially confirmed by each new leader, that constituted
their portion of the common feeding trough."[42] Absent that system, they
would necessarily be thrown into a dramatic crisis for survival as a class,
and the economic and social dispossession of this class in the 1990s emphasizes this point with dramatic clarity.[43] In short, what passed for a
middle-class, professionalized sector was far from it, was rapidly declassé
following the collapse of the state that gave rise to it, and – contrary to
what appeared to be the case in the late 1980s, when the Soviet state still
existed – was in no condition to form the tissue of a civil society that could
both participate with and monitor the state in shaping and consolidating
Russia's transit from communism.

Likewise, the rapid and widespread urbanization of Soviet society, itself a product and byproduct of Stalinization, represented something very
different from the phenomenon of urbanization in Western Europe and
North America. Urbanization thus had fundamentally different sociological consequences from those anticipated by theorists of the socioeconomic and political convergence of advanced industrial societies. The
Soviet Union, while certainly industrialized, was not exactly urbanized.
The development of urban civilization in Western Europe, the model for
concepts of modernity, implies an organic growth of an increasingly dif-
ferentiated and thus complex, interdependent social tissue, one in which
horizontal ties among citizens, guilds, professions, and corporations sup-
plant the essentially vertical, if often reciprocal, ties that characterized
feudalism in medieval Europe. Private property guaranteed by law plays
a key role in undergirding the relative decentralization of economic power,
social status, and ultimately political authority. Private commerce, based
on voluntary exchange sustained by contract and credit, and hence on

---

[42] Lorrain, op. cit., pp. 312–13.
[43] Sonja Margolina, *Die Fesseln der Vergangenheit* [The Chains of the Past] (Frankfurt am
Main: Fischer, 1993), pp. 137–39. Margolina observes that the Soviet and Russian intelligentsias were quintessentially state intelligentsias and that, to the extent that the Soviet
intelligentsia succeeded in delegitimizing the Soviet state in the 1980s, it thereby undermined the foundations of its own existence. Its entire social existence was defined in
opposition to a state power on which it in fact depended for its salaries. Daily life lay
entirely beyond its scope of theoretical reflection.

social trust, helps to give substance to a cosmopolitanism expressed by the very idea of being "urbane." In the late medieval world, *Stadtluft macht frei* [city air is the air of freedom], as the old German saying had it. In the continental context, liberty and the city are inextricably bound up with each other. Indeed, the very possibility of civil society as an autonomous social fact is profoundly rooted in the development of this kind of urban civilization.

As with "professionalization," so with Soviet "urbanization." With the partial exceptions of Moscow and St. Petersburg, Soviet cities were not, and post-Soviet Russian cities are not, urbane. Quite apart from the massive peasant influx into the cities in the 1930s, "prompting us," in Moshe Lewin's words, "to be cautious when assessing the effects of rapid urbanization on the disappearance of rural creeds, mores, and cultures," there is the specifically Soviet pattern of urbanization to take into account.[44] The development of Soviet cities went hand in hand with the forced industrialization of the Stalin period and therefore reflected the pattern of industrialization as provided for in the Five-Year Plans. Soviet urban development proceeded, as did industrialization and before that the political system itself, along centralized and vertical rather than decentralized and horizontal lines. Moreover, and reinforcing this tendency, Soviet cities developed not as comprehensive, integrated social organisms but overwhelmingly as a series of "camps" belonging to a particular ministry, industrial sector, political-administrative, military, or even scientific sector, most of which were based in Moscow and some of which subsisted "on just one branch of industrial activity or transportation."[45] Within these "mono-industrial" towns, these state agencies, based in and/or reporting to Moscow, organized whole quarters or indeed whole cities as Pullman towns – that is, the late-nineteenth-century U.S. phenomenon in which the company literally owns the town and exercises an essentially feudal authority over the residents, who are completely dependent on the company for an integrated set of services including job, pay, social security, provisions, housing, utilities, and so on.[46]

---

44 Lewin, *The Gorbachev Phenomenon*, p. 36.
45 Ibid., p. 40; Stefan Hedlund, *Russia's 'Market' Economy: A Bad Case of Predatory Capitalism* (UK: UCL Press, 1999), p. 358.
46 See Gerd Ruge, *Sibirisches Tagebuch* [Siberian Diary] (Munich: Knaur, 2000), p. 102 and passim, for an excellent description of a prototypical Pullman-like Russian town, Nerungri, a coal-mining settlement of one hundred thousand in southern Sakha (Yakutia); see also Per Botolf Maurself, "Divergence and Dispersion in the Russian Economy," *Europe-Asia Studies*, vol. 55, no. 8 (December 2003), pp. 1165–86.

This "departmentalist" approach to the development of Soviet cities was particularly marked in the new urban settlements developed after the onset of Soviet industrialization in the 1930s (such as Magnitogorsk, Bratsk, Padun, and Akademgorodok).[47] Likewise, Soviet factories provided not simply jobs, but job security, housing, nurseries, urban power grids, mass transit systems, leisure time possibilities, and so on. This had the effect of magnifying the dependence of Soviet workers and their families on these Soviet "Pullman towns," and worked against the development of the horizontal ties – not just between regions but within cities themselves – that sustain a genuine urban civilization. This no doubt helps to explain why, in spite of prolonged and massive nonpayment of wages in the post-Soviet period, Russian workers have been as a rule reluctant to leave their jobs: They evidently do not perceive economic and social alternatives that are implicit in a genuine city. The replication of these feudallike patterns perhaps clarifies the apparent paradox that post-Soviet Russia, though on the surface industrialized and urbanized, displays economic, social, and political patterns, including labor market inflexibility, that are more typical of poorly industrialized and weakly urbanized societies. Intersectoral and interregional labor action has also been weak, especially in light of the prolonged nonpayment of wages in the 1990s. In this context, it should not be surprising that Russian industrialization and urbanization have not seen the emergence of civic-oriented social forces, including the widespread associationalism that Alexis de Tocqueville saw as distinctive to American democracy and that are the byproduct of urban civilization properly conceived.[48] Relatedly, Robert Putnam concluded in his study of the conditions of responsive and effective government that, "By far the most important factor in explaining good government is the degree to which social and political life in a region approximates the ideal of the civic community."[49] To the extent that this is true, the sociology of contemporary Russia hinders rather than helps the establishment of good government, under any political auspices.

## VII. Tidal Waves of Violence

One should also consider the enormous toll of violence that the Russian people have paid throughout the twentieth century, which has in many fundamental respects exhausted them, physically and psychologically.

---

[47] Bater, *The Soviet Scene*, p. 123.
[48] Margolina, *Russland*.
[49] Robert Putnam, *Making Democracy Work* (Cambridge, MA: Harvard University Press, 1993), p. 120.

Consider, for example, the following assessments of the scale of violence inflicted on the Russian and Soviet peoples over the course of the twentieth century, made possible by work in the Soviet archives in the 1990s. This includes, but is by no means limited to:

- More than 1.5 million Russians killed in the First World War, and a far greater number wounded, maimed, or missing.
- Perhaps 13–15 million dead during the Russian Civil War of 1918–1920: 3 million deaths associated with battlefield causes (civilian as well as military deaths) in addition to 12 million dead as a result of the Spanish influenza epidemic that swept the world in 1919. Fully half of world deaths from that flu occurred in Russia, greatly assisted by the virtually complete breakdown of public order.[50]
- At least seventy thousand Russians in concentration and labor camps as early as September 1921.[51]
- Five million dead during the Volga famine of 1921–2, which was severely magnified by negligent and malignant state policies, including the forced seizure of grain in famine regions.[52]
- About 884,000 children in internal exile by 1954.[53]
- About 85,000 Orthodox priests murdered in 1937.[54]
- Six million deaths as a direct result of the famine of 1932–3, a catastrophe largely attributable to the policy of compulsory collectivization of agriculture and the seizure by the state of peasant harvests and seed grain.[55]
- Five million people deported or exiled in the Stalin years, of which half died on their journey into exile (including whole nations such as the Chechens and the Crimean Tatars, among others).[56]

---

[50] Orlando Figes, *A People's Tragedy: A History of the Russian Revolution* (New York: Viking, 1997), p. 773; Werth, *Le Livre Noir du Communisme*, p. 147; Aleksandr N. Yakovlev, *Omut Pamyati* [Vortex of Memory] (Moscow: VAGRIUS, 2000), p. 9; idem, *Krestosev* [Sowers of Graves] (Moscow, 1999), published in English as *A Century of Violence in Soviet Russia* (New Haven, CT: Yale University Press, 2002), p. 234; see also Martin Malia, *The Soviet Tragedy: A History of Socialism in Russia, 1917–1991* (New York: Free Press, 1994), p. 137.

[51] Werth, *Le Livre Noir du Communisme*, p. 116.

[52] Ibid., p. 177; see also Peter Christopher Mizelle, *"Battle with Famine": Soviet Relief and the Tatar Republic, 1921–1922*, Ph.D. dissertation, University of Virginia, Department of History, 2002.

[53] Based on a report of the Ministry of Internal Affairs to Soviet leaders Georgy Malenkov and Khrushchev in March 1954. Yakovlev, *Omut Pamyati*, p. 398.

[54] Ibid., p. 9.

[55] Robert Conquest, *Harvest of Sorrow* (New York: Oxford University Press, 1986).

[56] Werth, *Le Livre Noir du Communisme*, p. 294; Yakovlev, *Omut Pamyati*, pp. 389–441, passim. The archival-based research confirms in all essentials the nonarchival-based

- At least 680,000 executions during the Great Purge in the years 1937–8 alone (including most of the higher officer corps of the Soviet Army).[57]
- More than 150,000 Soviet soldiers executed by their own Army (more than one-third the number of all U.S. combat deaths in World War II) as well as more than 1 million Soviet prisoners of war and forced laborers transferred from Nazi to Soviet imprisonment after 1945.[58]
- More than 26 million killed and a greater number wounded, maimed, and missing at the hands of the Nazis and their allies during the Second World War.[59]

Beyond this nearly unfathomable scale of violence, there are also qualitative dimensions to consider. First, the Russian Civil War and then Stalin's Great Purge had the effect of killing or sending into emigration the bulk of Russia's propertied, cultured, and highly educated classes, those with the greatest knowledge of and exposure to the outside world, mainly Europe. By the early 1920s, three hundred thousand dispossessed and mainly aristocratic and bourgeois Russians were living in Berlin alone and 1.5 million outside of Russia generally.[60] Later, Stalin's terror purge of the Communist Party in the late 1930s was aimed principally at those communists who traced their political roots to the time before the Russian Revolution, when the Bolshevik Party still belonged to a European social democratic tradition. So, at the very outset, Russia's prerevolutionary bourgeois and nonbourgeois but cosmopolitan classes were largely eliminated physically from Soviet society and entirely as an autonomous social entity within Russia; by the end of the 1930s, the most highly educated, cosmopolitan wing of the Bolshevik Party had itself been subject

investigations of Conquest, *The Great Terror: The Reassessment* (London: Hutchinson, 1990 [first edition, 1968]), as well as a slew of other reports going back to the 1930s, e.g., David J. Dallinn and Boris J. Nicolaevsky, *Forced Labor in Soviet Russia* (London: Hollis and Carter, 1948); Ivan Solonevich, *Rossiya v Kontslagere* [Russia in a Concentration Camp] (Washington, DC, 1958), first published in the late 1930s); Merle Fainsod's archival-based study, *Smolensk under Soviet Rule* (Cambridge, MA: Harvard University Press, 1958), based on Soviet archives retrieved by the U.S. Army after the Nazis captured and shipped them to western Germany; Aleksandr Solzhenitsyn's magisterial work of "literary investigation," *The Gulag Archipelago* (New York: Harper & Row), in three volumes; see now Anne Applebaum's archive-based work, *Gulag: A History*, op. cit.

[57] Michael Ellman, "Soviet Repression Statistics: Some Comments," *Europe-Asia Studies*, vol. 54, no. 7 (November 2002), pp. 1151–72.

[58] Yakovlev, *Omut Pamyati*, pp. 418–23.

[59] Yu.A. Polyakov et al., *Lyudskiye poteri v period vtoroy mirovoy voyny* [Human losses during the Second World War] (St. Petersburg: Institut Rossiyskoy Istorii RAN, 1995), p. 41.

[60] Malia, *The Soviet Tragedy*, p. 137; Ernst Nolte, *La Guerre Civile Europeene*, p. 468.

to mass political murder. (To find a point of reference in the Western world, perhaps one would have to turn to the wholesale slaughter of tens of thousands of elite, highly educated young men from England, France, and Germany on the battlefields of Belgium and northern France in the first few months of the First World War, a bloodletting whose effects were felt decades thereafter in terms of lost creative energies in these societies.)

This twin destruction of Russia's educated elites, bourgeois and communist, arguably left Soviet Russia more isolated from world intellectual culture than Tsarist Russia had been in 1913. That whole fields of science such as genetics and cybernetics were banned for years and deformed for decades out of the political considerations of Soviet Russia's new, semi-educated rulers – rulers who were to rise and prevail over the Soviet system for half a century from the late 1930s until the mid-1980s – underscores another isolating effect of the Soviet legacy. (The outside world would be impoverished as well, as for many decades Western scholars studying Russia simply did not have counterparts in Russia with whom they could discuss matters of professional interest in which it could be presumed, as in other fields of European social and historical scholarship, that native scholars would bring unique and invaluable perspectives and sources to bear.)

Second, Russia's male population bore the brunt of this violence, from within and without, although women and children were by no means spared, a point that Aleksandr Yakovlev's archival-based and unbearable recounting of the persecution and imprisonment of hundreds of thousands of Soviet children in the 1920s and 1930s – most orphaned or dispossessed as a result of war and social cataclysm – brings home.[61] As a result, an enormous imbalance in the ratio of men to women became evident after the Second World War, with considerable reverberations on the fertility of the Soviet population. By the 1960s, the Soviet population was about 100 million people smaller than American demographers had projected during the Second World War.

Reflecting on this bleak tableau of mass violence, diplomat and Russian scholar George F. Kennan was quoted as the twentieth century was coming to a close:

Since the Thirty Years' War, no people have been more profoundly injured and diminished than the Russian people by the successive waves of violence brought to them by this past brutal century [ranging from two world wars, revolution and civil war, and then, extending over seven decades] 'the immense damages,

---

[61] Yakovlev, *Century of Violence*, pp. 27–48.

social, spiritual, even genetic, inflicted upon the Russian people by the Communist regime itself. In this vast process of destruction, all the normal pillars on which any reasonably successful modern society has to rest – faith, hope, national self-confidence, balance of age groups, family structure... have been destroyed. The process took place over most of an entire century. It embraced three generations of Russians. Such enormous losses and abuses are not to be put to rights in a single decade, perhaps not even in a single generation.'[62]

In sum, the cumulative impact of mass violence in twentieth-century Russia has been such as to propel an isolation from world currents that was exactly the opposite of the Bolsheviks' original, cosmopolitan intentions and then to induce a degree of physical and spiritual exhaustion that has left the Russian people without the energy – social, psychological, and even physical – to initiate grand projects of civic reconstruction.[63]

### VIII. Positive Legacies

This admittedly depressing picture should be tempered with a consideration of several other Soviet-era legacies of enduring significance. In 1917, the Tsarist order proved unable to withstand the crucible of total war with Germany. Had not American intervention rendered Germany's eastern conquests null and void (much in the way that the Soviet victory at Stalingrad in early 1943 made possible an American invasion of France the following year), Russia would have been shorn of its western and southern territories and reduced to the status of a tributary state of Imperial Germany. Tsarist Russia's failure of that critical power test made possible the Bolsheviks' seizure of power. That failure also provided a powerful signal to the Bolsheviks, and especially Stalin, that a campaign of industrialization without historical precedent in its tempo (and brutality) was required in order to avoid a repetition of 1917 on the military front. In the end, and by the skin of its teeth, with nearly unimaginable losses and with the considerable assistance of Great Britain and especially the United States, Soviet Russia passed the test that Tsarist Russia had failed: Whereas Germany had defeated Russia in 1917 and 1918, Soviet Russian troops raised the hammer and sickle over the Reichstag in May 1945. From that moment on, Soviet victory over Germany in

---

[62] Richard Ullmann, "The U.S. and the World: An Interview with George Kennan," *New York Review of Books*, August 12, 1999, p. 12.

[63] This point is supported by sociologists Bertram Silverman and Murray Yanowitch, *New Rich, New Poor, New Russia: Winners and Losers on the Russian Road to Capitalism* (Armonk, NY: M. E. Sharpe, 1997), p. 133.

the Second World War became the most important element legitimizing the communist regime at home and, to a very large extent, abroad as well.[64] To this day, that elemental experience, which includes tens of millions of a still living older generation of Russians and those raised by them, frames political attitudes toward the Soviet past and the importance of a powerful state. After all, had Soviet Russia failed that test, there would not today be a Russian people as a distinct cultural and national entity.

The Russians' experience with mass violence at home has also had a decisive impact on their socioeconomic and political attitudes. Russians are able to distinguish between the high value that they attach to the state as a guarantor of Russia's external sovereignty and internal order, and the terror state that took hold in the Stalin period. Certainly, security ranks high among Russians' public values: security against war, security against socioeconomic instability, and security against political terror at home. But Russians also have a nuanced range of views about the appropriate socioeconomic and political regime for their country, one shaped by their lives in the Soviet Union. At heart, Russians of all generations and level of education, going back several generations, have supported a strong role for the state in the management of the industrial economy and as guarantor of a minimum standard of living and job security. At the same time, most Russians accept the idea of wage inequality in relation to effort expended, and reject the idea that the state should be deeply involved in the service and agricultural sectors.[65] Viewed as a whole, the spectrum of Russians' social, economic, and political attitudes is not as far removed from the mainstream of continental European social democracy as many who would condemn the Russians to eternal autocracy would have it. Unfortunately, as we shall soon see, Russia's political rulers have not lived up to the promise contained within the population's attitudes; likewise, the population has not been able to find the means to induce the regime to become responsive to its needs.

Finally, there is the question of the middle class, which may even be considered the key factor "in the market reform of post-communist

---

[64] Francois Furet, *Le Passé d'une illusion. Essai sur l'idee communiste au xx-e siecle* (Paris: Robert Laffont/Calmann-Levy, 1995); see also the work of Nina Tumarkin on the impact of the victory in the Second World War on the functioning of the Soviet regime, *The Living and the Dead: The Rise and Fall of the Cult of World War II in Russia* (New York: Basic Books, 1994). Even today, Victory Day (May 9) is arguably the only genuine national holiday in Russia.

[65] Bahry, "Rethinking the Social Roots of Perestroika."

TABLE 4. *Middle-Class Potential of Select Postcommunist Countries*

| Country | Potential Middle Class, 1989 (%) | Per Capita GDP, 1997 | Average Monthly Wage, 1997 | Per Capita Foreign Direct Investment, 1997 | GDP Growth 1997 (%) |
|---|---|---|---|---|---|
| Czech Republic | 30% | 4,338 | 303 | 534 | 4.0 |
| Slovakia | 25 | 2,926 | 253 | 132 | 6.4 |
| Hungary | 20–5 | 3,882 | 328 | 971 | 4.0 |
| Poland | 15 | 3,167 | 307 | 155 | 6.5 |
| Romania | 5 | 1,380 | 110 | 79 | 3.8 |
| Bulgaria | 5 | 1,176 | 118 | 94 | 2.8 |
| Albania | 1 | 332 | 126 | negl. | 6.0 |
| Russia | 1 | 2,393 | 126 | [ca.100] | 2.0 |

societies."[66] If by middle class we mean that part of the population en-joying a "middle-class" material subsistence and lifestyle – that is, home ownership, an automobile, cultural activities, travel abroad, and so on – we see that late Soviet Russia was disadvantaged not just in relationship to Western Europe and North America but to a number of countries in East-Central Europe. In Poland, Hungary, and the Czech Republic, between 20–30 percent of the population can be considered to have belonged to the middle class by the late 1980s (compared to 60–70 percent in Western Europe and North America). By contrast, the middle class in late-Soviet Russia was extraordinarily weak, amounting to perhaps 1 percent of the population, apart from the higher party and state dignitaries (and even then their position depended on political power rather than income and private wealth enforced by law). The correlation between a country's middle-class potential in 1989 and the progress of market reform by the mid-1990s is remarkable. Consider Table 4, proposed by the Romanian social scientist Silviu Brucan.[67]

While Brucan almost certainly underestimated the extent and potential of a Soviet "middle class" at the end of the 1980s, especially if we define "middle class" by status and aspirations as well as property guaranteed by law, one of the tragedies of Russian history nevertheless becomes apparent from these figures. If in 1917 Russia's rulers attempted to initiate a socialist

---

[66] Brucan, *Social Change in Russia and Eastern Europe*, p. ix.
[67] Ibid., p. 62.

revolution in the general absence of the agency of such a revolution, that is, a strong working class, in the 1990s Russia's rulers committed the country to the construction of a market democracy in the absence of its most important sociological concomitant, that is, a reasonably strong middle class. In Brucan's formulation, Russia has always been one social class behind the historical process, that is, without a significant proletariat in 1917 and without a significant middle class in 1992.[68] Consequently, as we shall see, what passed for a middle class in Russia originated in the state economic bureacracy. That fact, and the simultaneous immiseration of Russia's existing and tenuous middle class, defined the political sociology of Russia in the 1990s.

## IX. The Legacy of Soviet Collapse: Stealing the State

To a large extent, the forms of Russia's political "transition," which generally correspond to post-1945 North Atlantic forms, have obscured the mechanisms and processes by which power over the acquisition and distribution of public (and private) resources has been obtained and maintained.[69] The chief motive force driving Russian politics since the late 1980s has not been so much the striving by state and society for democratic accountability but rather – spurred by the administrative chaos of the late Gorbachev period – the remarkably successful effort by strategically situated elements of the old Soviet service elite, and those with access to them, to convert its previous administrative control over the economic assets of the Soviet state into private control for themselves and their families.

This was not a monolithic process. As David Lane and Cameron Ross have shown, at the close of the Soviet era, control over assets was a zone of conflict between administrative incumbents seeking to preserve power by a mixture of administrative control and privatization (for example, natural gas baron Viktor Chernomyrdin, prime minister between 1992–8) and a new, aggressively acquisitive class originating from outside the old elites, from people in middle and lower executive positions, the shadow economy, and the professions (for example, mathematician and car exporter Boris Berezovsky, who became the personal manager of the Yeltsin family finances and a key mover behind the selection of Vladmir Putin as

---

[68] Ibid., p. ix.
[69] The phrase "stealing the state" is Stephen Solnick's, from his book of the same title, published in 1998 by Harvard University Press.

Yeltsin's successor – and protector).[70] In the process, many of those with administrative, political, or financial access to Soviet state assets that were liquifiable on world markets proved able to insulate themselves personally from the consequences of Soviet collapse, which explains in part why the system collapsed as peacefully as it did.[71] Not only did the disintegration of the USSR not threaten these elites' socioeconomic positions, it enhanced them; thus the present-day anticommunism of Russia's post-communist economic (as distinct from political) elites, who themselves are drawn mainly from the higher (though not usually the highest) levels of the now defunct Communist Party of the Soviet Union.[72] The fact that the USSR fell apart as peacefully as it did, avoiding the generalized violence that beset Yugoslavia, is no doubt related to the belief among many in the Soviet elite that they had thereby found a way to escape the personal consequences of the Soviet collapse.

Yet this triumph of private over public considerations, which helped the Russian people to avoid the worst consequences, also constrains Russia's political and economic prospects: In ways that will become evident in the course of this book, Russia's "new" political-economic elites have frequently proved either incapable or unwilling to assert the primacy of the public or even a state interest over the private interest in order to shepherd the Russian nation through its painful post-Soviet circumstances. Whether one speaks of the fate of economic reform, including the vaunted "success" of privatization; the capacity of the central government to raise taxes; the collapse of civilian control over the military, as well as the frequent collapse of the military's control over its own subordinate units; or the disintegration of the Russian Army as a coherent combat organization – in all of these areas and many more, the preconditions for minimally effective government in Russia (not to mention a government committed to economic or political reform) have been seriously undermined. The Russian state that emerged in the 1990s was extraordinarily

---

[70] David Lane and Cameron Ross, *The Transition from Communism to Capitalism: Ruling Elites from Gorbachev to Yeltsin* (New York: St. Martin's Press, 1999), pp. 19–20; Silverman and Yanowitch, *New Rich, New Poor, New Russia*, p. 113. On Berezovsky, see Lorrain, *La Mysterieuse Ascension de Vladimir Poutine*, passim; Alexander Rahr, *Wladimir Putin: Der "Deutsche" im Kreml* (Germany: Universitas, 2000).

[71] For the story in detail, see Brucan, *Social Change in Russia and Eastern Europe*; Steven Kotkin, *Armageddon Averted* (Oxford, UK: Oxford University Press, 2001); David Pryce-Jones, *The Strange Death of the Soviet Empire* (New York: Henry Holt, 1995), pp. 377–86; Steven L. Solnick, *Stealing the State: Control and Collapse in Soviet Institutions* (Cambridge, MA: Harvard University Press, 1998).

[72] Lane and Ross, *The Transition from Communism to Capitalism*, p. 182.

weak and unable to shape effectively much of its economic, social, and political environment. If Yeltsin's Russia appeared stable after late 1993, it was because those with the power to destabilize Russia – that is, the numerous alliances throughout Russia of the former communist industrial elite, military and police units, and openly criminal elements – were essentially satisfied with a weak state. Russian "stability" could be preserved so long as the state did not attempt a display of force, one that, as the first Chechen War (1994–6) shows, was likely to fail and that would make explicit the reality that the Russian government had little ability to reward its friends or punish its foes.[73] (We shall treat Russian President Putin's attempt to change this situation in Chapter 4.)

The mechanisms that guided the transformation of the Soviet economy from state to private ownership were contained within the structure of the Soviet system itself. For decades, even reaching back into the years of Stalin's terror, Soviet plant managers were regularly constrained to behave in ways that resembled those of principals of their own immediate organizations as distinct from faithful agents of the Central Plan as defined and enforced from Moscow. This meant that, at best, Soviet managers were "capable of mobilizing workers and employees in order to 'fulfill and exceed the plan', but they were not trained to deal with the constraints of a true economy," given the absence of market clearing prices. There was thus no need for a plant manager to take into account such factors as prices, costs of labor, profitability, and quality. In the end, the soft budget constraints of state financing would cover any accounting gaps. As a result, the main concern of the Soviet plant operator was not efficiency as such but "to succeed in obtaining the materials that he needed to guarantee the fulfillment of physical quotas."[74] Indeed, under conditions of perpetual shortages of supplies that were characteristic of Soviet economic planning ("taut planning"), plant bosses had no choice but to subvert the letter of the law to have a chance at fulfilling the number of the production quota assigned to them. Strategies employed including featherbedding in the labor force; accumulation of secret inventories; countless barter transactions with other, equally harried factory managers via the intermediary of the "expediter" *(tolkach)*; lobbying with higher ups in the ministerial bureaucracy; payoffs; falsification of data; and so

---

[73] Michael Thumann, *Das Lied von der russischen Erde: Moskaus Ringen um Einheit und Groesse* [The Song of the Russian Earth: Moscow's Struggle for Unity and Greatness] (Stuttgart: Deutsche-Varlags Anstalt, 2002), pp. 104–5.

[74] Lorrain, *La Mysterieuse Ascension de Vladimir Poutine*, p. 305.

on.[75] All of this was strictly illegal but at the same time absolutely indispensable to the functioning of an economy that ruled out market prices as a measure of value. Over time, and especially as the terror disappeared after 1953, such practices became virtually institutionalized.[76] By the mid-Brezhnev period, it was clear to Soviet managers that the capacity of the central Soviet party-state to monitor the functioning of the system had deteriorated to the point where they had increasingly less fear of sanctions from Moscow.[77]

Well before Gorbachev came to power, then, Soviet enterprise managers and often their ministerial supervisors were behaving as if their plants or even entire industrial sectors belonged to them. The destabilization of the system that Gorbachev's reform policies inadvertently brought about had the effect of presenting the Soviet Union's economic principals with a fateful choice: Assert real private control over what was merely their administrative responsibility, and in the process acquire something close to title over valuable assets, or see someone else do so and face the impoverishment that would soon be the fate of millions of Russians without privileged access to state property. A similar logic helped drive the movement toward secession presided over by a number of established Soviet elites such as Leonid Kravchuk in Ukraine: Given the legal monopoly on most property and capital still held by the state, and the evident decomposition of the central Soviet party-state, political secession would allow extant party-state elites in the union republics to control untold sums of wealth and patronage as heads of sovereign or even independent states.[78] In other words, had there been more private ownership of wealth and capital before the Soviet Communist Party came undone in 1990, communist elites, previously little noticed for their nationalist sympathies, would have had little incentive to collaborate with the genuine nationalist movements and accelerate the disintegration of the Soviet state itself. The structure of the Soviet political economy thus provided a powerful incentive and stimulus for the dessication of the Soviet state that took place in the years immediately before and after 1990.

---

[75] In many respects, it was corruption that allowed the Soviet as well as Imperial Russian systems to function at all. See Alain Besancon, "Eloge de la corruption en Union Sovietique," [In praise of corruption in the Soviet Union] in idem, *Present sovietique et passé russe* [Soviet present and Russian past] (Paris: Le Livre de Poche, 1980), pp. 289–318.

[76] James R. Millar, "The Little Deal: Brezhnev's Contribution to Acquisitive Socialism," *Slavic Review*, vol. 44, no. 4 (Winter 1985), pp. 694–706.

[77] Lane and Ross, *The Transition from Communism to Capitalism*, p. 39.

[78] See Jack F. Matlock, Jr., *Autopsy of an Empire: The American Ambassador's Account of the Collapse of the Soviet Union* (New York: Random House, 1995), p. 292.

This was no random occurrence but rather the final stage in a process of increasingly proprietary assertion by the Soviet nomenklatura that had been analyzed in detail by Charles Bettleheim in the 1970s and anticipated by Leon Trotsky in the 1930s.[79] In essence, Trotsky argued in the mid-1930s that in Stalin's USSR a twofold structure of political economy had emerged: On the one hand, there was a collectivist, or statist (socialist) structure of production, and on the other hand there had developed what he called "bourgeois" or private norms of distribution. Barring a socialist revolution from below or a capitalist restoration from without, Trotsky held that these two principles, of production and distribution, respectively, were not compatible over the long run. Institutional stasis, he felt, would lead the managers of the economy to attempt to convert their administrative control over assets into the equivalent of ownership, since their positions depended on their political location in the system, an obviously transient thing, rather than on wealth defined as private ownership and guaranteed by law.

Moreover, Trotsky held, without the ability to confer assets to one's blood heirs, managerial and administrative status was not half of what it seemed to be. Indeed, the behavior of Soviet elites since that time, and accelerating since the death of Stalin in 1953, resembled that of the rich in capitalist systems: Who was admitted to the best schools, who was able to avoid the draft, and who was able to secure privileged positions in Academy of Science research institutes and related prerequisites such as travel abroad were as closely correlated to the (invariably) father's location in the party-state hierarchy as in the West they are related to the (invariably) father's wealth, and probably even more so.[80] Functionally, Soviet elites were obtaining the rough equivalent of the right of bequeathal. So long as the party-state system retained its structural integrity, these tendencies were latent rather than explicit, although in hard-to-monitor regions such as Uzbekistan, the behavior of local party rulers often assumed especially outrageous forms, such as entirely fictitious cotton harvests.[81] Throughout the Soviet economy, by the 1980s, as Thane

---

[79] Charles Bettleheim, *Class Struggles in the USSR (1917–1923 and 1924–1930)* (London: Harvester Press, two volumes, 1977, 1979); Leon Trotsky, *The Revolution Betrayed: What Is the Soviet Union and Where Is It Heading?* (New York: Pioneer Publishers, 1945).

[80] In the United States, the rates of college graduation by income break down as follows (figures are for 1996): Eighty percent of children from families with incomes of more than $67,000 graduate from college, as compared to 20 percent from families with income between $20,000–67,000 and 9 percent for families with incomes lower than $20,000. *Washington Post*, February 3, 1997, p. A6.

[81] Lorrain, *La Mysterieuse Ascension de Vladimir Poutine*, pp. 308–9.

Gustafson has observed, "the local managers of the state economy were well on their way to becoming de facto owners."[82] The actual implosion of the Soviet system under Gorbachev confirmed Trotsky's vision: The collapse of the CPSU system removed the final constraints on strategically placed Soviet elites from translating their de facto property rights into *de jure* ones, with consequences that Trotsky also foretold, that is, the collapse of the Russian economy and culture (see Chapter 3 for details). Perhaps "[n]ever in human history," Gustafson writes, "has there been such a dramatic and sudden transfer of wealth, other than through military conquest."[83]

Between 1989–91, a substantial percentage of the Soviet economy, especially that part with assets that could be liquidated on world markets, such as energy, metals, the country's gold reserves, and so on, had already been seized by those with fiduciary responsibility for such property to the Soviet state and, thus the Soviet peoples. Given that the accumulation of private capital was censured and illegal in the Soviet Union, Russia's post-1989 "capitalists" made their fortune at the expense of state property and capital. What would pass for post-Soviet Russia's new middle and upper classes thus originated in the state's economic apparatus. Russia's first capitalists were in fact largely bureaucrats who kept their jobs. The resultant, largely spontaneous plunder of Russia's enormous riches and natural resources amounted to, in the French journalist Bernard Guetta's words, " Le plus grand 'hold up' de l'histoire."[84]

By 1988, the end of the Soviet state's monopoly on foreign trade triggered the first stages of the spontaneous privatization of Russia's vast exportable mineral resources. For example, in the course of 1991, while the Soviet Union still existed, one thousand tons of Soviet gold mysteriously disappeared from Soviet vaults. By 1993, Russia, which with South

---

[82] Thane Gustafson, *Capitalism Russian-Style* (Cambridge, UK: Cambridge University Press, 1999), p. 18.

[83] Ibid., pp. 26–8. Economic historians believe that Nazi Germany was able to milk the French economy of about 40 percent of its prewar GDP equivalent between 1940–4; by comparison, Anders Aslund estimates that Soviet elite profits from the collapse of the Soviet state amounted to over 70 percent of Russian GDP in 1992. Anders Aslund and Mikhail Dmitriev, "Economic Reform versus Rent-Seeking," in Anders Aslund and Martha Brill Olcott, eds., *Russia after Communism* (Washington, DC: Carnegie Endowment for International Peace, 1999), pp. 96–7.

[84] Bernard Guetta, "Russia: Pressures from the Past, Pressures toward a Different Future," in Centro Studi di Politica Internazionale, *Strategies for Stability in Europe: Interatlantic Relations since 1989* (Rome: Editore OA, 1995), pp. 13–17. See also Brucan, *Social Change in Russia and Eastern Europe*, p. xii.

Africa was one of the world's largest producers of gold, was ranked thirty-ninth of forty countries evaluated in terms of gold reserves, at $3.3 billion, versus $6.9 billion for Turkey, $11.1 billion for Indonesia, $20.1 billion for China, $43.6 billion for Singapore, $64.2 billion for the United States, and $103.9 billion for Germany.[85] Also in 1991, one aircraft plant making SU-25 ground attack planes sent its quota of aluminum abroad as a result of export licenses obtained through bribery of state officials. Given that on the Soviet domestic market, the price of aluminum was 1,500 rubles per ton (and a dollar to ruble exchange rate of 1:100), while on the world market the price was $1,500 per ton, the plant netted a neat 10,000 percent profit.[86] (The profit was actually greater, since the plant did not actually have to pay for its quota of aluminum.)

Another gauge of the magnitude of the transfer of wealth that took place as a consequence of Soviet disintegration is the Swedish economist Anders Aslund's calculation that revenues from Russian arbitrage transactions on the heavily regulated export market, where raw materials cost as little as 1 percent of the world market price, amounted to 30 percent of Russia's GDP in the first post-Soviet year of 1992.[87] Other forms of "rent-seeking" profits in the early years included bank loans at 10–25 percent interest while inflation raged at 2,500 percent; directed credits to enterprises from the Central Bank totaling 23 percent of the official Russian GDP in 1992; import subsides of 99 percent of the official exchange rate; as well as direct subsidies to firms, farms, and mines.[88] Anatoly Chubais, Yeltsin's periodic first deputy prime minister in charge of the economy, has confirmed that special customs privileges awarded in secret by Yeltsin to his cronies, who paid Yeltsin back in 1996 with massive infusions of cash for his presidential campaign, cost the government more than $800 million in lost revenue. More broadly, although 57 percent of Russian firms were privatized between 1992 and 1996 in an effort both praised and financially supported by the Clinton Administration, the Russian state budget received just $3–5 billion from the proceeds of these "sales." Essentially, the bulk of the Russian economy changed hands for the equivalent

[85] V. D. Andrianov, *Rossia v mirovoy ekonomike* [Russia in the world economy] (Moscow: Vlados, 1999), p. 189.

[86] Lorrain, *La Mystérieuse Ascension de Vladimir Poutine*, p. 310.

[87] Anders Aslund, "Social Problems and Policy in Postcommunist Russia," in Ethan Kapstein and Michael Mandelbaum, eds., *Sustaining the Transition: The Social Safety Net in Postcommunist Europe* (New York: Council on Foreign Relations, 1998), pp. 133–6; idem, "Russia's Collapse," *Foreign Affairs*, September/October 1999, p. 66.

[88] Aslund and Dmitriev, "Economic Reform versus Rent-Seeking."

of title fees. In one of the most dramatic but by no means untypical trans-actions, in 1996 Oneximbank, controlled by Vladimir Potanin, one-time first deputy prime minister of Russian President Boris Yeltsin's government and friend of Yeltsin's personal bodyguard, purchased the oil company Sidanco from the government for about $470 million at an auction or-ganized by Potanin's bank. In 1997, British Petroleum paid $571 million for a 10 percent stake, 20 percent of the voting rights, and a few posi-tions in Sidanco upper management.[89] The ratio of net worth to price of purchase was thus approximately 12:1, a fair gauge of the extent to which Russia's new capitalist class has plundered the Russian state and nation. By late 2000, the Russian natural gas monopoly Gazprom had been discovered siphoning off billions of dollars in marketable assets to a recently established affiliate, Itera, which was controlled by close relatives of Gazprom board members such as Chernomyrdin and Lev Vyakhirev. Before the board was reshuffled to allow Russian President Putin a more direct influence on the company, such asset stripping is thought to have cost Gazprom $2 billion per year from 1991–2001.[90]

The rise of oil magnate Mikhail Khodorkovsky, before his arrest in fall 2003 the richest man in Russia, is typical of this pattern. In fall 1995, the Russian president's office granted Khodorkovsky the right to hold an auction for a 45 percent stake in the state-owned oil giant Yukos. "Once foreign investors and rival Russian bidders had been disqualified," *Forbes* Journalist Paul Klebnikov (murdered in Moscow in July 2004) wrote:

... Mr. Khodorkovsky and his five partners ended up with a 78% stake in Yukos – for which they paid $309 million. How absurd was this sum? In the summer of '97, two months after this deal was finalized, Yukos was trading on the Russian stock exchange at a market capitalization of $6 billion. (Today [November 2003] its market cap is $24 billion.)[91]

Nor have Russian taxpayers been the only victims of the predatory practices of Russia's post-communist economic elite. Between 1992–8, the

---

[89] *New York Times*, August 13, 1999, p. C17; Dmitri Simes, *After the Collapse: Russia Seeks Its Place as a Great Power* (New York: Simon and Schuster, 1999), p. 180. By 1999, British Petroleum (BP) had written off $200 million of its investment in a company that was being rapidly stripped of its assets by its own management and suing for bankruptcy. BP has nevertheless maintained its commitment to the Russian market, increasing its purchase of Sidanco shares in spring 2002 and committing $7 billion to Russian energy development in 2003.

[90] Reuters (Frankfurt), "Russia Needs Help to Lead in Energy," May 3, 2002.

[91] Paul Klebnikov, "The Khodorkovsky Affair," *Wall Street Journal*, November 17, 2003, p. A20.

Russian Central Bank channeled as much as $50 billion in state funds – inevitably including a portion of the billions advanced to the Russian government by Western governments and the international financial institutions that they control – to Fimaco (Financial Management Company), a branch office that it established in 1989 under Gorbachev in Jersey in the Channel Islands, a noted banking and tax haven, to manage Communist Party finances. These funds, which were sent abroad ostensibly to protect the Russian government from creditor claims against unpaid Russian debt, were recirculated into Russia to buy Russian government bonds, which provided returns of up to 200 percent to bond holders (compared to a normal 5 percent), before the Russian bond market crashed in August 1998. This scheme was managed most recently by Russian Central Bank Director Viktor Gerashchenko (also the last central banker of the USSR; Gerashchenko was eventually fired in March 2002). An audit released by PriceWaterhouse Coopers in early August 1999 indicated that the Russian Central Bank also transferred credits committed by the International Monetary Fund (IMF), whose Russian activities were nominally the responsibility of the current prime minister, Mikhail Kasyanov.[92] While precise figures are difficult to come by, the IMF itself has indirectly confirmed that at least $1.2 billion of its funds were channeled to Fimaco. In the polite language of the IMF report on the matter, "the transfer of assets in the books of the central bank to Fimaco meant that the balance sheet of the central bank had given a misleading impression of the true state of reserves and monetary and exchange rate policies."[93] These transactions reflect "a fundamental lack of cooperation on the part of the Russian authorities, and [are] a serious violation of Russia's obligations to the IMF," according to an IMF communique.[94] A sense of the scale of international funds diverted may be gleaned from the fact that the Russian government has not to date provided an adequate accounting for the $4.5 billion in IMF funds provided to Russia in July 1998. What happened, in the language of a *Le Monde* editorial, is that "one of the great countries on the planet, one of the influential members of the UN Security Council, misappropriated money like common swindlers from the international community through companies set up in faraway tax havens, so that a few oligarchs might enrich themselves."[95]

---

[92] The report is summarized in detail in *Le Monde*, August 6, 1999, pp. 1–2, 13.
[93] As cited in Martin Wolf, "Price of Forgiveness," *Financial Times*, August 11, 1999, p. 10.
[94] *Le Monde*, August 6, 1999, p. 2; *Wall Street Journal*, August 20, 1999, p. A10.
[95] *Le Monde*, August 6, 1999, p. 13.

Instructively, the IMF, which is widely suspected of having been aware earlier of the diversion of Russian funds, later decided against providing its own money directly to the Russian government. In the summer of 1999, the next IMF credit to Russia, also for $4.5 billion, stayed within the IMF itself; the credit was now a bookkeeping entry to apply against previous Russian loans from the IMF, the money only going "from one IMF account to another," according to IMF head Michel Camdessus. Russian officials were no longer trusted with IMF money. The pretense of providing external resources for the development of the Russian economy had been abandoned. As Camdessus put it, describing a conversation with Yeltsin at the end of August 1999, "I alerted President Yeltsin that Russia will be treated exactly like Burkina Faso."[96]

## X. Russia's Path-Dependent Matrix

This triumph of private over public interests, that is, corruption, on the grand scale, while invaluable in constraining the chances for systemwide civil violence attendant on Soviet disintegration, also constrains Russia's political and economic prospects, democratic or otherwise. In the final analysis, Russia's postcommunist elites have proved incapable of asserting the primacy of the public interest or even the interest of the state over their private interests in order to shepherd the Russian nation through the necessarily painful aftermath of Soviet collapse.

This remains an historical development of the first magnitude. Key elements of the Soviet political, economic, and administrative elites managed to dissociate economic power from sovereign power, thereby undermining the distinctive pattern of Russian autocratic rule that prevailed in greater or lesser degree from the suppression of the princely boyars by Ivan IV ("the Terrible") in the second half of the sixteenth century until the disintegration of the USSR. This pattern, which prevailed in both the Imperial and Soviet periods, fused two forms of power that in other European countries were over time progressively disaggregated from each other: political power, in the form of sovereignty over a polity; and economic power, in the form of ownership over land, resources, and even people. It is precisely this distinctively Russian "patrimonial" system that was destroyed with the disintegration of the Soviet state. This means that, in principle, Russia's path toward more typical European and North American

---

[96] Interview in *Liberation* (Paris), August 31, 1999; see also Joseph E. Stiglitz, *Globalization and Its Discontents* (New York: W. W. Norton, 2002), pp. 133–94.

patterns of political and economic development is now open. Yet because of the manner in which that path was opened by the Soviet "boyars," the journey will be long and arduous, with possibilities for side trips all along the way. In this context, what is surprising is not the difficulties that Russia has experienced in making a "transition" to democracy, but that serious observers – knowing what they should know about the country's institutional and psychological inheritances and the wanton privatization of the nation's wealth – should ever have supposed that democratic cap-italism was ever a meaningful proposition for the Russian Federation in the early post-Soviet period.

This was the decisive context of Russian politics at the outset of the 1990s, not some institutional *tabula rasa* that might prove a receptive vehicle for liberal (or other) nostrums of economic and political transfor-mation. In this light, Western debates about "Who lost Russia?" appear to be beside the point. Russia's post-Soviet path of development was largely shaped by late-Soviet patterns of institutional decomposition and resource reallocation. Whether a better plan might have emerged is at the least a debatable proposition in light of the unprecedented challenges that a state such as Russia faced in charting its post-Soviet course.[97] If any criticism is to be made, it is that the Russian government that emerged from the Soviet rubble in 1992 was extraordinarily weak in terms of its administra-tive capacity and that, consequently, governmental policy was beholden to private interests that made any consistent policy – one that was both internally coherent and consistent with the public interest (if only with the interest of the state per se) – extremely difficult to sustain. Failure to recognize this meant that the policy interventions and resource com-mitments of Western governments and financial institutions were fated to be highjacked by the decomposition, if not the outright corruption, of Russia's entire governmental structure. Any post-Soviet strategy of political-economic development, whatever its political or ideological col-oration, would have to aim as a necessary precondition of success at estab-lishing and maintaining a system of public administration, including a civil service, that would enable the state to perform the essential functions of governance. Historically, these circumstances have provided a compelling justification for direct or indirect colonialism. It is interesting to note that several policy proposals advanced by Russians themselves in recent years – the idea of an international currency board for the ruble, or production sharing agreements with arbitration in foreign courts – do have the effect

[97] Ibid., p. 263, note 5.

of removing substantial amounts of operational sovereignty from Russian hands. Yet since contemporary ideology excludes imperialism as a solution to any kind of problem, the world will have to live for an extended period of time with a Russia whose government is something less than the sum of its individual parts.

# 3

# The 1990s in Russia

## A New Time of Troubles?

> Numerous bribe takers are also usually seen as corrupt. [This is wrong because] only those who have links with the organized criminal gangs can be regarded as corrupt officials. Do not mistake bribe-taking for corruption.
> – Russian Minister of the Interior Vladimir Rushaylo[1]

## I. Introduction

In the previous chapter, we established that the USSR itself represented a patrimonial society, albeit one that was both more comprehensive and intensive than Tsarist Russia ever was. The distinctive fusion of communist political monopoly and Soviet state monopoly ownership of capital, in the context of a generally hostile international environment, cemented the Soviet party-state system that was to last for the better part of the twentieth century. Given the virtual asphyxiation of organized public life outside the framework of the communist party-state system, down to the apparently most innocuous levels (such as fishing clubs), the sudden collapse of that system could be expected to have the most dramatic consequences for the integrity of the economy and the society, not to mention the country's international standing. The disintegration of the USSR in 1991 thus represented the end of a fixture in Russian life, with only brief interruptions (1917–20 and the early 1600s), since the emergence of Muscovy in the course of the fifteenth and sixteenth centuries: the presence of a powerful, highly centralized, militarized, and largely unaccountable patrimonial

---

[1] "Russia's Interior Minister Believes Bribe Taking Is Not Corruption," at *Johnson's Russia List* [hereafter *JRL*], #5157, March 17, 2001.

state. Interestingly, that state disintegrated (1989–91) precisely as the international political system was becoming the least threatening in the millennium of Russian statehood. If Russian absolutism, whether of the Tsarist or Soviet variant, arose in significant measure in response to the relatively high costs of establishing the security of the state, it seems that the lowering of those costs at the end of the 1980s played no small part in helping to propel the transformation and eventual collapse of the historical Russian state order.

One of the few observers to contemplate the political dynamics that could lead to the kind of Soviet collapse that occurred in 1991 was the U.S. diplomat George F. Kennan, who speculated in 1947 in *Foreign Affairs* magazine on what might happen if a post-Stalin leader should ever attempt to mobilize constituents outside of the Communist Party elite in the quest for higher power:

[I]f disunity were ever to seize and paralyze the Party, the chaos and weakness of Russian society would be revealed in forms beyond description.... Soviet power is only a crust concealing an amorphous mass of human beings among whom no independent organizational structure is tolerated. In Russia there is not even such a thing as local government. The present generation of Russians have never known spontaneity of collective action. If, consequently, anything were ever done to disrupt the unity and efficacy of the Party as a political instrument, Soviet Russia might be changed overnight from one of the strongest to one of the weakest and most pitiable of national societies.[2]

To what extent has Kennan's prophecy held true?

## II. Worst-Case Scenarios Failed To Occur

The Russian Federation that emerged from the debris of the USSR continues to exist, despite the prophesies of some,[3] while extreme scenarios of explosive social breakdown, the reactionary mobilization of embittered masses by ambitious demagogues, or even the widely discussed prospect of a "post-Weimar"–like Russia have failed to materialize. In spite of enormous problems in relations with its immediate ex-Soviet neighbors and largely frustrated expectations in its relationship with the United States and its main allies, Russia has neither striven to reimpose empire in central Eurasia nor to confront the advanced postindustrial

[2] "X" [George F. Kennan], "The Sources of Soviet Conduct," *Foreign Affairs*, vol. 25 (July 1947), pp. 169–82.
[3] Jessica Eve Stern, "Moscow's Meltdown: Can Russia Survive?" *International Security*, vol. 18, no. 4 (Spring 1994), pp. 40–65.

democracies.[4] Every major scheduled election at the national level has been held as planned. While the prospects of Russia consolidating a viable liberal or social democracy were undoubtedly more remote at the end of the 1990s than at the beginning, the bogeyman of a return to communism has been effectively banished, in spite of the fact that the Communist Party of the Russian Federation remained the largest (and perhaps the only true) political party in the country. Not only has Russia avoided most of the worst-case scenarios presented by Western and Russian observers, but the preservation of Russia's market-democratic institutional superstructure has encouraged influential U.S. and West European economists to declare Russia a successful market economy and political leaders such as William Clinton and Albert Gore repeatedly to praise the accomplishments of Russian democracy.[5] At the same time, the late 1990s witnessed the appearance, arguably for the first time, of a socially significant strain of anti-Americanism that was associated with Russia's difficult post-Soviet experience with the forms of political democracy and market economics and propelled by NATO's air war against Russia's client state Serbia in the spring of 1999.[6] By 1998, Russian conditions had reached the point where, in the words of a perceptive U.S. social anthropologist, it had become virtually impossible to find a pro-reform Russian nationalist.[7] How are we to understand this apparent contradiction?

## III. Another Russian Experiment

In a sense, the Russian experience of the 1990s has been a laboratory like examination of two major propositions of central concern to political science: (1) How might the institutions of a functioning market democracy be built on the ruins of a totalitarian political economy? (2) What happens to a society in the absence, under these circumstances, of a state that is able to exercise the minimal functions of governance? In Chapter 4, we attempt an explanation for the crisis of the state in Russia, one that helps to situate

---

[4] Allen C. Lynch, "The Realism of Russia's Foreign Policy," *Europe-Asia Studies*, vol. 53, no. 1 (January 2001), pp. 7–31.

[5] Anders Aslund, *How Russia Became a Market Economy* (Washington, DC: Brookings Institution, 1995); Stephen Cohen, *Failed Crusade: America and the Tragedy of Post-Communist Russia* (New York: W. W. Norton, 2000). See also the memoir published by President Clinton's chief Russia advisor, Strobe Talbott, *The Russia Hand: A Memoir of Presidential Diplomacy* (New York: Random House, 2002).

[6] As documented by William Zimmerman, *The Russian People and Foreign Policy* (Princeton, NJ: Princeton University Press, 2002).

[7] Janine Wedel, *Collision and Collusion* (New York: St. Martin's Press, 1999), ch. 5.

the experience of Russian society in the past decade and also suggests the paths of political development that are both open and closed to Russia in the immediate future. For the moment, we shall content ourselves with an empirical description of the impact of Soviet disintegration and post-Soviet "reform" upon a series of sectors that, taken together, outline the scope and depth of the Russian experience of the first post-Soviet decade. The period covered focuses on the years 1990–8; in a practical sense, the post-Soviet era began while Mikhail Gorbachev was still in power but unable to channel the energies that he had largely unleashed in his effort to revitalize the Soviet system, whereas the Russian financial crash of August 1998 serves as a natural divide, a watershed as Russians began to evaluate the relevance of policies adopted earlier in the decade for Russia's particular circumstances. The sectors to be treated include the Russian macroeconomy, the condition of Russian society, the state of the Russian military, the condition of Russian science, and aspects of the political economy of Russian crime.

## IV. The Russian Macroeconomy

From 1990 and through 1998, the year of Russia's financial crash, currency devaluation, and default on domestic and foreign obligations, the Russian economy suffered an economic contraction far eclipsing that of the Great Depression in the Western world in the 1930s.[8] The United Nations' International Labor Organization has minced no words: "There

---

[8] There has been an intense debate among experts about just how deep the decline has been, with skeptics pointing to relatively high electricity output, post-Soviet incentives to under-report production to avoid taxes and the "mafia," and the undoubtedly substantial shadow economy as evidence that the decline has not been as dramatic as it seems. While conceding the uncertainty about the exact extent of the decline, few doubt that it has been massive by any historical comparison; moreover, the oft-invoked electricity argument overlooks the fact that electricity usage is much less elastic than is industrial production – a relatively high and constant amount of electricity output is required for any industrial production at all. Thus wide fluctuations in industrial output would have much less effect on electricity usage, so long as the plants were kept open and running. With respect to the shadow economy, as useful as it undoubtedly is to most Russians, distribution predominates over production in this sector. Finally, while conceding the incentives for underreporting output, Russian statistics do not account for "black cash," that is, a transaction that is officially reported but does not in fact take place, to enable a firm to pretend to have expenses and thus to lower taxes. In this respect, there are also strong incentives to overreporting output that do not appear in the official statistics, which actually tends to inflate Russian GDP. See the article by Andrei Yakovlev, "'Black Cash' Tax Evasion in Russia," *Europe-Asia Studies*, January 2001, pp. 33–55.

should be no pretense. The Russian economy and living standards of the Russian population have suffered the worst peacetime setbacks of any industrialized nation in history."[9] Russians have argued that the "economic devastation [that] Russia suffered in the 1990s was even worse than during World War II. During 1940–46," Vladimir Radyuhin has written, "Soviet industrial production fell 24 per cent. In 1990–99, the fall was almost 60 per cent, while the GDP fell 54 per cent."[10] Moreover, while it is true that a significant decline was inevitable in the Russian case, as was true at the outset in all postcommunist transitions, and that the Russian decline would be magnified by the extraordinary share of the Soviet economy assumed by the military-industrial complex, very little progress was made in this period in restructuring the Russian economy to adapt to postcommunist incentives to produce. Thus, as stunning as it seems, the percentage of the Russian gross domestic product (GDP) occupied by heavy industry and the raw materials sector, the bulwarks of the old Soviet economy, actually increased throughout the 1990s, albeit in a much smaller economy.[11] Likewise, the number of Russian government officials at all levels appears to have increased significantly in recent years, to 2.8 million as compared to 1.15 million in the early 1980s, even as the share of GDP collected as revenues by the Russian state fell from 44 percent in 1992 to 31 percent in 1995 to approximately 29 percent in 1998.[12] By 2003, with state coffers awash in oil revenues since the rise in world oil prices after 1999, nearly 40 percent of Russia's GDP was being distributed through the state, according to prominent Russian economist Vladimir Mau.[13] This is a remarkably high level of state spending given the relatively low per capita income in the country. (By contrast, the government of nominally communist China typically spends no more than 17–18 percent of the country's GDP.) Indeed, in terms of the level of bureaucratization of the state, Russia exceeds Italy, Brazil, Venezuela, Indonesia, Mexico, India, Turkey, and Columbia, among forty others. Among forty-three states

9 Anders Aslund, "Social Problems and Policy in Postcommunist Russia," in Ethan B. Kapstein and Michael Mandelbaum, eds., *Sustaining the Transition: the Social Safety Net in Postcommunist Europe* (New York: Council on Foreign Relations, 1997), pp. 125–8.
10 Vladimir Radyuhin, "Russia's Economic Rebound," *Hindu* (India), at *JRL*, #7319, September 10, 2003, at www.cdi.org.
11 Efim S. Khesin, "The Intersection of Economics and Politics in Russia," in Aleksei Arbatov, Karl Kaiser, and Robert Legvold, eds., *Russia and the West: The 21st Century Security Environment* (Armonk, NY: M. E. Sharpe, 1999), pp. 111–13.
12 Reuters (Moscow), March 6, 2001; Thane Gustafson, *Capitalism Russian-Style* (Cambridge, UK: Cambridge University Press, 1999), p. 30.
13 As reported in *Moscow News*, September 24–30, 2003, at www.english.mn.ru.

measured along these lines, only China and Greece exceed Russia in the level of the bureaucratization of the state.[14]

More generally, the Russian government has lacked the necessary political strength to bring about genuine structural change in the economy. The annual report of the UN Development Program, 2000 *Human Development Report for the Russian Federation*, issued in March 2001, concluded that, despite a decade of attempts to construct a capitalist economic system, "Russia has not yet become a country with developed market relations."[15] Such problems as tax evasion, capital flight, "a crude social protection system," an "entirely inappropriate banking system," "a colossal shadow economy," and "rife corruption" have the effect of depriving Russia of what the UN report describes as "its natural advantage: a combination of of its natural resources and human potential."[16] As telling is that the raw materials sector represented a larger percentage of the Russian GDP at the end of the first post-Soviet decade than it did at the beginning, a striking indicator that the government failed in ushering in true structural reform of the economy.

Here are a few particulars: Fixed investment at the end of the 1990s was one-fifth of the 1990 level, with dramatic consequences for the integrity of the country's industrial, transportation, and communications infrastructures that will be detailed in Chapter 6.[17] Corrupt and incompetent financial administration as well as poor investor confidence has led to capital flight abroad that, in early 1997, was estimated conservatively at between $61 billion (according to the Economist Intelligence Unit) and $89 billion (according to the World Bank). The investment firm Deutsche Morgan Grenfell estimated that capital flight in 1996 was $22.3 billion, or 5 percent of Russia's GDP and a third of total private savings (or more than half of the Russian federal government's budget). (By contrast, net foreign investment in Russia totaled no more than $6 billion between 1989 and the first half of 1996.) This pattern continued through 2001 and

---

[14] V. D. Andrianov, *Rossiya v mirovoy ekonomike* [Russia in the world economy] (Moscow: Vlados, 1999), p. 216.

[15] Agence France Presse (Moscow), March 12, 2001, at www.AFP.fr.

[16] Ibid.

[17] To give just one striking particular, in the first three quarters of 1996, just 12 of 411 construction projects envisaged by the government's investment budget were completed. At 20 percent of the sites, no work was carried out at all. None of the seventy-seven construction projects in agriculture were finished, while that sector received only 20 percent of allocated investment monies. Dr. Herbert Levine, PlanEcon, presentation at the annual convention of the American Association for the Advancement of Slavic Studies, Boston, November 1996.

2002, when outflows of foreign direct investment (FDI) actually exceeded inflows.[18]

Before the rise in the global oil market in 1999, on which the Russian economy and federal budget remain disproportionately dependent, the central government struggled at times to collect, according to the Russian Finance Ministry, as much as half of the tax revenue needed to finance an admittedly unrealistic budget. In the first quarter of 1997, tax revenues were 58 percent of those budgeted. Whereas 1992 state revenue amounted to 44.2 percent of GDP, by mid-1996 that figure had fallen to 29 percent, underscoring the fiscal crisis of the Russian state. Workers who depend upon state-financed enterprises for a living have experienced lengthy delays in receiving their wages. A Russian survey conducted in late 1996 disclosed that only 30 percent of wages in Russia were paid on time and in full in 1996, down from 45 percent in 1995. Thirty-one percent of wages were delayed and 39 percent of workers were simply not paid at all, compared to 38 and 17 percent, respectively, in 1995. Those most likely to be affected are manual workers, inhabitants of rural areas, and those living in Siberia and the Far East. High-ranking government officials and managers, as well as residents of Moscow and St. Petersburg, were least likely to be affected. At current levels of Russian oil output, the federal government requires a global oil price of over $20 per barrel; the capacity of the state to meet its obligations remains precariously hinged on factors beyond its control.

Turning to the banking sector, according to the World Bank, before the August 1998 financial crash, Russia's top thirty banks had a negative net equity amounting to $10–15 billion. The failure of banking reform enabled many Russian banks to "transfer their remaining assets to other financial structures while leaving their liabilities to creditors." In extremis, the "unpaid staff of failed Russian banks have ripped out furniture and computers and sold them on the streets."[19] A significant percentage of large-scale transactions – at one point perhaps half of such arrangements – including the payment of salaries (when they are paid), was negotiated not with money but rather barter. Where money was involved, suitcases of cash transported across the country are far more common than instruments of credit. Unfortunately, for the foreseeable future the Russian

[18] Economist Intelligence Unit, "Russia's Long-Term Growth Prospects: Is Foreign Direct Investment the Key?" July 2003, at www.amcham.ru.
[19] John Thornhill, "EBRD: Bank Hits at Russia over Reform," *Financial Times*, April 27, 1999, at www.ft.com.

government will not have the resources to execute a successful restructuring of the banking system. It simply cannot at the same time pay off its foreign debt as well as recapitalize the banking system. Its tendency in recent years has been to keep foreign creditors at length while feeding favors to the best-connected domestic creditors, a tactic that will eventually liquidate the government's very limited resources without creating the basis for a healthy banking system.[20] By 2002, after three years of economic growth, Russian banks accounted for just 3 percent of all investment capital in the country. Lending in general accounted for just 40 percent of Russian banking assets, a striking indication of how far Russian banks have to go to serve their proper function in a coherent capitalist economy.[21]

Throughout the 1990s, two Swiss management firms published parallel studies of the leading economies in the world, including Russia's, by which they mean those most likely to affect the world's future economic growth. Both organizations – the Lausanne-based International Institute for Management Development and the Geneva-based World Economic Forum – consistently ranked Russia dead last in economic competitiveness (forty-eighth out of forty-eigth in 1995, forty-ninth out of forty-nine in 1996 and fifty-ninth out of fifty-nine in 1999). The two companies reviewed over one hundred criteria for each country, including openness to foreign trade; government budgets and regulations; development of financial markets; flexibility of labor markets; quality of infrastructure; technology; business management; and judicial institutions. The World Economic Forum has concluded in its justification of Russia's lowest ranking: "Russia is isolated from world markets, taxation is high and unstable and there is a general disdain for the infrastructure, technology, and management."[22] Correspondingly, the Economist Intelligence Unit has regularly listed Russia as the riskiest foreign investment destination among countries that it tracks.

## V. Paths Taken and Not

Three specific policies pursued by the Russian government beginning in January 1992 (and in preparation since the fall of 1991) framed Russia's

[20] Gustafson, *Capitalism Russian-Style*, p. 107.
[21] According to Petr Aven, president of Alfa Bank (Moscow), *JRL*, #6289, June 5, 2002, item no. 9, at www.cdi.org.
[22] Andrianov, *Rossiya v mirovoy ekonomike*, p. 87; *Moscow Times*, May 30, 1996, p. 15.

economic development from independence until the August 1998 crash: price liberalization, privatization of Soviet industry, and macroeconomic stabilization. In fact, these labels imply more coherence than was the case, as each policy was frequently pursued halfheartedly, with insufficient financial, administrative, and ultimately political support to sustain them along the lines originally intended by Russia's reformers. Moreover, Russia's capacity to act in any of these areas was significantly, if not decisively, influenced by patterns established as the communist system was breaking apart, as it is now recognized was true of all of the postcommunist transitions. In Russia's case, this meant, on the formal institutional level, an implicit tension between an executive branch temporarily under the sway of ideological liberals who saw the state (and political parties) per se as the major obstacle to overcome and a Soviet-era parliament whose majority, while in principle in favor of economic reforms, was wedded to the state as the guarantor of socioeconomic stability. On the informal sociological level, the locus of wealth had shifted from party-state institutions to private networks of power based upon the ability to exploit the still powerful nexus between state and property. As a result, Russia's early post-Soviet history came to be characterized by political instability between president and parliament and a creeping expropriation of larger and larger shares of the country's wealth by unaccountable private interests whose ability to affect the allocation of Russia's public resources often seemed to eclipse that of the Russian state itself.

In this light, many of the debates in the United States and Western Europe about the responsibilty for Russia's path of development in the 1990s are beside the point. Critics who charge that the Russian government mishandled the building of democracy and the development of a viable capitalist economy are correct,[23] as are those who criticize U.S. policy for supporting a narrow clique of unrepresentative politicians who enriched themselves and their networks at the expense of the Russian people.[24] Those who condemn policies of "shock therapy" as unsuited for Russian circumstances and undemocratic in essence, a kind of "market Bolshevism," in Peter Reddaway's words, are also correct, but also unpersuasive because Russia's post-Soviet path of development was largely shaped by late-Soviet patterns of institutional decomposition and resource

---

[23] Peter Reddaway and Dmitri Glinsky, *The Tragedy of Russia's Reforms: Market Bolshevism against Democracy* (Washington, DC: U.S. Institute of Peace, 2001).
[24] Especially Cohen, *Failed Crusade.*

reallocation.[25] This meant that first, all rhetoric aside, the Russian government never pursued a policy of "shock therapy" as envisaged by Western advisers, who did play a most important role in Russian economic policy making in the early post-Soviet years. Already by the late spring of 1992, the policy of radical reforms announced in January had met with such strong parliamentary opposition that the government retreated and acquiesced in a series of concessions that culminated in replacing the true radical reformer Yegor Gaidar with the old Soviet gas industry baron Viktor Chernomyrdin as prime minister in December 1992, less than one year into the reform process. Chernomyrdin would remain as prime minister until March 1998 and remained President Yeltsin's candidate of choice as late as that August. Large sectors of the Russian economy were governed by administratively set prices from the very beginning of price liberalization in January 1992. Even so, the attempt to free prices for a wide range of consumer products in the context of a heavily monopolistic structure of Russian industry – a process, moreover, that was announced several months in advance in the fall of 1991 – triggered an inflationary wave that hit 2,600 percent before 1992 was over and that wiped out the life savings of perhaps 90 percent of the Russian population. At the same time, insiders were able to borrow from the Russian Central Bank at interest rates of 10–25 percent and convert the credited rubles into dollars; these credits amounted to about one-third of Russian GDP for 1992 and constituted a major source of enrichment for Russia's well-placed elites even as the bulk of the population was sliding into general misery.[26]

It is the general aspect of the previously cited critiques rather than the programmatic ones that are to the point: What mattered most is that the Russian government, willingly but also encouraged by its Western supporters,[27] attempted to institute massive and complex socioeconomic reforms without an adequate legal, administrative, fiscal, or political foundation to sustain them.[28] This is significant because the critics imply that they had a better plan, a dubious proposition in light of the unprecedented

[25] An argument made convincingly by Steven Kotkin, *Armageddon Averted* (New York: Oxford University Press, 2001), and reinforced by Joseph Stiglitz, *Globalization and Its Discontents* (New York: W. W. Norton, 2002), pp. 133–65, 263, note 5.
[26] Anders Aslund and Mikhail Dmitriev, "Economic Reform versus Rent Seeking," in Anders Aslund and Martha Brill Olcott, eds., *Russia after Communism* (Washington, DC: Carnegie Endowment for International Peace, 1999), p. 96.
[27] Wedel, *Collision and Collusion.*
[28] For application to Russia in particular but also to struggling states in general, see Stiglitz, *Globalization and Its Discontents.* Stiglitz was chief economist at the World Bank for much of the 1990s.

challenges that a state like Russia faced in charting its post-Soviet course.[29] Moreover, the Western critics place major responsibility for Russia's fate in the 1990s with the United States government and the international lending agencies that it strongly influences, particularly the International Monetary Fund.

The critical turning point here appears to lie in the second half of 1990: At its July 1990 summit meeting in Houston, the Group of Seven (G-7) leading industrial democracies tasked the International Monetary Fund, the World Bank, the European Bank for Reconstruction and Development, and the Organization for Economic Cooperation and Development (OECD) to compile a report on the Soviet economy with recommendations on how Soviet Russia and the West might best proceed to reform the Soviet economy. In December 1990, the four leading international economic organizations presented their report, which focused on the following elements:

- A comprehensive and staged reform of the Soviet economy, not a sudden and radical change in parts of the system
- Relatedly, structural reforms in the fiscal, monetary spheres and systematic reforms in ownership, enterprise management, prices and the labor market
- An income policy to sustain a minimum standard of living during a necessarily painful transition period
- An overhaul of taxation and budgetary policies
- The creation and maintenance (that is, regulation) of competitive markets, so as to compensate for the monopolistic tendencies in many Soviet industries
- In respect of privatization, the establishment of procedures for reforming ownership rights, demonopolization, and enforcement of hard budget constraints on businesses
- Promulgation of monetary reforms but within a political context designed to ensure social equity and stability[30]

In effect, the Western international economic agencies were advocating a program of long-term, progressive, highly structured, and regulated reform of the Soviet economy, one in line not with the thinking of Western liberal economists such as Milton Friedman but with the more recent

---

[29] Gustafson, *Capitalism Russian-Style*, p. xiii, agrees.
[30] Stefan Hedlund, *Russia's 'Market' Economy: A Bad Case of Predatory Capitalism* (London: UCL Press, 1999), pp. 114–15.

work of economists Ronald Coase, Douglass North, and Robert Fogel (and implicitly of John Maynard Keynes), who stressed the importance of institutions and the legacy of the past in shaping economic futures.[31] Whatever chances such a program had to be implemented were probably eliminated by the fact and consequences of Soviet collapse in 1991, which completed the destruction of institutions that were required for the development of such a comprehensive reform.

If any criticism of Western policy is to be sustained, it must come to terms with the fact that the Russian government that emerged from the Soviet rubble in 1992 was extraordinarily weak in terms of its administrative capacity (for example, a genuine civil service) and that, consequently, governmental policy was beholden to private interests that made any consistent policy – that is, one that was both internally coherent and consistent with the public interest (if only with the interest of the state per se) – improbable.

In the second major area of economic reform policy, the privatization of Soviet economic assets, the spontaneous transfer of much of Soviet wealth from state to private hands by the beginning of the 1990s decisively shaped the contours and consequences of this program. Far from an equitable or merely effective transfer of title from the state to those who could develop the Russian economy, privatization, initially in the form of vouchers distributed to the Russian population that were largely absorbed by agents of Russia's industrial and political insiders, provided a license for those with a now legal title to wealth to plunder that wealth on behalf of narrow private as distinct from enterprise or shareholder interest. Once again, key institutional frameworks were absent: Whereas in Poland and the Czech Republic macroeconomic stabilization and the development of credible legal frameworks preceded the privatization process, in Russia the reverse took place.[32] And so, whereas countries throughout the world carrying out cash privatizations have typically managed no more than two hundred cases per year, in Russia privatizations totaled forty thousand each in 1992 and 1993 and five thousand each in 1995 and 1996.[33]

Clearly, no state, however well institutionalized, could manage such a gargantuan transfer of title on behalf of a public interest. The Russian government, being as we have seen far from adequately institutionalized,

---

[31] See especially Douglass C. North, *Institutions, Institutional Change and Economic Performance* (Cambridge, UK: Cambridge University Press, 1990).

[32] Stiglitz, *Globalization and Its Discontents*, pp. 181–8.

[33] Gustafson, *Capitalism Russian-Style*, p. 45.

gave little pretense of heeding public interests and allowed almost unlimited sway to well-connected private interests in the privatization process.
As noted in the previous chapter, revenues from Russian arbitrage transactions on the heavily regulated export market, where raw materials cost
as little as 1 percent of the world market price, amounted to 30 percent
of Russia's GDP in the first post-Soviet year of 1992.[34] More broadly, by
the mid-1990s, a majority of Russia's major firms were privatized at an
average of less than 10 percent of their existing book value and far below
their actual market value. Here are just a few typical instances:

- In 1995, Kremlin insider Mikhail Khodorkovsky's Menatep bank was
  able to obtain a 78 percent share in the oil company Yukos, then valued at at least $2 billion, for $309.1 million.[35] (By 2003, just before
  Khodorkovsky's arrest on Russian President Putin's evident orders,
  Yukos had a public value of more than $24 billion.)[36]
- Vladimir Potanin, once a deputy minister for economics in Yeltsin's
  government, used his firm Oneximbank to purchase, at an auction
  organized by that bank, virtually all of the oil company Sidanco for
  $570 million. A year later, Potanin sold a 10 percent share of Sidanco to
  British Petroleum (BP) for $470 million while secretly stripping assets
  that cost BP $200 million in irrecoverable losses by 1999.[37]
- In 2002, three years into the post-Yeltsin regime of Putin's "dictatorship
  of the law," Khodorkovsky's Yukos was able to purchase 100 percent
  control of the bankrupt gas firm Rosspan for $121 million, whose
  550 billion cubic meters of reserves had a market value at the time of
  $9 billion.[38]

Grigor Yavlinsky, a liberal economist and one of Russia's leading democratic politicians, has summarized the consequences of Russian privatization as follows:

Voucher privatization has had only limited success. A proprietary class was
not, strictly speaking, created; neither a change in management nor [significant]

---

[34] Anders Aslund, "Russia's Collapse," *Foreign Affairs*, September/October 1999, p. 66;
     idem, "Social Problems and Policy in Postcommunist Russia," pp. 133–6.
[35] See the report by Matt Taibi in *The Nation*, June 10, 2002, also at *JRL*, #6270, May 24,
     2002, at www.cdi.org.
[36] "Russia's $90 Billion Fortune Hunt," *Business Week*, August 5, 2002, p. 29; *Wall Street
     Journal*, November 17, 2003, p. 20.
[37] Silviu Brucan, *Social Change in Russia and Eastern Europe* (Westport: Praeger, 1999); Dmitri
     Simes, *After the Collapse* (New York: Simon and Schuster, 1999), p. 180.
[38] Brucan, *Social Change in Russia and Eastern Europe*.

investment took place. As a result we find ourselves in an exceptionally difficult situation and with an economically inefficient structure of property. Out of
the old forms of property have come ambiguous, intermediate forms of property relationships, which are neither state- nor private-property ones; this has
inevitably led to the growth of quasi-criminal, or if you prefer, an oligarchical
system. . . .[39]

Thane Gustafson, in his careful study of the Russian economy, has concluded that it will be a long time before the effects of the 1990s dissipates
and allows Russian entrepreneurial energies true leeway for their expression. Among the lasting legacies of the first post-Soviet decade are a large
illegal underground economy, prevalence of arbitragers and speculators,
siphoning off of profits by criminal and governmental organizations, and
so on. In this environment, it is nearly impossible to start a new business:
Whereas small business grew rapidly between 1991–3, reaching 900,000
enterprises by 1994, by 1996 this figure had dropped by 100,000 and
in mid-1997 stood at 838,000, accounting for just 9 million workers or
16 percent of the official workforce and 7–9 percent of industrial output.[40]
By 2002, after three years of long-awaited economic growth, small- and
medium-size businesses were still under 1 million and in fact declining as
a share of the total, constituting less than 15 percent of the labor force.
(By contrast, smaller businesses account for 49 percent of the workforce
in Great Britain and 54 percent in the United States.) In August 2002,
economists at UBS Warburg, a Swiss investment bank, calculated that
just eight business groups controlled 85 percent of revenue from Russia's
sixty-four largest private companies.[41] The number of state employees,
on the other hand, continues to rise, while in 2003 the Russian state disposed of nearly 40 percent of the country's official GDP compared to
17–18 percent in nominally communist China.[42]

---

[39] Grigor Yavlinsky, "Ne budet demokratii, esli ne budet svobodnoy pressy" [There will be
no democracy without a free press], *Vechernaya Moskva*, no. 17 (April 24–30, 1997), p. 3.
For an impressive theoretical explanation, see Paul B. Stephan III, "Toward a Positive
Theory of Privatization – Lessons from Soviet-Type Economies," *International Review of
Law and Economics*, vol. 16 (1996), esp. pp. 181–9.

[40] Gustafson, *Capitalism Russian-Style*, pp. 132–3.

[41] *International Herald Tribune*, August 14, 2002, p. 3. According to Forbes, thirty-six
billionaires control one-fourth of Russia's GDP. As reported in "Geld ist Macht" [Money
Is Power], *Sueddeutsche Zeitung*, July 8, 2004, p. 5.

[42] According to Petr Aven, president of Alfa Bank (Moscow), in *JRL*, #6289, June 5, 2002,
item no.9; as reported by Russian economist Vladimir Mau, *Moscow News*, September
24–30, 2003, at www.english.mn.ru.

In the area of macroeconomic stabilization policy, the Russian Central Bank, faced with a collapse of real production and thus of real incomes and real tax revenues, resorted alternatively to seemingly unlimited monetary emission (in 1992 and 1993) and later, in part in response to conditions insisted upon by the International Monetary Fund, to a monetary emission so restrictive that it appears in retrospect to have been a major reinforcing element, together with an artificially strong ruble, in Russia's decade-long economic depression. By the mid-1990s, the Russian government was pursuing a policy of comprehensive austerity in the midst of an unprecedented depression, reminiscent of Western policies in the early 1930s but certainly impossible to implement in a truly democratic polity.[43] In effect, the Russian government's budget was balanced, such as it was, by withholding scheduled wage, pension, and social security payments to large sectors of the most vulnerable elements of the population.[44] It is to these social consequences of the crisis of the Russian state that we now turn.

## VI. Social Aspects

The Russian government, which throughout the 1990s had been praised by the Clinton Administration and the international lending agencies (themselves strongly influenced by the United States) for its commitment to economic and political "reform,"[45] was thus failing to perform some of the elementary functions of governance and in the process jeopardizing not only Russia's democratic and market prospects but the essential coherence of society. That male life expectancy in Russia has fallen below sixty years, that deaths will vastly exceed births for the foreseeable future,[46] that less than a third of Russia's children (that is, those under the age of eighteen) are adjudged healthy by Russian medical authorities while a sixth have been diagnosed with chronic illnesses,[47] are just four of the most dramatic indices of the social devastation and despair that have

---

[43] Stiglitz, *Globalization and Its Discontents*, pp. 161–2.

[44] Padma Desai and Todd Idson, *Work without Wages: Russia's Non-Payment Crisis* (New York: Columbia University Press, 2000).

[45] See Talbott, *The Russia Hand*, pp. 56, 68, 86.

[46] *Sotsial'noye polozheniye i uroven' zhizni naseleniya Rossii* [The social conditions and living standards of the Russian population] (Moscow: Goskomstat, 1997), p. 10.

[47] *Segodnya* (Moscow), March 10, 1998, p. 2; Interfax (Moscow), September 10, 2003 at *JRL*, #7319, September 10, 2003, at www.cdi.org.

taken root in post-Soviet Russia. A definitive study of Russian poverty in the mid-1990s by economist Vladimir Mikhalev concluded as follows:

[L]ack of an effective safety net capable of alleviating the social hardships of the transition has been an important cause of growing popular disappointment, despair and even giving rise to the danger of social unrest. The results of the December 1995 parliamentary elections in Russia [where the communists won a majority of votes and the sole pro-government party won just 10 percent] and the collisions in the course of the presidential election in 1996 provided vivid evidence of the gravity of political backlashes against the reforms.

The following subsections detail some of the indicators of the economic and social price that much of the Russian population has been paying in recent years.

## A. Degree of Social Inequality

Economic inequality evidently tripled in the first years of the transition: Already by 1994, the richest top 10 percent of the population was earning fourteen times the income of the poorest 10 percent, compared to 5.4 times as much in 1991; by early 2001, it appeared that the gap between rich and poor in Russia had not changed significantly since the mid-1990s, while the middle 50 percent of the population had not seen its position improve, at best, since then[48]; by 2002, the top 20 percent of the Russian population earned 50 percent of money incomes (versus 30 percent in 1991), compared to 6.1 percent for the bottom 20 percent, a relationship more typical of Third World income distributions or the U.S. wealth (as distinct from income) distribution; the middle 60 percent earned 42.1 percent of money incomes.[49] (Russian economist Nikolai Shmelyov believes that the actual though unofficial ratio between the income of the top tenth to the bottom tenth is on the order of 60:1, not 14:1.[50])

---

[48] Based on an interview with Tatyana Maleva, a sociologist with the Russian Economic Analysis Bureau, in *Segodnya* (Moscow), March 6, 2001; also at www.wps.ru/e_index. html.

[49] V. Golovachev, "The Gap between Rich And Poor Is Narrowing In Russia," *Ekonomika i Zhizn'*, no. 6 (2001), *JRL*, #5150, March 14, 2001, item no. 2. Stanislav Menshikov, "Budget Policy Cautious But Ignores Rising Inequality," *Moscow Tribune*, June 14, 2002; www.tribune.ru. Bertram Silverman and Murray Yanowitch, *New Rich. New Poor. New Russia: Winners and Losers on the Russian Road to Capitalism* (Armonk, NY: M. E. Sharpe, 1997), p. 27.

[50] Nikolay Shmelyov, "Nekotorye klyuchevye rossiyskiye voprosy, otveta na kotorye poka net" [Some key Russian problems to which there are not yet answers], in IMEMO, ed., *God Planety: 2003* [World Annual: 2003] (Moscow: Ekonomika, 2003), p. 157.

Wealth was even more concentrated: Russian economist Dmitri Lvov has calculated that in 2003, 85 percent of the Russian population owns just 7 percent of the country's wealth.[51] Strikingly, by 2002, labor income constituted just 5 percent of all official Russian income growth (compared to 20 percent for capital and 75 percent for natural rent – mines, oil, gas, and so on), but accounted for fully 70 percent of all federal government treasury revenues, a ratio of 14:1.[52] One wonders whether the most exploitative fascist state could achieve a more disproportionate amount of revenues from the working population.

## B. Regional Inequalities

Inequalities between regions in Russia also rose dramatically, as the ratio of real per capita income between the richest and poorest regions increased from about 8:1 in 1992 to 42:1 by 1994, suggesting that the central government was losing the capacity to redistribute resources among Russia's regions so as to promote balanced national socioeconomic development. By 2000, in only nine out of Russia's eighty-nine regions was the average income higher than twice the minimum wage.[53] The average income of a Muscovite in 2002 was 4.2 times higher than that of residents of the rest of Russia and five times higher than residents in surrounding Moscow Province (a disparity that was evidently behind widespread soccer violence in Moscow during the World Cup in June 2002).[54] By 2003, after four years of impressive statistical growth, the city of Moscow (with 7 percent of the Russian population) still accounted for fully 28 percent of the country's retail trade and 21 percent of the country's GDP (compared to 14 percent in 1997), as well as 84 percent of all bank accounts, 25 percent of all Russian small businesses, and 40 percent of all privately owned cell phones.[55] Russian economist Dmitry Lvov has calculated the ratio of the per capita maximum to the per capita minimum in several

---

[51] Pravda online (*www.pravda.ru*), September 8, 2003, at *JRL*, #7317, September 8, 2003, item no. 16, at www.cdi.org.

[52] Academician Dmitry Lvov, "An Impartial View of the Russian Economy," *Versty*, no. 59 (2002), at *JRL*, #6313, June 18, 2002. Shmelyov states that wages account for 30 percent of Russian GDP, compared to the 70–5 percent that is typical in the G-7 countries. Shmelyov, "Nekotorye klyuchevye rossiyskiye voprosy," p. 156. (Data for 2002.)

[53] *Argumenty i fakty* (Moscow), no. 10 (March 2001), at www.wps.ru/_index.html.

[54] Menshikov, "Budget Policy Cautious But Ignores Rising Inequality."

[55] *Washington Post*, November 26, 2003, p. E10; "The Two Russias: Hinterlands Are Stuck in Post-Soviet Dysfunction," *Newsweek*, July 14, 2003.

TABLE 5. *Indices of Regional Inequalities in Russia*

| Sector | Ratio of Per Capita Maximum | Ratio of Per Capita Minimum |
|---|---|---|
| GDP | 64 | 1 |
| Investments | 2,000 | 1 |
| Consumption | 30 | 1 |

critical sectors across Russia's eighty-nine federal regions. His findings are summarized in Table 5.

By contrast, in the European Union, the consumption gap is no more than 6.5–7:1, allowing Lvov to conclude that "Europe, with its different countries, has more grounds to be called a single country than Russia with its regions now."[56] Characteristically, the cities of Moscow and St. Petersburg accounted for two-thirds of the country's limited Internet usage by mid-2002.[57] Investment resources were even more disproportionately concentrated in the city of Moscow, enabling one to speak of Moscow as a functional enclave of the oil and gas industry. In this respect, the post-Soviet Russian state has yet to perform one of the prerequisite functions of governance: to administer the society as a single whole.

## C. Compression of the Wage Structure

This period also witnessed the effective collapse of the wage structure. In real terms, the minimum wage had by 1996 fallen to 20 percent of its 1991 level and was equal to just 7 percent of the average wage; household consumption as a percentage of GDP fell from 47.4 percent in 1990 to 39.7 percent in 1994 while the percentage of income spent on food rose from 36.1 percent in 1990 to 46.8 percent in 1994[58]; moreover, by early 1996, the average real wage was worth 40 percent of its pre-reform level. These losses were compounded by widespread wage arrears, which amounted to nearly one-third of the wage bill by early 1996, 60.5 percent in 1999, and 32.5 percent in 2000; overall, the average purchasing power of individual incomes in 2000 was 1.7 times the officially defined subsistence level, compared to 3.4 times that level in the pre-reform year of 1991.[59] By 2002, wage levels had stabilized somewhat but were still

[56] Lvov, "An Impartial View of the Russian Economy."
[57] Interfax (Moscow), April 29, 2002, at www.interfax.ru.
[58] Silverman and Yanowitch, *New Rich, New Poor, New Russia*, pp. 23–4.
[59] According to the All-Russian Center of Living Standards, as reported in Vladimir Litvinov, "Statistika" [Statistics], *Ekonomika i Zhizn'*, no. 4 (2001), *JRL*, 5150, March 14, 2001, item no. 1.

40 percent of the 1990 level as well as lower than before the pre-crash level of August 1998. The highest basic wage remained below the official subsistence level.[60]

## D. Decomposition of the Soviet Middle Class

This period also saw the compression of the wages of professionals and engineers, who formed the backbone of Russia's aspirant middle class, and an important source of support for Gorbachev's democratizing reforms. Their wages – led by those of teachers and medical staff – have fallen to levels lower than those of unskilled workers; wage levels in education were 77 percent of the official subsistence minimum in mid-1995, 74 percent in culture and the arts, and 95 percent in the health care sector as a whole. While there are ongoing debates about the size of Russia's middle class and how to define it, there is broad agreement that Russia's old Soviet middle class has contracted dramatically, that the current Russian "middle" class – which sees itself as neither rich nor poor – is much closer in relative size to an early-twentieth-century middle class in continental Europe (that is, 10–20 percent of the population) than to its counterpart in the North Atantic world at century's end (that is, a majority), and that the middle class is remarkably insecure financially and psychologically.[61] Gordon Hahn estimates the Russian middle class at just 7 percent of the total society, while the dislocation of the educated classes of the late Soviet period may be seen in the fact that, whereas in the West most white-collar workers work in their chosen profession, in post-Soviet Russia just half do so.[62]

---

[60] Oksana Dmitrieva, "Economic Myths Debunked," *Moscow News*, July 3–9, 2002, at www.english.mn.ru.

[61] See Anna Raff, "Middle Class Is Back and Growing," *Moscow Times*, September 26, 2000, p. 1. Researchers at the Moscow-based Comcon marketing agency believe, based on income and spending surveys, that the middle class makes up 10 percent of the Russian population (and 20 percent in Moscow), compared to 15 percent before the financial crash of August 1998; 7 percent of the working-age population – that is, those between the ages of 18–50 – is considered middle class. See also Harley Balzer, "Russia's Middle Classes," *Post-Soviet Affairs*, vol. 14, no. 2 (1998), pp. 165–85; Igor Birman and Larisa Piyasheva, *Statistics of the Level of Living of the Russian Population* (Washington, DC: US Department of the Treasury, Office of Technical Assistance, 1997); Nataliya Tikhonova, *Russlands Sozialstruktur nach acht Jahren Reformen* (Cologne: Bericht des BIOst, no. 31, August 20, 1999). See also Brucan, *Social Change in Russia and Eastern Europe*, pp. ix–xiii, 64–7; see Gustafson, *Capitalism, Russian-Style*, pp. 172, 177–9, for a summary of and reference to the work of Russian sociologists Natalya Rimashevskaya and Tatyana Zaslavskaya that support this interpretation.

[62] Gordon M. Hahn, "Growing Middle Class Reinforces Civil Society," *Russia Journal*, April 26–May 2, 2002; *Profil* (Moscow), no. 17 (April 29, 2002), at *JRL*, #6226, May 6, 2002.

## E. High Poverty Rate

By the mid-1990s, Russia had a poverty rate commonly estimated at over
50 percent of the Russian population; moreover, working-age adults –
that is, the economically active population – rather than pensioners (as
is commonly assumed) form the majority of the poor (fully one-third of
the country in the late 1990s received a money income below the subsistence level).[63] The mortality rate increased more among the working-
age population in the 1990s (38.5 percent) than in the population as a
whole (31.8 percent).[64] Beyond this, regional data suggest that fewer than
20 percent of households eligible to receive some kind of locally provided
social assistance are actually getting it. In 1999, the incomes of more than
40 percent of the Russian population, or 60 million people, were below
the official subsistence level of 1,138 rubles per month, while fully half
of all families with one child lived below the subsistence level (this was
true of 75 percent of families with three children or more).[65] By 2003, after five years of economic growth following the 1998 crash, the Institute
of Interdisciplinary Social Research of the Russian Academy of Sciences
calculated that fully 72 percent of Russians were "poor or near poor."[66]

## F. Sharp Decline in Public Health

For the 1990s as a whole, the Russian death rate rose more than 30 percent, the highest of any major country, while the birth rate dropped by
nearly 40 percent, making it among the very lowest.[67] (In Italy, which has
a comparably low birth rate, there are 103 deaths for every 100 live births,
whereas in Russia there are 170 deaths per 100 live births.) Most strikingly, the population continues to decline in spite of the net in-migration of
5.5 million Russian immigrants in recent years, mainly from the Caucasus
and Central Asian states: The net decline in the Russian population from

---

[63] UN Development Program, *2000 Human Development Program for the Russian Federation*
(March 2001), at www.undp.ru.
[64] *Obshchaya Gazeta* (Moscow), March 1, 2001.
[65] *Izvestiya*, July 4, 2000, at www.izvestiya.ru; *Moscow Times*, October 18, 2000, at
www.moscowtimes.ru.
[66] "Highlights: Data on Russian Middle Class," *JRL*, #7427, November 19, 2003.
[67] For a comprehensive review of the state of Russian public health, see Mark G. Field,
"Health in Russia: The Regional and National Dimensions," in Peter J. Stavrakis et al.,
eds., *Beyond the Monolith: The Emergence of Regionalism in Post-Soviet Russia* (Washington, DC: Woodrow Wilson Center Press, 1997), pp. 165–80; Francesca Mereu, "Russia:
High Medical Costs Force Sick, Elderly To Do Without," and "Russia: Life Expectancy
Declining," *RFE/RL* (Moscow), July 5, 2002, at *JRL*, #6341, July 6, 2002, items no. 4
and 5, respectively.

1992–2002 was 4.2 million (from 148.7 million to 144.5 million).[68] As the main, Slavic source of immigration has been largely exhausted, the native population's decline of the 1990s will soon begin to intensify. As evidence, consider that the mid-1990s registered a decline in male life expectancy, from 63.8 years in 1990 to 58 years in 1995, and an annual excess of deaths over births approaching 800,000. This foreshadows a long-term decline in the Russian population, which historically had grown to become Europe's largest (as the year 2000 came to a close, male life expectancy in Russia was still below 60, at 59.75[69]; the overall Russian average life expectancy of 65.9 years in 1999 put Russia on a par with levels in Guatemala).[70] Since 1997, the mortality rate among women and children has also risen sharply, perhaps reflecting a growth in prostitution that has made that profession, at least in its hard currency version, a trade of preference among many Russian high school girls.[71] In only sixteen of Russia's eighty-nine federal regions do births exceed deaths,[72] while for the 1990s as a whole, Russia's child population declined by 4 million.[73] While the total number of Russians infected with HIV remains comparatively small, at 177,000 by the end of 2001, the rate of increase is alarming: HIV infections more than quadrupled from 1999–2001, with 20,000 new infections in 1999 compared to 87,000 in 2000.[74] If these trends continue unabated, Russia's population will decline from 144.2 million at the outset of 2002 to 86.5 million by 2050, a nearly 50 percent decline with obvious economic as well as geopolitical implications.[75] (By contrast, the population of the USSR was nearly 300 million at its demise in late 1991.) The UN Development Program has reported as its "medium" variant a Russian population decline of 21 percent between 2000–25.[76] In the short term, the merely economic dimensions of the problem may be grasped in the fact that between 1992–2002, the

---

[68] Nicholas Eberstadt, "The Emptying of Russia," *Washington Post*, February 13, 2004, p. A27; "First Results of 2002 Census Published," Rosbalt (Moscow), October 29, 2003.

[69] According to Yevgeny Andreyev of the Center for Human Demography and Ecology, Moscow, as reported by Interfax (Moscow), March 7, 2001.

[70] Ibid.

[71] According to an NTV report that the author watched, broadcast in Moscow, May 27, 2001.

[72] Dmitry Olshanksy, "Who Lives Well in Russia?" *Rossiya*, April 18, 2002, at www.wps.ru/e_index.html.

[73] RIA Novosti (Moscow), June 11, 2002, at *JRL*, #6303, June 12, 2002.

[74] *International Herald Tribune*, July 22, 2002, p. 5.

[75] For projections of Russian demographers, see *JRL*, #6318, June 20, 2002, item no. 7.

[76] Eberstadt, "The Emptying of Russia."

Russian labor force declined by 12 million; if current demographic trends continue, the Russian workforce will be reduced by an additional 10 million people by 2015.[77]

### G. Deterioration of Diet

Russians experienced a decline of more than 10 percent in daily calorie intake, from 2,589 in 1990 to 2,310 in 1995 (the UN Food and Agriculture Organization considers a daily calorie intake below 2,350 as going hungry); more specifically, survey research by the Western firm Russian Market Research Corporation has revealed that fully half of the Russian population report growing their own potatoes, onions, garlic, cucumbers, and tomatoes for personal consumption – an indicator of Russian adaptiveness, to be sure, but also of important pre-modern modes of survival in Russian society (that is, constraints on the division of labor and therefore of the chance to reap increases in living standards through the exploitation of comparative advantages).[78] Seventy to eighty percent of Russian families were raising a significant part of their own food. Relatedly, the percentage of consumer expenditure on food, increased from 36.1 percent in 1990 to 52 percent in 1995.[79]

### H. Increase in Suicide Rate

There was a dramatic increase in suicides, from 39,150 in 1990 to 56,136 by 1993, followed by an 11 percent increase the following year, leaving Russia with the third-highest suicide rate in the world. In 1992 and 1993, suicides accounted for nearly one-third of Russia's unnatural deaths. Overall, the Russian suicide rate increased by a third in the 1990s. Some sixty thousand Russians committed suicide in 2002, continuing the trend of the previous decade and placing Russia with the second highest suicide rate in the world (after Lithuania).[80] Comparatively, the Russian suicide rate in 2002 was 38.4 per one hundred thousand inhabitants, versus rates of 26.4 for the USSR as a whole in 1990, and 20, 16.4, and 13.4 for France, Canada, and the United States, respectively, in 2002.[81]

---

[77] "Russian Workforce Declines by 12 Million over Last 10 Years," Rosbalt (Moscow), September 5, 2003, at *JRL*, #7314, September 6, 2003, item no. 3, at www.cdi.org.

[78] Balzer, "Russia's Middle Classes," p. 177.

[79] Gustafson, *Capitalism Russian-Style*, p. 172.

[80] According to the World Health Organization, at *JRL*, #7313, September 5, 2003, item no. 8, at www.cdi.org.

[81] "Social Reasons behind High Russian Suicide Rate," *Agence France Presse*, August 11, 2003.

## VII. Russia's Silent Scream

These trends, which reflect the dramatic shock administered to the integrity of Russian social life by the sudden collapse of the Soviet institutional order, have continued, in some cases in somewhat attenuated form, as Russia entered the twenty-first century. The previously adumbrated evidence suggests that a dramatic decomposition of the social order took place in the first years following the Soviet collapse. By 1994 and 1995, the bottom had been reached. While the social situation as a whole has not dramatically deteriorated since then, neither has it improved significantly, thus lending a morbid credence to President Putin's statement that Russia is on the verge of becoming "a senile nation."[82] Overall, Russia is in one hundred and thirty-fourth place in the world in male life expectancy and one hundredth in female life expectancy, with 80 percent of the deaths among men taking place in the working-age population. The implosion of the Russian health care system, in the context of a Soviet health care system that itself spent just 3 percent of its GDP on health (compared to 12 percent for a typical, much richer, North Atlantic state) is plain from a visit to virtually any Russian hospital where, as I have witnessed, plumbing and toilets may be completely out of commission. In the majority of the cases, many life-threatening diseases appear to be undiagnosed while the patient is alive. In the macabre words of what has seemingly become a Russian medical folk saying, "An autopsy will tell."[83]

Another personal experience may be instructive. In the summer of 1995, during a visit to Russia, I happened to see a Russian-language version of the American anti-abortion film, *The Silent Scream*, broadcast on Russian television. The clip, sponsored by a U.S. religious organization, was evidently intended to discourage Russian women from having abortions, which are the main form of birth control in the country and regularly exceed the number of births by a factor of two or three. The film is quite graphic and focuses on the effects of an abortion procedure on the fetus itself. It turned out that most Russian women, instead of reexamining their attitude toward abortion, became more positively attuned to the idea after having watched the film. My U.S. students are incredulous when I tell them this but are themselves caused to reexamine their attitudes toward Russia, and the ways in which foreigners interact with

[82] Michael Wines, "An Ailing Russia Lives a Tough Life That's Getting Shorter," *New York Times*, December 3, 2000, p. 1.
[83] "Russian Health Experts Present Latest 'Shocking' Figures," *Obshchaya Gazeta, JRL*, #5141, March 9, 2001, item no. 1.

Russian society, when they hear the explanation. The obvious intent of the producers of the film is to induce the viewer to focus on the abortion procedure and provoke a reaction of physical and moral revulsion. At the least, they succeed in making Americans focus on the procedure, whatever their views on abortion may be. But what do Russian viewers, especially women, focus on? What strikes Russian women is not the depiction of the procedure and the torment of the fetus but rather the antiseptically clean operating room; the state of the art technology employed in the abortion, including the use of rapid and effective anesthesia; the professionalism and mutual respect characterizing relations between doctor and nurse; and the privacy and respect accorded the women undergoing the abortion. The typical Russian woman emerges from viewing the film with the idea, "Wouldn't it be great to have an abortion in the West!" This episode conveys by implication both the state of the Russian health care system and the difficulties that one culture has in translating its intentions into the understanding of another, a point to which we shall return.

## VIII. How Do Russians Get By at All?

At this point, the Western reader may justifiably ask, "How can Russians get by at all if things are that bad?" Since many Russians are obviously getting by, is the picture really that bleak? The answer lies in the fact that Russians do not live in a socioeconomic system that is comparable to Western systems, where legal norms, institutionalized and depersonalized public relationships, contractual reciprocity, and transparent economic transactions tend to predominate. British social scientists Richard Rose and Ian MacAllister have pointed out that there are in fact nine different economies in a country like Russia. The complexity of this system, which defies simple analogy to West European and North American norms, has undoubtedly allowed millions of Russians to devise economic strategies for themselves that, if they are not exactly conducive to the economic development of the country, do help ensure personal and family survival. The "density and scope of [these] social ties that can be converted or used as a substitute for economic resources" constitute what Michael Stedman has termed "intangible resources of adaptation" for societies "under stress," and they can in fact be quite considerable, when taken in conjunction with legalized economic transactions.[84]

---

[84] Michael Stedman, "Society under Stress," April 16, 2002, at www.strana.ru.

In this respect, Rose and MacAllister distinguish between civil economies, which are legal and monetized; social economies, which are legal and nonmonetized; and uncivil economies, which are illegal and monetized. The civil economy, where law and money prevail, covers (1) official employment and (2) pensions. For many Russians, this civil economy provides just a fraction of their real income. In Russian universities today, many professors depend upon their official teaching appointment as a tax dodge – that is, they pay their official taxes on their official university income while devoting the bulk of their energies to other, nontaxed, income-producing activities.[85] The social economies, which exist outside the pale of both law and money, provide much of the social grease that makes life livable for many Russians. The social economy, which has roots deep in Soviet times, includes (3) growing one's own food (on one's dacha) and making one's own repairs; (4) finding help among friends and relatives; (5) exchanging free favors; and (6) standing in line for more than half a day per week. The uncivil economies, which operate beyond the pale (and often the reach) of the law but not of money, encompass (7) working in the black market, (8) taking tips and bribes, and (9) using hard currency (mainly dollars and euros) instead of rubles in economic transactions.[86] According to a 1992 survey, whereas 94 percent of Russians said that they derived income from the civil economies, 96 percent stated that they were active in one or more of the social economies and 48 percent stated that they were involved in one or more of the uncivil economies. The average Russian household was involved in 3.7 of the nine economies listed, which implies that the unofficial economy is at least as important for most Russians as the official one. This helps to explain the ability of many, if not most, Russians to survive and adapt to the consequences of the crash of state finances, the collapse of the ruble, and default on state obligations in August 1998: Since most Russians were not yet dependent on the legalized money economy (and had not been so in Soviet times), the crash had less severe consequences for them than Western observers – imagining the impact of such an event on their own economies – anticipated at the time. This also helps explain why Russian public opinion studies to this day regularly chart expenditures by

---

[85] Based on privileged personal communication.

[86] Richard Rose and Ian McAllister, "Is Money the Measure of Welfare in Russia?" *Review of Income and Wealth*, vol. 42, no. 1 (1996), pp. 83–9. For a discussion, see Hedlund, *Russia's "Market" Economy*, pp. 359–60.

the public that significantly exceed reported "income."[87] This no doubt also helps to explain the almost complete absence of concerted civic and political action on the part of the Russian population in the aftermath of the crash: Most, apart from the small "middle class" that had committed itself to the new cash- and credit-based market economy, were just not affected.[88]

To give some specific examples, the Russian government's Auditing Commission has estimated that nonlegal economies as a whole had quintupled in size over the past decade, amounting to perhaps half of Russia's real gross domestic product. (By contrast, in Germany, "shadow" economic activities account for about 16 percent of the GDP.[89]) In a poll conducted in spring 2002, fully 81 percent of Russian business respondents said that they cannot operate without violating laws and regulations whereas only 15 percent said that they could. Several particulars reported by the Auditing Commission as well as the Central Statistical Administration stand out, including the following:

- Whereas 185 million deciliters of vodka are "sold" annually, at least 215 million are drunk.
- In 2001, Russia officially exported 1 million tons of oil less than was imported by other countries from Russia, based on the sum of other countries' import manifests.
- Whereas just 597,000 television sets were officially sold in 2001, fully 3 million sets were actually purchased, based on consumer respondents' information.
- Whereas only 30 million Russian workers are registered in the country's official pension fund system (social security), 70 million are actually employed.[90]

This picture undoubtedly helps explain patterns of social adaptation after the collapse of communism, based on skills learned in the communist

---

[87] Yevgeny Andreyev, "The Shadow Economy," *Moscow News*, October 2003, 22–8, at www.english.mn.ru.
[88] Gerd Ruge, *Sibirisches Tagebuch* [Siberian Diary] (Munich: Knaur, 2000), p. 286. There is a parallel in the effects of the Great Depression of the 1930s: Those countries that were most closely connected to open international trading and financial flows, such as the United States and Germany, were most deeply affected. Those that had erected substantial barriers against free trade in the form of high tariff walls (such as France) and imperial preferences (such as Great Britain), suffered much less.
[89] "Schattenwirtschaft waechst ungebremst [The Shadow Economy Grows Out of Control]," *Frankfurter Allgemeine Zeitung*, July 27, 2002, p. 10.
[90] *Argumenty i fakty*, no. 18–19 (2002), at *JRL*, #6226, May 16, 2002, at www.cdi.org.

economy of planned consumer scarcity. It also helps explain the dissociation of money from actual income and perhaps even the lower mortality rates of Russian women, whose better social skills should serve them better in the social economy.

It should be self-evident from the picture of Russian society that emerges from these trends that economic inequality has increased dramatically in just a few years, that the wage structure of the former Soviet Russian middle class has effectively collapsed, and that, even where Russians have been able to maintain some semblance of subsistence and dignity, they have done so through a sudden, thorough, and traumatic change in their working hours and lifestyle. The adaptations that have taken place are the kind that help ensure personal and family survival but contribute little to the development of a truly modern society, at least as the term is understood throughout the Western world. Russian society, in short, is under tremendous stress. A Soviet-era middle class that is growing smaller and increasingly insecure – even as elements of a post-Soviet entrepreneurial class are being established – is most unlikely to serve as the social foundation for stable political democracy in a country where neither the institutions nor the values of democracy have taken very deep root.

## IX. The Military

The German political sociologist Max Weber famously observed that the irreducible criteria for adjudging a government to be an actual government lay in a monopoly of effective taxation and a monopoly of control over the use of armed force for public purposes. In fact, the two standards are deeply interdependent, as the loss of a state's control over the power of the fisc tends to be associated with its loss of control over the armed forces. The Russian experience of the 1990s underscores the truth of Weber's dictum, as the difficulties that the Russian state has had in raising sufficient revenue to fund the operations of government have seriously undermined the capacity of the Russian armed forces to act as a coherent combat organization, one that is integrated into the purposes of the state. (The same may be said about the institutional integrity of the Russian police.) The consequence has been the transformation of the Russian military from an organization once feared for its aggressive strength vis-à-vis the outside world to one whose very weakness underscores the main preoccupation of the broader world with post-Soviet Russia, that is, the spillover of instability from Russia and more generally, the post-Soviet region whose overwhelming challenge is governing itself.

The external, quantitative indicators are dramatic enough. NATO today has a degree of "conventional" (that is, nonnuclear) military superiority vis-à-vis Russia that is almost the exact inverse of that which the Soviet Union and its Warsaw Pact allies had over NATO in the late 1980s. With the addition of Poland, Hungary, and the Czech Republic, NATO now possesses a quantitative preponderance over Russia of 1.7:1 in the area of combat aircraft to 3.7:1 in tanks. Taking into account scheduled and mainly budget-driven reductions in the Russian armed forces in the foreseeable future, this balance will shift even more dramatically in NATO's favor by 2005. The progressive obsolescence of most Russian military equipment, given an 80–90 percent reduction in military procurement since the 1990s, will accelerate this trend. Even in the critical strategic nuclear sphere, Russian military and arms control policies are mainly driven by budgetary constraints that rendered the bulk of the Russian missile fleet technically obsolete by the late 1990s.[91] Measured in constant 1995 U.S. dollars, the post-Soviet Russian military budget declined by more than 75 percent throughout the 1990s, from $47.5 billion to $11.2 billion in 1998.[92] Under these circumstances, Russian specialists consider that the defense budget, which itself is often not fully funded in practice, covers at best one-third of the minimally necessary expenses for maintaining the armed forces. Less than 20 percent of the military budget in recent years has been devoted to procurement, with the bulk going to salaries, operating costs, pensions, and housing.[93] Russian force levels declined from 3.3 million in 1992 to 1.2 million in 2000; even so, many civilian Russian defense analysts believe that this lower level cannot be sustained under the existing military system.[94]

But the internal, qualitative signs of Russian military decomposition are more striking still. Even while the USSR still existed, Soviet authorities, amid the political and administrative chaos of Soviet disintegration, lost track of a nuclear bomb scheduled for test explosion in the deserts of

---

[91] Vladimir G. Baranovsky and Aleksei G. Arbatov, "The Changing Security Perspective in Europe," in Aleksei Arbatov et al., eds., *Russia and the West: The 21st Century Security Environment* (Armonk, NY: M. E. Sharpe, 1999), pp. 49–50.

[92] Stockholm International Peace Research Institute, *The SIPRI Yearbook 1999: Armaments, Disarmament and International Security* (Oxford, UK: Oxford University Press, 1999).

[93] Aleksei Arbatov, Karl Kaiser, and Robert Legvold, eds., *Russia and the West: The 21st Century Security Environment* (Armonk, NY: M. E. Sharpe, 1996), pp. 108–9.

[94] A. Mikhailova, "Statistics on the Age Structure of the Russian Population," *Ekonomika i Zhizn'*, no. 7 (2001), translated by RIA Novosti, at *JRL*, #5156, March 17, 2001, at www.cdi.org.

Semipalatinsk in Kazakhstan. It took eighteen months before the device in question was located. In early 1994, in an incident that exemplifies the cash crisis afflicting the Russian military in the 1990s, Russian bomb squad soldiers in Petersburg demanded cash from the city authorities before they would agree to dismantle an unexploded bomb just unearthed from the Second World War siege of Leningrad. This story illustrates the extent to which civil–military relations, once a matter of exclusive (civilian) Communist Party authority, could become a matter of negotiation between the military and politicians in post-Soviet Russia and thus the degradation of the proper function of the military as an agency of governance. In March 2001, a bipartisan commission chaired by former GOP Senate Majority Leader Howard Baker and ex-White House Counsel Lloyd Cutler (and including defense specialist Sam Nunn) concluded that the risk of the theft of Russian nuclear materials is "the most urgent unmet national security threat" facing the United States, requiring $30 billion on the part of the U.S. government over the next decade.[95] Subsequent studies published in mid-2003 reinforced the message.[96]

Relatedly, stranded Russian army units had acted, on their own, even apart from the Ministry of Defense, to decide the course of a secession crisis in Moldova in early 1992, while in Georgia in 1993 the Defense Ministry appears to have acted largely on its own to support a secessionist movement in Abkhazia against a Georgian government led by the despised former Soviet foreign minister Eduard Shevardnadze. In the spring of 1994, the Russian Defense Ministry expressly contradicted Foreign Ministry negotiations with the government of Latvia on the withdrawal of Russian troops, as well as the scheduled phase-out of a radar site at Skrunda, and announced that Russia was committed to preserve a string of thirty military bases in ex-Soviet republics, including Latvia. From time to time, the Defense Ministry would announce that it was pursuing "its own" policy in the Balkans, an attitude that presaged the June 1999 dispatch of two hundred Russian paratroopers to occupy the airport in Pristina, Kosovo, and to deliver a fait accompli not merely to NATO but to the Russian Foreign Ministry, which had been cut off from pertinent communications on the issue.

---

[95] H. Josef Hebert, "Budget Cuts for Russian Nuke Program," Associated Press (Washington, DC), March 13, 2001.

[96] See the report conducted by Harvard University's Nuclear Threat Initiative, "The Threat in Russia and the Newly Independent States," at: www.nti.org/e_research/cnwm/threat/russia.asp; Nunn and Richard G. Lugar were cochairs of the board that oversaw the report.

The extreme difficulties that the Russian military has experienced in subduing Chechnya, where during the first Chechen War of 1994–6 the Russian army suffered more casualties in the first month than did the Soviet army during the first six months after the invasion of Afghanistan in December 1979 and whence it eventually withdrew in defeat and humiliation, underscores the fragility of the power of the contemporary Russian state. Many of the reasons for the numerous setbacks encountered by the Russian army, reminiscent of the USSR's difficult campaign against Finland in the Winter War of 1939–40, are already clear. They include disastrous military tactics (relying on tanks to take the capital city of Grozny, the same mistake the Serbs made in Slovenia in June 1991), reflecting the failure (or inability) to execute Russia's new military doctrine, which places a premium on highly maneuverable rapid deployment forces; poorly trained troops, many of whom had never exercised together (some marine units had to be brought in from Vladivostok, whereas comparable units were also available in the nearby Black Sea fleet); lack of coordination between units and services; low morale and combat readiness; and strong divisions of view among the military high command (comparable to those that undermined the coup d'etat of August 1991) and, consequently, lack of unified military support for the operation.[97]

In fact, many of these characteristics of Russia's armed forces were clear to careful observers many months before the invasion of Chechnya. The unexpected and unplanned collapse of the Soviet Army from a force of 3.5–4 million men in 1990–1 to Russian armed forces approaching 1 million today has been part of a broader picture that underscores the disintegration of the once vaunted Red Army (now mainly the Russian Army) as a capable combat organization. Consider the following evidence:

- It took the Russian Army nearly one year to organize an expeditionary force of fifteen thousand men to police the frontier between Tajikistan and Afghanistan in 1993.
- Draft dodging has become rampant and virtually unpunishable, leaving the Russian Army with the least-educated, least-fit elements of Russian society to draw on and a ratio of officers to enlisted men at times approaching 1:1.[98]

[97] See the Russian journalist Anna Politovskaya's firsthand account, *A Small Corner of Hell: Dispatches from Chechnya* (Chicago: University of Chicago Press, 2003).
[98] Boris Makarenko, "Commentary," *Rossiyskaya Gazeta*, June 19, 2002, at *JRL*, #6319, June 21, 2002.

- Military procurement has fallen catastrophically. Whereas in the early 1980s the USSR produced one hundred different kinds of military aircraft, by 1993 the Russian government purchased just seventeen military aircraft of all kinds. In 1996 and in several years thereafter, the Russian military purchased not a single new combat aircraft. In 2002, just 30 percent of the Russian Air Force planes were considered in good repair. Between 2002–7, half of these will be scrapped, with few replacements in prospect.[99]

- Today, a typical Russian Air Force pilot receives at best twenty-three to thirty hours per year of flying time, versus a minimum of one hundred twenty (and more typically two hundred) for an average NATO-country pilot. It is estimated, moreover, that between 2002–5, 70 percent of trained pilots will quit the military with precious few replacements (not more than 10 percent).[100]

- A major source of weapons for Chechen soldiers in the first Chechen War was Russian soldiers themselves, who often sold their weapons for dollars or marks upon completion of their tour of duty. This signified either that the Russian military had lost inventory control over their weapons, underscoring its decomposition as a combat organization, or that it had not lost inventory control, in which case local officers were complicit in this suicidal trade in order to gain "off-budget" revenues not forthcoming from the Russian government. More generally, according to General Anatoly Kvashnin, chief of the Russian General Staff, 21 of the 170 tons of silver allocated to the Air Force in 2001 were stolen. The Russian armed forces, in Kvashnin's authoritative words, are "overwhelmed with theft and embezzlement."[101]

- In 1995, in response to a scheduled and prenotified Norwegian launch of a scientific rocket toward the North Pole, the Russian air command interpreted the radar signals as possible evidence of a hostile nuclear attack and informed President Yeltsin, who had to decide within minutes on whether and how to respond, underscoring the Russian military's loss of both vertical integrity (that is, institutional memory) and horizontal integrity (that is, coordination within the institution).

- By the end of the 1990s, three-fourths of Russia's strategic nuclear missiles had outlived their intended service life, propelling a process

---

[99] "Surrender of Chechnya," *Zavtra*, July 4, 2002, at *JRL*, #6340, July 5, 2002, item no. 8.
[100] Ibid.
[101] Artem Vernidub, "Corrupt Army Incapable of Defending Fatherland," May 31, 2002, at www.gazeta.ru.

of de facto disarmament independent of Russian governmental policy one way or another.

- Finally, as if to emphasize the eclipse of the Russian Army, the bulk of the second Chechen War was fought by armed units of the Ministry of Internal Affairs and contract soldiers. Even so, just one in four soldiers there were receiving their promised pay of $1,000 per month.[102] In fact, Interior Ministry troops, border troops, and the Presidential guard now outnumber the troops of the regular Russian Army in Russia as a whole (in 1999, Russia's paramilitary forces totaled 478,000 compared to 348,000 for the regular army).[103]

In part as a consequence of the state's loss of the power of the fisc (combined with the general institutional chaos set in motion during the last months of Gorbachev's tenure in office), the state has also lost control over the military. From time to time, whole months have gone by before the Defense Ministry received its allocated funds from the federal government. Moreover, as the Chechnya operation reminds us, the military high command has also lost considerable control over its own subordinate units. This systematic underfunding of the Russian military highlights a central aspect of post-Soviet Russian politics. What was once thought of, correctly, as an integrated military-industrial complex in Soviet times has split into those parts of the old Soviet economy that have the prospect of hard currency exports on the world market and those that have not. The former include the fuels and energy complex and a few other sectors such as diamonds and other precious and semiprecious metals. Also included are some arms production sectors, while the bulk of the Russian military and the industries that serviced them cannot possibly sustain themselves based on market criteria.

As a result, the Russian ground forces are capable only of internal use – and even here with considerable difficulties, as the Chechen wars show – or against a third-rate power. They lack the capacity to project power or to engage in sustained combat operations against a competent, modern military force, such as that of Turkey. Yury Baturin, secretary of the Russian president's advisory Defense Council, concluded in February 1997 that the army was "in a critical state.... If things continue in this way for another two years we could have a navy without ships, an air force without aircraft and [a] defense industry unable to make weapons."

[102] *Zavtra*, July 4, 2002.
[103] The International Strategic Institute for Strategic Studies, *The Military Balance 1999–2000* (Oxford, UK: Oxford University Press, 1999); *The SIPRI Yearbook 1999*, op. cit.

The eclipse of the Russian Army in Chechnya and in the country at large suggests that Baturin was right.

By late 2003, after five years of economic growth, this legacy remained essentially unaddressed. For the fifth year in a row, 2003 saw more Russian servicemen killed in noncombat circumstances (more than 1,200) than in combat, in spite of a brutal war continuing in Chechnya. The Ministry of Defense cited "accidents, carelessness, bullying and suicide" as the main causes.[104] On November 19 of that year, Russian Defense Minister Sergei Ivanov stated that the ministry had "not yet managed to stop the relative aging of our accumulated technology and weapons . . . ; [at most] one can speak only of a gradual re-equipment of the armed forces." Thus, at best, 70–85 percent of the military's weapons and technology are considered to be in "working order," while just 20 percent are considered to be up to contemporary standards. Air Force pilots were still averaging twelve to forty-four hours of flying time per year, compared to a norm of one hundred sixty to one hundred eighty. "Because of the poor training of pilots and the lagging technology of our [air] fleet, not a single unit of our air forces . . . meets the requirements of full readiness."[105] (In February 2004, the Russian Navy failed to launch two long-range ballistic missiles in a major strategic exercise, in the presence of President Putin, that was billed – a month before Putin's reelection – as a sign that Russia could still compete with the United States.[106])

## X. The Condition of Russian Science

If the military has not been spared the effects of the general collapse of state authority in Russia, it is little wonder that the former Soviet scientific establishment is in a struggle for survival as well. When the USSR collapsed, the scientific community fell into disarray. Today, its very survival is at risk, with two-thirds of Russia's scientific infrastructure having disappeared since 1991.[107] The OECD has described the condition of research and development in Russia as being one of "profound crisis." This reflects both the disintegration of a previously integrated scientific network across the territory of the ex-USSR as well as the extreme poverty

---

[104] Stephen Dalziel, "Death Rate High in Russian Army," BBC, September 13, 2003.
[105] "Defense Chief Bewails Unreadiness of Russia's Military," Rosbalt (Moscow), November 19, 2003, at *JRL*, #7427, November 19, 2003.
[106] Agence France Presse (Moscow), February 17, 2004, at *JRL*, #8071, February 17, 2004, item no. 11, at www.cdi.org.
[107] Shmelyov, "Nekotorye klyuchevye rossiyskiye voporosy," p. 152.

of the contemporary Russian state. Severe cuts in state spending on science have left scientific institutes, including prestigious ones, struggling simply to pay their electric bills and salaries. Wages are often paid months behind schedule. The once-prestigious science city of Akademgorodok now has an emergency food program servicing 10 percent of the population.[108] As a result, by 1995, as much as one-fifth of the sixty thousand scientists who had skills in electronics, rocketry, or other fields useful to nuclear weapons programs had abandoned their research laboratories in favor of more lucrative opportunities in the private sector, as well as abroad. Of an estimated 950,000 people working in research and development in Russia in 1991, two hundred thousand to three hundred thousand are thought to have left the system altogether by the mid-1990s, while by some calculations between five hundred thousand to eight hundred thousand Russian "scientists" are thought to have left Russia between 1991–2001, few of whom have returned for good.[109] The youngest and most talented are leading the way. In all, by 1999, one-fourth of Russia's scientists were thought to have left the country; another fourth, though in Russia, had left science as a field altogether; while another fourth were preparing to leave or retire.[110]

Overall, state financing for the Academy of Sciences and its numerous institutes, observatories, expeditions, libraries, publishers, and so on, has declined by as much as 80 percent over the last decade.[111] With a science budget of approximately $1 billion per year, the Russian state spends as much on science as does an average U.S. university.[112] Senior scientists at Russia's most prestigious institutes earn as little as the equivalent of $95 per month (3,000 rubles in 2002), which means that a typical scientist cannot afford on his monthly salary a round trip ticket between Novosibirsk – a leading scientific center – and Moscow.[113] By contrast, a Russian emigre scientist in the West can easily earn between $3,000–7,000 per month, that is, thirty to seventy times his or her nominal Russian salary.[114] All told, between 1989–93, the number of people employed in

---

[108] Andrew Jack, "Off Centre," *Financial Times*, March 31, 2001, at www.FT.com.

[109] Interfax (Moscow), June 20, 2002, at *JRL*, #6319, June 21, 2002.

[110] [Gustav Weber], "Brain Drain: Die Intelligentzia wandert aus," [Brain Drain: The Intelligentsia Is Leaving] *Ost in West: Politik und Wirtschaft in GUS und Baltikum*, no. 18, 1999 (September 6), p. 20. The figures are according to Sergei Kapitsa, head of the International Division of the Union of Russian Scientific Establishments.

[111] Jack, "Off Centre."

[112] *Sueddeutsche Zeitung*, August 14–15, 2002, p. 11.

[113] Interfax (Moscow), June 20, 2002, at *JRL*, #6319, June 21, 2002.

[114] Pravda Online (www.pravda.ru), May 21, 2002.

science in all of the countries of the ex-USSR decreased by more than 1 million. The dismal material conditions and prospects also mean that, for the most part, talented young people are simply no longer attracted to science as a vocation. Indeed, by 2000, young researchers between the ages of twenty-five and thirty-five made up just 11 percent of those engaged in scientific research, while the average age of researchers (fifty-five) is close to the pensionable age, and that of academicians in the Russian Academy of Sciences is seventy-two.[115] This has happened in spite of the fact that, in dollar terms, the expense of conducting science in Russia is about one-twentieth of the cost in the United States. Russian sociologist T. V. Naumova has described the situation as follows:

A typical Russian emigrant is a scientist who is engaged in fundamental science. That contingent includes specialists in the fields of information science, physics, computer mathematics and programming, genetics, and biotechnology.... The greatest level of emigration occurs among young representatives of the intelligentsia between the ages of 25 and 35, [reflecting also] a decline in the prestige of a number of professions involving intellectual labor.... The emigration of one specialist results in a loss to our country of ca. $300,000.[116]

In the area of nuclear energy, one can only be amazed that another Chernobyl has not happened. The Siberian chemical combine known as Tomsk-7 has accumulated twenty-three thousand containers of nuclear materials – plutonium and enriched uranium – from obsolete nuclear warheads that exist in conditions that the Russian government's Security Council described in late 1994 as "extremely unfavorable." The drastic deterioration of wages in the Russian Ministry of Atomic Energy has led to a number of alarming developments since 1992, including strikes by scientific and engineering personnel begun in 1993 and 1994 because of delays of months in the payment of salaries. Such stoppages have since become common, and in 1996 it was reported that delays in wage payments of two to six months were common in the nuclear industry. In late 1996, the director of the Russian Federal Nuclear Center in Snezhinsk, Vladimir Nechai, committed suicide in despair over shortfalls in state funding of such magnitude that he concluded he could no longer ensure the safety of the operations or pay the staff. Moreover, in 1993, eleven attempts to steal uranium from nuclear facilities were averted. There were also nine

---

[115] Agence France Presse, "Alarm Sounded for Science," *Moscow Tribune*, February 16, 2001, p. 4; Weber, "Brain Drain."

[116] T. V. Naumova, "Utechka umov' iz Rossii" [Russia's Brain Drain], *Sotsiologicheskiye Issledovaniye*, no. 6 (1996), pp. 138–40.

hundred instances in which illegal penetrations of closed nuclear facilities were cut short, and seven hundred instances in which enterprise employees tried to take out secret documents and were caught. All such attempts were made by employees with a thorough knowledge of the technology concerned. Finally, it is an open secret that the safety standards of Russia's nuclear industry, as well as those of all of Russia's ex-Soviet neighbors, are set by the available budgetary resources rather than by internationally accepted minimum criteria, which are deemed too costly to enforce.

Science has followed the pattern that we have identified in the macroeconomy, society, and the military, that is, a dramatic and rapid shock administered in the immediate aftermath of the collapse of the Soviet state and a subsequent gradual deterioration. By 2000, research funding for Russian science was one-sixth of what it had been a decade before, and the total number of researchers was down by half, to 910,000. Russian funding for research and development in general had declined from 1.03 percent of the GDP in 1991 to 0.32 percent in 1997 (compared to the 2.5–3 percent that is typical of North Atlantic countries).[117] President Putin has proposed to increase Russian government spending on science to 1.5 percent of the GDP; this compares to the 4 percent that is typical of much richer countries like the United States, Germany, and France.[118] Average research spending per capita stood at one-twenty-fifth the sum allocated in the world's industrialized nations. Whereas Russian law stipulates that the space program should receive 1 percent of the GDP, in 2000 it received 0.014 of the GDP, or $114 million (compared to $12.6 billion for the United States' NASA program).[119] The cumulative effect of this (unplanned) dessication of Russian science has led international scientific bodies to rank Russia's scientific potential now with states such as Hungary, New Zealand, Poland, and Spain, according to Russian Minister of Science Aleksandr Dondukov. Consequently, the share of Russian scientists' publications in scientific journals worldwide has dropped by 30 percent in the last decade, a slide that seems destined to accelerate given the dramatically advancing age of the Russian scientific community.[120] Given the central role that Russian technological development would have to play in Russia's ability to compete in the international economy, especially in terms of value-added exports, this is sobering news indeed.

[117] Arbatov et al., *Russia and the West*, p. 100; Naumova, "Utechka umov' iz Rossii," p. 51.
[118] *Sueddeutsche Zeitung*, August 14–15, 2002.
[119] Karl E. Hanuska, "Mir End Leaves Russian Space Program in Doubt," Reuters (Moscow), March 19, 2001.
[120] *Moscow Tribune*, op. cit.

## XI. The Rise of Post-Soviet Russian Crime

It should be clear by now that the debility of Russia's public institutions, particularly the Russian state, has meant that key elements of post-Soviet economic and social order have been distorted far beyond the intentions of those in Russia and the West who have attempted to plant market democracy in Russian soil. Significantly, organized crime – in various forms – has stepped into the breach of state authority and dominated the privatization of Russian industry, one of the most highly advertised success stories of the Russian government. In what Bernard Guetta of the French daily *Le Monde* has termed the "biggest holdup in history," Russia's criminal "mafia," in combination with many in the old communist elite, has taken over much of the economically valuable property in Russia, with consequences – such as massive capital flight – that are far from helpful to the future productiveness of the Russian economy. By 1994, Russia's Tass-Krim press agency was reporting that the Russian mafia had already "privatized between 50 and 80 percent of all shops, storehouses, depots, hotels, and services in Moscow." According to Yeltsin adviser Piotr Filipov, who at the time headed the Center for Political and Economic Analysis, by the mid-1990s criminal elements already controlled forty-thousand privatized enterprises and collected protection money from 80 percent of the country's banks and private enterprises. In August 1995, the Russian Ministry of Internal Affairs conservatively estimated that criminal groups controlled over four hundred banks and forty-seven financial exchanges. Infiltration of the financial sector has helped to provide the assets needed to infiltrate Russian industry. In April 1997, Lawrence Summers, U.S. deputy secretary of the treasury, stated that three-fourths of Moscow shops paid security firms for protection and that Russian businesspeople routinely had to pay bribes to secure import or export licenses, lease commercial space, or register their firms. Illegal payments designed to circumvent regulatory problems amount to as much as 15 percent of Russian wage costs, according to Summers. Russian and Western experts have estimated that more than half of Russia's capital "and 80 percent of voting shares are in the hands of criminal clans."[121] By 1997, forty-one thousand industrial companies and 80 percent of joint ventures were believed to have criminal connections while up to half of criminal profits may have been spent on corrupting (poorly paid) state officials.[122] Of the

---

[121] Tanya Frisby, "The Rise of Organized Crime in Russia: Its Roots and Social Significance," *Europe-Asia Studies*, vol. 50, no. 1 (1998), p. 35.

[122] Ibid., pp. 35, 37.

TABLE 6. *Percentage of Criminal Control of*
*Various Sectors of the Russian Economy*

| Sector | % of Criminal Control |
|---|---|
| Private business | 40 |
| State-owned business | 60 |
| Banks | 50–85 |

scores of contract murders of prominent bankers, journalists, politicians, and their aides that have occurred since the mid-1990s, including that of the distinguished legislator Galina Starovoitova, not one case has been successfully prosecuted. To give just one particular, in 1999, fifty-four Russian journalists were beaten, stabbed, or gassed in apparent reprisal for reports critical of authorities, according to the Moscow-based Center for Journalism in Extreme Situations. By early March 2001, fifteen more attacks (including six murders) had been reported, a situation that has led the Paris-based World Association of Newspapers to assess Russia as the most dangerous country in the world for journalists, after Colombia, the world's cocaine base.[123] In June 2002, Russia's Ministry of Internal Affairs estimated that by 2000, organized crime controlled 40 percent of private businesses, 60 percent of state-owned businesses, and 50–85 percent of Russia's banks,[124] as illustrated in Table 6.

More specifically, the organized criminal sector in Russia, motivated by the prospect of huge profits to be made from exploiting the still thick intersection of politics and economics, has successfully insinuated itself into a series of Russian business and related sectors, including finance and business, industry and trade (especially in natural and strategic resources, food and fisheries), production and trade in alcohol, sport, advertising and leisure industries, state and public administration, legal institutions, agriculture, and even charities. Narcotics trafficking and production occupies an increasingly important part of Russian crime's international connections.[125] International ratings of corruption levels in various countries, based on detailed surveys with foreign businesspeople, rank Russian corruption (0.98 on a scale of zero to ten) as far worse than such countries as

---

[123] Anna Dolgov, "Media in Russia Suffers Attacks," Associated Press, March 8, 2001.
[124] *Rossiyskaya Gazeta*, June 29, 2002, at *JRL*, #6338, July 5, 2002, item no. 10.
[125] Frisby, "The Rise of Organized Crime in Russia," p. 32.

Venezuela (1.58), Brazil (1.74), Italy (1.81), Colombia (2.38), Indonesia (2.68), and Turkey (3.08).[126]

Finally, one should keep in mind that arguably the largest "criminal" transfers of economic and state assets took place in plain view, presided over by Russia's legally elected and appointed officials. These include the following:

- The loans-for-shares program of 1996, in which a few magnates obtained the bulk of Russian industry in exchange for loans to Yeltsin's government during his reelection campaign
- The diversion of billions in International Monetary Fund credits to private purposes
- The sale of whole weapons arsenals to Chechen leader Dzhokar Dudayev by the Russian military leadership in 1991 and 1992
- The widespread and continuous conversion of state stockpiles of industrial assets and raw materials to private exports
- The default by the Russian government on state and commercial obligations to Russian and foreign creditors in August 1998
- The establishment by Yevgeny Adamov, at the time minister for atomic energy (who initiated an $800 million contract with Iran to build nuclear power reactors there), of a front company designed to profit from U.S. government contracts aimed at improving the safety of Russia's nuclear plants (that is, to tighten the security of the nuclear nonproliferation regime that Adamov was undermining with his ministry's policy toward Iran)[127]
- The juggling of railroad freight rates by then Railroads Minister Nikolai Aksyonenko to benefit companies owned by his son and nephew[128]

From this point of view, it is not just that organized crime has penetrated the Russian state but that Russia now possesses a state that by any Western definition of the term is itself a criminalized state.[129]

---

[126] Andrianov, *Rossiya v mirovoy ekonomike*, p. 218. New Zealand ranked first as least corrupt at 9.50, followed by Denmark (9.48), Singapore (9.25), Sweden (9.09), Finland (8.94), Canada (8.67), and Ireland (8.63). The United States ranked fourteenth, at 7.21, placing it between Germany and Austria.

[127] *International Herald Tribune*, July 19, 2002, p. 2.

[128] Ibid.

[129] See the work of David Satter, especially his *Darkness at Dawn: The Rise of the Russian Criminal State* (New Haven, CT: Yale University Press, 2003); also Vadim Volkov, "Who Is Strong When the State Is Weak? Violent Entrepreneurship in Russia's Emerging Markets," in Mark R. Beissinger and Crawford Young, eds., *Beyond State Crisis? Postcolonial*

There are some striking parallels between what is occurring in Russia today and the conditions that led to the rise of the Italian mafia in Sicily toward the end of the nineteenth century. In both the Sicily of that time and the Russia of ours, there existed social, economic, and political systems in which almost all property, social privileges, and political power, including control over the use of force, were held in the hands of a very small elite, whose power was enhanced by the fact that it was the same small elite in each country that combined economic, social, and political power (that is, the landowning class in late-nineteenth-century Sicily, and the Communist Party in Soviet Russia). In both countries, this feudal structure of power collapsed very rapidly under the pressure of the forces of modernization. The details of this process are less important than the consequences: the rapid fragmentation of property, so that it was almost overnight held in many individual hands instead of a few; the disintegration of traditional political authority, so that there was no effective legal and police protection of the new social and economic order; and many suddenly unemployed or underemployed military or paramilitary forces, who now found themselves in need of gainful employment. This process was under way even before the formal collapse of the Soviet state in December 1991, as demonstrated by the theft by Communist Party officials of one thousand tons of Russian gold in the course of 1991,[130] for which to date not one criminal charge has been brought.[131]

Thus both the demand for security and the supply of security increased rapidly and simultaneously both in late-nineteenth-century Sicily and in contemporary Russia. The result, in both cases, has been the rise of a powerful mafia, which is at heart an industry of private protection or security.[132] To employ the striking metaphor of Thane Gustafson, what turned a crime endemic in the USSR into a crime epidemic in Russia was the combination of a state that is both weak in enforcement but obstructive in

*Africa and Post-Soviet Eurasia in Comparative Perspective* (Washington, DC: Woodrow Wilson Center Press, 2002), pp. 81–104.

[130] See Pierre Lorrain, *La Mystérieuse Ascension de Vladimir Poutine* (Monaco: Editions de Rocher, 2000), pp. 307–10, for the Soviet context for the emergence of Russian organized crime.

[131] V. V. Luneyev, "Korruptsiya" [Corruption], *Gosudarstvo i Pravo*, no. 8 (1996), p. 85. For one illustration of Soviet-era sources of contemporary organized crime, see Anatoly Rubinov, "Soblaznennyi i rasstrelyannyi: Mafia v Moskvu prishla ne iz Italii" [Tempted and Shot: The Mafia Didn't Come to Moscow from Italy], *Literaturnaya Gazeta*, November 22, 1995.

[132] Diego Gambetta, *La mafia siciliana* (Turin: Einaudi, 1993); Federico Varese, "Is Sicily the Future of Russia?" *Archives Europeenes de Sociologie*, vol. 35, (1994), pp. 224–58.

the economy, a weakened society in disarray, an inexperienced private sector unable to manage its own affairs, and tremendous opportunities for material gain. In other words, "the legal vacuum which appeared as a result of the disintegration of the previous Soviet legal system (as well as the state itself) and the rapid redistribution of wealth in Russia . . . created basic preconditions for primitive accumulation of a criminal kind."[133] "Russia," Gustafson concludes, "is like an organism whose immune system has broken down and which succumbs to opportunistic infection by a microbe that previously lived more or less quietly in its gut." The infection will subside if the key enabling conditions are addressed, that is, a more settled society, stable relations between the state and the private sector, and a halt to the massive transfer of rents and property.[134]

Unfortunately, in Russia today, developments sometimes leave one in a mood of nostalgia for the disciplined criminality of La Cosa Nostra – the Italian mafia – as there are virtually no accepted rules or limitations on the behavior of organized crime in a Russia whose greatest deficit is one of security, and whose public institutions have proved unable to fill this critical gap. For example, there were three hundred contract killings in Moscow in 1998, forty tax policemen killed in the line of duty in 2000, and six journalists killed in 2000, without a single successful prosecution to date.[135] From this angle, "crime is not only a consequence of the social situation. It is also a barometer of social instability and a reflection of the weakness of the state, its legal base and institutions of law enforcement.... The inadequacy of legal mechanisms helps to create a system of administrative arbitrariness and corruption," in which, according to British crime sociologist Tanya Frisby, the "creators of capitalism, i.e., bankers, entrepreneurs, property developers, manufacturers, etc., depend not so much on government policies and decisions as on the actions of corrupt state administrators and organized criminals."[136] The consequences of this takeover of much the state's taxation and enforcement functions are dramatic for the economic development of the country: aggravated inflation due to higher transaction costs; fewer tax receipts for the poor; reduction in investment as against immediate consumption; capital flight and dollarization of the economy, in the process weakening the ruble and

133 Frisby, "The Rise of Organized Crime in Russia," p. 41.
134 Gustafson, *Capitalism Russian-Style*, p. 136.
135 Anna Bodkhen, "Russia's New Press Freedom Finds a Taint from Old Source," at *Boston Globe*, March 18, 2001, www.boston.com/news/globe; Hedlund, *Russia's "Market" Economy*, p. 330; RIA Novosti (Moscow), March 18, 2001.
136 Frisby, "The Rise of Organized Crime in Russia," p. 35.

TABLE 7. *Estimated Bribes by Sector in Russian Society*

| Sector | Bribes Paid per Year |
| --- | --- |
| Business | $33.5 billion |
| Medical care | $600 million |
| Courts | $274 million |
| Traffic police | $368 million |
| Admission to university | $449 million |

aggravating inflation further; proliferation of inefficiencies in production and distribution; and the reinforcement of attitudes and expectations that threaten the foundations of a viable market economy, such as distrust and discounting the future.[137]

On the most prosaic, day-to-day level, Russian criminologists have estimated that Russians spend nearly $40 billion per year to bribe government officials, who at an average salary of $113 per month are among the lowest paid government officials in the world. (Chinese civil servants are paid significantly more than their Russian counterparts.[138]) This figure is comparable to the size of the Russian federal budget in recent years. These figures break down in part as shown in Table 7.[139]

In a very important sense, then, Russia today is like Sicily, but a Sicily without the rest of Italy behind it to limit the scope of the mafia's power. Russian economic crime is parasitic, not productive. For the most part, Russia's new rich have accumulated their wealth by exploiting privileged access to resources for which they have paid precious little to acquire or develop. Under these circumstances, tremendous profits for individuals or individual firms may be obtained by selling items on the world market at dumping prices, which still brings income far exceeding any investments already made. On the whole, those profits, beyond the funds needed to sustain a sumptuous lifestyle within Russia and to maintain this parasitic

---

[137] Gustafson, *Capitalism Russian-Style*, pp. 147–8.

[138] *International Herald Tribune*, July 19, 2002, p. 2. The calculation is based on salary in relation to per capita GDP. On June 2, 2002, President Putin decreed a 50 percent increase in civil service salaries. The extent to which this will be put into effect remains to be seen. (In Chechnya, only one-fourth of Russian soldiers were receiving their promised pay increases in the first half of 2002.)

[139] *Argumenty i fakty*, May 29, 2002, at www.aif.ru; Interfax (Moscow), May 21, 2002, at www.interfax.ru; Yulia Latynina, "Redistributing the Blame," *Moscow Times*, April 17, 2002, at www.moscowtimes.ru; www.strana.ru, May 21, 2002, at *JRL*, #6260, May 21, 2002. It is commonly known in Moscow that a payment of $5,000 (U.S.) can obtain exemption from the draft for a son. This is the same sum for which a contract killing could be arranged in the mid-1990s.

type of economy, are being invested outside of Russia. (See Chapter 6 for details.) Ironically, it may even be the case that Russian capital, in spite of the vastly superior resource base of the Russian economy, is contributing more to the development of the Chinese than of the Russian economy. In any event, in the estimation of an Interior Ministry general, "the damage from criminal activity to our economy is comparable to the revenue side of the national budget. Our economy has in fact become a zone of total criminal aggression."[140]

The phenomenon of post-Soviet Russian crime thus both reflects and propels Russia's structural economic crisis: Within broad limits, Russia's criminals observe the logic of market economics. Illegal capital flight in the form of money laundering is in critical respects the counterpart of the legal export of capital from the Russian Federation. This explains in part why Russian domestic capital investment is down over 80 percent since the Soviet collapse and why the Russian economic, social, military, and scientific infrastructures are themselves close to collapse. In effect, Russia's criminal class too lacks the confidence in Russia's legal prospects that is prerequisite to large-scale productive investment in Russia's economic future. In turn, the extent of criminal penetration of the economy has the effect of undermining international business confidence in investing in Russia, which further reduces the availability of precious capital required to revive the Russian economy.

## XII. Conclusion

In summation, the 1990s were indeed a Time of Troubles for Russia; the country will not soon recover.

---

[140] General Dr. Pavel Ponomarev, "Chtoby prognoz ne opravdalsya" [Lest the prognosis bear out], *Militsiya*, no. 8 (1996), p. 19.

# Russia's "Neopatrimonial" Political System, 1992–2004

I stand above the court!

– Russian President Boris N. Yeltsin, April 1996[1]

The long and the short of it is that Russia, after fair and democratic elections in December of 2003, legitimately rejected democracy in favor of an updated authoritarian Soviet-type regime.[2]

– Russian political sociologist Olga Kryshtanovskaya

## I. Introduction

It was the first of the two Russian revolutions of 1917 that gave substance to Woodrow Wilson's call for the United States to "make the world safe for democracy" through its intervention in the First World War. The sudden collapse of the Tsarist monarchy and the establishment of a liberal democratic Russian government under the leadership of Alexander Kerensky in the winter of 1917 gave credence to the hopes of American democrats that Allied military victory over Imperial Germany would usher in an age of universal democracy and with it an age of universal peace. The tide of democratic sentiment also flowed westward from the Russian capital Petrograd, where Kerensky's government, anxious to convince its British, French, and now American allies of Russia's newfound democratic allegiance, kept a grievously weakened Russia engaged in the fourth year of war with Germany and launched ill-conceived offensives that by the

---

[1] As cited in Stefan Hedlund, *Russia's "Market" Economy: A Bad Case of Predatory Capitalism* (UK: UCL Press, 1999), pp. 60–1.

[2] As cited in *Vedomosti*, December 9, 2003; available at www.cdi.org/Russia/286–6.cfm.

summer of 1917 had resulted in the disintegration of the Russian Army as an effective combat force. Sir George Buchanan, the British ambassador in Petrograd, wondered in his diary whether it might not have been prudent of the Western democracies to have withdrawn the military pledges they had extracted from what had become a gravely weak Russia and let the country negotiate its own path out of the war. In the end, the continuation of Russia's involvement in the "war for democracy" proved to be perhaps the decisive trigger for the second Russian revolution of 1917 and the establishment of a communist regime that fall.[3]

The sudden disintegration of Mikhail Gorbachev's Soviet Union in December 1991 and the emergence of an independent Russian Federation that, under its president, Boris Yeltsin, was openly committed to the ideals and institutions of Western democracy, appeared to take up the promise of that first, February revolution of 1917. Political democracy, and with it the establishment of an economy along Western capitalist lines, were now the avowed and urgent aims of Russia's post-Soviet government. In this connection, Russia's government sought a broad diplomatic and economic partnership with the advanced industrial democracies, including, where possible, integration into Western political, economic, and even security institutions. The policies of many governments, including those of the United States, were now aimed at bolstering what they saw as the "reform" government of Russian President Yeltsin: By cementing Russia's democratic and capitalist foundations, they believed, they were laying the groundwork for a stable and reasonably harmonious relationship between Russia and the advanced capitalist democracies. Then-U.S. Secretary of State Warren Christopher summarized this policy in March 1995 by noting, "The successful transformation of the former Soviet Union into a region of sovereign, democratic states is a matter of fundamental importance to the United States."[4]

The purpose of this chapter is to examine the premises of this approach to post-Soviet Russia in light of the evolution of the Russian political system during the two terms of Yeltsin's presidency and the first term of his

[3] Stephen Cohen, *Failed Crusade: America and the Tragedy of Post-Communist Russia* (New York: W. W. Norton, 2000), pp. 251, 277.
[4] Warren Christopher, "US Policy Toward the New Independent States: A Pragmatic Strategy Grounded in America's Fundamental Interests," *US Department of State Dispatch*, no. 6 (1995). For extensive analysis, see James Goldgeier and Michael McFaul, *Power and Purpose: U.S. Policy toward Russia after the Cold War* (Washington, DC: Brookings Institution Press, 2003), as well as the memoir of U.S. President William Clinton's chief Russia adviser Strobe Talbott, *The Russia Hand: A Memoir of Presidential Diplomacy* (New York: Random House, 2002).

successor, Vladimir Putin. We are in particular interested in how the effort to install in Russia a liberal political economy, as in 1917 inspired by and supported by the most powerful Western states, resulted instead in the emergence and eventual consolidation under Putin of a "neopatrimonial" political system. This system, as with its Soviet and Tsarist predecessors, rests upon the tight nexus of wealth and political power (even if state ownership of the economy as a whole has been abandoned) and is distinguished by the following characteristics:

- The holding of regular elections in which nevertheless (a) public choice is severely constrained by the raw administrative power of the state and (b) there is little accountability – institutional or popular – of the head of state once elected.
- The domination of government at the national level by the presidential administration, which has become increasingly a paramilitary body in terms of the military and intelligence agency origins of key officials – for example, fully two-thirds of the staff of President Putin's administrative offices have a background in the security services.[5]
- Government at the regional level is mediated by extraconstitutional deals between the president's office and regional governors, most of whom are even less accountable by legal methods than is the Russian president himself.
- Major economic decisions of private businesspeople (for example, mergers with foreign firms) must be coordinated with the government, especially where the energy sector is concerned.
- There is hardly a senior official in the Russian federal government who could not have been a trustworthy administrator of the Soviet Union, had it survived (this may be even more pronounced at the regional level).
- Public and elite support for a liberal model of democratic-capitalist development has collapsed, even while strong support for the ideas of democracy and the market per se persist.[6]

How has this situation, so far removed from the original intentions of Russian reformers and their supporters in the Western world, come to pass?

---

[5] Interview with Russian political sociologist Olga Kryshtanovskaya in *Nezavisimaya Gazeta*, August 19, 2003, as translated in *Johnson's Russia List* (hereafter *JRL*), #7294, August 19, 2003, item # 3, at www.cdi.org.

[6] Lilia Shevtsova, *Putin's Russia* (Washington, DC: Carnegie Endowment for International Peace, 2003), pp 163–276.

## II. General Prerequisites of Democracy

As we shall shortly discuss, all contemporary stable democratic political systems rest on a capitalist economic foundation. Moreover, a functioning rule of law is required for the holders of capital to assess the risks that necessarily follow investment in an economy's future. Not all capitalist economies sustain political democracies, however, and in this respect capitalism may be considered a necessary but not sufficient precondition for the establishment of political democracy. Indeed, questions of institutions are only one part of the democratic equation. The other concerns what we might call the democratic spirit, that is, the basic attitudes, values, and conception of humanity and its place in society. Political theorist Hans Kohn has distinguished between the attitudes, method, and institutions of democracy as follows.[7]

In terms of fundamental attitudes and values, democracy "presupposes the existence of opposition as a legitimate partner in the democratic process, it accepts a pluralistic view of values and associations and it rejects any totalitarian or monolithic identification of the state with one party or dogma." Considered as a way of life, democracy reflects that attitude "by which the members of a community are led to secure to every one his rights, to look upon all fellow citizens without distinction of color or race as brethren in a common enterprise, and to give spontaneous support to projects which enhance civic excellence and promote the general welfare." In this respect, then, tolerance and civic-mindedness are core components of democracy.

The "method of democracy" Kohn defined as "the method of discussion, of open-minded critical inquiry, and finally and frequently of compromise." Yet it is also true that critical inquiry and even compromise, as well as tolerance and civic-mindedness, are compatible with nondemocratic political systems, such as the benevolent despotism that Aristotle considered the ideal form of polity. But since none can predict when the admittedly rare enlightened despot will emerge, or, rarer still, that his or her power will be bequeathed to an equally enlightened successor, democratic values and methods require certain types of institutions to survive and flourish. At heart, as Harvard University's Samuel Huntington has observed in his 1991 book, *The Third Wave*,[8] democracy requires institutions that allow effective choice over who shall rule and meaningful

---

[7] Following Kohn's essay on "Democracy" in the *Encyclopedia Britannica*, 14th edition (Encyclopedia Britannica, 1947).

[8] Published in Tulsa by the University of Oklahoma Press.

participation in the process of government. If, as Kohn wrote, political democracy be conceived as a form of government "based upon self-rule of the people and . . . upon freely elected representative institutions and an executive responsible to the people," then a number of institutions are necessary for democratic values to express themselves. These include:

- A popular constitution that expresses the consent by which the people establish the state, establishes a specific form of government, and both grants and limits the powers that the government is to possess.
- A system of representative government based on a parliament that is chosen through elections run on the principle of universal suffrage.
- A relatively disciplined system of political parties that connects popular opinion to the governmental process and frames meaningful public debate and legislation on issues of civic importance.

A key social precondition for stable political democracy is the existence of a relatively large, prosperous, well-educated, and secure middle class – or at least one that, if small, is growing rather than contracting – that believes that its interests and values are and will continue to be protected by the democratic process. In this respect, a degree of economic well-being and socioeconomic equality are critical to the democratic enterprise.

To summarize, then, political democracy has a political-institutional foundation in the agencies and procedures of representative government,[9] a social-psychological foundation in the prevalence of toleration and civic spirit in the citizenry,[10] and a social-economic foundation in economic well-being and a reasonably large and secure middle class.[11]

### III. Specific Tensions in Postcommunist Reform Processes

These preconditions, or at least concomitants, of democratic political development are difficult enough to consolidate and integrate so as to form enduring democracies. Consider the collapse of the Weimar Republic or the enduring instabilities of France's political regime until well into the 1960s, not to mention the absence of civic (as distinct from racial) democracy in the American South until all too recently. To the inherent

---

[9] Kohn, "Democracy"; Samuel J. Huntington, *The Third Wave: Democratication in the Late Twentieth Century* (Norman, OK: University of Oklahoma Press, 1991).

[10] Robert Putnam, *Making Democracy Work* (Princeton, NJ: Princeton University Press, 1993).

[11] Aristotle, *Politics*, Book IV; Harley Balzer, ed., *Russia's Missing Middle Class* (Armonk, NY: M. E. Sharpe, 1997).

fragility of democratic progress must now be added the particular challenges emerging from the collapse of communist regimes throughout Europe. The legacy of the Soviet/Russian imperial party-state and the nature of its collapse have framed the choices facing all of the governments and peoples in the post-Soviet states, Russia included. As Alexander J. Motyl has noted,[12] all of these states are compelled by force of circumstances to face two enormous political challenges that were not faced in the lengthy and by comparison organic evolution of democracy in the Western world. These are, first, the need to build effective political, economic, and legal institutions practically from the ground up in the wake of the collapse of the Soviet economy and state (the challenge of mechanical construction rather than organic growth). Second, and even more difficult, postcommunist states must build all of these institutions at the same time (the challenge of simultaneous as opposed to sequential institutional development). Consider only that the existence of certain kinds of institutions is a precondition of the effectiveness of others, and the fragilities of post-Soviet political-economic development become apparent. That is, while "democracy" may be the ultimate aim (for many, it clearly is not), an effectively functioning market economy appears to be a historically demonstrated prerequisite for political democracy itself. Likewise, it is hard to see how a modern market economy can be established without an effectively functioning legal system, which is itself predicated upon the existence of a strong and competent state and state administration. In the final analysis, strong democracies are also strong (that is, competent) states.

It is difficult to see how, in the post-Soviet wasteland of effective public institutions, a rapid and stable progression from formerly totalitarian and imperial to recognizably pluralist political systems could have been made. Without a state that is able to perform the minimum functions of governance (raising sufficient taxes, controlling the military, enforcing the law), the legal and economic prerequisites for constitutional government, not to speak of democracy, cannot be laid. Unfortunately, so many of the voices calling for a strong state in the post-Soviet region are also those most opposed to democracy, the market, and the rule of law.

Moreover, the simultaneous introduction of market economics and electoral democracy means that the broad swaths of Russian society that are being economically and socially disenfranchised are also being

---

[12] Alexander J. Motyl, *Dilemmas of Independence: Ukraine after Totalitarianism* (New York: Council on Foreign Relations, 1993), pp. 51–75.

enfranchised politically. In this context, one of two outcomes are likely: Either the economically and socially disenfranchised majority will express its interest in maximum social security through the ballot and elect representatives far less favorable to market economics than the Russian government has recently been (that is, political democracy at the expense of market economics – Russia's 1993 and 1995 elections lend strong support to this view, as does the electoral ouster of the early reformers in Poland, Hungary, and Lithuania in 1993) or the new economic and social elites will seek to protect their gains by direct and indirect subversion of the democratic process (that is, market economics at the expense of political democracy, the prime example being the post-1973 Chilean dictatorship and perhaps post-Soviet Russia itself). The best case is thus implausible.[13]

The same, however, is true for what many Americans imagine to be the worst case. Because of the collapse of the Soviet political economy, there is simply no way back to the Soviet past, in terms of a party-state monopoly of the political and economic system or the revival of a challenge for global or even Eurasian hegemony. Yet absent this extremity, almost all of the futures that one could imagine for Russia are plausible, save perhaps for the rapid and stable transformation of the Russian Federation into a functioning democracy and mature market economy. In many respects, post-Soviet Russia remains faced with the same problem as bedeviled Gorbachev: How to maintain the integrity of what remains in Russia a federal, multinational state while at the same time reorganizing the distribution of power within that state so as effectively to modernize politically, economically, and socially? It was in this historical and institutional context that post-Soviet Russia and its foreign supporters embarked on Russia's experiment with political democracy.

## IV. The Early Course of Reform

The spontaneous privatization of Russia's economic resources that was made possible initially by the disintegration of communist authority under Gorbachev framed the choices of the early Yeltsin government with respect to economic policy and political behavior in general. Determined to dismantle the communist political-economic order as rapidly as possible, and in the absence of either (a) a receptive parliamentary majority, (b) a

---

[13] Adam Przeworksi, *Democracy and the Market: Political and Economic Reform in Eastern Europe and Latin America* (Cambridge, UK: Cambridge University Press, 1991); Daniel Yergin and Thane Gustafson, *Russia 2010 – and What It Means for the World: The CERA Report* (New York: Random House, 1993).

presidential political party, or (c) any social consensus on the nature of economic reform, the early Yeltsin government moved rapidly on a broad front, with two enduring effects: First, it succeeded in rendering organizationally impossible the reestablishment of anything resembling the old Soviet order. Second, it at the same time and through the same means radically reduced whatever chances there may have been to establish responsive and responsible constitutional government in Russia for the foreseeable future.

Indeed, the three pillars of Russia's post-Soviet economic reform – price liberalization (and the four-digit inflation that ensued), privatization (and the plundering of the economy that we have already discussed), and macroeconomic stabilization (that is, austerity amid depression, reinforcing the widespread impoverishment of the population) – were as much imposed upon the Russian population as was Stalin's brutal "Revolution from Above" in the late 1920s and 1930s. As Dimitri Simes has observed, initially, in 1991 and 1992, Yeltsin and his key economic advisers Yegor Gaidar (prime minister in 1992) and Anatoly Chubais (who directed the privatization program) could not count on the backing of existing social groups, most of whom had no hope of acquiring significant private wealth in the foreseeable future. In the absence of such support, they attempted to create a new class of property owners who could be relied on to support radical change because of the immense personal benefits of governmental policy. As a result, Russia's market reforms proceeded without adequate legislative foundation (because the legislature would not support the policy) through presidential decree without a candid explanation to the Russian people of the likely hardships to be endured (Yeltsin promised higher living standards to the population within a year); without popular support; without significant new investment, domestic or foreign; without a credible mechanism to ensure meaningful restructuring of the privatized government enterprises and without giving the majority of the population a real stake in the reform process. "Had Yeltsin, Gaidar, and Chubais accepted what every politician in the West takes for granted," Simes writes:

...namely, that voters cannot be forced to make major sacrifices against their will and that imperfect but democratically sustainable reforms are better than more radical changes imposed autocratically – they would likely have found many opportunities for dialogue with those elements of the Russian political spectrum who are supportive of reform but uncomfortable with shock therapy.[14]

---

[14] Dmitri Simes, *After the Collapse: Russia Seeks Its Place as a Great Power* (New York: Simon and Schuster, 1999), p. 158. See also Cohen, *Failed Crusade*, passim.

*[handwritten margin note: use of force to resolve the crisis]*

Instead, the distinguishing mark of Yeltsin's presidency is his use of Russian tanks in October 1993 to destroy the Russian parliament, thereby resolving Russia's most important dispute over policy and the nature of the regime by the bullet rather than the ballot. Russia's authoritarian constitution, which vests highly concentrated powers in the hands of the (elected) executive, is a direct consequence of that failure of policy.

The initial years of independence of 1992 and 1993 – culminating in the crisis of October 4, 1993 – were plagued by perpetual political warfare between the executive and legislative branches of government. Not only were the president and the legislature pursuing mutually exclusive policies – focused on the scope and pace of price liberalization and the privatization of industry – they were each claiming mutually exclusive jurisdiction within the political system. Furthermore, there were no generally accepted constitutional procedures (such as a vote of confidence) for resolving such a governmental impasse. The explosive culmination of the Russian political stalemate in the streets of Moscow in early October 1993 thus represented the functional (if violent) equivalent of a vote of confidence, in that it "resolved" the crisis of power in favor of the Russian president, who assumed classically dictatorial powers pending parliamentary elections in December 1993 (which in fact proved to be a decisive defeat for Yeltsin's political supporters).

If 1993 saw the emergence of a new political order in Russia, 1994 saw that order put to significant tests. Throughout 1994 and frequently since, many Russian and outside observers have remarked on the puzzling stability that has seemed to prevail in Russian politics and society. The comprehensive disintegration of the previous, Soviet-era institutions of public authority, the continued collapse of the industrial economy, and a growing polarization in the society as well as in the polity did not lead to the sorts of political confrontations typical of 1992 and 1993, which seemed destined to become endemic to post-Soviet Russian politics. Had Yeltsin's Russia reached some sort of precarious equilibrium, one that eluded Gorbachev as well as Yeltsin himself in his first two years as president of the independent Russian Federation?

Before 1994 was out, certain events had occurred, most prominently the Russian invasion of Chechnya, which suggested that post-Soviet Russia was failing some fundamental tests of political viability. The calamity of the Russian government's invasion of the secessionist province of Chechnya in December 1994 underscored in the most dramatic fashion the failure of Yeltsin's government to impart the minimum of institutional coherence to the activities and functioning of government in

postcommunist Russia. Taken by a handful of Yeltsin's security ministers,[15] the decision to invade showed just how weak was Russia's parliament and civil society; the defeat eventually suffered by the Russian armed
forces in failing to suppress the Chechen rebellion showed just how weak
the Russian state as a whole had become.

*weak decision-making*

## V. Foreign Reinforcements

Through its political and material support, the United States throughout the Clinton years demonstrated its backing for Russian policies that,
whatever one thinks about their advisability and results, had the effect
of making the United States party to one faction in the Russian government, a faction, moreover, that by the end of the decade had lost virtually
all of the limited electoral support it once enjoyed.[16] In the process, the
United States has become controversial in postcommunist Russian society
in ways that were never true in the USSR.[17]

Throughout the Clinton Administration, the United States did not wa-
ver in its rhetorical support for democratization and marketization in
Russia.[18] In practice, this came to mean support for one particular vision
of democracy and the market, one associated with the immediate abol-
ishment of price controls, rapid and comprehensive privatization of the
Russian economy, and tight state budgets and monetary emission during
a prolonged depression. Because such policies were supported by a small
cohort of Yeltsin associates and opposed consistently by democratically
elected Russian parliaments (and without any base of support in the population at large), their implementation polarized Russian politics, isolated
the president's party vis-à-vis the legislature and public opinion and, by

---

[15] Carlotta Gall and Thomas de Waal, *Chechnya: A Small Victorious War* (London: PAN,
1997); Anatol Lieven, *Chechnya: Tombstone of Russian Power* (New Haven, CT: Yale
University Press, 1998); Michael Thumann, *Das Lied von der russischen Erde: Moskaus
Ringen um Einheit und Groesse* [The Song of the Russian Earth: Moscow's Struggle for
Unity and Greatness] (Stuttgart: DVA, 2002), pp. 104–15.

[16] In a representative expression of U.S. policy premises toward Russia, Deputy Secretary
of State Strobe Talbott stated, in March 1998, "I regard Russia as a peaceful democratic
state.…" Cited by Jim Hoagland, "Foreign Policy by Impulse," *Washington Post*, March
19, 1998, p. A21. Vice President Albert Gore, about the same time, identified himself
with the "optimism" that he believed all those who knew Russia well shared. Cited in
Cohen, *Proval Krestovogo Pokhoda S.Sh.A.* (Moscow: AIPO-XX, 2001), p. 19. In August
1998, the Russian economy crashed, entailing a forced and massive devaluation of the
ruble and default on Russia's domestic and foreign obligations.

[17] William Zimmerman, *The Russian People and Foreign Policy* (Princeton, NJ: Princeton
University Press, 2002), pp. 187–215.

[18] As is demonstrated by Talbott, *The Russia Hand*.

concentrating extreme power in the executive necessary to carrying out such unpopular policies, set back the cause of Russian democracy that the process of democratization was supposed to advance. To the extent that ordinary Russians identify democracy and capitalism now with the violent suppression of the parliament and the immiseration of large sectors of society while the government virtually "appoints millionaires," the social foundation for market reform, not to mention those directly associated with Yeltsin's government, became weaker by the month.[19] Moreover, insofar as the United States identified itself with these policies, Russian society's traditional pro-Americanism has now become controversial for the first time.[20]

It is important to stress that U.S. support for Russian "reform" has not been limited to rhetorical encouragement for liberal market changes in general. Instead, the United States and the international financial institutions that it strongly influences repeatedly provided Yeltsin's government with strong, specific, and invaluable political cover and material resources in order to sustain its position and policies.[21] In October 1993, President Clinton used the diplomatic channel to indicate to President Yeltsin that the United States understood his position in his physical confrontation with the Russian parliament, thereby emboldening Yeltsin in his decision to resort to force of arms to resolve a political disagreement.[22] In early December 1994, on the eve of the Russian Army's invasion of Chechnya, President Clinton specifically noted in public that the Russian–Chechen conflict was entirely Russia's internal affair, again reassuring the Yeltsin government that Russia would not have to pay a significant price in its relations with the United States for the large-scale (and in the end disastrous) use of force in Chechnya. In May 1995, President Clinton traveled to Moscow, but not to London, in celebration of the fiftieth anniversary of the end of the Second World War, again underscoring the depth of the administration's commitment to Yeltsin's government. Indeed, a year later, during a meeting of the Group of Seven advanced industrial democracies in Moscow designed to emphasize Western financial support for Russia during Yeltsin's presidential campaign, President Clinton went out

[19] Igor Klyamkin and Lilia Shevtsova, *The Omnipotent and Impotent Government: The Evolution of the Political System in Post-Communist Russia* (Moscow: Carnegie Moscow Center, 1999).

[20] Allen C. Lynch, "The Realism of Russia's Foreign Policy," *Europe-Asia Studies*, January 2001, pp. 7–31.

[21] Michael Cox, "The Necessary Partnership: The Clinton Presidency and Post-Communist Russia," *International Affairs* (UK) Vol. 70, no. 4 (Fall 1994), pp. 635–58.

[22] Cohen, *Failed Crusade*, pp. 130–40.

of his way – in a phrase apparently inspired by his "Russia hand" Strobe Talbott – to compare Yeltsin to Abraham Lincoln and relatedly Russia's war in Chechnya to the U.S. Civil War, again seeking to legitimize Yeltsin's government and policies.[23] In the spring of 1996, the Clinton Administration approved the dispatch of four political campaign strategists – including Richard Dresner, who had previously worked with Clinton's personal political "guru" Dick Morris to get Clinton elected governor of Arkansas – to assist in Yeltsin's reelection campaign, a fact that the Russian government strove mightily and successfully to keep secret until after the elections.[24]

Most controversially, perhaps, the U.S. government, through the U.S. Agency for International Development (AID), effectively turned its Russian reform programs over to the hands of a single group of reformers within the Russian government: that group associated with the circle of Anatoly Chubais, Yeltsin's privatization chief. Subcontracting through Harvard's Institute for International Development (HIID), U.S. AID channeled $40 million in direct funding and $300 million in indirect funding through Russian agencies controlled by Chubais. The majority of U.S. AID contracts were awarded to HIID without competitive bidding. The impact of such programs was far larger than their relatively modest sums suggest, as the political power of Chubais's office, as of Chubais himself, was critically dependent upon his ability to leverage large sums of foreign capital for the creation of a new, pro-Yeltsin Russian upper class through rapid, comprehensive privatization of the Russian economy. Foreign and especially U.S. aid agencies became the external constituent that Chubais's policies were lacking at home. In the end, U.S. AID spent a total of $58 million dollars to underwrite the Russian privatization effort.

In the absence of parliamentary or popular support, privatization and its consequences required rule by presidential decree rather than agreement with parliament. U.S. AID's subcontractor, HIID, drafted many of these decrees, thereby making the U.S. government a direct party in the most controversial part of Russia's post-Soviet economic transformation. In its 1996 annual report, U.S. AID praised Russian privatization, noting that 150,000 firms were privatized in 1994 alone.[25] (Worldwide, countries carrying out cash privatizations have typically

[23] Talbott, *The Russia Hand*, p. 149.
[24] Michael Kramer, "Rescuing Boris," *Time*, July 15, 1996, pp. 17–26.
[25] *The USAID FY 1998 Congressional Presentation: Russia* (Washington, DC: US GPO, 1997), p. 6.

managed no more than two hundred per year.[26]) By contrast, in 1997 the Russian parliament voted 288 to 6 to denounce the privatization program undertaken between 1992–6. By identifying the United States so closely with one faction within the Russian government instead of seeking to make the institutions of government more effective in general, U.S. AID both made the United States a party in Russian politics and undermined the effectiveness of the liberal reform process that it was trying to support. As social anthropologist Janine Wedel – who has studied the Western aid process to post-communist Europe closely – has observed, "Building lasting, non-aligned institutions is a tough assignment in any context.... To foster reform, donors need to work to develop a market infrastructure that all relevant parties can support – not just one political faction."[27] The result? Through its efforts to shape the specific contours of the Russian political economy, the United States has helped to make it, in Wedel's words, "virtually impossible to conceive of a pro-reform Russian nationalist."

## VI. Russia's Political Institutions

Russia's postcommunist institutions have been shaped decisively by the early confrontations between president and parliament in 1992 and 1993. At first glance, Russia possesses all of the institutions that we have said are characteristic of political democracies: a written constitution approved by popular vote, a bicameral representative parliament selected on the basis of universal suffrage, multiple political parties broadly reflecting the range of political opinion in the country, an executive presidency accountable to the people through direct elections, and a multitude of newspapers expressing often highly critical views of government policy. What is the nature of Russia's political institutions and how do they work in actual practice? In particular, what does the functioning of Russia's institutions imply about Russia's democratic prospects?[28]

### A. The Constitution

Russia's written constitution, adopted in December 1993 after a nationwide referendum, is a direct product of the struggles between parliament

---

[26] Thane Gustafson, *Capitalism Russian Style* (Cambridge, UK: Cambridge University Press, 1999), p. 45.

[27] Janine Wedel, *Collision and Collusion* (New York: St. Martin's Press, 1998), pp. 162–3.

[28] For the argument at length, see Allen C. Lynch, *Does Russia Have a Democratic Future?* (New York: Foreign Policy Association, 1997).

and president in 1992 and 1993 over the ultimate source of power.[29] These struggles, which were intensified by the absence of a mechanism, such as a vote of confidence, in the Soviet-based constitution of the time, were ultimately resolved by bullet instead of ballot. Armored units of the Russian Army, at President Yeltsin's orders, shelled the Russian parliament building and forced the surrender of the coalition of communists and extreme nationalists who had defied Yeltsin's authority and had themselves begun to resort to force of arms to press their cause. Yeltsin, who had by his own admission unconstitutionally suspended the parliament in September 1993, sought to justify his actions by calling for early parliamentary elections and a referendum on a new constitution. As we shall see, the elections of December 1993 resulted in a crushing defeat for the Russian president's allies and brought to parliament a majority not very different from the coalition that Yeltsin had physically destroyed just three months earlier. At the same time, in a procedure that remains controversial to this day, Yeltsin's government claimed a majority vote for a constitution that would establish a superpresidentialist form of government, thereby ratifying in constitutional terms Yeltsin's recent military victory over his political opponents. (Curiously, the vote for the constitution – which many specialists regard as rigged – and for the legislature, which could come into being only if the proposed constitution were in fact approved, was held at the same time, suggesting a certain disregard for legal procedure and popular opinion.)

Drawing from aspects of the U.S. and French presidential systems, the post-1993 Russian constitution firmly establishes the supremacy of president over parliament, even if certain checks and balances are formally included.[30] For example, whereas previously a simple majority in parliament could override a presidential decision, now a two-thirds vote of both the State Duma – (representing the population as a whole) and the Council of the Federation – (representing Russia's federal units), is required. Whereas before president and parliament contested the authority to appoint the government, the new constitution gives this power clearly to the president. While the parliament may reject the president's choice for prime minister, should it do so three times, the president may dissolve the parliament and call for new elections. Similarly, the parliament may vote no confidence in the government, but the president may ignore

---

[29] For specialist treatment, see Rita Moore, "The Path to the New Russian Constitution," *Demokratizatsiya*, vol. 3, no. 1 (Winter 1995), at www.heldref.org/dem.php.
[30] For the text of the constitution, see *Izvestiya*, November 10, 1993, pp. 3–5.

the first such vote. If the vote is repeated within three months, the president is obligated to respond but he may choose to dismiss the parliament instead of the government. Moreover, the president may simply dismiss the government without taking into account the views of the parliament. The president is also granted the power to declare a state of emergency and govern (temporarily) by unfettered presidential *diktat*. The budget is determined by the presidentially appointed government, not the parliament, although the latter must approve of the state budget. It must also be recalled that any temptation that parliament may have had to confront the president was undoubtedly tempered by the precedents that President Yeltsin set for employing military force to resolve political disputes within Russia – that is, the conflict with parliament itself in October 1993 and the invasion of Chechnya in December 1994.

Perhaps most importantly, the Russian president is empowered with broad authority to govern by executive decree. This device quickly evolved from a device of presidential governance to perhaps the mainstay of presidential rule in Russia by 1995. Gordon Smith has calculated that, whereas President Yeltsin issued an average of twelve to thirteen decrees per month before the clash with parliament in fall 1993, this had quintupled to sixty-five in December 1993 and by 1996, following the election of an even more anti-Yeltsin parliament in December 1995, Yeltsin had virtually given up attempting to govern with parliament and had resorted to de facto rule by decree. Issuance of presidential decrees had tripled in 1996 by comparison with previous years: In the first seven months of 1996, there were 591 presidential decrees – which retain the force of law unless overriden by a two-thirds vote of both houses of parliament – raising serious questions about the decision-making process of such an overloaded system of presidential governance.[31] Two questions arise here: First, who was drafting, and reading, this sea of decrees? How could the Constitutional Court even judge them at the rate they were being produced? Second, it is clear that rule by decree places the center of political gravity on access to the Russian president, who in the Yeltsin period was often seriously ill and physically unfit to govern much of the time. (In the second half of 1996, a sick Yeltsin spent no more than fifteen days at work in the Kremlin.)

Much of Russian politics has thus come down to lobbying the presidential staff, which is barely mentioned in the constitution. Not surprisingly, in such an unstructured situation, individuals play a disproportionate role

---

[31] Paper presented by Gordon Smith to the annual convention of the American Association for the Advancement of Slavic Studies, Boston, November 1996.

in the decision-making process. Throughout the critical presidential election year of 1996, two stood out in this respect: Anatoly Chubais, then Yeltsin's chief of staff, and President Yeltsin's daughter Tatyana, who appears to have been one of the very few individuals to have had the president's confidence.[32] In the early Putin years, a more assertive leader and a more favorable fiscal balance for the state have witnessed a more definitive presidential stamp upon national decision-making, but the office of the presidency itself is if anything even more insulated from accountability to the rest of the government, not to mention the rule of law, than was true under Yeltsin.[33] Under these circumstances, Russia's written constitution must be regarded as a poor guide to the actual distribution of political power and the process by which decisions are made.

## B. *The Parliament*

Russian parliamentarism has a brief and unhappy history. First established after the Russian Revolution of 1905, Russia's first Duma, as the parliament was then (and now) called, was unable to persuade the Tsar to relinquish autocracy in practice. Then, as now, Russian politics centered around the head of state and personal and extralegal access to him. The establishment of communist power in Russia signaled the end of efforts to introduce significant parliamentary influence on government for three-quarters of a century, until the establishment of the first, relatively representative Soviet parliament by Gorbachev in spring 1989. Up to that point, the Supreme Soviet, as the Soviet parliament was styled, was simply a rubber-stamp body for decisions previously made in the higher councils of the Soviet Communist Party. Meeting twice a year for several days and without a staff of any note, it was manifestly impossible that the Supreme Soviet could evolve into a meaningful deliberative body, much less influence the affairs of state.

The immediate antecedents of the current Russian Duma lay in the establishment by free election of a two-level Soviet parliament including an umbrella body, the Congress of People's Deputies (1,050 delegates), and the smaller Supreme Soviet (250 delegates). In principle, the Congress was the supreme agency of government according to Soviet-era legislation. Yet the unwieldiness of that body, the heavy representation within it of Soviet officials, and in particular the absence of any mechanism to resolve disputes between parliament and the executive – which after Yeltsin's

---

[32] Shevtsova, *Putin's Russia*, pp. 17, 19, 26–8.
[33] Ibid., pp. 104–86.

election as Russian president in June 1991 granted him substantial non-Soviet legitimacy – rendered the Congress a highly unstable structure for governance. At first, this mattered little, as parliamentary leaders such as Speaker Ruslan Khasbulatov rallied to Yeltsin's side to defeat the attempted coup d'etat by the communist old order in August 1991. As Russia assumed real independence in 1992, however, major policy differences between president and legislature placed what proved to be unbearable burdens on post-Soviet Russia's constitutional structure. The major issue over which president and parliament split was the scope and pace of economic reform, begun in January 1992, which was aimed at liberalizing prices and privatizing as much of the old Soviet state-owned economy as quickly as possible. Yeltsin's own vice president, former Air Force General Alexander Rutskoi, joined the parliamentary opposition in alarm at the impact that the withdrawal of government subsidies was likely to have on the Russian economy's large military-industrial sector.

A perilous confrontation was thus joined. An armed clash seemed to be narrowly averted in March 1993 when Yeltsin withdrew a threat to impose direct presidential rule in exchange for referenda on his rule and policies to be held in April 1993. Although Yeltsin received broad popular support in the four referendum items, the opposition majority in parliament remained unreconciled and on September 21, 1993, Yeltsin dissolved the parliament by decree. With this admittedly unconstitutional act, Yeltsin triggered a chain of events that led to a violent clash between parliament and president that culminated in the shelling of the Russian White House, home of the parliament, by Yeltsin's troops on October 4. This act was tacitly welcomed by the Clinton Administration, which had cemented its partnership with Yeltsin at a Russian–American summit meeting in Vancouver, Canada, the previous March. About two hundred people are thought to have died in the fighting, and the leaders of the fighting opposition, including Khasbulatov and Rutskoi, were sent to jail.

It was on this basis that Russia's current parliament was established in the elections of December 12, 1993.[34] The constitution that was at the same time adopted provided for a weak parliament, thereby ensuring

---

[34] For specialist treatment, see Thomas F. Remington and Steven S. Smith, "The Development of Political Parties in Russia," *Legislative Studies Quarterly*, vol. 20, no. 4 (November 1995), pp. 457–89; Stephen White, *Russia's New Politics: The Management of a Postcommunist Society* (Cambridge, UK: Cambridge University Press, 2000), pp. 62–9.

Yelstin's domination of the governmental structure. Yet the elections themselves were a striking defeat for Yeltsin's political allies. In the half of seats allocated according to political parties, an extreme nationalist group, named the Liberal Democratic Party and led by Vladimir Zhirinovsky, captured nearly 23 percent of the vote. Russia's Choice, the president's party, received just 15.5 percent of votes cast for parties. When votes for individual candidates are taken into account, President Yeltsin could expect little support from a Duma in which his strong supporters accounted for less than 16 percent of seats (70 out of 450) while his strong opponents in Zhirinovsky's party, the Communist Party, and its ally, the Agrarian Party, made up nearly one-third (145 out of 450). In combination with other, smaller parties and the 31 percent of seats occupied by independents, antigovernment forces could count on frequent majorities *stalemate* in the new parliament.

Still, with a new constitution in which a two-thirds vote of both houses of parliament are needed to overturn presidential acts, a certain stalemate obtained. While Yeltsin could not count on real support from the parliament, neither could the parliament – whose other federal chamber was noticeably less hostile to Yeltsin than the Duma – expect to obtain the kinds of supermajorities needed to wrest control of the government from Yeltsin. So long as this situation prevailed, a certain stability settled over relations between the executive and legislative branches. Moreover, Yeltsin's prime minister, the pragmatic power broker Chernomyrdin, who replaced the ideologically inspired market reformer Yegor Gaidar in response to parliamentary pressure in December 1992, was much more disposed to work with rather than against parliament wherever possible. The years 1994 and 1995 thus saw a number of important acts of cooperation between parliament and president, as a substantial part of a post-Soviet legal infrastructure developed, including the elaboration of a new criminal code, a code of civil procedure, a tax code, and a maritime code.

Free elections, however, upset the political balance when in December 1995, in response to the growing impoverishment of much of Russian society and the prolonged and highly unpopular war in Chechnya, a parliament that was even more hostile to Yeltsin was elected. The Communist Party, led by presidential aspirant Gennady Zyuganov, increased its vote by half over the previous elections and obtained 22.3 percent of the popular vote. Zhirinovsky's party receded in correspondence to Communist gains and received just over 11 percent of the vote, while the government's party, Our Home Is Russia, received just over 10 percent. Economist Gregory Yavlinsky's liberal reform bloc received just under 7 percent. Combined with votes for individual candidates and translated into seats in the Duma, Yeltsin's strong opponents now controlled a solid majority of parliamentary seats. Combined with splinter groups generally hostile to governmental policy, this meant that the Duma was much closer to obtaining the two-thirds threshold required by the constitution to challenge Yeltsin's government and perhaps – through invoking the constitution's impeachment clause – even Yeltsin himself.

The strength of the opposition was reflected in a stronger anti-Yeltsin attitude and a greater willingness to challenge governmental policy. In response, as noted earlier, Yeltsin and his advisers resorted to de facto presidential rule by relying on executive decrees rather than legislative initiative to govern the country. The increasing removal of the governmental process from parliamentary influence led the Duma in mid-November 1996 to approve by a vote of 344 to 1 a resolution calling for greater parliamentary oversight over the cabinet. Such a measure, because it would entail a change in the 1993 constitution, could probably not pass the test of judicial review by Russia's Constitutional Court. It is, however, an accurate indicator of the clear polarization between parliament and president throughout the Yeltsin years and specifically of the inability of both sides to devise a collaborative approach to problems of governance. This tension would eventually be removed by Putin's orchestration, under state-nationalist auspices, of compliant parliamentary majorities in the elections of December 1999 and 2003, respectively.

### VII. Russia's Electoral History

Perhaps the most positive feature of recent Russian politics, and one of the few that bode well for the country's eventual democratic evolution, is the fact that free and regular elections have been held, on schedule, since 1989, on the parliamentary, presidential, provincial, and local levels.[35] Through the election of Putin as Russian president in March 2000 and his reelection in March 2004, more than thirteen major sets of popular

---

[35] For specialist treatment, see Timothy Colton, *Transitional Citizens: Voters and What Influences Them in the New Russia* (Cambridge, MA: Harvard University Press, 2000); Michael McFaul and Nikolai Petrov, "The Changing Function of Elections in Russian Politics," in Anders Aslund and Martha Brill Olcott, eds., *Russia after Communism* (Washington, DC: Carnegie Endowment for International Peace, 1999); Stephen White, Ian McAllister, and Richard Rose, *How Russia Votes* (Chatham Press, 1997).

votes had been held in Russia going back to the Soviet era in early 1989. These include:

- *March 1989*: The entire USSR, Russia included, elected a Congress of People's Deputies in the freest elections since 1917. In spite of many protected seats, a number of leading Communist Party officials were defeated, sending shock waves throughout the party establishment. Fully 88 percent of the successful candidates were elected to public office for the first time. Voter turnout was 87 percent in Russia.
- *1990*: Soviet republics held their own elections, in the process legitimizing nationalist politics, especially in the western and southern republics (the Baltic states, the Caucasus states, and Ukraine). Russian voter turnout was 77 percent.
- *March 1991*: Gorbachev and Yeltsin conducted competing referenda on the Soviet and Russian levels, respectively. Sixty-one percent of the Soviet electorate (and 76 percent of actual voters) supported a vaguely worded concept for a reformed USSR while a comparable percentage in Russia (52.5 percent of the electorate and 70 percent of actual voters) endorsed the idea of electing a Russian president by direct popular vote, thereby legitimizing Yeltsin's Russian challenge to Gorbachev and his concept of the union. Turnout for Gorbachev's referendum was 80 percent throughout the USSR; 75 percent of the Russian electorate turned out for Yeltsin's referendum.
- *June 1991*: Yeltsin was elected president of Russia with nearly 60 percent of the vote in a six-man race. (Gorbachev, in a fundamental miscalculation, never submitted himself to a direct popular vote for statewide office.) Turnout was 75 percent.
- *April 1993*: In a four-point referendum, Yeltsin received broad majority support for his presidency and policies in the midst of his political conflict with the Russian parliament. Turnout was 64 percent.
- *December 1993*: Yeltsin received a major setback as his political opponents garnered half of the seats in the Duma, less than three months after Yeltsin's tanks shelled the Russian White House, forcing the parliament to surrender after the loss of two hundred lives. Voter turnout continued to decline to 55 percent.
- *December 1995*: Yeltsin and his government received an even greater shock as the pro-government party, Our Home Is Russia, led by Prime Minister Chernomyrdin, received just 10 percent of the vote in nationwide parliamentary elections. Turnout increased to 64.4 percent.

- *June and July 1996:* In a remarkable comeback, Yeltsin, whose popularity was in single digits earlier in the year, outpolled Communist Party leader Zyuganov 35.3–32 percent in the first round of presidential elections. Former General Aleksandr Lebed, whose campaign was financed and led by key Yeltsin aides, drew 14.5 percent of the vote and thereby guaranteed Yeltsin's first-place finish. Yeltsin immediately awarded the post of national security adviser to Lebed, who in effect threw his supporters behind Yeltsin, helping the latter to cement a 54–40 percent victory over Zyuganov in the two-man second-round race in July. Turnout jumped to nearly 70 percent in both rounds of elections. (Lebed would be dismissed in October 1996, after negotiating an armistice to the Chechen War and evincing clear presidential ambitions himself.)
- *September–January 1996–97:* Forty-five gubernatorial and five other regional elections took place that saw governors chosen by direct popular vote instead of presidential appointment. The ballots were a disappointment for the government, which saw a majority of pro-Yeltsin incumbents defeated. (Gubernatorial elections have taken place on a regular basis since then; in September 2004, Putin called for the president to appoint all regional governors.)
- *December 1999:* National parliamentary elections took place that saw Putin's recently created Unity Party take second place to the Communists and emerge with a de facto majority in combination with other parties and groupings.
- *March 2000:* Putin was elected by an absolute majority in a five-candidate race after the surprise resignation of Yeltsin as Russian president on New Year's Eve and the convening of elections three months earlier than anticipated.
- *December 2003:* Parties sympathetic to Putin's pragmatic state-nationalist program gained close to a supermajority of two-thirds of the votes in the Duma, effectively enabling Putin to govern without concern for parliamentary obstruction (even possibly to introduce constitutional amendments that would have the effect of allowing Putin to govern Russia beyond his currently constitutionally mandated two terms of four years each).
- *March 2004:* Putin was overwhelmingly reelected by a large majority in a multicandidate race in which a number of candidates were encouraged and even financed by Putin's office in order to lend greater legitimacy to Putin's reelection.

What can be said about the significance of this apparently impressive electoral history? First, it is, of course, positive in itself that the electoral principle has been adopted, and rather consistently practiced, in Russian politics since the late 1980s. As legislative and especially presidential elections are repeated, the precedent thereby set will tend to raise a progressively higher barrier to those who might seek simply to seize and appropriate political power. It should be noted, however, that the acid test of the durability of electoral procedure has yet to be passed in Russia – that is, elections that involve a transfer of effective political authority. As we have seen, the two victories for Yeltsin's opponents in the parliamentary elections in December 1993 and December 1995 had little impact on fundamental governmental policy. Indeed, such a momentous decision as that to invade Chechnya in December 1994 was made without any consultation with the Duma at all. Moreover, the second Russian presidential election in summer 1996 confirmed the incumbent in office in circumstances that, as we shall see, raised serious questions about the fairness of the procedure. A number of signs in the spring of 1996 – such as Yeltsin aide (actually, his bodyguard) Alexander Korzhakov suggesting that the June and July 1996 presidential elections be canceled – indicate that the prospect of expelling the incumbent government from office could meet with serious resistance, throwing the country, and with it Russia's electoral prospects, into upheaval.

Second, as encouraging as Russia's nascent electoral tradition is, the fact remains that the single most important political conflict in post-Soviet Russia – the impasse between president and parliament in mid-1993 – was resolved by force of arms rather than by vote or compromise. The subsequent constitution, which enshrines a presidentially dominant political order, reflects that brutal fact. As a result, the parliaments that have been elected have had little real influence upon governmental policy. As we have observed that a critical test for democracy is not just the holding of elections whereby representatives are selected, but meaningful, if indirect, constituent influence on the state, it is clear that the severe imbalance between executive and legislative agencies of government in Russia hinders the evolution of Russia's democratic possibilities. An elected parliament that broadly represents the spectrum of popular opinion (as I think the Duma does) but that has no real impact on the composition and course of the government is hardly an improvement on the rubber-stamp Supreme Soviet of communist days. Indeed, to the extent that the population identifies the concept of democracy with such hollow institutions, democracy itself will be the loser. The issue is compounded by the fact that important political parties, such as the Russian Communist Party and the Liberal Democratic Party of

Russia are far from unambiguously committed to democratic procedure itself.

Third, the early pattern of Russia's elections, presidential as well as parliamentary, demonstrated that in current Russian conditions the extension of electoral participation and structural market reform in the economy – that is, democratization and marketization – tend to proceed at the expense of one another rather than in tandem. The large share of the Russian population, indeed perhaps the majority, that has not been able to adapt to Russia's post-Soviet market economy,[36] has thrice expressed its dissatisfaction at the direction of government policy: by the humiliation of pro-government parties at the legislative polls in December 1993 and December 1995 and by a disturbing generational split during the presidential elections in summer 1996. A majority of the Russian population over the age of forty-five voted for the communist candidate Zyuganov in the presidential runoff of July 1996, while a majority under forty-five voted for Yeltsin. Such a split need not be a dangerous one in terms of the stability of the system. After all, revolts and riots are seldom made by the older generations. But it does raise questions about the capacity of Russian politicians and Russia's political institutions to establish a political order that is responsive to broad sectors of the population, one that is based on tolerance and compromise for the sake of the system rather than on efforts to seize (or maintain seizure of) the state for the ends of one faction and its clients. Indicatively, by the turn of the century, Yeltsin's successor Putin had abandoned even the rhetoric of liberal reform in favor of a state-nationalist stance that effectively spanned the generational divide and served to insulate Putin himself from specific failings in the economy and social system. (Putin has typically enjoyed approval ratings of 70–5 percent throughout his presidency.)

Fourth, the Russian presidential election of summer 1996 was far from the free and fair vote proclaimed by the government and its diplomatic

---

[36] For evidence, see Michael Stedman, "Society under Stress," at www.strana.ru, April 16, 2002. Stedman examined the adaptation of Russian society to post-Soviet circumstances in relation to "intangible resources of adaptation" that individuals did or did not possess. These include: (a) attained level of education, (b) professional skill levels, (c) aptitude in using cultural and information resources, (d) social ties, and (e) residence, that is, urban versus rural. Stedman concludes that the 60 percent of the population with "low resource potential" has adapted poorly to post-Soviet circumstances; moreover, the one-third of the population with average resource potential has also not fared well. Twenty percent of those with high resource potential also failed to adapt successfully. Stedman's research suggests that just 5–6 percent of the Russian population has adapted successfully to post-Soviet circumstances.

supporters in the U.S. government and elsewhere abroad. This is not to say that the vote was a pure sham, or to deny that Yeltsin conducted a vigorous and effective campaign, especially as compared to those of his chief rivals in the Communist and Liberal Democratic camp. Yeltsin was able to polarize the choice presented to the Russian electorate: In effect, choose Yeltsin and vote for the future, or vote Zyuganov and bring back the dark, totalitarian past. Such tactics did much to structure the vote in Yeltsin's favor. In the end, he edged out Zyuganov 35.3–32 percent in the multicandidate first round in June and by 53.8–40.3 percent in the two-man runoff in July.

Having said that, Yeltsin enjoyed, and created for himself, a number of advantages through the direct and indirect use of his governmental powers that seriously distorted the choices before the voters. These were not simply the "powers of incumbency" that so many Western observers complacently attributed to such tactics. Yeltsin enjoyed something close to a monopoly in the television coverage and much of the press coverage of the campaign. Some of this was accomplished through the apparently voluntary support of Yeltsin by many journalists, who felt themselves threatened in the event of a Communist victory. In a number of cases, it turned out that key corporations under clear governmental influence, such as the gas giant Gazprom with very close connections to Prime Minister Chernomyrdin, soon bought major shares of key television networks (such as NTV – "Independent Television"). Most blatantly, the Yeltsin government funded and guided the candidacy of another candidate, former General Lebed, who acquired 14.5 percent of the vote in the first round and – by siphoning off part of the anti-Yeltsin protest vote that otherwise would have gone to the Communist Zyuganov – assured Yeltsin's narrow edge over Zyuganov (a difference of 1.7 percent of the vote would have placed Zyuganov ahead of Yeltsin). Moreover, the comments of some of Yeltsin's closest aides cast serious doubt on the government's commitment to the electoral process. Although Korzhakov, the most notorious among these, was later fired, the government was apparently prepared, if only as a contingency, to circumvent the polls in the event of an impending defeat.[37] In short, the 1996 presidential election is a highly fragile precedent by which Russia's electoral future may be judged, especially in light of the fact that the selection of Putin in 1999 as Yeltsin's successor must be regarded as a form of palace coup. Whatever Russia's ultimate electoral course, it must be remembered that elections, however free, without reliable means for representatives to influence policy, do not form the basis

---

[37] White, *Russia's New Politics*, pp. 95–106.

for democracy, much less constitutional government. For now, there are few ways by which the constitutionally established agencies of government, even within the executive branch, can affect the decision-making process without direct access to the president's staff. That so much attention in Russia and throughout the world is focused on the activities of one man – first Yeltsin, now Putin (and before that Gorbachev) – suggests just how little confidence there is in the capacity of Russia's institutions to guide the ship of state through the admittedly unchartered waters of the postcommunist transformation.

## VIII. The *"Pays Reel"*: The System of Presidential Authority

The most significant line in the Russian constitution is perhaps Article 83, section i, which states simply that, "[The president] shall form his administrative staff." This provision, which was intended to provide for the routine administrative needs of the president's office, has turned out to be the operative key to understanding high politics in Russia in recent years.[38] In brief, faced with an unsympathetic parliament and weak governmental ministries, and given Yeltsin's own personal disinclination to systematize the decision-making process, the Russian presidency has developed an informal staff structure that has become the linchpin of Russian politics, in many respects duplicating the formal structure of government ministries and agencies. (Remarkably, it seems that there has been a major increase in the number of Russian bureaucrats since the disintegration of the USSR, with 1.2 million bureaucrats added to the state system between 1992–8, the bulk at the local levels.[39])

In Russia's superpresidentialist system, the word of the president is decisive. Access to the president is therefore critical in advancing the agenda of any office of government. Yeltsin's office devised a structure of presidential access in which nearly all governmental and extragovernmental agencies compete with each other for the scarce and precious commodity of presidential time and/or imprimatur. In this respect, the real structure of decision making finds the Russian president in the position of Tsar: Nothing of importance happens without presidential approval; moreover, access to the president is all. In principle, such a system, authoritarian as it is,

[38] Ibid., pp. 87–95.
[39] Anders Aslund and Mikhail Dmiriyev, "Economic Reform versus Rent Seeking," in Anders Aslund and Martha Brill Olcott, eds., *Russia after Communism*, p. 105; Gustafson, *Capitalism Russian Style*, p. 30.

can work as a vehicle of governance, but it requires a highly competent, informed, skillful, and interventionist chief executive to function. (Otto von Bismarck's chancellorship in Imperial Germany and Henry Kissinger's administration of U.S. foreign policy in the Nixon period come to mind as models. Putin seems intent on assuming such a leadership role.) In the absence of such a political virtuoso, however, the political system tends to decompose, as all actors await responses from the top that seldom come. In this respect, Yeltsin's personal disinclination to attend to the administration of government, reinforced by the lengthy absences from affairs of state that his frequent illnesses required, was exactly the wrong match of political personality to political system. In effect, Yeltsin had developed an authoritarian system of power. Until the president at the top did something, nothing happened in the pyramid of power.

What happened instead is that government was run for the most part by informal and usually covert cabals of claimants on the resources and protection of the state, who were able to obtain access to the presidential chain of command, frequently through the outright purchase of officials' time and accord. U.S. diplomat Thomas E. Graham, who was responsible for analyzing Russian internal affairs at the U.S. Embassy in Moscow, characterized this system in late 1995 in an article published in a leading Russian newspaper as "clan" politics, in which an oligarchic collection of economic interests struggle for access to the president and thus state resources in order "to engineer a political stability that would insure their hold on power and the country's financial resources."[40] The contesting clans included a group of oil and gas industrialists under the aegis of Prime Minister Chernomyrdin; a "Moscow group" under the aegis of Mayor Yuri Luzhkov and based upon the city's banking and real estate interests; a military-industrial and security circle responsible for the war in Chechnya led by Korzhakov (later fired), Yeltsin's close personal adviser and security chief until June 1996; an "agrarian" group controlling the mainly unreformed Soviet-era farm sector; and a group of "Westernizers," such as Yeltsin's deputy prime minister for the economy Chubais, whose power stemmed from their involvement in the privatization of the Russian economy and their access to Western financial institutions, such as the World Bank and the International Monetary Fund, which have played important roles in sustaining the Russian state budget through difficult times. The principal mechanism by which these clans' interests were advanced was the promulgation of presidential decrees, which often

[40] *Nezavisimaya Gazeta*, November 25, 1995, www.ng.ru.

established tax or import/export advantages for particular interests. It is quite obvious that with more than five hundred such decrees issued in the mid-1990s, when Yeltsin was too ill to govern for extended periods of time, the Russian president had in effect ceded enormous economic and political power to private interests, or clans, whose access to the Russian government was mediated by his staff.

These clans, Graham wrote, "contain few staunch supporters of democracy, and none of the clans are devoted to democratic ideals, despite public assurances to the contrary." Indeed, elections "present a danger to [this] elite because even though they retain the levers of power, they understand less and less of what is going on in society." In principle, a healthy and activist president able to impose the general interests of Russian society on the Russian political process might be in a position to advance the interests of society and of the system as a whole. (Putin seems to be attempting something like this. A detailed discussion of this follows.) In practice, his absence meant that, with a presidential camarilla embedded within a superpresidentialist constitution, Russian politics became the prisoner of a new post-Soviet economic and financial oligarchy that has seen the interests of its individual sectors, and often the pecuniary interests of its leading individuals, become the focal point of the political system. Thus, the writer Aleksandr Solzhenitsyn concluded, a stable and tight oligarchy of 150–200 people, including the most cunning representatives of the top and middle strata of the former communist ruling structure, along with numerous *nouveaux riches* who amassed their recent fortunes through banditry, had been established.[41] Before Yeltsin's second term was over, one of those new magnates, Boris Berezovsky – a former mathematician whose power derived from a fortune made through the automobile import-export industry and thus being cash rich at the right time – would play a decisive and entirely extraconstitutional role in determining the contours of the Russian political succession.[42]

[41] As reported by Radio Free Europe/Radio Liberty Research Service, March 6, 2000, www.rferl.org/newsline/2000/03/l-rus.

[42] Pierre Lorrain, *La Mystérieuse Ascension de Vladimir Poutine* [The Mysterious Rise of Vladimir Putin] (Monaco: Editions de Rocher, 2000), p. 311. Berezovsky understood earlier than most that the difference in costs in Russia as compared to the rest of the world could generate astronomical profits. Berezovsky thus obtained a license to export the Zhiguli (Lada abroad) car and in 1991 established a company named Logovaz toward that end. Cars at the time sold on the domestic market for the equivalent of $250 at the official exchange rate but could be sold abroad for $7,000, a differential of 28:1. Berezovsky employed a similar strategy at Aeroflot, where he managed to appoint Yeltsin's son-in-law as director.

## IX. From Yeltsin to Putin

The extreme and virtually unaccountable concentration of political power in Yeltsin's hands was illustrated by the political crisis of March 1998, in which Yeltsin sacked his prime minister of more than five years' standing and appointed a virtual unknown, the young Sergei Kiriyenko, in his stead.[43] Recall that according to the Russian constitution the president may submit a candidate to the Duma three times for approval; if the Duma thrice refuses, the president may dissolve the parliament. This would seem to be a formidable enough imbalance of power favoring presidential supremacy, even by Gaullist standards. Yet what Yeltsin did in the spring of 1998 demonstrated the extent of presidential contempt for parliamentary prerogatives, as well as the potential fragility of the presidentialist constitution: Yeltsin actually submitted Kiriyenko's name three times to the parliament, in effect daring the parliament to turn down his candidate. On the third vote, the Duma, given Yeltsin's record of violence and the risk of losing a number of valuable privileges attendant upon parliamentary status (including housing in Moscow, free travel throughout Russia, payoffs for key votes from the presidential administration, and – last but not least in today's Russia – immunity from prosecution), gave in and allowed the installment of Kiriyenko as head of government.

Yet this open flaunting of executive power was only the surface of the story. Behind the scenes, in what amounted to Yeltsin's court, key members of what Russians called "the family" were desperately searching for an eventual successor to Yeltsin who could constrain the communists and extreme nationalists from coming to power and thereby also protect them from expropriation of their newly privatized wealth and criminal prosecution.[44] Yeltsin too appears to have been sensitive to such considerations, given the privileged role that financier Boris Berezovsky was playing in managing the Yeltsin family finances. (Eventually, the first act of state of Acting President Putin was to sign a decree granting Yeltsin full immunity from prosecution.[45]) Increasingly alarmed at the deteriorating state of Yeltsin's health and the Russian economic crash of August 1998, and

---

[43] For extended treatment, see Lorrain, *La Mystérieuse Ascension de Vladimir Poutine*, pp. 397–447; Shevstova, *Putin's Russia*, pp. 7–103, and Alexander Rahr, *Wladimir Putin: Der 'Deutsche' im Kreml* [Vladimir Putin: The "German" in the Kremlin] (Munich: Universitas, 2000), pp. 202–52.

[44] For an informed and thoughtful Russian account consistent with this one, see Shevtsova, *Putin's Russia*, pp. 7–68.

[45] Ibid., p. 69.

unconvinced of the political fortitude of Kiriyenko, Yeltsin's entourage acceded to the appointment of the parliament's candidate, Yevgeny Primakov, as prime minister in September 1998, only to undermine him as soon as possible in spite of a defensible record in stabilizing the economy after the August 1998 crash. In May 1999, Primakov was replaced by Sergei Stepashin, a career police official, who in turn was replaced at the end of August by Putin, a middle-ranking career intelligence officer who had previously been deputy in charge of Kremlin property (under Pavel Borodin, arrested in New York by the FBI under Swiss warrant for embezzlement in February 2001).

The prime criterion in the advancement of Putin appears to have been personal loyalty to Yeltsin and to those advancing his career toward the top as well as an apparent determination to wield power aggressively in light of another war looming in Chechnya.[46] Putin's signature on Yeltsin's "pardon" in January 2001 seemed to bear out the hopes that were evidently placed in Putin.[47] He would soon take actions that would force Berezovsky and other "oligarchs" such as Vladimir Gusinsky into foreign exile and even arrest; yet without Yeltsin's court, and in disregard of Russia's formal constitutional mechanisms, a Putin – a middle-ranking career intelligence officer with no political constituency, a complete unknown upon assuming office in August 1999 – could never have come to power. Such was the dessication of the Russian political system after nearly a decade of political and economic "reform."

Dramatic developments dominated Russian politics at the turn of the century. At the end of December, Russian President Yeltsin announced suddenly that he would resign effective January 1, 2000, in favor of Prime Minister Putin, whom Yeltsin had appointed at the end of August as the fifth prime minister in seventeen months. According to the Russian

---

[46] Lorrain has assembled a plausible circumstantial case that the original intention of Yeltsin's circle in arranging the resignation of Stepashin was to spare him the criticism expected from the forthcoming Chechen campaign. In this scenario, Putin would do the dirty work of fighting the war and would be forced out in time to reestablish Stepashin as the family's presidential candidate for the scheduled June 2000 elections. By late September 1999, however, the explosion of two apartment buildings in Moscow resulting in nearly three hundred deaths convinced most Russians that the Chechen problem was now a national problem and not simply an elite-driven phenomenon. Putin proved able to exploit this sentiment to catapult himself to the presidency. See Lorrain, *La Mystérieuse Ascension de Vladimir Poutine*, pp. 431–5.

[47] For details, see Rahr, *Wladimir Putin*, pp. 182–242. For Putin's own perspective, see *Ot pervogo litsa: Razgovory s Vladimirom Putinom* [In the first person: Conversations with Vladimir Putin] (Moscow: Vagirus, 2000).

constitution, presidential elections must be held within three months of the sitting president's resignation. Thus Putin, who also became acting president pending those elections, submitted himself to the electorate and, in a multicandidate race held before opposition candidates could effectively mobilize, received 52 percent of the vote in the first round, ensuring his inauguration as president of the Russian Federation in May 2000, for a four-year term.[48]

The confidence of Yeltsin's entourage that Putin might be able to win the presidential election was based on the remarkable surge of nationalist sentiment in favor of Putin following the government's prosecution of the second war against Chechnya in the 1990s. A series of four bomb blasts in the first half of September 1999 in Moscow and southern Russia, which killed nearly three hundred people in Moscow, galvanized public opinion behind the government, which now (unlike in 1994–6) saw the government's war in Chechnya as a war in defense of the interests of the Russian nation and not merely of those of the regime currently in power. In addition, tight media control, the appearance of limiting Russian casualties by unleashing massive artillery and aerial bombardment of the Chechen capital Grozny (in the process leveling much of the city), and fear about the spread of Chechen insurgency to neighboring areas of Russia's north Caucasus region (such as Dagestan, which was invaded by Chechen fighters in August 1999) united Russian opinion behind the government and sustained a wave of pro-government political support. This support propelled the pro-Putin Unity Party (created only in September 1999) to 23.3 percent of party-list votes in the December 19, 1999, parliamentary elections (in second place just behind the Communist Party, with 24.3 percent) and Putin to election as Russian president at the end of March.[49] Through alliances with other Duma parties, blocs, and independents, Unity was able to forge pro-government majorities for the first time since the early 1990s.

Once again, Russia held national elections on schedule, as it has since 1989. Yet also once again, the government has shown that it is capable of using the executive power of the state to structure electoral situations so as to favor the government strongly and also to insulate the government from serious accountability once it is in power. Following a pattern that

---

[48] See the report of March 28, 2000, of U.S. Undersecretary of State for Political Affairs Timothy Pickering (also former U.S. ambassador to Russia), "Russia after the Elections," at www.state.gov., p. 1.

[49] Troy McGrath, "Political Shifts in Russia's Duma: A December to Remember," *ACE: Analysis of Current Events*, vol. 11, no. 11–12 (December 1999), pp. 1, 3.

was established in the 1996 Russian presidential elections, Western governments, including the United States, confirmed publicly that the Russian elections were essentially free and fair.[50] At the same time, the International Election Observation Mission of the Organization of Security and Cooperation in Europe (OSCE) characterized the December parliamentary elections as follows:

- Lack of discipline and ethics was rife among the participants.
- Russia's civil code failed to provide sufficient and timely penalties for violations of the electoral code.
- Campaign expenditures regularly exceeded the legal limits.
- Executive authorities frequently interfered in the electoral process.
- Candidates from opposition parties were often prevented from arranging public meetings.
- Supporters of opposition parties were threatened with dismissals from employment.
- In a number of regions, broadcast media and regional editions of national newspapers had great difficulty expressing views critical of local power structures.
- In at least four regions (Kalmykia, Bashkortostan, Tatarstan, and the Maritime province), broadcasters and publishers lost their leases on premises controlled by the local administration, and some journalists lost their jobs; other measures included special tax investigations, administrative fines, and criminal investigations.
- Military personnel were encouraged to vote for the pro-Kremlin Unity Party, in clear violation of the electoral laws.
- Members of the electoral committees frequently were involved in actual campaigning.
- Finally, and perhaps most importantly, Russian state television, which alone reaches households across all of Russia, sustained a scandalously libelous media attack on key opposition figures, especially Moscow Mayor Luzhkov and former Prime Minister Primakov, that carried over into the presidential campaign of January–March 2000.[51]

That campaign, which propelled Putin to executive power, followed lines similar to the parliamentary elections. Most important was not the

[50] Pickering, "Russia after the Elections." For an extensive discussion of the ways in which Western political interventions have helped to sustain Russian incumbents in power, see Sarah E. Mendelson, "Democracy Assistance and Political Transitions in Russia: Between Success and Failure," *International Security*, vol. 25, no. 4 (Spring 2001), pp. 68–106.
[51] McGrath, "Political Shifts."

outright stealing of votes but rather the structuring of electoral choices through the use of the executive power of the government. Thus, the government – and government-controlled and government-friendly media (especially television) – orchestrated (as it did for Yeltsin in 1996) a pro-Putin blitz of positive coverage, while excoriating opponents with libelous charges and with little or no right of reply. More broadly, the government ably exploited the nationalist sentiments of Russians in the wake of the Moscow apartment bombings in September and used the second Chechen War of the 1990s to mobilize public opinion behind Putin; in this context, antigovernment views were easily portrayed as antipatriotic, even treasonous.[52] Thus, the one presidential candidate who dared to express even mild dissent from the government line on the Chechen War, the liberal reformer Gregory Yavlinsky, saw his public support drop immediately and precipitously. The often wanton brutality displayed by the Russian Army in Chechnya, warranting a rebuke by the United Nations Human Rights Commission on April 26, 2000,[53] has had no appreciable effect on Russian public opinion, which appears to see the vital national interests of an increasingly isolated Russia (in the wake of NATO expansion and NATO's war against Russian ally Serbia) at stake. In a similar atmosphere and employing similar tactics, although now under a more perfect state control of the television networks, Unity's successor party United Russia and its allies achieved a supermajority of approximately two-thirds of Duma seats in the December 2003 parliamentary elections.

## X. Putin and the Consolidation of Russia's Neopatrimonial System

It is beyond the scope of this work and in any event too early to analyze the specific contours of Putin's policies in authoritative detail. Suffice it to note that almost immediately upon election as Russian president, Putin began to "streamline" the operations of Russian government. Russia now had that dynamic and energetic leader who, unlike the decrepit Yeltsin, just might be able to make the highly centralized presidentialist system work. Putin quickly set to work to do so, aided in the task by the much greater inflow of oil-based revenues into state coffers made possible by the rise of world oil prices since the August 1998 crash, when the price

---

[52] Thumann, *Das Lied von der russichen Erde*, pp. 146–193.
[53] *New York Times*, April 29, 2000, at www.nytimes.com.

of oil had sunk to $10 per barrel. By mid-2004, that price had quadrupled to approximately $45 per barrel.

Putin was no doubt moved to create a single economic and legal field to improve the conditions for investment in the Russian economy; reduce the power of regional governors, who wielded substantially more power than did the federal center in their respective locales; and in the process strengthen the chain of command emanating from the Russian president's office, what Russians call "the power vertical." The effect has been to amass even more formal power in the office of the Russian president in what Vladimir Shlapentokh has termed an authoritarian reaction to the "liberal feudalism" of the Yeltsin years. The aim of such a reaction was to restore effective state power and bring under control all forms of Russian "civil society," democratic or elite.[54] For instance, even before calling for the replacement of gubernatorial election by presidential appointment in September 2004:

- Putin had reorganized Russia's eighty-nine regions within the framework of seven new super regions, corresponding to existing military districts and supervised by the president's superprefectural appointees, who have been drawn mainly from the military and intelligence services.

- He induced the Duma to allow the president the authority to dismiss elected regional leaders if a court deems that they have violated federal law more than once.

- He reorganized the upper house of the Federal Assembly by removing regional governors from the body and making tenure subject to presidential appointment, thereby depriving regional leaders of a national forum and input on federal legislation.[55]

- He managed the progressive merging of Russian political parties to form one omnibus pro-government party, as reflected in the decision of Moscow Mayor Luzhkov, viciously attacked by Putin's side in the parliamentary and presidential campaigns, to combine his Fatherland-All Russia Party with Putin's Unity Party. By the December 2003 parliamentary elections, several pro-state and pro-Putin forces merged in the form of the United Russia Party, essentially fusing the parliamentary majority with Putin's office. In the process, the parliament – and

---

[54] Vladimir Shlapentokh, "Hobbes and Locke at Odds in Putin's Russia," *Europe-Asia Studies*, vol. 55, no. 7 (November 2003), pp. 981–1008.

[55] Julie A. Corwin, "Has a Year without Yeltsin Been a Year without Change?" *RFE/RL Research Report*, March 14, 2001, at www.rferl.org.

more uncertainly, regional leaders through federal influence on local elections – would be rendered even more of a tool in the hands of the Russian president.[56]

• In mid-2000, Putin passed a tax reform aimed not simply at streamlining revenue flows and encouraging a better business climate (the flat tax of 13 percent, passed in mid-2000) but at shifting the flow of tax revenue away from local governors into the federal treasury (where necessary, other federal tools such as the withdrawal of oil from refineries in Bashkortostan are used to shift the revenue balance in favor of the federal center).[57]

• Putin had effectively destroyed the remaining independence of the television networks by exploiting the financial and administrative power of the Russian state to change the management of NTV, the last occasional critic of the government's positions on the national airwaves, in the process cementing the presidency's ability to monopolize mass circulation news and opinion.

• Increased oil-export revenues have allowed the creation of a multibillion dollar emergency fund that, while certainly desirable *in se*, underscores the indispensability of the office of the president to the welfare of the nation.

• Putin had staffed the presidential administration, government, and parliament with allies and clients drawn increasingly and overwhelmingly from Russia's military and paramilitary organizations, especially the intelligence services, successors to Putin's erstwhile employer, the KGB. Five of seven heads of Russia's macrofederal districts are military or security officers, as are 35 percent of all deputy ministers appointed between 2000–3, and 25 percent of the Russian political elite as a whole for the same period (compared to 11 percent for business elites), representing a sixfold increase in military and security representation in governmental leadership posts since the late Soviet period. As previously noted, two-thirds of Putin's presidential staff have backgrounds in the security services.[58]

[56] "2-Party Merger Bolsters Putin," *International Herald Tribune*, April 13, 2001, at www.iht.com; Thumann, *Das Lied von der russichen Erde*, pp. 194–211.

[57] Shevtsova, *Putin's Russia*, p. 141.

[58] Olga Kryshtanovskaya and Stephen White, "Putin's Militocracy," *Post-Soviet Affairs*, vol. 19, no. 4 (October–December 2003), pp. 289–306. For background on the capacity of the intelligence agencies to preserve their organizational integrity amid the debris of Soviet collapse, see Amy Knight, *Spies without Cloaks* (Princeton, NJ: Princeton University Press, 1996).

- The administration of the government itself reflects the presidentialist prerogative: Before a streamlining of governmental administration in early 2004, fully twenty of sixty-one government ministries reported directly to the office of the Russian president, whereas the remainder of the government, mainly the economic ministries, were the responsibility of the prime minister (whom the president can dismiss at any time).[59]
- Finally, and as befits a former intelligence operative, Putin had ordered a series of spectacular arrests and prosecutions of businesspeople (such as Berezovsky and Mikhail Khodorovsky) who concluded that their mere wealth entitled them to political influence in the absence of coordination with the Kremlin. In the process, the principle that businesspeople should stay out of politics (except on the Kremlin's terms) has been convincingly demonstrated.

One should not exaggerate the degree of recentralization of authority in the hands of the Russian president. First, unlike the Soviet period, the bulk of Russia's economy now lies outside the direct purview of the state; much of Russia's liquid capital, in fact, is held abroad by private parties. Second, at the operational level of Russian government, there remains a symbiotic interpenetration between Russian ministries and officials, on the one hand, and private business elements, on the other (both legal and illegal), that complicates the simple execution of the president's will. Third, and in part as a consequence, Russia now experiences the lobbying of interest groups, especially among Russian industrial manufacturers, that has, for instance, already complicated Russia's early entry into the World Trade Organization. Fourth, Russia has yet to develop a well-articulated administrative state, based on generally applicable rules; Russian administration, like Russian politics, remains the sphere of men, not law, thereby hindering the exercise of even highly centralized formal executive power. Finally, since elections are held, public opinion does count for something. Indeed, Putin's authority is almost entirely charismatic. As a result, bold reforms such as the reform of prices for housing and utilities have had to be put on hold in the face of evident and widespread public dissatisfaction.[60]

Moreover, for every action that Putin has taken, there has often been a countervailing reaction or constraint on the extent of federal-executive

[59] Kryshtanovskaya and White, "Putin's Militocracy."
[60] Vyacheslav Nikonov, "Putinizm" [Putinism], in idem, *Sovremennaya Rossiyskaya Politika* [Contemporary Russian Politics] (Moscow: OLMA-PRESS, 2003), p. 41.

authority. For example, whereas Putin was able to remove the regional governors from the Federal Asssembly, the governors won the right to extend their terms of office, in the process cementing the local power bases of governors with their own independent resource flows.[61] The appointment of seven presidential superprefects in the regions is much less significant than appears at first glance due to the limited administrative infrastructure available to these federal envoys. The federal center can often use its administrative powers to hinder or even remove an undesired candidate for regional office but it cannot reliably control voters' behavior; voters have often enough spurned the federal candidate in favor of a protest candidate. While Putin can control the national parliament to get his legislation passed, it is another thing altogether to get that legislation enforced on the local level (the law on the sale of agricultural land passed in July 2002, for example, depends critically on implementation by local governors).[62] Perhaps most importantly, the ability of the central Russian state to spread its influence throughout the country's eighty-nine regions depends critically on the extent to which local leaders have access to resource flows that make them relatively immune from Moscow's financial blandishments and pressures. What has undoubtedly happened under Putin, no doubt reinforced by the impact of the second Chechen War and the significant increase of oil revenues since 1999, is to reassert the interest and presence of the central government that had seriously waned throughout the 1990s and especially in the aftermath of the economic crash of August 1998, which rendered the central government broke and thus virtually powerless throughout much of Russia. Yet when all is said and done, the question remains, as ever, can a Russian leader amass sufficient political and administrative authority on the basis of a sufficient political and social consensus to induce the influx of capital investment that is vital to Russia's prospects as a state, a nation, and a civilization? That is, assuming that Putin has the degree of power that he desires, what can he do with it?

## XI. Conclusion

By the end of Putin's first term as Russian president in early 2004, it seemed that a certain stability had been imparted to Russia's post-Soviet

---

[61] *Le Monde*, July 12, 2002, p. 4.

[62] "Putin unterzeichnet Agrarland-Gesetz: Regional unterschiedliche Umstezung [Putin Signs Land Law: Differing Regional Reactions]," *Die Neuer Zuercher Zeitung*, July 26, 2002, p. 19.

political-economic structure. The forms of democracy and capitalism had been preserved, perhaps indefinitely. The power of the national state – or at least of the presidency – had been asserted convincingly as against all comers, including the parliament, the television broadcast media, regional gubernatorial barons, Russia's infamous economic "oligarchs," and even the Russian military, as is shown by Putin's stunning alignment of Russia with the United States after the September 11, 2001, terror attacks on U.S. soil. Only in Chechnya had the Russian state yet to make its writ prevail; there it could destroy but not govern. Even so, this was no mean feat, especially when set against the debilitating paralysis of the Russian government throughout the 1990s.

Yet there were reasons to be wary of confounding the consolidation of the power of the Russian president with the stabilization of Russia as a whole. For one, the early Putin years have been favorable ones economically for Putin's government and the Russian state, for reasons that have more to do with externally determined conjunctural factors than they do with sound structural fundamentals in the Russian political economy. Much of the stimulus to Russian economic growth since 1999 has been due to the one-time effects of the massive devaluation of the ruble in late summer 1998 – making native Russian production much cheaper as compared to imports – followed by an average tripling of the world oil price between 1999 and 2004. In 2004, this sector accounted for a larger percentage of the Russian economy and the state's budget revenues – nearly half of which come from energy export receipts – than was true at the outset of the post-Soviet period. In other words, the ability of the Russian state to fulfill its various internal and external obligations depends on the  course of key world commodity prices. Moreover, reactions by Putin and Russian officials to a series of crises – the sinking of the atomic submarine Kursk in August 2000, the fire in the Ostankino television tower the same month, the storming of the Chechen terrorists in the Moscow theater in fall 2002, and the Beslan school massacre of September 2004 – suggest that Soviet-era instincts of secrecy, deniability, and servility remain strong among Russian officialdom, above all in the ranks of the military and paramilitary personnel that make up a major part of Putin's system of governance. In short, it is far from clear that the Russian state has settled upon a mechanism that can encourage a broadly based, self-generating economic recovery that might make Russia into a moderately prosperous country and accountable political system.

In this light, Putin's first term (2000–4) may be seen, even against the evident failure of the second, post-Soviet Chechen War, as the period in which the Russian state halted the progressive decomposition of the Yeltsin years. Putin himself ably exploited the new national-patriotic mood after the deadly Moscow apartment explosions to establish his authority on charismatic grounds in compensation for the weakness of Russia's formal institutions of governance. Increased oil revenues allowed the state to meet pressing internal obligations such as wage and pension arrears as well as external ones such as the foreign debt that consumes fully one-fourth of the Russian national budget, all the while prosecuting a costly war in Chechnya. Politically, an energetic Russian president whose office was now flush with cash could face down the economic "oligarchs" who controlled the financing of the state in the Yeltsin years as well as clip the wings of regional barons and media critics. Toward the end of his first term, Putin and his political "technologists" had engineered a fully compliant parliament and a triumphant reelection for Putin himself. Yet what this represented above all was the consolidation of the hyperpresidentialist political system that Yeltsin had fashioned out of the barrel of a gun in late 1993 rather than a formula for the regeneration of Russia.

Indeed, such a neopatrimonial system, resting as it did on a frail institutional foundation and fickle foreign commodity exchanges, could prove to be quite brittle should its key permissive condition – high world oil prices – disappear. Twice before in recent Russian political history, in the mid-1980s and in the late 1990s, the collapse of world oil prices condemned Gorbachev and Yeltsin to failure. The key question as Putin began his second term thus seemed to be whether the office of the Russian presidency could broaden its political-institutional foundation while at the same time encouraging a broadening of the productive foundation of the Russian economy so that Russia might absorb such a shock should it happen again.

# 5

## The Russian 1990s in Comparative Perspective

Spread the truth-the laws of economics are like the laws of engineering. One set of laws works everywhere.

> – Lawrence Summers, then chief economist of the World Bank, October 1991.

There are no special countries from the point of view of economists. If economics is a science, with its own laws – all countries and all economic stabilization plans are the same.

> – Pyotr Aven, Russian Minister of Foreign Economic Relations, February 1992.[1]

Russians compensate for the severity of their laws by ignoring them.

> – Anonymous

## I. Introduction

To what extent has the Russian exit from communism been unique? After all, Russia is only one of more than two dozen states to have charted an independent path since the disintegration of communist power in Europe between 1989 and 1991. From the perspective of initial starting conditions, then, post-Soviet Russia had much in common with post-Soviet Ukraine, post-Soviet Estonia, and the other republics of the USSR as well as with a number of the formerly communist states of Eastern Europe. Given the apparent similarity of key starting points, a comparison of

---

[1] Both as cited in Stefan Hedlund, *Russia's "Market" Economy: A Bad Case of Predatory Capitalism* (London: UCL Press, 1999), p. 112.

the post-communist states should shed useful light on whether Russia possesses any distinctive features that may have shaped its postcommunist path of development. Likewise, many social scientists have defined the exit from communism as part of a broader, global process toward democratization that began with the end of authoritarian rule in Spain, Portugal, and Greece in the mid-1970s, so that the Russian "transition" may also be compared to a series of states with noncommunist but authoritarian political legacies. As the epigrams cited at the beginning of this chapter suggest, the attempted application across a decade of market formula derived from Economics departments at the University of Chicago, Harvard, and other centers of liberal economics warrants examination of whether or not there are not specificities of Russian development that might necessitate a reevaluation of the allegedly universal laws of economics, at least in the manner in which they are frequently applied. There is also the dramatic contrast of the Russian case with another major communist state that attempted far-reaching economic reforms in the absence of structural political reform, that is, the People's Republic of China. Finally, there is the frequently invoked historical comparison with another transitional regime attempting to consolidate democracy under comparably trying circumstances, that is, Weimar Germany, as well as with societies that appear to have adapted well to life parallel to, if not apart from, the state, for example, contemporary Italy. In the discussion to follow, we shall review the similarities and differences entailed in these several comparisons in an effort to situate postcommunist Russia along a range of conditions, enabling and disabling, and likely outcomes of the transition from communism and/or authoritarian rule.

A social system, though not an organism, is more like an organic than a mechanical thing. The workings of a social system are thus best understood in ecological rather than engineering terms. The garden rather than the machine better conjures the essence of social life. Individuals, their families, social groups, classes, private and public organizations, and so on, live and develop in constant interaction with their environments, natural, social, and institutional. Patterns of adaptation do not emerge accidentally or irrationally. Rather, they represent what appear to those with the ability to influence a given society as reasonable (if also usually self-interested) responses to environmental circumstances. Efforts to change behavior without addressing the environmental circumstances that gave rise to and reinforce that behavior tend to run aground on the resistance of the culture that developed in a process of enduring exchange with that environment. That culture invariably entails not merely the formal rules by which it proclaims itself to be bound but, and invariably more importantly, the informal, unwritten but generally understood rules and enforcement mechanisms by which the society is actually run. At some level it is undoubtedly true, as Harvard's Lawrence Summers would have it, that economics is a universal science; the challenge, however, is to make as explicit as possible the entire set of assumptions about the nature and range of rules, formal and informal, and enforcement mechanisms peculiar to a given society. Thus, while from afar the predominance of communal peasant farming in old Russia may seem a wasteful allocation of social energies and economic resources, to most peasants, living as they did in harsh conditions on the margins of survival, the commune represented vital social insurance.[2] Sacrifice of individual freedom to farm as one would wish would seem well worth the gain of much higher assurance of individual and family survival that communal farming entailed under Russian conditions of climate, soil, and rainfall. Under these circumstances, peasant resistance to technological innovation represents a reasonable skepticism to a process that must inevitably take current resources out of production on a gamble of greater future yields, in the process rendering the group more vulnerable than ever. In order to change peasant resistance to such innovation, either technological or in terms of the social structure of the commune itself, convincing evidence of a change in environmental circumstances would be required. In the end, tragically, only the Stalinist state acquired the raw power to change decisively the social structure of peasant Russia by in effect presenting itself as a totally new environmental factor with which the peasants had to contend. (Russian agriculture has yet to recover fully from that shock.[3])

It is thus difficult to change prevailing patterns of social behavior, in particular by simply changing the formal rules by which society functions. Unless the environmental circumstances can also be changed, the informal rules and enforcement mechanisms developed over long experience will tend to absorb and defeat the purposes of the best-intended rules.[4] Historically established patterns of social behavior are thus extraordinarily difficult to change from without, as the research of Nobel laureate economists Douglass North and Robert Fogel, with their

[2] Edward L. Keenan, "Moscovite Political Folkways," *Russian Review*, vol. 45, no. 2 (April 1986), pp. 115–81.
[3] James C. Scott, *Seeing Like a State: How Certain Schemes to Improve the Human Condition Have Failed* (New Haven, CT: Yale University Press, 1998), pp. 193–222.
[4] Hedlund, *Russia's "Market" Economy*, pp. 35–6.

emphasis on "path dependency," as well as political scientists such as Robert Putnam, have convincingly shown.[5] Anthropologists, of course, have long known this. Interestingly, one of the most penetrating studies of foreign involvement in the postcommunist reform process was written by a social anthropologist, Janine Wedel.[6] In his remarkable 1993 study entitled *Making Democracy Work*, Putnam examined the consequences and sought to account for the differences in implementation of wide-reaching administrative reforms in each of Italy's twenty provinces since 1970. One of his unexpected conclusions reflected the continuing influence of distant history and thus the reproduction of social relations over time. It turned out that the most reliable indicators of how effectively a particular region or city had exploited the opportunities of the greater freedom allowed by centrally decreed administrative decentralization was that area's level of civic development in the late Middle Ages. While nearly all of Italy's regions benefited in absolute terms from the devolution of power from Rome, the gap in political, civic, and relatedly economic development between Italy's north and south remained as large, if not larger, after the experience of reform as before. A comparable perspective on Russian political-economic development would reveal that, since that time, the predominant tendency in Russian institutional life has been the erosion of the distinction between private property and political power, if indeed not the actual fusion of the two spheres, as was true for much of Imperial Russian history and most of Soviet Russian history. The persistence of this patrimonial paradigm in Russian political history has had decisive consequences for the role of the state in relationship to property and persons. As Swedish economist Stefan Hedlund has argued:

... the path dependence that links old Russia with the Soviet system may be seen to rest, above all, in the continued failure of the state to serve as a guarantor of the rule of law. Though there were differences in the respective modes of repression and censorship, the continued absence of rights, reciprocity and participation looms large. And actors under both regimes logically would invest in skills that improved their performance under such rules. And the associated process of learning would

[5] Ronald Coase, "The Institutional Structure of Production," *American Economic Review*, vol. 84, no. 3 (1995), p. 366; Douglass C. North, *Institutions, Institutional Change and Economic Performance* (Cambridge, MA: Harvard University Press, 1990); idem, "Economic Performance through Time," *American Economic Review*, vol. 82, no. 4 (1992), p. 714; Robert Putnam, *Making Democracy Work: Civic Traditions in Modern Italy* (Princeton, NJ: Princeton University Press, 1993).
[6] *Collision and Collusion* (St. Martin's Press, 1998).

serve, on both sides of the fence, to rationalize these collectively irrational types of behavior.[7]

Russia's path of political development, in this light, has been one of (a) concentration of virtually unaccountable power in the hands of the executive, a concentration that at times is able to mobilize resources to perform extraordinary tasks but is not conducive to legal rationality in respect of persons and property; and (b) the absence of a clear line between property and political power.[8] The fundamental test for Russia in the 1990s, then, was to change this essential unaccountability of executive power and with it the chance of establishing the rule of law that is the prerequisite of both capitalist and democratic development. That Russia entered the twenty-first century with an executive authority that was largely unaccountable to the formal institutions of state and a continued merger of political power and economic wealth (albeit in new forms) suggests just how powerful Russia's historical path of development was and the difficulties that Western-oriented Russian reformers and Western friends of Russian reform have confronted in trying to make Russia into a liberal market democracy.

## II. Institutions and Values

It may be helpful at this point to clarify several points that are often obscured in discussions about democracy and democratic transitions. The first and foremost is that an important distinction exists between democracy as a set of values and democracy as a set of institutions.[9] It is far from clear that the kinds of values that today many consider democratic (for example, equality, liberty, and tolerance) are as a matter of principle best and always advanced by democratic politics. As noted earlier, Aristotle held that the ideal form of government, one that would advance the common weal and respect that which was due the individual, was an enlightened despot of Solomonic judgment and capabilities. Conceding for the moment the difficulty of finding such an individual, not to mention ensuring that his or her successors would maintain the tradition, the fact remains that it has very frequently been the case that indisputably democratic institutions have thwarted as well as advanced democratic values.

---

[7] Hedlund, *Russia's "Market" Economy*, p. 36.

[8] Ibid.

[9] For a fuller discussion, see Allen C. Lynch, "Introduction," in *Nations in Transit 1997* (New York: Freedom House, 1998), pp. 29–38.

Conversely, indisputably authoritarian institutions have often promoted liberal values, both politically and economically.

Consider, for instance, that slavery was abolished in the United States through the vehicle of the bloodiest war that had been experienced in either Europe or North America in the century between 1815–1914, whereas Tsarist Russia abolished its comparable institution of serfdom in 1861 by decree, quite peaceably and with remarkable administrative effectiveness at that.[10] Moreover, U.S. democratic institutions proved insufficient to guarantee the civil rights of emancipated slaves for fully a century thereafter. In Latin America, the modeling of postcolonial constitutions after 1825 on the U.S. Constitution, with its emphasis on checking and blocking the accumulation of central state power, served under the very different economic and social conditions of the region to perpetuate feudalistic elites' grip on power; such imported democratic structures hindered rather than advanced the democratization of society. In recent times, the sudden convening of (genuinely) free elections in multinational Bosnia-Herzegovina in the early 1990s had the (predictable) effect of providing democratic legitimacy to three purely and exclusively nationalist political parties (that is, Croat/Catholic, Serb/Orthodox, and Bosniak/Muslim), thereby fueling the genocidal war that soon ensued. Civil wars in the multi-ethnic societies of Georgia and Moldova were also triggered by the institution of free elections in societies that lacked a sufficient preexisting social and political consensus to make elections a factor for stability and unity rather than discord and strife.[11]

The Napoleonic civil code, which remains central to the legal structures of contemporary democratic Western Europe, was of course imposed by Napoleonic means. Likewise, some of the most outstanding successes in democratic development have been imposed by foreign conquest, occupation, and rule; the Allied conquest and domination of Germany and Japan between 1945–9/50, in which both states were compelled to adopt democratic institutions, is only the most recent and dramatic case of this kind. Previously it was the British Empire, through foreign conquest and imperial administration, which laid the groundwork for democracy in North America, Australia, New Zealand, India, South Africa, the Caribbean, and

[10] George L. Yaney, *The Systematization of Russian Government: Social Evolution in the Domestic Administration of Imperial Russia, 1711–1905* (Urbana, IL: University of Illinois Press, 1973), pp. 230–48.
[11] For a broader analysis along these lines, see Amy Chua, *World on Fire: How Exporting Free Market Democracy Spreads Ethnic Hatred and Global Instability* (New York: Doubleday, 2003).

elsewhere (even Ireland), in the process becoming the greatest propagator of democracy in history (as Winston Churchill once taunted Franklin Roosevelt as he was pressing him for Indian independence). The relatively liberal yet undoubtedly imperial administration of the late Habsburg era – by contrast to the harsher rule of the Ottomans and the Russian Tsars – is itself one of the historical factors that work in favor of Czech, Slovene, Hungarian, and even Croat efforts to establish liberal economic, social, and political institutions in the postcommunist period.

Finally, there are some pressing issues of democratic participation that most democracies, as currently structured, seem ill prepared to address. In most industrial democracies, the majority of the population is middle class and thus relatively prosperous. It is increasingly clear that comfortable democratic majorities are not necessarily sensitive to claims for economic and social inclusion from poor and marginal minorities, especially when such majority-minority cleavages are associated with ethnic and/or racial divides as well. (Most social welfare programs in countries such as the United States and Germany are politically viable only when the middle classes can obtain a disproportionate share of the benefits.) Democratic theory assumes that majorities and minorities are complex and will alternate over time. A social, economic, and political condition in which entrenched minorities do not effectively participate in the common life of the polity, in part because they do not see how such participation can address their social and economic circumstances, is not easily compatible with democratic values (even if is not threatening to the stability of that democratic order). Yet it is far from clear that current liberal democratic institutions and practices are capable of mobilizing majority coalitions on behalf of such marginalized economic and social minorities. If this is true of such established democracies as France (see the rise of the anti–Arab Front National), Germany (see the longstanding German resistance to citizenship for its long-resident Turkish inhabitants) and the United States (see the intersection of race and poverty), one should not be surprised that the incomparably more fragile institutions of the many multinational societies of postcommunist Europe have encountered substantial difficulties in reconciling ethnic/national heterogeneity with liberal politics. (Perhaps indicatively, five of the seven consolidated democracies in the region – Poland, the Czech Republic, Hungary, Slovenia, and to a somewhat lesser extent Lithuania – are virtually ethnically homogeneous.)

I state the preceding not to make the case for an authoritarian transition to democracy but rather to suggest the complexity of the relationship between democratic values and democratic institutions. Clearly, each is organically dependent upon the other. Precisely because of this, it is difficult to see how one model of democratic governance can be transplanted from the North Atlantic experience to the postcommunist experience without substantial adaptations and unexpected consequences. Discussion about the transition to "democracy" often overlooks just how varied democratic experience is within the North Atlantic world itself. Consider just a few of the variations that are typically found among democratic polities:

- Presidential versus parliamentary systems
- Direct versus proportional representation, or as is also common, a mix of both
- Unitary versus federal, or federal versus confederal
- Written versus unwritten constitutions
- Common law versus civil code legal foundations
- Bipolar versus multipolar (and sometimes unipolar) party systems
- Active judicial review versus judicial restraint
- Thresholds for representation in parliament or not
- Absolute versus qualified or supermajorities
- Liberal democratic versus social democratic versions of capitalism

Without wishing to underestimate the flexibility of democratic procedures, the possible combinations of these existing features of democratic systems totals 3,456. Under these circumstances, the effectiveness of particular democratic institutions needs to be viewed in light of local circumstances as well as democratic principles, as has in fact always been the case in the Western world. It should also be noted that, since the states under review are undergoing economic and social as well as political transformations, historically an even wider variation in political systems is associated with the functioning of market economies. Whereas all democracies have a capitalist economic foundation, many capitalist economies do not operate with democratic political systems. Market economics are a historically demonstrated and necessary prerequisite to liberal political development, but they are very far indeed from being a sufficient enabling condition for democracy. This is of particular importance since the attempt throughout postcommunist Europe to construct democracy and capitalism at the same time is historically unprecedented and arguably one that is fraught with tensions and dilemmas not captured by the notion of a linear "democratic-capitalist transition."

## III. Russia in the Postcommunist Context

More generally, the evident patterns of political and economic development in postcommunist Europe during the first post-Soviet decade suggest

that history and politics are strongly intertwined in these states' transit
from their recent and common communist experience. Each state's experience under communism, which itself was conditioned by particularities
of history and circumstance, continues to project a major if perhaps declining influence upon the prospects for freedom, prosperity, stability, and
security in the years ahead. To be sure, specific policy choices and ongoing political and economic configurations are serving to differentiate the
postcommunist states; *ex uno plura* is a plausible summary of this emerging reality. But the differentiation across the postcommunist landscape is
not random. The emergence of four relatively distinct groups of states
that are defined in terms of geographical regions – corresponding to the
nature and degree of postcommunist development toward economic and
political freedom – implies that deeply rooted forces are at work that im-
pel or constrain a given state's political and economic prospects. The four
regions may be defined broadly as:

- East-Central Europe, extending to the Baltic states and including
  Slovenia and Croatia
- Southeastern Europe, with Bosnia and Albania being understood as
  wards of the great powers
- The Slavic core of the former Soviet Union
- The Caucasus and Central Asia

As a general rule, it appears that the closer a given state is to "the West"
(conceived as the Group of Seven advanced industrial democracies) –
geographically, historically, economically, culturally, and diplomatically –
the greater are its chances for managing the intrinsic challenges of establishing simultaneously political democracy and market capitalism in a
mutually reinforcing and self-sustaining fashion. Interestingly, the countries that we may consider as consolidated capitalist democracies are
all located in East-Central Europe, whereas the consolidated repressive
regimes, with the exception of Belarus, are all located in Central Asia.
What we might consider the "in-between states" – those whose fundamental political and economic directions remain fluid, indeterminate, and
potentially unstable in the short- to medium-term future – are for the most
part located literally "in between" East-Central Europe and Central Asia.
(These classifications, which are detailed in this chapter based on research
conducted by the author in 1997 and 1998, are confirmed by the practical
test of preparedness of interested states in fulfilling the exacting political,

economic, legal, and institutional requirements for joining the European Union as of spring 2001.[12])

How are we to explain this close correspondence between political-economic direction and geographical location? Five factors appear to account for a given state's capacity to manage the dilemmas of the postcommunist transition. Two factors are historical in nature and concern the impact of the communist political-economic legacy and the legacy of imperialism in a given state; two additional factors concern political choices made in the last decade but are conditioned by the exit from both communism and imperialism, that is, the degree of political democratization and the degree of economic marketization undertaken; the fifth and final factor concerns the impact of the international environment – economically, diplomatically, and militarily – on a given transitional state. As we shall see, beyond a certain threshold of economic and political development, external factors arguably have had the greatest single impact upon a given state's ability to negotiate the path of economic, political, and social revolution in the wake of the communist collapse.

In this respect, Alexander J. Motyl has advanced a compelling explanation of the trajectory of postcommunist outcomes, arguing that the capacity of governments to undertake effective political and economic reforms is strongly influenced by historical legacies and in particular by two factors stemming from the legacy of the communist period: (a) the degree of totalitarianism experienced by a particular country, and (b) the degree of imperial rule experienced.[13] These legacies are important because it appears that the stronger the impact of totalitarianism and imperialism, the smaller the scope for the development of civil society and the growth of competent local governmental elites, respectively. As Motyl has framed the issue, countries that have a lesser degree of imperial rule have a greater capacity to embark on reform (in the form of qualified indigenous elites), whereas countries that avoided the harshest extremes of the totalitarian system over longer periods of time possess a greater capacity to respond to the reform process (in the form of a relatively active civil society). Polities with both features – less stringent totalitarian rule and predominance of native elites – are thus most able to embark successfully upon the path of reform. The East-Central European states, which alone have consolidated

---

[12] See the detailed table entitled "Status of the EU Accession Negotiations," *Frankfurter Allgemeine Zeitung* (English language edition), March 31, 2001, at www.FAZarchive.FAZ.net.

[13] Alexander J. Motyl, "Introduction," *Nations in Transit* (New York: Freedom House, 1997).

liberal political and economic systems, tended to exercise the most autonomy under the communist system. Motyl has noted that the actual degree of reform since 1989–91 correlates closely with the extent of totalitarianism and imperial rule, with the exceptions being mainly those states that have been involved in desperate military conflicts (that is, the former Yugoslavia, Armenia and Azerbaijan, Georgia and Tajikistan).

In short, the nature of the imperial legacy influences the nature and capacity of the state, whereas the nature of the totalitarian legacy influences the capacity of civil society. Both an effective state and a vital civil society are essential to a stable consolidation of democratic authority. To ask which comes first is to engage in "chicken and egg" argumentation: The relationship is an organic one that evolves over longer rather than shorter periods of time. Still, the skill of the gardener can make a decisive difference to the nature and prospects of the garden, so long as an organic rather than a mechanistic perspective is maintained.

In this respect, it seems warranted to take up a point mentioned but not developed by Motyl, that is, the relative impact of the international environment upon the political and economic transformations of the postcommunist states. Many of the dilemmas and difficulties of postcommunist reform have been analyzed by a broad range of scholars: the difficulty of building so many new social, economic, political, and other institutions from the ground up in the wake of the communist collapse; the problem of simultaneity, that is, constructing these new institutions at the same time when some – as the long and often painful evolution of the West suggests – are demonstrated prerequisites for the success of others; as well as the apparent tension between democratization and marketization, that is, in the short term disenfranchising large sectors of the country economically and socially while at the same time giving them the ballot to express their resentment at the putative cause of their immiseration. All postcommunist countries have been confronting these dilemmas. Certainly, some have been more successful than others in negotiating their way around the numerous pitfalls to earnest reformers. Yet are the differences in initial conditions among the postcommunist countries sufficient to account for the greater success of the East-Central European states in consolidating political and economic transformations? (Czechoslovakia, for instance, along with the German Democratic Republic and Romania, was arguably the most strictly controlled communist state between 1969–89, with almost no scope for civil society or economic experimentation before the collapse.) Consider also that the most successful case of democratization and marketization, as between 1945–9, has been imposed in Germany, that is, the incorporation of the German Democratic Republic – perhaps the most totalitarian of all the ex-communist countries – into the Federal Republic of Germany. By transferring about $100 billion per year over a decade into eastern Germany, the German state has fulfilled the function of a super Marshall Plan in the region.

Clearly, no other ex-communist state has remotely comparable prospects for economic integration into the G-7 world as has the ex-GDR. Yet just as clearly, some are much better positioned than others to obtain resources that can help them absorb some of the inevitable costs and instabilities of the postcommunist transition. It is now evident that Germany (and hence NATO and the European Union), out of an understandable interest in stabilizing its new eastern frontiers, will simply not allow Poland, the Czech Republic, and Hungary to remain outside the sphere of North Atlantic economic, political, and even security integration. Geography and size, as well as legacy and policy, matter. A comparison of trade, investment, and aid flows eastward underscores that a few countries, which happen to be those that are also able to make best use of the resources, are exceptionally well positioned to become absorbed into the North Atlantic world's political-economic-security community. Thus, direct foreign investment in Hungary between 1989–96, which amounted to just under $15 billion, accounts for about 10 percent of its GDP, while the figure for Russia, which attracted approximately $6 billion for the same period, is less than one-half of 1 percent of the country's GDP. That trend has continued through 2004.

Purely diplomatic attention matters as well. Across the southern periphery of the former Soviet Union, from Moldova through Georgia, Armenia, Chechnya, and Tajikistan, the Russian state has employed military force unilaterally without concern that by doing so it might call its broader relationship with the G-7 world into question.[14] By contrast, the persistent and demonstrable message from Western Europe and the United States in 1993 and 1994 that Russian resistance to withdrawal from the Baltic states would jeopardize Russian–Western relations reinforced rather than undermined a developing consensus in Moscow that the Baltic states were "different," in significant measure because the most powerful Western governments plausibly declared that they were different. The prospects for democracy in both the Baltic states and in Russia were thereby improved. Likewise, the admission, actual and prospective,

---

[14] Allen C. Lynch, "The Realism of Russian Foreign Policy," *Europe-Asia Studies*, vol. 53, no. 1 (January 2001), pp. 7–31.

of Hungary and Romania into NATO and the European Union have impelled these states to insulate the delicate issue of the substantial Hungarian minority in Romania from their bilateral relationship.

This should not be surprising. The period since 1989–91 is not the first or even the second liberal moment of the twentieth century. In the years before 1914 as well as in the mid-1920s, the fact that the most powerful states and empires in the world were also democracies in their core polities made it appear that liberal democracy was the wave of the future throughout much of the world. This emulation effect is quite common in world politics. Success is imitated, failure spurned. It was the inability of the Western world to manage its international relations more than the specific failure of democracy that saw the rise of new authoritarian and even fascist regimes throughout East-Central Europe in the mid-1930s, as the international successes of Nazi Germany and Fascist Italy (and fear of Bolshevism) appeared to presage an antidemocratic wave throughout the world. Today, in the postcommunist and post–cold war world order, the leading democratic state, the United States, is arguably more powerful relative to the next most powerful states than has been true of any Occidental polity since Imperial Rome during the Hadrian-Trajan apogee. (The U.S. military budget, for example, is larger than that of the next fifteen most powerful states combined; it is more than ten times that of the People's Republic of China; California's GDP is as large or larger than that of France and just smaller than that of Great Britain, depending on the dollar:euro exchange rate; 75 percent of all living Nobel Prize winners live and work in the United States, whereas the top ten U.S. universities outpace any foreign rivals.[15]) Among the next dozen or so most prosperous and powerful states, only China is not a democracy or aspiring to become one.

It flatters most Americans to imagine that the United States is strong because it is special; most of the world concluded long ago that the United States is special because it is strong. Democrats should actually take heart from such a reality, because it means that the power of the democratic world can serve to counteract and absorb some of the inevitable tensions and costs of the postcommunist transitions. The exercise of power, however, is never cost-free and seldom cheap. Absent the kinds of resources

---

[15] Stephen Brooks and William C. Wohlforth, "American Primacy in Perspective," *Foreign Affairs*, vol. 81, no. 4 (July/August 2002), pp. 20–33; "Das letzte Rom. Die Hypermacht: Ist Amerika zu stark fuer diese Welt? [The Last Rome: Is Hyperpower America Too Strong For This World?]" *Frankfurter Allegemeine Zeitung*, July 15, 2002, p. 29.

that the German state has been pumping into eastern Germany since 1990 (nearly $1 trillion), the choice of interventionist strategy becomes all important.

But where to focus attention? The European Bank for Reconstruction and Development (EBRD) has concluded that one of the main reasons for pessimism about economic prospects throughout the postcommunist region is the weakness of "institutions, policies and practices which underpin a well-functioning market economy and the investment that supports growth. In responding to these challenges, good governance will be crucial." In other words, the establishment of a competent state, one that is able to exercise the regulatory functions and legal consistency requisite to a modern market economy, is essential to translate the privatization of the former communist economies into productive and self-sustaining economic growth. In the critical area of financial institutions (banking reform, interest-rate liberalization, securities markets, and non-bank financial institutions), the EBRD adjudged that by the late 1990s not a single country among the twenty-five that it examined possesses "standards and performance norms of advanced industrial countries." The focus here is clearly on strengthening the state.[16]

On the other hand, a careful reading of recent annual editions of the U.S. State Department's Country Reports on Human Rights Practices shows that, outside of the East-Central European region, human rights are frequently abused by states that are too strong (because unaccountable) in the wrong areas, that is, in the ways that they treat their own citizens. Political and civil society are too weak to compel responsible human rights behavior on the part of the state. Consider the gravamen of abuses contained in a recent U.S. State Department Report on a state that the U.S. government throughout the 1990s considered one of the more hopeful democratic aspirants, that is, the Russian Federation:

- "Many members of the security forces, particularly within the internal affairs apparatus, [have] continued to commit human rights abuses...law enforcement and correctional officials tortured and severely beat detainees and inmates...virtually without restraint...."
- "[B]etween 10,000 and 20,000 detainees and prison inmates may die in penitentiary facilities annually...."

[16] European Bank for Reconstruction and Development, *Transition Report, 1997* (Paris: EBRD, 1997), www.ebrd.org.

- "Police and other security forces [have] continued their practice of targeting citizens from the Caucasus and darker-skinned persons in general for arbitary searches and detentions. . . ."
- "Lengthy pre-trial detention [has] remained a serious problem.[17] The Government made little progress in the implementation of constitutional provisions for due process, fair and timely trial, and humane punishment. In addition, the judiciary was often the subject of manipulation by political authorities. . . . Authorities infringed on citizens' privacy rights. . . ."[18]
- "While the President and the Government have supported human rights and democratic practices in their statements and policy initiatives, they have not institutionalized the rule of law required to protect them. While most abuses occur at lower levels and not by central direction, government officials do not investigate the majority of the cases of abuse and do not dismiss or discipline the perpetrators. . . ."
- "The judiciary does not yet act as an effective counterweight to other branches of government. . . ."
- "Domestic violence [against women] remains a major problem, as victims rarely have recourse to protection from the authorities. . . ."
- "The law establishes minimum conditions of workplace safety and worker health, but these standards are not effectively enforced."[19]

While the preceding language is taken from a U.S. government report on the Yeltsin period, it should be noted that Russian President Vladimir Putin specifically confirmed a number of these points in his annual address to the Russian nation on April 3, 2001, especially those concerning abuse of pretrial detention, ineffectiveness of the judiciary, and unreliability of the rule of law.[20] The Council of Europe reinforced these findings in a detailed report of June 2003.[21] (Incredibly, the acquittal rate in

---

[17] Those arrested may be held up to one and a half years pending pretrial investigation.

[18] See also Ana Uzelac, "Russia Reevaluates Court Sentencing and Amnesties," *Transitions Online* (Prague), March 30, 2001, www.tol.cz. Amnesties have become an economic necessity for the Russian prison system due to rampant overcrowding and the poverty of the system itself, which has become a breeder of tuberculosis and other infectious diseases.

[19] U.S. Department of State, *Country Reports on Human Rights Practices for 1996* (Washington, DC: US Government Printing Office, 1997), section on the Russian Federation. See subsequent annual volumes as well.

[20] See Putin's address to the Russian Federal Assembly of April 3, 2003, BBC Monitoring Service, Russia TV (Moscow), in Russian, 0800 gmt, April 3, 2001.

[21] "Le Conseil de l'Europe denonce les mauvais traitements dans les prisons russes," *Le Monde*, July 2, 2003, p. 5.

postcommunist Russia was reported in early 2001 at less than 1 percent of cases going to trial, as compared to the 5–7 percent that was typical of the ersatz justice of the Stalin period, which assigned quotas for acquittal.[22])

Clearly, under such conditions, an improvement in human rights practices involves the exertion of effective pressure upon existing governments, from within in the form of a stronger civil and political society and from without in the form of sustained international attention and appropriate incentives, positive and negative. In broad terms, an apparently contradictory picture emerges: The improvement of long-term economic prospects involves a strengthening of the state (within appropriate regulatory spheres), whereas the improvement of respect for human rights involves a weakening of the capacity of the state to act in arbitrary and capricious ways against its citizens, through a strengthening of civil society. Such a tension is real and cannot be wished away. Nevertheless, a careful comparable analysis of the postcommunist states suggests certain avenues of approach that may increase the scope of both economic progress and individual freedom. Consider the following rankings of these states that I have constructed, based on data and evaluation from the European Bank for Reconstruction and Development and the U.S. Department of State, as well as my own research. The rankings include an economic rating, based on a combination of GDP per capita (measured in terms of purchasing power parity), the coherence of the financial as well as legal institutions necessary for the functioning of a modern market economy, as well as the state's prospects for accession to the European Union, given the latter's exacting set of economic and institutional requirements. The political ranking is based on degree of respect for human rights, civil liberties, and due process of law by the government. The rankings are in descending order, according to the degree to which governmental practices promote modern market practice and respect for human rights and due process of law. Thus:

- The states performing at or very close to Western standards economically are the Czech Republic, Estonia, Hungary, and Poland; such states politically are the Czech Republic, Lithuania, and Slovenia.
- Those states approaching Western standards economically are Slovakia and Slovenia; politically, they are Estonia, Hungary, Latvia, and Poland.

[22] Uzelac, "Russia Reevaluates Court Sentencing and Amnesties."

- States that have made substantial progress in establishing and implementing Western standards of performance economically are Croatia, Latvia, and Lithuania; politically, they are Bulgaria, Macedonia, Romania, Moldova, Croatia, and Ukraine.
- A state where contradictory progress has been made in establishing and implementing Western standards economically is Russia; politically, it is also Russia.
- Substantial difficulties in establishing and implementing Western standards economically have been witnessed in Bulgaria, Georgia, Kazakhstan, Kyrgyzstan, Macedonia, Moldova, and Romania; politically, such states are Azerbaijan, Georgia, and Tajikstan.
- States where little or no progress is evident in establishing and implementing Western norms are, economically Albania, Armenia, Azerbaijan, Belarus, Bosnia-Herzegovina, Serbia/Montenegro, Tajikistan, Turkmenistan, and Ukraine; politically, Albania, Armenia, Belarus, Bosnia-Herzegovina, Kazakhstan, Serbia/Montenegro, Turkmenistan, and Uzbekistan.[23]

What inferences may be drawn from these comparisons? First, there is a broad, but by no means complete, correspondence between the coherence of governmental institutions in the economic area and respect for human rights and due process of law. In principle, then, strengthening the administrative capacity of the state need not mean weakening society or the rights of its constituent individuals. Second, a number of states with poorer economic records and less coherent state institutions in the financial and legal sectors generally respect the human rights of their citizens and observe due process of law. These include Bulgaria, Lithuania, Macedonia, and Romania. Third, certain states, especially Croatia, perform much less well in respect to human rights and due process than their levels of economic development and coherence of government institutions would otherwise suggest. Fourth, a number of states are either at, approaching, or making substantial progress toward approaching Western standards of both economic and human rights performance. These include the Czech Republic, Slovenia, Hungary, Estonia, Poland, Latvia, Lithuania, as well as Slovakia. Progress toward consolidating market democracy seems assured in these countries. Current Western policies of progressively integrating these states into North Atlantic

---

[23] See the annual publication of Freedom House, entitled *Nations in Transit*, for detailed evidence that largely supports these conclusions.

political, economic, and security institutions will only accelerate their consolidation of Western political and economic norms and practices. Fifth, a number of states have few prospects (or apparent desire) to establish Western-oriented norms in politics or economics. States whose leaders appear ill disposed in these directions include Turkmenistan, Tajikistan, and Belarus. Albania may have different intentions, but its state capacity is, like Bosnia's, so weak that it has few medium-term liberal prospects. Finally, a number of states are experiencing contradictory or slow progress in establishing Western-oriented economic and political norms, including Croatia, Russia, Bulgaria, Romania, Kyrgyzstan, Kazakhstan, Georgia, Macedonia, Moldova, Armenia, and Azerbaijan.

## IV. Conclusions on Russia Compared to East-Central Europe

What conclusions may we draw from these findings? First, in spite of a common starting point from the exit from communism between 1989–91, after a decade or so of experience with postcommunist political-economic dynamics, Russia finds itself in a fundamentally different situation from countries in East-Central Europe, including Poland, Hungary, the Czech Republic, Estonia, and Slovenia. These countries have consolidated recognizably democratic and capitalist institutional orders, whereas Russia's, at best, languishes in a kind of no-man's land of ambiguous and ambivalent political and economic transformations. By century's turn, governmental power in each of the latter countries had changed hands at least once without endangering democratic and capitalist foundations, whereas this had yet to happen in Russia. The emergence of a middle-ranking career intelligence officer in the form of Putin as the second Russian president is best understood in terms of a palace coup rather than in those of established electoral procedures.

In stark contrast to the East-Central European countries, where several prominent ex-dissidents in communist times had become heads of state (in Lithuania, Poland, and the Czech Republic), not one dissident has risen to the ranks of governmental authority at any level of importance in the post-Soviet Russian Federation. Strong private economic sectors, reinforced by rule of law and reasonably able civil services, were in place and significant sums of foreign direct investment were flowing into many East Central European countries to reinforce their market development and general orientation toward the North Atlantic world. According to our framework of analysis, this was possible because, although both Russia and the East European states may be scored low on the scale of "imperialism," that is, because native elites governed within the framework of the communist system, the East European experience of communism was significantly different from the Russian one, and can therefore be scored much lower on the scale of "totalitarianism." This is not simply a question of time, that Russia spent three-quarters of the twentieth century under communism compared to about forty years in Eastern Europe, years that were furthermore punctuated by popular uprisings in 1953 (East Germany and Czechoslovakia), 1956 (Poland and Hungary), 1968 (Czechoslovakia and Poland), and 1970 and 1980–1 (Poland). More to the point, compared to Russia, there was far greater scope throughout Eastern Europe for (legal) private agriculture, (legal) private niches in the service sector, for social forces such as Solidarity and institutional forces such as the Catholic Church, both in Poland, as well as for a much more intensive interaction with Western culture and societies.

Moreover, national memories and myths in the East European societies bound them up much more closely with Western Europe and North America than was true of either Russian elites or society. In effect, the political alternatives to the established communist elites were stronger in much of East-Central Europe between 1989–91 than was true in Soviet Russia, and there was more substance to the idea of a civil society in these countries as well. As a result, there tended to be a stronger commitment to break with the past throughout the political system than was true in Russia, and the society was somewhat better organized to reinforce the postcommunist elites in that undertaking. To this must be added the reinforcing effect of Western resources in the form of aid, investment, and debt relief (in the case of Poland amounting to half of its foreign obligations) that provided highly tangible incentives and impulses toward continued marketization and democratization. Although reform communists would come to power in Hungary, Poland, and Lithuania as early as 1993, thus confirming the tension between simultaneous democratization and marketization, in no country did this lead to, or even threaten to lead to, a reversal of the fundamental commitment to market-based economies and political democracy. In Russia, although communists have not taken power, the fact that the 1996 election was conducted in terms of choice of regime (as opposed to the performance of the government) and that the second president was chosen in a way to minimize exposure to the vicissitudes of a true electoral campaign suggests that the nature of the regime is far from settled. In this respect, Russia is indeed a case apart from the former communist countries of East-Central Europe. There was simply not enough time in the few years of the Gorbachev epoch (the reforms of which were in any event almost entirely driven from above) to develop the institutional and social mechanisms to compensate for the handicaps of the communist legacy. Political power and property were as intertwined at the end of the Gorbachev era as they were at the outset, and under the more chaotic circumstances of the disintegration of the state and its enforcement capabilities. Alternative elites and society were insufficiently strong and available external resources were insufficiently massive to improve Russia's prospects for a liberal democratic or even a social democratic future after communism, in spite of the evident will to do so under Gorbachev and in the early Yeltsin years.

At the same time, Russia has certainly progressed further in terms of both market and democratic development than have many other states in the former Soviet Union, even excluding those states such as Armenia, Azerbaijan, Moldova and Georgia that have been mired in interstate or interethnic conflict. Central Asian states such as Turkmenistan and Uzbekistan, as well as Belarus under President Aleksandr Lukaskenko, have made no pretense of liberalization in either the economic or political spheres. No doubt the institutional inheritance of the non-Russian republics of the Soviet Union was constrained by the predominance of Russian or russified Soviet elites in the Communist Party of the Soviet Union, the country's true governing agency. Unlike Russia, then, the formerly non-Russian republics of the Soviet Union thus score high on the scale of "imperialism," implying that their state structures face especially severe challenges in managing a transition to liberal politics and/or economics. Yet like Russia they also score high on the scale of totalitarianism, implying that their societies are ill suited to the task of civic participation and aggressive monitoring of the state that the transitional reform paradigm entails. Russia does share some striking similarities with Central Asian states such as Turkmenistan in the strength of each country's energy sector. The resources available from extraction of oil, natural gas, and so on, provide a relatively easy, steady, and impressive stream of funds into and through the hands of the ruling elites in each country, rendering those elites less interested in and less susceptible to popular accountability. The cushion that Russia's raw materials sector provides Russia's ruling elites tends to insulate those elites from difficult choices about the structure of the system that more resource-poor states cannot afford to delay.[24]

---

[24] Xavier Sala-i-Martin and Arvind Subramanian, "Addressing the Natural Resource Curse: An Illustration from Nigeria," National Bureau of Economic Research, Working Paper 9804, June 2003, at www.nber.org/papers/w9804.

From this point of view, Russia's situation, while possibly hopeless, is not necessarily serious.

## V. Russia Compared to the G-7 World

An implicit comparison of Russia to the West is contained in the liberal aspirations that both Russians and Westerners had for Russia at the turn of the 1990s. The basic assumption of radical market reform was that Russia, once rid of its communist institutional superstructure, would witness the virtually spontaneous emergence of market forces and democratic practices as they are known in the Western world. This expectation was no doubt reinforced by the dramatic success of democratization after the collapse of authoritarian regimes in Spain, Portugal, and Greece in the mid-1970s. These implicit analogies led to a drastic underestimation of the institutional requirements not so much for a successful exit from communism as for the successful consolidation of market democracy. Yet virtually the entire institutional structure of Soviet communism, which from a superficial angle might seem to differ from Western democratic and even authoritarian practice only in degree, was unsuited to function apart from the political conditions that gave rise to and sustained it, that is, the Communist Party's monopoly of political-economic power.

Soviet elections, for instance, were obviously not elections in the Western sense. Neither was the Communist Party a political party as the term is normally understood, but rather an agency for the perpetual and comprehensive control of the state, economy, and society. Soviet enterprises, while often creative in their solutions to the problems imposed by the central plan, could in no way be entrepreneurial in the capitalist sense of responding to market stimuli as defined by opportunity cost and marginal value (since there was in fact no way to calculate marginal value in the absence of a market).[25] Trade unions were not unions but rather agencies of the integrated planning mechanism designed in theory to extract maximum productive effort for minimum cost for the sake of the plan. Even Soviet cities were for the most part not cities in the Western sense of highly integrated and interdependent, organic socioeconomic and cultural concentrations but instead an agglomeration of Pullman settlements corresponding to the segmented and vertical interests of industrial, administrative, military, and ministerial

---

[25] Hedlund, *Russia "Market" Economy*, pp. 35–6.

interests.[26] Soviet-era institutions were thus not in a position to evolve organically in market democratic directions once the communist system disintegrated. Moreover, and unlike the postauthoritarian transitions to democracy in southern Europe, all of the postcommunist countries, and especially those in the former Soviet Union, were compelled to negotiate not simply a political transition but simultaneously an economic transition as well. An enormous institutional counterweight, sustained by massive resources, would thus have been required to lay the groundwork for a stable and coherent Russian transition to market democracy. Something comparable in impact to the Allied administration of Germany or the U.S. administration of Japan after 1945 would have been required. This challenge was in itself daunting enough. It seems clear that whatever chances there may have been for a more hopeful post-Soviet evolution, the actual strategies chosen by Russians and Westerners alike – deemphasis of the state, disregard for building institutions, conscious destruction of political consensus – decreased rather than increased those chances. As a result, Russia at the turn of the twenty-first century finds itself with a neopatrimonial rather than a liberal democratic or even a social democratic political economy, even though the forms of private property and representative democracy have been preserved (see Chapter 4 for details).

Is it true, though, that there are no instructive points of reference for Russia in the Western world? Johnathan Adelman has argued forcefully and thoughtfully that "Italian democracy offers hope for a distinctive Russian road to democracy."[27] Between 1944 and 1994, there was no alternation of political parties in Italy, as the Christian Democratic Party, able because of the cold war to neutralize the chance that the powerful Italian Communist Party might come to power, dominated every government over that half century, an impressive political feat by any standard. In spite of more than fifty formal changes of government in those fifty years, the Christian Democratic system stayed intact. In addition, this Italian quasidemocracy emerged from highly unfavorable historical antecedents, given the legacies of fascism, the Mafia, and civil war (1943–5) before

---

[26] James H. Bater, *The Soviet Scene: A Geographical Perspective* (London: Croom Helms, 1989), p. 132; Fiona Hill and Clifford Gaddy, *The Siberian Curse: How Soviet Planners Left Russia out in the Cold* (Washington, DC: Brookings Institution, 2003); Moshe Lewin, *The Gorbachev Phenomenon* (Berkeley, CA: University of California Press, 1990), p. 36; Sonja Margolina, *Russland: Die Nichtzivile Gesellschaft* [Russia: The Uncivil Society] (Hamburg: Rowohr, 1994); Gerd Ruge, *Sibirishces Tagebuch* [Siberian Diary] (Munich: Knaur, 2000), p. 102 and passim.

[27] Johnathan Adelman, *Torrents of Spring* (New York: McGraw-Hill, 1994), pp. 334–5.

1945, and constant corruption, again the Mafia, political scandal, political alienation, and terrorism after 1945. Moreover, votes for nondemocratic parties (the communists and the neofascists) regularly amounted to 40 percent of the electorate. As in Russia, the Italian economy has been characterized by a massive and inefficient interweaving of state and property, with the government regularly disposing of more than 50 percent of the country's (legal) GDP, and a politicized judiciary. Adelman concludes that, even taking the obvious differences into account, especially the overall level of economic development and membership in the European Union, "the case of troubled, and even at times bizarre, Italian democracy in the postwar era shows that democracy can flourish in many diverse settings. This offers some genuine hope for Russia creating its own form of democracy."[28]

Allowing for the force of this argument, it may be instructive to return to Putnam, whose work on good government in the Italian setting frames the introduction to this chapter. The focus of Putnam's work is why northern and southern Italy came to have such different political cultures and governing capacity. Adelman's invocation of the Italian example should thus be qualified by this geographical dimension: Which Italy do we have in mind when we speak of "Italy" – north or south? Putnam concludes, with Russia in mind:

> Where norms of civic engagement are lacking, the outlook for collective action appears bleak. The fate of the [Italian south] is an object lesson for the Third World today and the former Communist lands of Eurasia tomorrow, moving slowly [as they are] toward self-government. The "always defect" social equilibrium may represent the future of much of the world where social capital is limited or nonexistent. For political stability, for governmental effectiveness, and even for economic progress, social capital may be even more important than physical or human capital. Many of the formerly Communist societies had weak civic traditions before the advent of Communism, and totalitarian rule abused even that limited stock of social capital. Without norms of reciprocity and networks of civic engagement, the Hobbesian outcome of the [Italian south] – amoral familism, clientelism, lawlessness, ineffective government, and economic stagnation – seems likelier than successful democratization and economic development. Palermo may represent the future of Moscow.[29]

Southern Italy is still part of Italy. While northern Italians complain about it, the fact is that the rest of Italy is able to bring economic and administrative resources of various sorts to bear to contain the implicit

---

[28] Ibid., p. 335.
[29] Putnam, *Making Democracy Work*, p. 183.

ungovernability of the Italian south. Sicily and its environs are just part of the Italian whole. The afflictions that we have diagnosed in Russia affect Russia as a whole. The next chapter addresses the question: Whence are the resources to come to move Russia toward a viable economic and political equilibrium?

## VI. Other Points of Comparison

### A. *Weimar Germany*

Perhaps the most popular comparison to have been made with post-Soviet Russia is that with Weimar Germany, the classic case of the failure of a transitional democratic regime. Certainly, there are a number of unsettling similarities in the situations that the two countries found themselves in after the collapse of German authoritarianism and Soviet totalitarianism, respectively. Generally, both Weimar Germany and postcommunist Russia can be situated within the following conditions:

- Collapse of empire
- Loss of historical borderlands
- Old elites unreconciled to a lost war
- New elites frustrated by difficulties in integration into the Western world
- Political dependence on military and/or paramilitary forces
- Weak democratic traditions
- Strong authoritarian roots
- Episodes of high inflation destroying savings of population
- A massive depression followed by a collapse in living standards

In some respects, one could argue that the situation in Russia is even more dramatic than that in Weimar Germany insofar as Russia had to create an entirely new kind of economic order with the political, foreign policy, and other challenges adumbrated previously. It seems fair to accept that the accumulated weight of these circumstances dooms Russia's chances to develop a politically responsive democracy and a legally regulated capitalism in any foreseeable future. But this is a long way from accepting a second implication of the Weimar analogy, that is, that Russia is likely to follow the Weimar example in giving rise to an extremist government actuated by militarist ambitions. At this point, the analogy becomes much less convincing, for reasons that do not help Russia's democratic and market prospects. There are sufficient differences in the economic, military, social, and political spheres to suggest that the reconstitution of a strong and centralized Russian state should be among the least of our worries. First, given the generalized collapse and obsolescence of the Russian industrial base, the kind of military Keynesianism used to revive the Nazi German economy in the mid-1930s is simply not possible. Germany, like the United States at the time, faced a depression rooted in a massive macroeconomic disequilibrium between supply and demand; government spending, for social or military purposes, could temporarily substitute for that lagging demand. Each country's industrial base was fundamentally intact and highly competitive internationally. By contrast, the Russian depression is rooted in a decade-long process of unreplenished capital depreciation. Russia's physical infrastructure is disintegrating. Even if the will to remilitarize were present, the means to do so would not be present.

Second, the Russian military appears to be too divided to act as an independent force in the political system. Political intervention would likely shatter the military's remaining organizational integrity, a fact of which the military's leadership appears to be all too well aware. Latin American coup scenarios thus do not apply. Third, Russian society itself remains mostly poorly organized and perhaps more importantly deeply cynical about the proposition that collective action can make any positive difference to their lives, a despair about the future that is no doubt reflected in Russia's frightening demographic trends.[30] Relatedly, with the partial exception of the Communist Party of the Russian Federation, no reasonably well-organized crossnational or crossregional political parties are capable of mobilizing significant constituencies on behalf of reasonably coherent agendas with an aim to assume responsibility to govern.[31] Paradoxically, the very weakness of Russian society, so unlike the highly structured (and polarized) political society of Weimar Germany, gives reason to suppose that, while a democratic outcome for Russia is improbable, so is the post-Weimar scenario of an adventurist, militarist Russia.

### B. Communist China

Since 1979, the People's Republic of China has shown that reform communism is possible. A series of reforms, predominantly economic but

---

[30] On the eve of the December 2003 parliamentary elections, the independent Russian polling agency VTsIOM found that 70 percent of respondents had little or no interest in the campaign. According to sociologist Oleg Saveleyev, "many people are indifferent to the campaign because they think they already know the results." Oksana Yablokova, "Most Voters Don't Care, Survey Finds," *Moscow Times*, November 24, 2003, in *Johnson's Russia List*, #7434, November 24, 2003, item 3, at www.cdi.org.

[31] Stephen E. Hanson and Jeffrey S. Kopstein, "The Weimar/Russia Comparison," *Post-Soviet Affairs*, vol. 13, no. 3 (1997), pp. 252–83.

extending to political reforms at the local level and legal reform more broadly, resulted in a doubling of China's GDP every decade, leading arguably to the greatest improvement in human living standards in history. By the turn of the twenty-first century, China's GDP, as measured in terms of purchasing power parity, was five times that of Russia's, while amazingly China's per capita GDP was beginning to approach that of Russia. Why has China succeeded where first the Soviet Union and now the Russian Federation have failed?

Certain aspects of China's reforms seem inapplicable to Russia. Perhaps most importantly, because China was still 80 percent rural (compared to 80 percent urban for Russia) at the outset of the reforms, it was possible to secure significant early gains from efficiencies in the agricultural sector.[32] Only later was the reform extended to the service sector and urban areas, and even so the unfolding of the reform process has been carefully regulated.[33] For example, the Chinese government, unlike the Russian government, has made a critical distinction between freeing the movement of trade and freeing the movement of capital. Second, and implicit in this, Chinese reformers were able to consolidate their political authority rapidly at the end of the 1970s largely because of the discrediting of the old guard caused by the massively disruptive Cultural Revolution toward the latter years of Mao Tse-Tung's rule. The Soviet old guard, which traced its origins to the consequences of Stalin's purges in the late 1930s, was by comparison much more intact upon Gorbachev's coming to power in 1985. The attempted coup of August 1991 demonstrates just how unreconciled powerful elements of the Soviet establishment had been to Gorbachev's reform efforts from very early on and thus how much energy Gorbachev had to expend upon tactical political maneuvers.

Where the Chinese reforms appear instructive for a country such as Russia is in the nature of the reforms as distinct from their specific programmatic content. China's economic reforms have been sector-specific, they have been gradual, and they have been extended to other sectors in stages, all while the political sphere has been held relatively constant. This is not to make a brief for communist politics. Rather, it was the unimpeachably anticommunist philosopher Karl Popper who cautioned against wholesale and complex social engineering, due to the impossibility of controlling for the interdependent and inevitably unanticipated,

[32] Alexei D. Voskressenski, *Russia and China: A Theory of Inter-State Relations* (London: RoutledgeCurzon, 2003), pp. 197–9.
[33] Thane Gustafson, *Capitalism Russian Style* (Cambridge, UK: Cambridge University Press, 1999), p. xi.

unintended consequences of such interventions in the body social.[34] In retrospect, it appears that it was Gorbachev's effort to revolutionize simultaneously the Soviet economic and political systems that triggered the Soviet collapse; the same appears true of the Russian 1990s. President Putin appears to have learned that lesson.

## C. *The Postcolonial World*

It may appear provocative to compare Russia's post-Soviet circumstances to the postcolonial world, but consider the following characteristics of Russian political-economic life in relationship to what much of formerly colonial Asia and especially Africa experienced upon independence between the late 1940s and late 1960s:

- The collapse of empire (true of Russia and the entire postcolonial world, by definition)
- The collapse of an entire institutional order (true of Russia and especially of the post-Belgian Congo and post-Portuguese Angola and Mozambique; not true, for example, in post-British India)
- The predominance in the economy of extraction and export of natural resources over manufacturing for the domestic market; a high level of dependence on international financial institutions, as exemplified by high ratios of debt servicing to GDP; an economic pattern characterized by the predatory depletion of resources made available by antecedent investment supporting luxury lifestyles for the elites rather than investment in future production; macroeconomic policies designed to please creditor G-7 states and the international lending agencies rather than revive domestic production (true of Russia and much of sub-Saharan Africa)
- An unresponsive political order characterized by elections without accountability, poor institutional development, powerful executives and weak legislatures, and no evident will of elites to lose power through genuinely free elections.

Indeed, compared to British India, where liberal empire prevailed and a very small British contingent of soldiers and administrators ruled for the most part indirectly through local Indian notables, thus paving the way for a pluralist postcolonial political order, post-Soviet Russia may be at a disadvantage in terms of democratic possibilities. Given Russia's

---

[34] Karl Popper, *The Open Society and Its Enemies* (Princeton, NJ: Princeton University Press, 1963).

persistent challenge of establishing effective public authority and the parasitic rather than productive patterns by which so much of Russia's wealth is accumulated, analogies with postcolonial sub-Saharan Africa and states such as Haiti appear instructive.[35] Of course, Russia disposes of certain distinctive advantages. These include, first, a still massive reserve of natural resources, especially oil and natural gas, that tend to cushion the impact of Russia's economic malaise, reduce the political urgency of instituting far-reaching structural reforms, and lend political credence to the argument that Russia can go it alone, if need be, as a resource-rich, continental economy. Second, in spite of "protracted state crisis" in both Africa and post-Soviet Eurasia, the remnant of the state is still much stronger in Russia than is the case throughout sub-Saharan Africa, a fact that – together with energy receipts – has allowed Putin to consolidate a neopatrimonial, hyperpresidentialist political order.[36] Third, unlike most countries, Russia possesses thousands of nuclear weapons, many of which can easily strike the United States. This leads many Russian elites to conclude, not without considerable justification, that the Western world will treat Russia as a special case, to which the normal rules of international intercourse need not apply. The experience of the 1990s, in which an insolvent Russia received $200 billion in capital resources from Western governments and creditor institutions, is instructive in this regard.[37] It is another question altogether as to whether either Russia or the West actually benefits from this peculiar dispensation.

## VII. Conclusion

This discussion of post-Soviet Russia in comparative perspective has the aim not only of attempting to improve our understanding of Russia's location and likely trajectory along the path of postcommunist political and economic development but also of clarifying our thinking about how the outside world might engage Russia to maximize the advancement of its interests in respect to Russia. Implicitly or explicitly, our points of comparison with Russia entail focal points for the orientation of policy toward Russia. If, for example, our main terms of external reference in

---

[35] See Mark Beissinger and Crawford Young, eds., *Beyond State Crisis? Post-Colonial Africa and Post-Soviet Eurasia in Comparative Perspective* (Washington, DC: Woodrow Wilson Center Press, 2002).

[36] Ibid., pp. 6, 118–20.

[37] Ibid., p. 123; also Joseph Stiglitz, *Globalization and Its Discontents* (New York: W. W. Norton, 2002), pp. 133–79.

thinking about Russia derive from the experience of the North Atlantic world, we shall be tempted to urge the adoption of rules and practices that appear to have proven their worth in that particular historical and institutional context. For much of the 1990s, this meant urging from without and reinforcing from within Russian choices to liberalize prices, privatize state property, and achieve macroeconomic balance, with little regard for the institutional prerequisites and political sensibilities that make those policies reasonable ones in the Western world.[38] In any event, the premise that viable markets and responsive polities would emerge almost spontaneously from the miasma of Soviet disintegration has been decisively falsified and no longer has any takers in Russian politics. If, by contrast, we take as our external point of reference postcolonial Africa, we shall be sensitive to the requirement of establishing and consolidating effective governmental jurisdiction over the state, legal system, and macroeconomy. The challenge in Russia, as in much of sub-Saharan Africa today, is to find a way to accomplish this without access to the kinds of external resources comparable to those that were historically brought to bear by responsible imperial rule. If our external reference point is Weimar Germany, we should be concerned with integrating, appeasing, and subsidizing Russia so as to compensate for the dearth of civic, social, and political capital in the country. But if so, which middle-class majorities in which Western polities are going to agree to be taxed in order to subsidize which parasitic Russian elites? Finally, if our external point of comparison is communist China, we shall tend to focus on stabilizing the political order as a precondition to improving the economic order. The question that then arises is how to accomplish this under Russian circumstances and how the state should go about bringing order and direction to the economy. The next chapter is devoted to this question.

---

[38] Chua, *World on Fire*; Stiglitz, *Globalization and Its Discontents*.

# 6

# What Future for Russia?

## Liberal Economics and Illiberal Geography

> The whole history of our state has been a search for ways to settle and provide stimuli to settle Siberia.
>
> – Leonid Drachevsky, Russian President Putin's plenipotentiary "prefect" for Siberia.[1]

> Thanks to the industrialization and mass settlement of Siberia . . . Russia's population is scattered across a vast land mass in cities and towns with few principal connections between them. . . . One-third of the population has the added burden of living and working in particularly inhospitable climatic conditions. . . . Costs of living are as much as <u>four times as high</u> as elsewhere in the Russian Federation, while costs of industrial production are sometimes higher.[2]
>
> – Fiona Hill and Clifford Gaddy, authors of *The Siberian Curse: How Communist Planners Left Russia out in the Cold*

## I. Introduction

Having experienced a probably unprecedented economic decline throughout the 1990s, Russia finished the decade and entered the new millennium with unexpectedly good economic news. After the 70 percent drop in the ruble's value in August 1998, Russian domestic production picked up. The multiplication of world oil prices since then – between January 1999 and summer 2000, the price of oil increased from $9 to $35 per barrel,

---

[1] Ian Traynor, "For Siberia, a Return to Wasteland," *Guardian* (UK), June 12, 2002, p. 1.
[2] Fiona Hill and Clifford Gaddy, *The Siberian Curse: How Communist Planners Left Russia out in the Cold* (Washington, DC: Brookings Institution Press, 2003), p. 2.

TABLE 8. *Russian GDP Growth, 1992–2003 (in %)*

| 1992 | 1993 | 1994 | 1995 | 1996 | 1997 | 1998 | 1999 | 2000 | 2001 | 2002 | 2003 |
|------|------|------|------|------|------|------|------|------|------|------|------|
| −14  | −8.7 | −13  | −4   | −3.5 | +1.5 | −5.5 | +6.5 | +10  | +5   | +4   | +6   |

while in mid-2004, after the U.S.-led invasion of Iraq, the price approached $45[3]) – has filled Russian state coffers to an unanticipated extent, enabling the state to finance the war in Chechnya and still meet its external debt-servicing obligations as well as wages and pension arrears at home. Russian gross domestic product (GDP) has experienced five consecutive years of impressive growth, following a decade of progressive contraction, as Table 8 illustrates.[4]

Russia's fledgling stock market was the highest performing in the world in 2001 and 2003, while in January 2004 Standard and Poor's upgraded Russia's international rating to "top speculative grade" and its domestic debt to the lowest investment grade level.[5] Investment, real income, and exports increased steadily between 2000–3 while Gazprom, the state-dominated natural gas monopoly, has posted impressive profits while also sustaining a significant investment profile, scheduled for $8.5 billion in 2004.[6] In addition, long-term gas contracts totaling $250 billion were concluded between Russia and the European Union, guaranteeing Russia one-fourth of the West European natural gas market for the next ten to fifteen years. New oil and gas pipelines were opened in the Baltic and the Black Sea regions. Correspondingly, Russian state coffers remained in the black, reflecting an impressive current account surplus of $39–40 billion in 2003 (that is, 9 percent of the dollarized GDP) and larger surpluses in preceding years going back to 2000. Foreign exchange reserves totaled more than $82 billion as of late January 2004, thus enabling Russia to continue servicing an external debt (at about $120 billion) comparable to that which caused the Argentine government to default at the outset of 2002.[7]

---

[3] *Le Monde*, January 7–8, 2002, p. 2; *Neue Zuercher Zeitung*, July 19, 2002, p. 24.

[4] Associated Press (Moscow), May 3, 2001, citing a report by Goskomstat, the Russian state statistical agency; Oksana Dmitrieva, "Economic Myths Debunked," *Moscow Times*, July 3–9, 2002, at www.moscowtimes.ru; *Economist*, July 27, 2002, p. 90; David Owen and David O. Robinson, "Russia Rebounds," December 11, 2003, at www.imf.org; Prime-Tass (Moscow), January 8, 2004, at www.amcham.ru.

[5] *Financial Times*, January 28, 2004, at www.ft.com.

[6] Ibid.; Prime-Tass (Moscow), November 20, 2003.

[7] *Economist*, July 27, 2002, p. 90; *Moscow Times*, January 30, 2004, p. 6; *Rossiyskaya Gazeta*, December 28, 2001, citing Russian Prime Minister Mikhail Kasyanov, at www.rg.ru.

The 2003 foreign trade surplus approached $60 billion, also reflecting the pattern of recent years.[8]

On the political front, the news was equally striking. After the terror bombings of September 11, 2001, Russian President Putin placed his country foursquare behind U.S. policy in the war against international terror. Openly disregarding the views of his senior generals, eighteen of whom published an open letter in the Russian press protesting the alignment of Russia's foreign policy with that of the United States and the stationing of U.S. forces in the formerly Soviet republics of Uzbekistan and Tajikistan, on the Afghan border, Putin proved to be one of the United States' most important allies in the U.S. war in that unfortunate country. This remarkable shift in the tenor of the bilateral Russian–American relationship was reflected in the relative equanimity with which the Russian president reacted to the U.S. announcement in December 2001 that it would abandon the 1972 Anti-Ballistic Missile (ABM) Treaty, as well as in the restraint with which Russia (unlike France) dissented from the U.S. war policy toward Iraq in late 2002 and early 2003. Putin appeared to be committed to shaping a truly substantial bilateral relationship with Washington, one in which no particular issue could be deemed worthy of undermining that relationship and in the process jeopardize Russia's standing in the Western world, where Putin had clearly placed his bets.[9] Domestically, Putin's approval ratings stood at 70–80 percent throughout his first term in office,[10] while some of his policies seemed to be yielding fruit. For instance, the establishment of a "flat" tax rate of 13 percent on personal income appeared to trigger a 50 percent increase in tax revenues from individuals, thereby further solidifying the fiscal balance of the Russian government.[11] The federal government's budget for 2002 was thus the first of the post-Soviet era with a targeted surplus.[12] The government was even able to establish for the first time a small contingency fund of approximately $3 billion.

[8] Peter Westin, "Opinion: 2003 Balance of Payment Numbers Need Extra Analysis," Prime-Tass (Moscow), January 12, 2004, at www.amcham.ru.

[9] For a supporting analysis by the chair of Russia's advisory Foreign Policy and Defense Council, see Sergei Karaganov, "Novye vyzovy bezopasnosti i rossiyskaya politika" [New Security Challenges and Russian Policy], in Vyacheslav Nikonov, ed., *Sovremennaya Rossiyskaya Politika* [Contemporary Russian Politics] (Moscow: OLMA-PRESS, 2003), 185–97.

[10] Interfax (Moscow), December 26, 2001.

[11] "Russian Economic Situation: What Should We Expect?" *Trud* (Moscow), December 27, 2001, at *JRL*, #5617, December 27, 2001, item no. 7.

[12] Owen and Robinson, "Russia Rebounds."

## II. Structural or Conjunctural Factors in Russia's Favor?

The short-term picture for the Russian economy is thus rosier than many anticipated in the aftermath of the Russian financial crash of August 1998. Yet, as the effort in January 2001 by the Russian government to escape responsibility for its Soviet-era debt implies, the structural fundamentals of the Russian economy are hardly as strong as the recent conjunctural data would appear to suggest.[13] For example, the Economist Intelligence Unit has calculated that fully 60 percent of Russian economic growth since 1999 is accounted for by the rise in world oil prices and the devaluation of the ruble in 1998.[14] For all of 2003, following five years of consecutive economic growth, net direct foreign investment in the Russian economy actually declined, with an outflow of $100 million for the year.[15] Overall, as of early 2004, Russia was calculated to have the lowest ratio of accumulated foreign direct investment of any country in postcommunist Europe, save possibly Tajikistan and Uzbekistan.[16]

These and other indicators – for example, an increase in imports due to the real increase in the ruble's value as a result of relatively high domestic inflation – suggest that the robust performance of the Russian economy in 1999–2003 is the product of temporary conjunctural factors rather than of sound fundamentals in the economy itself, as Table 9, detailing the share of imports in Russian retail trade, suggests.[17]

---

[13] On January 5, 2001, the Russian government announced that it would withhold payments of $1.5 billion on $48 billion of intergovernmental debt owed to the Paris Club of creditor states that was due in the first quarter of 2001. Clearly, this represented a diplomatic gambit, not pressing financial necessity (the government subsequently backed down from its claim, faced with universal Western rejection): In 2000, the Russian government serviced $10.5 billion of external obligations without borrowing; the government also paid Cuba $200 million to operate an electronic intelligence center, and on his December 2000 visit to Havana Russian President Putin granted the Cuban government a credit of $110 million. *Frankfurter Allgemeine Zeitung*, January 16, 2001, at www.FAZ.DE; *Le Monde.*

[14] Laza Kekic, "How Dependent Is Growth on the Oil Price?" *St. Petersburg Times*, February 3, 2004, p. 9.

[15] Westin, "Opinion."

[16] Alex Nicholson, "Foreign Capital Sinks to a New Low," *Moscow Times*, January 12, 2004, at *JRL*, #8009, January 12, 2004, item no. 7, at www.cdi.org; Westin, "Opinion." Also *International Herald Tribune*, August 17–18, 2002, p. 3.

[17] Economist Intelligence Unit, *Country Forecast for Russia* (July 2003), available at www.amcham.ru; "Schelte des russischen Regierungschef: Ruegen wegen zu hoher Teuerung [The Russian Prime Minister Scolds: Blame for Too High Taxes]," *Neue Zuercher Zeitung*, July 19, 2002, p. 19.

TABLE 9. *Share of Imports in Russian Retail Trade, 1997–2002*

| Period | Share (%) |
|---|---|
| Before August 1998: | > 50 |
| 1999 | 30 |
| 2000 | 35 |
| 2001 | 45 |
| 2002 | 45 |

The question therefore arises of the extent to which the Russian economy's undoubted strong performance in the past five years can be separated from such conjunctural and largely external factors that can neither be replicated nor planned for.[18] Indeed, Swedish economist Stefan Hedlund – reinforcing the view of the Economist Intelligence Unit – has calculated that once one takes into account the stimulus to domestic production provided by devaluing the ruble against the dollar from 8:1 to 24:1 in August 1998, as well as the subsequent boost to Russian coffers provided by the trebling of world oil prices from $10 to $35 per barrel between August 1998 and 2000, there were in fact few other sources of growth in the Russian economy.[19] (World Bank calculations for mid-2003 sustained this view.[20]) Russia's ability to meet its external debt and internal social obligations, as well as levels of domestic investment, hinges on a satisfactory price for world oil. In 2004, Russia's federal state budget was targeted to balance at an average world price of oil of $20 per barrel, while projections of economic growth of 4.1 percent hinged on an oil price of $23 per barrel.[21] Given that oil and gas receipts account for the majority of profits of Russian firms as well as 40–50 percent of Russian governmental revenues – though employing just 3 percent of the Russian workforce – the continuing and precarious dependence of the Russian economy and the Russian state on the energy sector and thus the global energy market

---

[18] For a comprehensive overview of Russia's economic condition and prospects, see John Hardt, ed., *Russia's Uncertain Economic Future: Compendium of Papers Submitted by the Joint Economic Committee of the U.S. Congress* (Washington, DC: U.S. Government Printing Office, 2002), also at www.access.gpo.gov/congress/joint/sjoint03.html.

[19] For a supportive analysis, see Boris Kagarlitsky, "The Riddle of Putin," December 22, 2001, at www.zvet.org.

[20] World Bank, *Russian Economic Report* (August 2003), at www.worldbank.org.ru.

[21] Prime-Tass (Moscow), December 12, 2003. See also Erin E. Arvelund, "Russian Growth Accelerated, Stoked by Oil," *New York Times*, January 7, 2004, at www.nytimes.com.

becomes readily apparent.[22] (In both 1986 and 1998, the near collapse of
the global oil market to $10 per barrel threw the Soviet and then Russian
economies into a tailspin that upended the political programs of Mikhail
Gorbachev and Boris Yeltsin, respectively.)

Second, the weight of the evidence indicates that Russian economic
growth and profits are mainly concentrated in the energy and raw materials sectors, which have rich export possibilities, as opposed to the still
physically massive manufacturing sector, on which most Russian employment depends and which, outside of parts of the arms industry, has few
export opportunities. Boom times in the raw materials export sectors do
have a kind of "trickle-down" effect to other sectors of the economy and
society (as well as to the government), but they remain of a secondary
nature and exceptionally sensitive to changes in the external terms of
trade. To a large extent, the budgeting projections of the Russian government, its external debt servicing, and its ability to meet certain basic
social obligations (such as pensions), as well as the political standing of
the government, are governed by the international energy market, reflecting typical Third World patterns of political-economic development. The
Russian population as a whole simply does not possess the purchasing
power to act as a sustained stimulus for the economy. The consumer
poverty of Russia at large is reflected in the fact that fully 30 percent of all
retail spending in the country takes place in Moscow, with no more than
7 percent of the country's population, while 25–45 percent of turnover
in the service sector is accounted for by just two cities, Moscow and St.
Petersburg.[23] Russia's two historical capitals also account for 54 percent
of Russia's imports.[24] Based on consumption patterns, fully 60 percent of
the Russian population may be considered to be poor, while 25 percent
of the population earns less than the officially determined "subsistence
minimum." The Russian "middle class" remains almost exclusively a
Moscovite phenomenon.[25]

---

[22] Moises Naim, "If Geology Is Destiny, Then Russia Is in Trouble," *New York Times*,
April 12, 2003; idem, "Russia's Oily Future," *Foreign Policy*, January/February 2004,
pp. 96–7.

[23] Karl Emerick Hanuska, "Amid Global Gloom, More Russians Have Cash To Shop,"
*Reuters*, December 31, 2001; A. Yu. Skopkin, *Ekonomicheskaya Geografiya Rossii* [Russian
Economic Geography] (Moscow: Prospekt, 2003), p. 317.

[24] Gabriele Lueke and Gustav Weber, eds., *So Kommen Sie nach...Russland: Der
Wirtschaftswegweiser fuer den Mittelstand* [Guide to the Russian Economy for the Small-
and Medium-Sized Businessperson] (Munich: Primeverlag, 2003), p. 397.

[25] Economist Intelligence Unit, *Country Forecast for Russia.*

Third, the state of Russia's public health continues to deteriorate at an alarming rate, further suggesting that Russia's recent economic growth is far from a recovery and narrowly rather than broadly based. Continuing a trend that began in the first post-Soviet years, deaths continue to exceed births by seven hundred thousand to eight hundred thousand per year, while male life expectancy remains under sixty years.[26] Paradoxically, perhaps, Russian polls register exceptionally low levels of societal trust in public institutions, including now the army, yet Russians have not engaged in any significant political mobilization to assert the views and interests of social groups or classes as against other groups or the government itself.[27] In another paradox, Russia has held every major election as scheduled since 1989, yet the executive branch of the Russian government, under Putin perhaps even more so than under Yeltsin, remains largely unaccountable to the formal agencies of government or to what counts as civil society in Russia. Indeed, it was this very autonomy of his office that allowed Putin to align Russia so clearly and so rapidly with the United States in September 2001, against the clearly expressed preference of the bulk of Russia's foreign policy and national security elites.[28]

## III. Infrastructure, Asset Depreciation, and Direct Capital Investment

Finally, Russia remains confronted by a profound structural problem that, if not solved, has the potential of perpetuating Russia's economic status as a peripheral raw materials state critically dependent on external terms of trade for its economic and political viability: the crisis of Russia's capital infrastructure, which has been allowed to deteriorate to the point where in time it may be possible to speak of Russia as little more than an enclave economy. In spite of the first significant upsurge in capital investment in a decade,[29] the Russian economy possesses an increasingly obsolescent capital stock requiring annual investment of at least $50 billion per year over the next two decades simply to rebuild the existing infrastructure grid,

---

[26] Mikhail Antonov, "Money Tests," *Rossiyskaya Gazeta*, December 28, 2001, at *JRL*, #5618, December 28, 2001, item no. 8.

[27] Alexei Vladimirov, "The Investment Situation in Russia," June 6, 2001, at *JRL*, #5282, June 4, 2001, item no. 10.

[28] For an analysis of their views, see William Zimmerman, *The Russian People and Foreign Policy* (Princeton, NJ: Princeton University Press, 2002), p. 55.

[29] As detailed in *Investitsii v Rossii, 2003* [Investment in Russia, 2003] (Moscow: Goskomstat, 2003), covering the period 1995–2002.

TABLE 10. *Indices of Russian Capital Investment*

| | |
|---|---|
| Foreign Investment in Russia, Jan–June 2002: | $8.368 billion |
| Russian Investment Abroad, Jan–June 2002: | $10.046 billion |

*Source:* Interfax (Moscow), August 12, 2002.

not to mention develop one that is more appropriate to a market-based economy.[30] Unless Russia can reverse the massive net outflow of capital, it is hard to see how Russia as a whole, as distinct from certain raw materials-based enclaves, and the sectors associated with them, can be developed. Unlike in the Soviet past, capital can no longer be coerced, even if at exorbitant human and economic costs, from society at large. Rather, as is the case almost everywhere else in the world, holders of capital, whether they be Russian or not, must be persuaded that their chances of acceptable return are greater in Russia than in other investment locales. As Sergei Witte, Russia's great modernizing finance minister at the turn of the twentieth century put it:

Capital, like knowledge, knows no fatherland. Once wealth is created, it flows where it is needed the most, where it is valued the highest, where it can best be utilized....

Without solid confidence in the security of his person and property, without a clear assurance about property rights and a reliable defense of these rights through the law ... [the potential investor] will be paralyzed by fear of losing his money and savings will in the best case be limited to the flight to gold and silver, as well as precious metals, in other words, to the accumulation of dead capital.[31]

Tables 10 and 11 illustrate the challenge facing Russia in attracting net investment and reversing the widespread depreciation of the country's capital infrastructure.

It is essential to Russia's prospects that the recent upsurge in capital investment be maintained. Yet it should be noted that fully three-fifths of Russia's direct capital investment are in sectors tied closely to the state, that is, oil and gas (for example, Gazprom), electricity (UES), transportation (including the oil and gas pipeline network), as well as housing and utilities. By contrast, the machine-building sector received just 3 percent

---

[30] For an overview of Russia's infrastructure requirements, see V. D. Andrianov, *Rossiya v mirovoy ekonomike* [Russia in the world economy] (Moscow: Vlados, 1999), pp. 222–46, as well as Hill and Gaddy, *The Siberian Curse.*

[31] As cited in N. V. Kurys', *Inostrannye Investitsii: Rossiyskaya Istoriya* [Foreign Investment in Russian History] (St. Petersburg: Yuridicheskiy Tsentr, 2003), pp. 7, 64.

TABLE 11. *Rate of Growth in Russian Capital Formation, 1995–2003*

| Year | 91 | 92 | 93 | 94 | 95 | 96 | 97 | 98 | 99 | 00 | 01 | 02 | 03 |
|---|---|---|---|---|---|---|---|---|---|---|---|---|---|
| Growth (in %, Rounded) | –15 | –40 | –12 | –? | –8 | –19 | –6 | –10 | +5 | +13 | +11 | +3 | +13 |

*Source:* Prime-Tass (Moscow), January 27, 2004, at www.prime-tass.ru; www.imf.org; Russian Ministry of Finance figures, at www.minfin.ru; A. Yu. Skopkin, *Ekonomicheskaya Geografiya Rossii* [An Economic Geography of Russia] (Moscow: Prospekt, 2003, pp. 45–6; World Bank, *Russian Economic Report* (August 2003), at www.worldbank.org.ru.

TABLE 12. *Share of Direct Investment by Sector, 2003*

| Sector | Share (%) |
|---|---|
| Fuel & energy | 27.0 |
| Electricity | 4.7 |
| Transport (includes pipelines) | 15.0 |
| Housing & utilities | 14.6 |
| Machine building | 3.0 |

of direct investment in 2003, less than half its share of Russian GDP, as Table 12 illustrates.

The World Bank concluded in August 2003 that in spite of the notable increase in capital investment that year, "Neither domestic consumption nor domestic investment [is] yet strong enough to guarantee a self-sustained recovery.... Fresh capacity [is] created mostly in the natural resource sectors."[32]

Perhaps most dramatically, a comparison of flows of foreign direct investment into Russia versus other, much smaller postcommunist states, in times of boom as well as bust, illustrates the difficulties that Russia has had in attracting significant investment capital from the free market. In good times as well as bad, Russia performs poorly, suggesting that capital inflow is a phenomenon distinct from the macroeconomic prospects of a mainly fuels-based economy, as Tables 13 and 14 show.

In consequence, Russia's accumulated stock of foreign direct investment is perhaps the lowest in the world among major economies; at

[32] World Bank, *Russian Economic Report* (August 2003), at www.worldbank.org.ru.

**TABLE 13.** *Direct Foreign Investment, 1990–8*

| Country | Foreign Investment |
| --- | --- |
| Russia | $10 billion |
| Hungary | $16 billion |
| Poland | $20 billion |

*Source:* Economist Intelligence Unit, *Country Forecast: Russia* (July 2000), p. 40; Stefan Hedlund, *Russia's "Market" Economy: A Bad Case of Predatory Capitalism* (London: UCL Press, 1999), p. 8.

**TABLE 14.** *Gross Inflows of Foreign Direct Investment, 2001–3 ($ Billions)*

| Country | 2001 | 2002 | 2003 |
| --- | --- | --- | --- |
| Russia | 2.5 | 2.4 | 5.2 |
| Czech Rep. | 5.6 | 9.3 | 5.6 |
| Poland | 5.7 | 4.1 | 4.1 |
| China (PRC) | 46.8 | 52.7 | 57.0 |
| Brazil | 22.5 | 16.6 | 9.1 |
| Ireland | 15.7 | 19.0 | 41.7 |
| Netherlands | 51.2 | 29.2 | 30.5 |

**TABLE 15.** *Accumulated Stock of Foreign Direct Investment, 1989–2003*

| Country | FDI |
| --- | --- |
| Russia | $29 billion |
| China (PRC) | $385 billion |
| Brazil | $186 billion |

$26 billion for the period 1991–2003, Russia's stock of foreign direct investment is less than half of the flow of foreign direct investment into The People's Republic of China (PRC, exclusive of Hong Kong) in either 2002 or 2003.[33] Russia's global disadvantage is stark, as shown in Table 15.

[33] Valeria Korchagina, "EIU Says Superpower Ego Hurts Investment Climate," *Moscow Times*, July 7, 2003, p. 5; www.unctad.press/pr/2004/001.

## IV. The Decision to Invest

In making the investment decision, the business agent must take into account *inter alia* the extent to which factors of political stability/instability and legal reliability/unreliability affect the costs of production. This production function is viewed in terms of "the ability to establish an institutional structure that is conducive to an efficient transformation of available resources into marketable goods and services."[34] The costs of production, in turn, are also affected, as they are everywhere, by environmental aspects of economic geography. In the Russian case, as we shall argue in detail later, these geographic factors tend to make large-scale industrial production and infrastructure development significantly more costly than elsewhere, thereby raising the burden of proof that the political and legal system must meet in order to attract large-scale capital investment. The state, therefore, continues to occupy a central position in the Russian political economy. Beyond simply setting the rules and policing the transactions of a market economy, the Russian state must (a) in effect find ways to compensate prospective investors for the higher degree of risk that they are likely to assume under Russian circumstances, and (b) redistribute a portion of the wealth from those few sectors of the economy that can realistically be competitive on the global market in the short term to those sectors that might be competitive in the medium term (that is, industrial policy) as well as to the bulk of the country that cannot (that is, socialism). It remains to be seen whether this moderately interventionist state can be constituted under conditions at home of weak public institutions and abroad of an increasingly liberal and integrated global capital market.

## V. The Influence of Late-Soviet Developments on Post-Soviet Prospects

Russia possesses approximately 13 percent of the world's crude oil; 35 percent of its natural gas (with more reserves than the rest of the world combined); 32 percent of iron; 31 percent of nickel; 30 percent of coals; 21 percent of cobalt; 16 percent of zinc; 14 percent of uranium; 5–30 percent of world supplies of gold, platinum, and diamonds; 11 percent of renewable water resources; 65 percent of the world's nontropical forests; and so on.[35] It is the second largest producer of brown coal; third in timber

---

[34] Hedlund, *Russia's "Market" Economy*, pp. 2–3.
[35] Skopin, *Ekonomicheskaya Geografiya Rossii*, p. 44.

logging; fourth in production of electric energy, cast iron, steel, iron ore, cereals, and meat; fifth in black coal and mineral fertilizers; and so on.[36] In such areas of production and reserves as gold, silver, diamonds, platinum, chromium, nickel, tin, lead, zinc, copper, rubber, sugar, paper and board, and bauxite, Russia is regularly among the top five in the world.[37] Unfortunately, Russia's economic performance has not lived up to the promise of its resource endowment. From 1990 through 1998, the Russian economy was mired in a depression far greater than that which struck the capitalist world in the 1930s. Even today Russia has little prospect of participating in the global market as a competitive industrial or postindustrial economic power.[38] Russia has a dollarized gross domestic product less than that of the Netherlands (around $417 billion in 2003) and a foreign trade turnover similar to Denmark's. Russia's exports are dominated by the sale of oil and gas and are virtually nonexistent in other, value-added sectors.[39] Oil, for instance, accounts for 70 percent of Russia's stock market valuation.[40] The Russian natural gas monopoly Gazprom alone, which is about ca 40 percent state-owned, accounts for 8 percent of Russia's official

---

[36] Martin Wolf, "Price of Forgiveness," *Financial Times*, August 11, 1999, p. 10.

[37] For an overview of Russia's resource endowment, see Andrianov, *Rossiya v mirovoy ekonomike*, pp. 12–18; Yu. N. Gladkin, V. A. Dobrosok, and S. P. Semenov, *Sotsial'no-Ekonomicheskaya Geografiya Rossii'* [A socioeconomic geography of Russia] (Moscow: Gardariki, 2000), pp. 117–56.

[38] See V. S. Bard, *Investitsionnye Problemy Rossiyskoy Ekonomike* [Investment Issues in the Russian Economy] (Moscow: Ekzamen, 2000), pp. 211–21, for a thorough discussion of the problem of Russian economic decline and how to gauge it. Judging by physical production indicators in the construction and consumption areas, and comparing 1997 to 1985, the decline has been massive: for example, the production of excavators fell by five-sixths, of bulldozers by six-sevenths, of oil and gas condensates by two-fifths, of meat by one-third, of sausage products by one-half, of sugar by one-fourth, of cheese and related dairy products by three-fifths, and of eggs by one-fourth. A common view that much smaller declines in electricity output reflect less dramatic real declines in growth overlooks the minimal level of electricity production needed for any production at all. Electric power is in effect much less sensitive to recession and depression than is industrial and consumer production.

[39] Valuing the Russian gross domestic product at the official exchange rate (as opposed to purchasing power parity [PPP] estimates) understates the actual extent of economic activity but is an accurate gauge of the economy's capacity to service its dollar-denominated external sovereign debt. Actual GDP is certainly higher in light of the significant volume of unregistered economic transactions. Still, while Russia's shadow economy may account for as much as 40 percent or more of all transactions, it is generally agreed that the unofficial economy involves much more distribution than production. See Bard, *Investitsionnye Problemy Rossiyskoy Ekonomiki*, pp. 211–12. Economist Intelligence Unit, *Country Forecast: Russia* (July 2000 and July 2003).

[40] Reuters (Frankfurt), "Russia Needs Help To Lead in Energy," May 3, 2002; "Russia on a Roll," *Financial Times*, October 10, 2003, at www.ft.com.

GDP, 25 percent of the country's exports, and 20 percent of the Russian government's budget revenues.[41] The energy sector as a whole makes up 15 percent of the country's GDP, 55 percent of exports by value, and half of government revenue. More broadly, the Russian federal budget must generate more than $20 billion per year from energy-related taxes and income in order to remain in balance; this sum was fully half of the government's 2003 budget and only slightly higher than its annual debt service payments to the G-7 economies. In order to earn that $20 billion from oil income, the Russian government's 2002 budget balanced at a world price of oil of $18.50 per barrel. In 2003, it balanced at $21.50. By contrast, in 1997 and 1998, a revenue flow of $20 billion required – given the lower level of Russian oil output then – a world price of oil of $26.28 per barrel, compared to the extant price of $10. No wonder, then, that the Russian government's finances collapsed in August 1998, quite apart from the audacious manipulations of senior members of the Russian government.[42] Russia's macroeconomic stability thus remains a hostage to the global energy market.

The consequences of such dependency, especially given the country's substantial debt-servicing burden, can be dramatic indeed. As a result of the August 1998 financial crash, which saw a 70 percent devaluation of the ruble, the dollar value of Russia's GDP is estimated to have declined from $436 billion in 1997 to $278 billion by the end of 1998.[43] Relatedly, the ratio of Russia's foreign debts to its (again, dollarized) GDP increased from 28 percent in January 1998 to nearly 90 percent in the year 2000.[44] Annual debt service as a percentage of dollarized GDP increased from 6.2 percent in 1997 to 11.8 percent in 1998 to 14 percent in 2000 and, as an absolute sum, peaked in 2003 at $17 billion, when it represented one-fourth of Russia's federal budget.[45] No wonder that the Russian government in early 2001 was seeking some way to avoid servicing its inherited Soviet-era debt. Table 16 summarizes the volatility of the country's fiscal stability.

[41] Jerome Guillet, "Fix Gazprom's Fatal Leak," *Wall Street Journal*, May 31, 2002, at www.wsj.com.

[42] Ben Aris, "Weaning off the Barrel," *Moscow Times*, June 3, 2002, at www. moscowtimes.ru.

[43] *Financial Times Annual Survey: Russia*, April 30, 1999, p. 1.

[44] Economist Intelligence Unit, *Country Profile: Russia 2000*, p. 22; Economist Intelligence Unit, *Country Forecast: Russia* (July 2000), appendix; *Journal of Commerce*, July 26, 1999.

[45] Andrianov, *Rossiya v mirovoy ekonomike*, p. 184; Peter Ivanov, "Survival Instinct Attracts Capital to Russia," at www.gazeta.ru, at *JRL*, #6307, June 14, 2002, item no 11, at www.cdi.org; Economist Intelligence Unit, *Country Forecast: Russia* (July 2000).

TABLE 16. *Impact of 70 Percent Devaluation of the Ruble (August 1998) on Capacity to Service the External Debt*

| Year | GDP ($) | GDP Growth | Debt Service/GDP ($) |
|------|---------|------------|----------------------|
| 1997 | $436b   | +1.5%      | 6.2%                 |
| 1998 | $278b   | −4.6%      | 11.8%                |
| 2000 | $198b   | +10.0%     | 14%                  |

## VI. Long-Term Consequences of Russia's Decade-Long Depression

The crisis that dominated the Russian economy through 1998 cannot be adequately explained by exclusive reference to specific policy decisions that were made by the Russian (or the U.S.) government from the fall of 1991 on. Certainly, the manner of formulation and execution of the three central policies of price liberalization, privatization of Soviet-era industries, and macroeconomic stabilization were basic to the ways in which the Russian economy made its way from the disintegrated communist planned economy.[46] Yet these policies themselves and their consequences took form in a political-economic context that was heavily influenced by specific legacies inherited from the Soviet past. These include:

- The predictable effects of liberalizing prices given the monopolistic structure of much of Russian industry, leading to a 2,600 percent inflation rate in the first year of reform (1992) and the evaporation of the life savings of most Russian citizens.
- The effect of the largely spontaneous seizure of liquifiable Soviet state assets between 1990–1 by strategically situated (by no means all or most or even the most powerful under the Soviet regime) elements of the Soviet nomenklatura, which had a decisive impact on the forms and consequences of Russian privatization, as well as on the character of the Russian political system itself. Indeed, from one angle, the privatization process may be seen as the legalization of this extralegal private expropriation of wealth.[47]

---

[46] For a penetrating discussion of these policy aspects, see Peter Reddaway and Dmitri Glinsky, *The Tragedy of Russia's Reforms: Market Bolshevism against Democracy* (Washington, DC: U.S. Institute of Peace, 2001).

[47] For a sophisticated sociological analysis of the composition of the new Russian elites as compared to the old Soviet elites, see David Lane and Cameron Ross, *The Transition from Communism to Capitalism: Ruling Elites from Gorbachev to Yeltsin* (New York: St. Martin's Press, 1999).

TABLE 17. *Some Economic Comparisons between China and Russia*

|  | China | Russia |
|---|---|---|
| GDP ($, 2001) | $1.16 trillion | $310 billion |
| GDP (PPP, 2002) | $5.989 trillion | $1.409 trillion |
| Per capita GDP ($) | $1,230 | $2,137 |
| Per capita GDP (PPP, 2002) | $4,700 | $9,700 |
| Avg. annual growth, 1980–2001 | +9.9% | <0% |
| FDI Stock, 1989–2003 | $390 billion | $30 billion |
| Foreign Exchange Reserves | $200 billion | $70 billion |
| GDP, 1999:1990 | 2:1 | 1:2 |
| Main Exports | Machinery, transport | Raw materials |
| Population | 1.3 billion | 145 million |

*Source:* Economist Intelligence Unit, *Country Forecast: Russia* (July 2000); *Financial Times Annual Survey: China*, November 13, 2000; *Handbook of World Statistics, 2003* (Geneva: UNCTAD, 2003) at www.unctad.org; www.cia.gov/cia/publications/factbook.

- The influence of the disproportionately militarized structure of the Soviet economy, which, combined with the fact of Soviet disintegration itself, magnified and prolonged the inevitable economic depression that must follow the transition from noncapitalism to noncommunism, to borrow phraseology from Martin Malia.[48]

While elements of each of these factors were present in many post-communist states in Europe, including the East-Central European ones, few if any outside states of the former Soviet Union experienced the depth of impact in each of these areas. Russia, in this respect, does stand apart.

The consequences of this decade-long economic decline have been dramatic, not only for Russia's internal condition but also for its international standing. By the end of the 1990s, China, which had more than doubled its national income during the decade after having doubled it also in the 1980s, was beginning to approach and perhaps even to exceed Russia in several indicators of economic development. Consider the comparisons in Table 17.

Even were these trends not to continue, the 1990s would have witnessed one of the most astounding changes in the economic balance of power to have taken place between two major countries in such a short period of time.

---

[48] Martin Malia, *Comprendre la Revolution Russe* (Paris: Editions du Seuil, 1980), p. 218.

## VII. After the Crash

President Putin faces the same set of problems and the same narrow margin for maneuver, both domestically and internationally, as did his predecessor, Boris Yeltsin. The Russian economy, in spite of what appears to be a conjunctural rebound after the double effect of ruble devaluation and oil price appreciation, is still suffering the effects of an economic depression following Soviet disintegration that has witnessed capital flight upwards of $350 billion. The progressive obsolescence of the country's capital stock continues as capital investment – at the turn of the twenty-first century still one-fourth of the 1990 level[49] – has dried up. The problem lies in the fact that neither Russian firms nor the Russian government appears to have been using this temporary respite to correct fundamental imbalances in the Russian micro- and macroeconomy, rendering the economy more vulnerable when oil prices decline and/or the ruble appreciates (as it has in fact been doing in real terms under the impact of Russia's rate of inflation – 12–20 percent in recent years compared to 2–3 percent for the United States).[50]

A key indicator of Russia's economic prospects lies in the possibility of injecting massive amounts of capital investment in order to repair, maintain, and develop the country's industrial, transportation, and communications infrastructure.[51] Without such investment, former Russian Prime Minister Mikhail Kasyanov has stated, Russia "will remain in the backyard of the world economy."[52] Yet, as noted, in spite of Russia's privileged position in many natural resources, human capital and wage structure, capital investment in Russia in the late 1990s was less than one-fifth of the 1990 level and at most one-third by 2003.[53]

Using 1990 as a base year doubtlessly may exaggerate the subsequent decline, given the disproportionate place occupied by investment, especially military-related investment, in the Soviet economy. Even so, the consequences of the capital drought that has afflicted the country since

---

[49] Skopin, *Ekonomicheskaya Geografiya Rossii*, pp. 45, 351; Valerie Sperling, ed., *Building the Russian State* (Boulder, CO: Westview, 2000), p. 17.

[50] Interfax (Moscow) in English, 1502 GMT, April 20, 2000; BBC Monitoring Service, April 21, 2000; Ruben Vardanyan, "The Dangers of Market Manic Depression," *Moscow Times*, June 4, 2002.

[51] Hans-Hermann Hoehmann and Christian Meier, "Conceptual, Internal, and International Aspects of Russia's Economic Security," in Alexei Arbatov, Karl Kaiser, and Robert Legvold, eds., *Russia and the West: The 21st Century Security Environment* (Armonk, NY: M. E. Sharpe, 1999), p. 83.

[52] RIA news agency (Moscow), in Russian, 1127 gmt, November 22, 2000.

[53] See also Bard, *Investitsionnye problemy rossiyskoy ekonomiki*, pp. 154–234, for an excellent overview of the Russian investment crisis in its various dimensions.

then are dramatic enough; the capital stock of the country is rapidly wearing out. The average age of industrial equipment in 1995 was 14.1 years, as compared to 10.8 in 1990, 9.5 in 1980, and 8.5 in 1970. Just 4.7 percent of industrial equipment in 2000 was less than five years old, compared to 26.6 percent in 1992, 29.4 percent in 1990, 35.5 percent in 1980, and 40.8 percent in 1970. Fully 38.2 percent of the capital stock of industry was older than twenty years in 2000, compared to 10.8 percent in 1990, 9.5 percent in 1980, and 8.4 percent in 1970.[54] Another gauge, the rate of renewal of fixed capital stock, was 6.9 percent in 1990 compared to 1.0 percent in 1998. Only in the fuels and food sectors did the capital replacement rate reach as high as 2 percent.[55] Research and development declined from 1.03 percent of Russian GDP in 1991 to 0.32 percent in 1997 (compared to the G-7 norm of 2–2.5 percent.)[56] Consequently, some Russian economists have calculated that fully 75 percent of the country's productive assets in entire industries would have been obsolete by 2003.[57] Table 18 summarizes these 1990s trends.

Current indices for specific sectors suggest that the pattern continued through 2003.[58] For instance, fully one-half of Russia's oil pipelines are more than twenty years old (a third are older than thirty), while a third of natural gas pipelines are older than twenty years.[59] There are seventy-five to eighty ruptures in the oil pipeline network in a given year, resulting in large-scale leaks and ecological damage.[60] In mid-February 2004, Sergei Stepashin, former prime minister and at the time chair of the Russian Audit Chamber, confirmed that few Russian oil companies are carrying out significant exploratory research or drilling new wells but rather exploiting Soviet-era wells to the maximum feasible limits.[61] Clearly, the bulk of Russia's investment challenges lies before it.

---

[54] Bard, *Investitsionnye Problemy Rossiyskoy Ekonomiki*, pp. 187–98; M. T. Mkrtchyan et al., *Sostoyaniye i protivorechiya ekonomicheskoy reformy* [The Condition and Contradictions of Economic Reform] (Moscow: Ekonomika, 1998), p. 175; Jean Radvanyi, *La Nouvelle Russie* (Paris: Armand Colin, 2000), p. 145.

[55] Ibid., pp. 145, 149. The centrality of the energy sector may be gauged by the fact that in 1999 it constituted 35 percent of Russian GDP, 12 percent of industrial employment, 45 percent of the country's capital stock, 42 percent of state budget revenues, and 46 percent of exports.

[56] Alexei Arbatov, Karl Kaiser, and Robert Legvold, eds., *Russia and the West: The 21st Century Security Environment* (Armonk, NY: M. E. Sharpe, 1999), p. 100.

[57] Ivanov, "Survival Instincts Attract Capital to Russia."

[58] *JRL*, #7446 (December 1, 2003), item no. 12, at www.cdi.org.

[59] Skopin, *Ekonomicheskaya Geografiya Rossii*, pp. 179, 188.

[60] Ibid., p. 179.

[61] Rosbalt (Moscow), February 17, 2004, in *JRL*, #8071 (February 17, 2004), item no. 9, at www.cdi.org.

TABLE 18. *Indices on the Russian Capital Infrastructure*

|  | **Average Age of Industrial Equipment** |
|---|---|
| 2000 | Indeterminate but older than the following |
| 1995 | 14.1 years |
| 1990 | 10.8 years |
| 1980 | 9.5 years |
| 1970 | 7.5 years |
|  | **% of Equipment Less Than 5 Years Old** |
| 2000 | 4.7% |
| 1996 | 9.7% |
| 1995 | 10.9% |
| 1991 | 26.6% |
| 1990 | 29.4% |
| 1980 | 35.5% |
| 1970 | 40.8% |
|  | **% of Industrial Equipment Older Than 20 Years** |
| 2000 | 38.2% |
| 1995 | 23.0% |
| 1990 | 10.8% |
| 1980 | 9.5% |
| 1970 | 8.4% |
|  | **Rate of Renewal of Fixed Capital Stock** |
| 1998 | 1.0% |
| 1990 | 6.9% |
|  | **Research and Development as a % of Russian GDP** |
| 1996 | 0.32% |
| 1991 | 1.03% |

The lion's share of direct investment in Russia since 1999 has been concentrated in the oil and gas industries (about $20 billion in 1999–2002), and even there recovery of existing fields has tended to predominate over new exploration efforts.[62] The rest of the economy, above all the nonenergy-related industrial sector, remains starved for vital capital resources.

The implications of this draining of Russia's productive substance are dramatic: Whereas a team of Russian economists in the late 1990s prepared a best-case scenario in which Russia might attain its 1990 GDP around the year 2008, these figures and the trends they reflect suggest

---

[62] Sophie Lambroschini, "Russia: The Economics Behind the Yukos Crisis," *RFE-RL* (Moscow), November 26, 2003, at www.rfe-rl.org.; Reuters (Frankfurt), "Russia Needs Help To Lead in Energy," May 3, 2002.

that even their worst-case scenario – in which Russia attains its 1990 GDP in 2015 – may be optimistic. Russian President Putin himself is on record as stating that Russia would need fifteen consecutive years of growth at 8 percent per annum to enable the Russian economy to attain the current per capita income levels of Portugal.[63]

Here are some specifics: In the fall of 2000, economists estimated that Russia required at least $50 billion per year for the modernization of the Russian capital stock for the foreseeable future, with $20 billion per year over the next twenty years for the energy sector alone.[64] (Only beginning in 2003 do such levels appear to have been attained.[65]) If we break down Russia's investment requirements by sector, we shall have a better sense of the urgency of the problem and the scale of investment required if Russia is to have any chance of developing its economy in a comprehensive and balanced way in the decade to come.

Western observers consider much of the Russian railway system, which accounts for three-fourths of all freight moved in Russia (when measured in terms of tons per kilometer), to be in "very poor repair." Indeed, by Russian standards, 71 percent of the railroad system was considered obsolete in 2001.[66] On the highways, "poor road quality" – just one-fourth of Russia's federal highways (that is, the best) are deemed to be in acceptable condition, whereas 40 percent are in various stages of decomposition – means lower truck speeds and thus higher transport costs, which can often attain 50 percent of the costs of production.[67] Forty percent of Russia's villages cannot be reached on tarmac roads, and there are no Western-type highways in the whole country (except the ring roads *around* Moscow). The main road between Moscow and St. Petersburg is a two-lane affair, vastly overloaded and unable to cope with the traffic between Russia's two most important cities.[68] Beyond a radius of sixty miles from the larger cities, asphalted roads are generally replaced by graveled lanes.[69]

[63] Mkrtchyan, et al., *Sostoyaniye i protivorechiya ekonomicheskoy reformy*, p. 185.

[64] Masaaki Kuboniwa (Hitotsubashi University, Japan), "FDI and Capital Flight in Russia," paper presented to the 2000 National Convention of the American Association for the Advancement of Slavic Studies, Denver, CO, November 11, 2000.

[65] World Bank, *Russian Economic Report.*

[66] Skopin, *Ekonomicheskaya Geografiya Rossii*, p. 288.

[67] Gabriele Lueke and Gustav Weber, eds., *So Kommen Sie nach ... Russland: Der Wirtschaftswegweiser fuer den Mittlestand* [Come to Russia: Guide to the Russian Economy for the Small and Medium-Sized Businessperson] (Munich: PrimeVerlag, 2003), p. 451.

[68] Galina Stolyarova, "Highway Gets Putin's Nod," *St. Petersburg Times*, February 3, 2004, p. 5.

[69] Ibid., p. 91.

Russia's ports are generally in a "poor state of repair," and the Russian maritime fleet is the oldest in the world.

Fully half of Russia's electricity generation and distribution network and the industry's fixed assets are past their intended productive lives, the consequence being that "Russia could face serious supply squeezes by the middle of the decade. Electricity generation threatens to become a major constraint on growth."[70] Standard and Poor's has calculated Russian investment requirements in the electrical industry at $5–10 billion annually until 2010.[71] Indeed, summing up the indicators of the condition of Russia's economic infrastructure – including electricity generation, quality of ports, the cost and availability of office space, retail and wholesale distribution networks, general technological endowments, railroads, and roads – the Economist Intelligence Unit in July 2000 forecast that "in none of these areas is major progress expected in Russia in the forecast period [that is, through 2004]."[72]

Even in the critical oil and gas sector, which typically earns half of Russia's hard currency export receipts and accounts for as much as half of the federal government's budget revenues, the average volume of exploratory drilling in the 1994–8 period was 1.4 million meters per year, compared to 5.3 million meters in 1990; the figure for 1999 was 1.16 million meters, about one-fifth of the 1990 levels, a figure that corresponds to the depreciation of the Russian capital stock across sectors. As existing oil fields were depleted and fewer new ones were coming into production, Russian oil production continued to decline throughout the 1990s, as it did from 569 million tons in 1988 and 462 million tons in 1991 to 303 and 305 million tons in 1998 and 1999, respectively.[73] Annual investment of $10–11 billion over the next twenty years is required in the oil sector alone, compared to $2–4 billion in the 1990s.[74] By contrast, Russian oil companies have been quite active in Western investment markets. Lukoil, for example, has opened thirteen hundred gas stations in the United

---

[70] Economist Intelligence Unit, *Country Forecast: Russia*, pp. 29–30. Also available at www.eiu.com.

[71] Reuters (Frankfurt), "Russia Needs Help."

[72] Economist Intelligence Unit, *Country Forecast: Russia*.

[73] A. P. Parshev, *Pochemu Rossiya ne Amerika* [Why Russia is not America] (Moscow: Krymsky Most, 2000), p. 64; Radvanyi, *La Nouvelle Russie*, p. 148.

[74] Alexei Mastepanov, "Main Points of Russia's Energy Strategy," *International Affairs* (Moscow), vol. 47, no. 2 (2001), p. 45; Thane Gustafson, *Capitalism, Russian Style* (Cambridge, UK: Cambridge University Press), p. 223.

States (originally under the Getty name); through the Italian firm Avanti, Lukoil has completed the purchase of seven hundred gas stations in Europe and is contemplating the purchase of several refineries in the United States and the Czech Republic. The state-controlled company Slavneft saw a $1.3 billion revenue turnover in 2000 from its joint venture with a Belgium partner in Belgium.[75]

This picture began to change after the 1998 currency devaluation – which overnight made Russian producers among the cheapest in the world – and the dramatic increase in world oil prices in 1999 and 2000, as Russian oil companies, suddenly flush with cash, began to invest in domestic infrastructure and foreign technologies in order to take advantage of the trebling of prices. In the first half of 2001, for instance, Russian spending on exploration and drilling increased 50 percent while government-sponsored pipelines opened in the Baltic and Black Sea regions. As a result, Russia was able to increase its oil exports in 2001 by half a million barrels per day. Still, Russian energy companies are believed to invest about two-thirds of their assets outside of the country. Most domestic investment has been in recovery rather than in the much more expensive and risky exploration for new fields.[76] Indeed, the volume of geological prospecting has fallen even as oil production increased from 1999–2002. (Overall, Russian oil reserves fell 13 percent from 1991–2001.[77]) So long as this is the case, Russia can expect to increase oil production in the short run while risking long-run productivity. Indeed, more intensive recovery operation of fields that are already more than half depleted tends to result in dramatic drops in output after brief short-term increases, a problem for which more sophisticated foreign extraction technologies have no answer.[78] As with the economy as a whole, the question remains: Can these positive

[75] Milana Davydova, "Accelerated Capital Flight," *Segodnya* (Moscow), March 16, 2001, from World Press Service (WPS) Monitoring Agency, at www.wps.ru/e_index.html. In general, Russian companies invested $15.154 billion in property abroad in 2000, compared to $4.43 billion in direct foreign investment in Russia for that year. In 1999, the ratio was $8.38 billion in Russian capital directly invested abroad, compared to $4.26 billion in FDI in Russia. See also Daniel Bases, "Russia Creates Cautious Investor Optimism," *Reuters* (New York), March 16, 2001.
[76] Skopin, *Ekonomicheskaya Geografiya Rossii*, pp. 174–84; J. Robinson West, "We Can't Get Along without Saudi Oil," *Washington Post*, April 9, 2002, p. A19. West is chair of the Petroleum Finance Corporation and former assistant secretary of the interior of the United States.
[77] Agence France Presse, "Russian PM Urges Bigger Market Role in Energy Sector," May 28, 2002.
[78] Lambroschini, "Russia"; Skopin, *Ekonomicheskaya Geografiya Rossii*, pp. 174–84.

investment effects be increased and sustained independently of exchange-rate manipulations and relatively high global prices for oil?

Under these circumstances, Russia's short- to medium-term economic prospects are highly constrained. A decade or more of neglect of infrastructure cannot be made up easily. For example, in 2000, in response to the rise in world oil prices, Russian producers decided to increase production significantly. Yet they could at most squeeze an extra 20 million tons of production (about 7 percent of total production), mainly by opening old wells that had been mothballed. Much bigger gains were achieved in 2001 and 2002, mainly through more intensive recovery operations as well as significant capital investment that put Russia temporarily on a par with Saudi Arabia as the leading world oil producer. Yet only Russia's Far Eastern oil fields can significantly compensate for the long-term decline in Russian production; for that to happen, massive amounts of venture capital will have to be invested in remote regions with severe climatic conditions and little to no existing industrial, transportation, and communications infrastructure.[79]

The capital requirements for the recovery and development of Russia's economic infrastructure are thus massive. In the oil and gas sector, the typical cost of bringing a new field upstream is $8–10 billion; in November 2000, the Russian government approved a document establishing Russia's investment requirements in the natural gas sector as between $165–170 billion over the next twenty years.[80] Unified Energy Systems, the state electricity monopoly, requires $30–50 billion in capital investment over the next decade but is constrained from investing in future expansion of capacity due to $5 billion in unpaid bills from (mainly industrial) customers.[81] Vladimir Ushakov of Alstom, which sells power stations, calculates that Russia needs to invest $7 billion per year over the next fifteen years to repair and replace increasingly worn out power stations; in 1999, for instance, Russia invested just $1 billion.[82] An authoritative report issued by Russian electricity specialists in 1999 reached some alarming conclusions: Half of Russia's thermal power generators, which account for 64 percent of Russian electricity generation, had outlived their intended service lives of twenty-five years; 60 percent of the country's

---

[79] "Russian's Natural Resources Running Out Fast," *Rossiyskaya Gazeta*, March 30, 2001, at *JRL*, #5180, April 1, 2001, item no. 1.

[80] Mastepanov, "Main Points of Russia's Energy Strategy."

[81] Radvanyi, *La Nouvelle Russie*, p. 42.

[82] "Russia's Infrastructure: Crumble, Bumble," *Economist*, September 2, 2000, at www.economist.com.

hydroelectric power generators, which account for 19 percent of Russian electricity generation, were older than twenty-five years and have not undergone significant capital repair. Sixty-one percent of local electric power substations are obsolete, while 30 percent of the system's transformers and 43 percent of the high voltage switches are beyond their intended service life of twenty-five years. The report concludes, "A sharp decline in the reliability of the switches is expected in the next few years."[83]

Some of the consequences of neglecting capital repair and replacement may be seen in the widespread collapse of the power infrastructure in Arctic Russia and the Far East, where in mid-January 2001, amid temperatures of –4 degrees Fahrenheit (that is, –20 degrees Centigrade), there were daily fifteen-hour-per-day power cuts. Anatoly Chubais, head of the Unified Energy System, stated that the cause of the energy supply crisis in the city of Artem was the destruction of the municipal energy system: "Locking attachments and materials of nonferrous metals have been stolen. The pipelines are run down. They have been hit by the freezing temperatures. The heating units lack essential parts. The basements in buildings are partially flooded."[84]

In other areas, approximately $40 billion in capital investment in the telecommunications industry is required over the next decade.[85] Railroads will require $28 billion in capital investment between 2003–8, the highway system $75 billion between 2002–10, and so on.[86]

These sums would appear in principle to be within the capacity of the Russian state to start financing, in light of the current world price of oil (about $40–45 per barrel), a current account surplus of nearly $40 billion (or 9 percent of dollarized GDP), a large foreign trade surplus ($60 billion in recent years), $3–4 billion in foreign arms sales per

[83] Svodni tekhnicheskiy otchet po itogam otraslevykh meropriyatiy po sboru informatsii, analizi i obobshcheniyu sostoyaniya elektrotekhnicheskogo oborudovaniya energosistem Rossii [Summary technical report on the results of a multilevel study of the condition of the electro-technical infrastructure of the Russian energy system] II (Moscow: RAO "YeES Rossii," 1999).
[84] International Herald Tribune, January 16, 2001, www.iht.com.; Washington Post, November 23, 2000, at www.washingtonpost.com.
[85] The illegal export of nonferrous metals has become a major crisis affecting Russia's power and transport infrastructure. Of Russia's 700,000–750,000 tons of nonferrous scrap metal exported each year, only half is genuine scrap. The rest is composed of stolen railroad track, copper overhead power lines, and so on. Theft from power lines resulted in seven hundred cases of nonfatal electrocution throughout Russia in 1999 and more than five hundred deaths from electric shock. Moscow Times, May 27, 2000, at www.moscowtimes.ru; Nezavisimaya Gazeta, November 18, 2000, at www.ng.ru.
[86] Lueke and Weber, So Kommen Sie nach, p. 453.

year,[87] as well as several hundred billion dollars in Russian capital secreted in foreign bank accounts. Indeed, to some extent, this has been happening, as 1999 saw a 4.5 percent increase in gross fixed investment – the first time that there had been an increase in gross investment in the 1990s – with an apparent increase of 13 percent in 2000, 11 percent in 2001, and 3 percent in 2002. Investment reportedly increased 12.5 percent in 2003, even as foreign investors were removing their capital from the country.[88]

Several points are worth noting, however. First, these are increases from a very low level, one determined by the unprecedented depression that Russia suffered in the 1990s. In the words of Economic Development and Trade Minister German Gref, the current volume of foreign direct investment "is absolutely insufficient for accomplishing the tasks facing the country."[89] Second, the sectors that are attracting the lion's share of capital investment are food, trade/catering, and transportation (69 percent of total investment in 1999 and 80 percent of all foreign direct investment); to a lesser extent, fuels and power are attracting this investment.[90] Public sector infrastructures that are critical for private sector economic development (such as ports, highways, railways, domestic aviation, public buildings, the educational system, and so on) remain poor orphans even within a relatively impoverished investment climate. Third, most of this recent investment derives from firms' internal resources, which in the view of former Prime Minister Kasyanov, is simply not enough.[91] The banking system has yet to be reformed and made into a viable source of venture and investment capital for the country's enterprises. Russia's banks account for less than 10 percent of the country's investment activity, whereas lending accounts for less than 15 percent of the activity of Russia's banks. (Relatedly, in the consumer sector, just 2 percent of Russians have purchased a mortgage to finance their dwelling.[92]) In the words of a recent International Monetary Fund report, the Russian banking system is "an accident waiting to happen."[93]

*(handwritten margin note: ★ company's investment insufficient)*

---

[87] The figure for 2000 is $3.7–3.8 billion, as reported in *Wall Street Journal*, January 24, 2001, www.wsj.com.

[88] Prime-Tass (Moscow), December 12, 2003.

[89] *Business Review* (Moscow), September 2000, p. 57.

[90] "Russia's Economy: False Calm," *Economist*, November 8–14, 2003, at www.economist.com.

[91] RIA news agency (Moscow), in Russian, 1127 gmt, November 22, 2000.

[92] According to the Analytical Department of RIA RosBusiness Consulting. See *JRL*, #8036, January 28, 2004, item no. 10, at www.cdi.org.

[93] Andrew Jack, "IMF Mission Leaves Russia with No Agreement," *Financial Times*, November 23, 2000, p. 2.

TABLE 19. *Net Foreign Direct Investment*
*Per Capita, 2003*

| Region | FDI |
|---|---|
| East-Central Europe & Baltics | $1,400 |
| Ex-USSR (excluding Baltics) | $200 |
| Russia | $52 |

*Note:* End-of-year calculations would reduce
Russia's figure to $22 if FDI from Cyprus, that
is, repatriated Russian capital, were discounted.
*Source:* International Monetary Fund, *Finance
and Development* (December 2003), p. 56.

Finally, Western investment experience in Russia has been less than
satisfactory. Western oil companies experienced at least $10 billion in
costs and losses in the 1990s, according to energy specialist Thomas Walde
of Dundee University,[94] while Western direct investment in Russia has
been a fraction of investment in such countries as Hungary, Poland, and
the Czech Republic.[95] In East-Central Europe, foreign direct investment
typically equals 4–5 percent of GDP compared to less than 1 percent in
Russia.[96] Table 19 summarizes this situation.

Cumulative U.S. investment in Russia amounted to $6.3 billion in
2002, a sum comparable to that invested by U.S. firms in Costa Rica.[97]

Moreover, Russian enterprises have invested significantly more capital abroad, typically in short-term instruments of less than three-months'
duration, than foreigners have been investing in Russia ($7.66 billion
versus 4.78 billion, respectively, for the first half of 2000, and $10.04 bil-
lion versus $8.36 billion in the first half of 2002).[98] This is quite apart
from the question of illegal capital flight, which the Russian Security
Council conservatively estimates at more than $20 billion in 1999 and
more than $30 billion in 1999 and 2000, respectively; such capital flight,
which resumed in 2003 after a brief hiatus, probably totals at least

---

[94] "Oil Change," *Economist*, September 21, 2000, at www.economist.com.
[95] Radvanyi, *La Nouvelle Russie*, p. 227. The rest of foreign investment in Russia was constituted by portfolio investment (2–5 percent of the total per year) and credits (50–60
percent); the city of Moscow, with 8 percent of the country's population, is the recipient
of 50–70 percent of all foreign investment in Russia, as of all Russian capital investment
itself.
[96] Economist Intelligence Unit, *Country Forecast: Russia* (July 2000), p. 40; Hedlund, *Russia's
"Market" Economy*, p. 8.
[97] According to U.S. Ambassador to Russia Alexander Vershbow, *JRL*, #6262, May 22,
2002, at www.cdi.org.
[98] Interfax (Moscow), August 12, 2002; ibid., August 30, 2000.

$350 billion in Russian capital secreted abroad, through both legal and illegal channels.[99]

What, then, are the conditions that would trigger the release of capital investment – private and public, Russian and foreign – that is required in order to underwrite and sustain a Russian economic recovery?

## VIII. Enabling Conditions of Russian Recovery: Politics versus Geography?

It is almost a truism among Western and even most Russian observers that the root causes of Russia's prolonged economic decline in the 1990s and the chief barriers to Russian economic development in the future lie in the political and administrative sphere, that is, "high levels of political uncertainty," and consequently high degrees of political risk for investors, reams of burdensome and contradictory regulations at all levels of government, an uncertain and volatile legal environment, unstable ownership rights, excessive taxation, poor corporate governance, corruption, and so on. Russian economist Vladimir Mau, rector of the Academy on the National Economy, has stated explicitly his view that, "The entire problem of economic efficiency has its roots in the political sphere."[100] In the words of the Economist Intelligence Unit, "institutional ineffectiveness remains the main constraint on improving Russia's performance."[101] In this view, political stability, rule of law, and sound money would enable Russia to reap the benefits of several factors that would appear to work in favor of a rapid and substantial Russian economic recovery, such as reserves of underemployed labor, raw materials, plants, and equipment; productivity gains from new market sectors; shifts from defense to consumer production; and substantial reserves of domestic savings, mainly

---

[99] *Rossiyskaya Gazeta*, November 17, 2000, at www.rg.ru. The 1999 estimate breaks down as follows:

| | |
|---|---|
| Nonreturn of foreign exchange earnings: | $2.3 billion |
| Nonreceipt of goods or nonreturn of advance payment on imports: | $3 billion |
| Transfer of advance payments for fictitious import contracts for provision of services: | $5.5 billion |
| Export of cash dollars in Xerox boxes, etc.: | $12 billion |
| (the figure for 1998 was $21.6 billion) | |
| Nonreceipt in Russia of foreign exchange earnings from sale of goods in "duty-free zones" such as the Black Sea: | Indeterminate |

[100] Antonov, "Money Tests."
[101] *Country Forecast: Russia*, p. 9.

in dollars.[102] As someone who has written extensively and early on the "crisis of the Russian state," I shall not dispute that the establishment of a system of state administration capable of performing the requisite tasks of governance, especially the provision of public goods, is a necessary precondition for Russian economic development.[103] Without doubt, the precipitous collapse of the authority of the CPSU in 1990 and 1991 and the difficulties that Russian leaders have faced since then in establishing a state that can adequately perform the minimal functions of government have seriously constrained Russia's ability to implement a consistent and effective economic policy of any coloration. These irreducible tasks of governance include:

- Raising tax revenue sufficient to fund the agencies and activities of the state, such as the following
- Exercising an effective monopoly on the use of force for public purposes
- Enforcing the law and public order
- Policing the frontiers
- Suppressing, or better yet deterring, secessionist rebellion
- Regulating the macroeconomy
- Honoring the fiduciary obligations of the state, at home and abroad

The difficulties that the Russian state experienced throughout the 1990s in fulfilling these tasks of governance tended to undermine the government's ability to manage the unprecedentedly complex and interdependent "factors" implied by the idea of the transition from communism to capitalism. One enduring consequence of state failure in Russia, apart from the general incoherence of various economic "reforms," has been capital flight and reluctance to invest directly in the country, which has propelled the obsolescence of the capital stock described in the previous section. This lack of investor confidence, combined with the indifference of the state, has allowed key elements of Russia's economic infrastructure – ports, roads, railways, the electricity grid, telecommunications, and even to some extent the oil sector – to deteriorate to the point where they are close to physical collapse as integrated national systems. Russia's economic future, indeed whether there is a future for Russia at all as we have known it in recent centuries, depends centrally on whether substantial sums of investment capital can be committed to the salvation, maintenance, and development

[102] Gustafson, *Capitalism, Russian Style*, pp. 224–5.
[103] Allen C. Lynch, "The Crisis of the State in Russia," *International Spectator* (Rome), April–June 1995, pp. 21–34.

of Russia's industrial, transportation, communications, and energy infrastructure. This involves less the renewal of the existing infrastructure grid of the country, which corresponds to conditions of planned, nonmarket economics, than it does the establishment of a largely novel infrastructure appropriate to the conditions of a market-based economy.

Yet it is at least debatable whether the stabilization of the political system and the development of the legal system are sufficient conditions to trigger the magnitude of investment needed to develop Russia as a whole, as distinct from privileged raw materials enclaves within it. First, the question of the state cannot be separated from the kind of state that we are speaking about (for example, liberal or social democracy) and the relation of that state to a particular political-economic environment (such as liberal or state capitalism) and the inevitable gradations between these respective poles. Second, the investment decision is shaped by this simple question: What should be invested in, over what period of time in order to derive acceptable revenues in relation to the costs of production? In this respect, the costs of production are influenced not simply by the political and legal uncertainties involved but by all factors that determine the costs of doing business, including those related to economic geography. Because the investment decision involves a guess, however calculated, about the future, political stability and legal reliability are essential. Yet because this decision involves profits, it also entails a guess about the ratio of revenues generated by production compared to the costs of production.

Those costs of production in Russia tend to be quite high, quite apart from the question of Soviet legacies of inefficiency. In short, the combined and mutually reinforcing impact of (a) the severity of Russia's climate, (b) the vastness of the Russian space, and (c) the predominance across this bi-continent of expensive land transport over cheap sea transport means that in most areas of the Russian economy the intrinsic and irreducible costs of infrastructure as of production itself are two to three times that of almost any other country in the world. Consequently, it is questionable whether Russia can develop as an entire socioeconomic unit under predominantly liberal market auspices. An administratively strong and interventionist state even in a market-based economy – one that protects Russian industry and directs resources from profitable (mainly natural resource – based) sectors to unprofitable but arguably vital sectors and regions (for example, Arctic and Siberian settlement and development) – seems to be an essential prerequisite to Russian welfare, as the normal costs of production will not normally be assumed by private investors with free access to the world's generally more attractive investment possibilities.

In other words, to what extent does economic geography make Russian economic development incompatible with the free movement of capital?[104]

We shall not advance an argument of strict geographic determinism. The Russian economy experienced the fastest growth rate in the world between 1880–1914, averaging 5 percent growth for the period as a whole and 8 percent for the decade of the 1890s;[105] by 1914, Russia was the fourth largest industrial power in the world and the sixth largest trading state by volume. Likewise, Stalin's Soviet state modernized sufficiently, if brutally, to survive the Nazi onslaught and thereafter to harass the United States for nearly half a century. (Interestingly, though, Russia's late-nineteenth-century economic boom was focused on the climatically more favorable Russian South: Russia's railroad network was most dense toward southern Russia so as to facilitate the export of Russian grain to the world market; Baku, in the deep south of the Caucasus, became the world's leading center of oil production around 1900; while Russian Turkestan became the source of cotton and other raw materials for the economically vital textile industry.[106] Only in the Soviet period, with an incomparably more powerful state apparatus, was Russia's North developed in any systematic way.) Russia has thus modernized when it has been open to the West and when it has been closed to it; it has also modernized in the presence of the market and without it. Yet in each of these cases, the Russian state – in one case a mercantilist state emphasizing high tariff walls, state orders, and state guarantees of superior return on foreign capital (4.5 percent compared to the 2–2.5 percent typical in London

---

[104] This question was first broached publicly by Joseph Stiglitz, then chief economist at the World Bank, in a report issued in April 1999 in which he contrasted the implications of open capital accounts in Russia versus closed capital accounts in China for each state's ability to shape its economic environment during the transition from comprehensive central planning. For a discussion, see Reddaway and Glinsky, *The Tragedy of Russia's Reforms*; Joseph Stiglitz, *Globalization and Its Discontents* (New York: W. W. Norton, 2002), p. 260; Shinichiro Tabata, "The Great Russian Depression of the 1990's: Observations on Causes and Implications," *Post-Soviet Geography and Economics*, vol. 41, no. 6 (2000), pp. 389–98. It was of course also the case that most postwar countries in Western Europe, including the Federal Republic of Germany, maintained highly regulated capital accounts until the late 1950s and beyond.

[105] Mikhail Pokrovskiy, *Russkaya Istoriya* [Russian History] (St. Petersburg: Poligon, 2002), vol. 3, p. 270, 294–304, for indices of Russian economic growth between 1880–1914 and in particular the role of the state in guaranteeing foreign investors higher rates of capital return than in the West, the importance of tariff policy in protecting Russian industry and agriculture, and in general the significant role played by foreign capital in triggering Russia's industrial modernization under mercantilistic circumstances.

[106] Michel Heller, *Histoire de la Russie et de son empire* (Paris: Plon, 1997), p. 842.

and Paris in the late 1890s) invested in the Russian economy,[107] in the other a monopolist state – played a decisive role in framing the modernization process.[108] More to the point, Russia has never developed under conditions of free movement of capital and possibly cannot do so.

Why not? The three mutually interacting factors of economic geography mentioned previously – severity of climate, distance (including the growing dislocation between population and natural resources), and predominance of expensive land over cheap water transport – have sustained the case for the state in Russian economic development.[109] First, Russia cannot be compared to Canada, an analogy often made by those with a passing knowledge of geography and by many Russian intellectuals themselves.[110] Russia's climate is the most severe in the world, with the exception of Mongolia's. That severity is measured not by the coldness of the winters but by the contrast between the length and coldness of the winters with the brevity and heat of the summers in Russia's continental climate. Through much of Siberia, for instance, the temperature differential normally reaches 100 degrees Celsius, that is, the temperature swings between lows of 60 below Celsius in the depths of winter to 40 above in midsummer.[111] By contrast, Canada, though a large country with an ostensibly northern location, has a small population (about a fifth the size of Russia's), excellent river and other transport possibilities that provide easy access to the world's oceans (that is, the St. Lawrence Seaway, connecting the Atlantic to the North American heartland at Lake Superior), and a moderate climate where the bulk of the population lives. That is, 80 percent or so of the Canadian population lives within a two-hour drive of the U.S. border, making Canada economically the northernmost periphery of the richest country in the world. The industrially developed parts of Canada correspond to the climate of Rostov oblast' or Krasnodar krai, in Russia's deep south, although the Canadian climate is more humid. In this respect, economic geography favors Canada immensely over Russia. Still, it is interesting to note that the productivity of Canadian farming

[107] N. V. Kurys', *Inostrannye Investitsii. Rossiyskaya Istoriya* [Foreign Investment in Russian History] (St. Petersburg: Yuridicheskiy Tsentr, 2003), pp. 38–116; Pokrovskiy, *Russkaya Istoriya*, pp. 294–301.

[108] James H. Bater, *The Soviet Scene: A Geographical Perspective* (London: Edward Arnold, 1989), p. 26.

[109] For an overview of the impact of geography on Russia's historical development, see Richard Pipes, *Russia under the Old Regime* (London: Penguin Books, 1995), pp. 1–24, as well as the work of the French geographer Radvanyi, *La Nouvelle Russie*, pp. 31–54.

[110] Gladkin et al., *Sotsial'no-Ekonomicheskaya Geografiya Rossii'*, p. 90.

[111] Gerd Ruge, *Sibirisches Tagebuch* [Siberian Diary] (Munich: Knaur, 2000), p. 78.

is roughly comparable to that of the later Soviet period (about 20 centners per hectare compared to 70–80 centners per hectare in northwestern
Europe), that Canada employs (like the Soviet *sovkhoz*) industrial-scale
farming as a rule, and that in those areas such as Edmonton and Winnipeg
where the climate is colder than in Moscow, the economy (as in much of
Russia) is devoted mainly to raw materials extraction (timber and petro-
chemicals).[112] Thus, climatewise, Russia should be compared to Mongolia
and perhaps North-Central Canada and not the Canada that is geographically and economically integrated with the United States.

   Fiona Hill and Clifford Gaddy, in their impressive study *The Siberian
Curse*, report research findings on the U.S. and Canadian economies
that each extra degree (Celsius) of cold would cost the North American
economies 1–1.5 percent of their GDP. While comparable studies have
yet to be done in the Russian case, a measure of the Russian "cold index"
can be seen in the breakdown of standard industrial machinery in the
Siberian cold, where such machinery breaks down three to five times as
fast it does in the rest of Russia, where construction costs are three to
eight times as high and labor costs two to seven times as high.[113]

   The second factor of economic geography that Russians contend with
is the country's size – not simply the vast expanse of territory spanning
eleven time zones, but the discrepancy between the main population centers, still in European Russia, and the location of Russia's treasure of natural resources, which are predominantly located in Asiatic and Siberian
Russia. As British geographer James H. Bater has observed, "the location
of resources for industry of sufficient scale to sustain long-term development is generally far removed from the main markets of European Russia.
The cost of resource development in ever more remote frontier regions
simply compounds the cost of overcoming distance."[114] Distance itself
thus becomes a kind of cost of production under these circumstances, as
food, fuel, machinery, and virtually everything needed to sustain organized modern life must be brought in from the outside over enormous
distances and frequently by air in large parts of Siberia and virtually all of

---

[112] Parshev, *Pochemu Rossiya ne Amerika*, p. 45. At the same time, Canadian agricultural
productivity per worker is incomparably higher than Russia's, at more than $25,000 in
value added per worker in Canada compared to less than $500 in Russia in the early
1990s. See Andrianov, *Rossiya v mirovoy ekonomike*, p. 26. Gorbachev's impressions
of Canadian agricultural efficiency during a ten-day trip to Canada in 1983 became a
significant stimulus to his reform efforts once in office.

[113] Hill and Gaddy, *The Siberian Curse*, pp. 47–51.

[114] Bater, *The Soviet Scene*, p. 209.

the Far North.[115] For example, in order to sustain the coal-based urban settlement of Nerungri in Sakha (Yakutia) with its population of one hundred thousand, developers would have to build a transcontinental railroad through a land without roads, through swamps and hills in a condition of perpetual permafrost. To date, under market conditions, there is no evidence that private investors are willing to take that plunge.[116]

Moreover, the size of the country combined with the low population density means that per capita costs of public infrastructure tend to be higher than elsewhere. To give one instance, the density of Russia's road network is measured at 25 kilometers per 1,000 square kilometers, compared to 1,000 kilometers of road per 1,000 square kilometers in Western Europe (and 800 kilometers of road per 1,000 square kilometers in the United States).

Yet the hindrance of distance is magnified by the third geographical factor, and that is that due to the south-north flow of most of Russia's rivers and the difficulty of access to the world's oceans, land transport predominates over sea transport. As every student of military logistics knows, the latter is vastly cheaper than the former.[117] In Russia, land transport tends to be five times as costly as sea transport.[118] (Fully 80 percent of Russian freight and 44 percent of Russian long-distance passengers are carried by the railroads.[119] Indicatively, whereas fully 51 percent of Western Europe lies within 200 kilometers of the sea, this is true for only 2 percent of European Russia.[120]) Taken together, these three constants of Russian economic geography – an extremely severe climate, vast distances between resources and consumers, and costly means of transportation over these distances – mean that, as a rule, the costs of production in Russia – especially for large-scale infrastructure projects – tend to be several times higher than in almost any other country of the world.[121] Reinforcing the problem, the disintegration of the Soviet Union saw the center of gravity of the Russian state shift farther northward in terms of both land mass and population (if we compare the USSR to the Russian Federation): The

---

[115] Ruge, *Sibirisches Tagebuch*, p. 73.

[116] Ibid.

[117] W. Scott Thompson, "The Persian Gulf and the Correlation of Forces," *International Security*, vol. 7, no. 1 (Summer 1982), pp. 157–80.

[118] Bard, *Investitsionnye Problemy Rossiyskoy Ekonomike*, p. 282.

[119] Radvanyi, *La Nouvelle Russie*, p. 200; Skopin, *Ekonomicheskaya Geografiya Rossii*, p. 268.

[120] Gladkin et al., *Sotsial'no Ekonomicheskaya Geografiya Rossii'*, p. 96.

[121] Bard, *Investitsionnye Problemy Rossiyskoy Ekonomike*, pp. 282–3.

geographic center of the USSR was 57°25' north compared to 60°25' north for the Russian Federation, while the population center shifted from 52° north in the USSR to 55°30' north in the Russian Federation.[122] (Recall that the northern border of the continental United States runs along 49° north between Minnesota and Washington State.) In addition, Russia lost many ports and half of its merchant fleet after the Soviet collapse.[123]

The argument can be illustrated by any number of sectors in the Russian economy. Most famously, the productivity of Russian agriculture in terms of value added has historically been much lower than in Western Europe.[124] Poor soil, unreliable rainfall, and brief growing seasons tended to keep Russian agriculture near the subsistence level in premodern times and to perhaps one-third (at best) the productivity of Central European farming.[125] Relatedly, whereas in Western Europe in the sixteenth to eighteenth centuries, the work of several dozen peasants was required to support one soldier or official, in Russia the labor of several hundred was needed.[126] If anything, the destruction of the peasant culture during Stalin's catastrophic collectivization campaign of the 1930s lowered the productivity of Soviet agriculture further: It was not until after 1953 that 1913 levels of per capita agricultural production were attained and in the 1990s, with the collapse of state subsidy, the productivity of Russian farming fell from a Soviet-era high of 20 centners per hectare to 14 between 1992–7 (as compared to 70–80 in northwestern Europe). The low marginal productivity of most Russian farming has historically hindered the development of agricultural surpluses that in West European countries sustained the rise of a reasonably prosperous peasant and yeoman farmer class, the development of trade and cities, and the associated infrastructure of modernity captured under the rubric of "civic capital" and civil society."[127] This is dramatically illustrated in Table 20, which

---

[122] Ibid., pp. 90–1.

[123] *Ekonomicheskaya Geografiya* (Moscow: Ekzamen, 2003), p. 58.

[124] Parshev, *Pochemu Rossiya ne Amerika*, pp. 117–18. Costs of production were calculated in terms of fuel and electricity, raw materials, pay, and depreciation.

[125] Gladkin et al., *Sotsial'no Ekonomicheskaya Geografiya Rossii'*, pp. 89–98.

[126] See L. V. Milov, *Velikorusskii pakha i osobennosti rossiyskogo istoricheskogo protsessa* [Russian Tillage and Particularities of Russian Historical Development] (Moscow: Rosspen, 1998), expanding upon idem, "Prirodno-klimaticheskiy faktor i osobennosti rossiyskogo istoricheskogo protsessa" [The Natural and Climatic Factor and Particularities of Russian Historical Development], *Voprosy Istorii*, no. 4–5 (1992), pp. 37–56. See also Parshev, *Pochemu Rossiya ne Amerika*, p. 392.

[127] For provocative thoughts along these lines, see Ryszard Kapuscinski, *Imperium* (Paris: Feux Croises/Plon, 1994), p. 339. French translation from the Polish by Varonique Patte.

TABLE 20. *Value-Added per Agricultural Worker, 1991*

| Country | Value-Added per Worker |
|---|---|
| Netherlands | $41,338 |
| Finland | $37,803 |
| USA | $29,544 |
| Norway | $26,586 |
| Canada | $25,153 |
| Japan | $17,253 |
| South Korea | $7,384 |
| Hungary | $3,508 |
| Poland | $1,210 |
| Indonesia | $545 |
| Thailand | $504 |
| Russia | $476 |

outlines the relative productivity of agricultural labor in several countries in the last Soviet year of 1991, as measured in added value (in dollars) per agricultural laborer.[128]

In energy and related areas, comparable economics apply. Consider that permafrost covers 59 percent of the territory of the Russian Federation (10 million square kilometers), extending continuously from Arkhangel in the northwest through the Russian Far East. Rocks and permanently frozen soil can attain considerable thickness, ranging from a few meters to 500 meters in western Siberia and in Yakutia (Sakha) up to 1,000–1,500 meters. In this region there are about seven months of continuous frost. As the French geographer Jean Radvanyi has noted, "This requires sophisticated construction techniques to avoid the effects of thermal conduction induced by the construction of buildings or pipelines on permafrost soils."[129] Outfitting and building oil and other infrastructure in Siberia and the Russian North, where most of the new energy and other mineral reserves are located, are unimaginably expensive by prevailing

---

[128] Andrianov, *Rossiya v mirovoy ekonomike*, p. 26. Possibly employing a different calculus and no doubt influenced by the prevailing artificially high exchange rate for the Soviet ruble (which almost had parity with the U.S. dollar), the *Economist* magazine estimated that in 1987 Soviet agricultural labor productivity was one-fourth that of Western Europe and one-eighth that of the United States. "The Soviet Economy," *Economist*, April 9–15, 1988.

[129] Gladkin et al., *Sotsial'no Ekonomicheskaya Geografiya Rossii'*, p. 94; Radvanyi, *La Nouvelle Russie*, p. 40.

global practice. Before the currency devaluation of August 1998, a barrel of West Siberian crude oil cost about $14 to produce compared to $4 for Kuwaiti crude and U.S. oil drilled from the Gulf of Mexico, about $10 for North Sea crude, and a projected $16 for oil drilled from the Alaskan wilderness preserve, suggesting, in spite of higher costs to observe environmental restrictions in Alaska, that the extremity of Arctic and sub-Arctic conditions makes Russian (as with Alaskan) oil intrinsically expensive compared to other producers and exporters.[130] In 2002, some Russian oil companies – for example, Yukos – began to report production costs of $4–5 per barrel (in fact the average worldwide), which seems unlikely if all of the costs of production, including the massive Soviet-era investment in infrastructure, are factored into the accounting balance.[131] Certainly, in the future, new startup costs cannot be factored out of the decision to invest and produce, under market conditions; this is reflected in Exxon's estimated cost of production for the Sakhalin I complex of nearly $17 per barrel.

Under these climatic conditions, basic construction costs are in general higher than elsewhere; thicker walls require more massive foundations, all of which multiplies the basic costs of production. (For example, a typical Russian one-story house is equivalent to a three-story English house in terms of construction materials used, not because Russian labor is more wasteful – even if it is – but because English houses cannot be lived in under Russian conditions.) Moreover, depreciation costs are higher since buildings as well as machinery are also shorter lived in the Russian climate. As a result, construction costs of all kinds are generally two to three times more expensive in Russia than in Western Europe and much more in most of Siberia.[132]

The intrinsically high costs of Russian oil production have been compounded by the general obsolescence of Russian drilling technology, which through the 1990s was still largely based on a turbo-drill technology developed before the Second World War. The turbo drill, which uses high-pressure water and mud injections to soften the soil, does not rotate and can be made with relatively low-quality steel. Drilling below 3,000 meters requires rotary drills, demanding higher-quality steel from domestic or foreign producers. The stagnation of the Russian steel industry and

[130] www.worldwildlife.org/arctic-refuge/goerold_paper.pdf.
[131] David Ignatius, "Check That Oil," *Washington Post*, November 14, 2003, p. A29.
[132] Gladkin et al., *Sotsial'no Ekonomicheskaya Geografiya Rossie'*, p. 89; Parshev, *Pochemu Rossiya ne Amerika*, pp. 54–6.

the paucity of foreign investment saw Russian oil production continue
to fall throughout the 1990s. Three-fifths of Russia's oil fields are now
of the "difficult-to-recover" type, yielding fewer than ten tons of crude
per day.[133] In many regions, there are more repair brigades than production brigades in the field. As Bater notes, new "fields discovered tend to
be smaller, and almost by definition in more remote and hostile environments, and therefore are more costly to tap."[134] As noted, investment
by Russian oil companies in state-of-the-art foreign technologies between
2000–2 helped to raise short-term output by more intensively exploiting existing fields, but it should be pointed out that when oil fields have
been drained of more than half of their recoverable reserves, exponential
declines in production rapidly follow, as the experience of North Sea oil
shows. New technology cannot help this. Russia's long-term energy future
thus lies in massive new exploration projects in remote and harsh areas
with little or no existing infrastructure (that is, roads, ports, pipelines,
power cables, and so on).[135] For instance, the infrastructure costs alone
that foreign firms are expected to assume in connection with the development of oil deposits on Russia's Sakhalin Island in the Sea of Okhotsk –
that is, pipeline construction, a gigantic gas liquifying plant, storage
facilities, as well as roads and airports to ship oil and gas to world markets – are expected to amount to $13 billion between 2003–6.[136] Costs of
oil production are correspondingly higher.

*inefficient*        Relatedly, Russia expends five times more fuel and electricity and twice
as many raw materials to make $100 of finished product than do the G-7
countries.[137] No doubt, as in all of these areas, there is room for efficiencies. But there are also limits. Thus, it takes about four tons of heating
fuel to heat a typical Moscow apartment of four persons during a year
that includes a seven-month "heating season" (compared to the seven-
month growing season in my home state of Virginia); this would cost
about $2,000 – about the average annual dollarized Russian wage – at
world market prices. Were Gazprom and the oil companies to insist on
world market prices for their product (Gazprom sells gas to the European
Union at a price ten times higher than it sells it for in Russia[138]) most of

[133] Mastepanov, "Main Points of Russia's Energy Strategy." p. 44.
[134] Bater, *The Soviet Scene*, pp. 203–4.
[135] *Petroleum Review*, April 2002, at *JRL*, #6225, item no. 7, at www.cdi.org; Jeanne Whalen,
      "Russia Pumps Up Oil Exports," *Wall Street Journal*, June 13, 2002, at www.wsj.com.
[136] *International Herald Tribune*, August 7, 2002, p. 9, at www.iht.com.
[137] Skopin, *Ekonomicheskaya Geografiya Rossii*, p. 45.
[138] Guillet, "Fix Gazprom's Fatal Leak."

Russia would not survive the winter. The same holds true for electricity: On purely market grounds, why should Russian electricity producers supply to Russians at all, given that the domestic price has been 1–2 cents per kilowatt hour compared to 12–15 cents in most of the rest of the world? Fully 80–90 percent of the cost of mining Siberian gold is defined by expenses on energy, the infrastructure of which was established under decidedly nonmarket Soviet auspices. Likewise, the mining of copper and nickel in Norilsk is dependent upon nearby gas installations, without which prices would become unsustainably high. The 80 percent of Russia's massive energy reserves that consists of coal may be unrecoverable under market conditions – there is simply no profit to be made. In a dramatic but by no means atypical case, while Russia possesses huge deposits of bauxite – in the Kolyma Peninsula, near Volkhov, in the Urals region – under free-market conditions it is cheaper to purchase bauxite in Tunisia and Guinea and ship it to the Altai region to produce aluminum.[139] Likewise, the editor of a Siberian newspaper in a gold mining center in Sakha (Yakutia) as well as local engineers have noted ruefully that, given the price of gold on the world market, it would be cheaper to buy gold on the London Exchange and bring it to Sakha.[140] Similarly, Russia is able to harvest just 15 percent of its massive timber reserves. Ex-Russian Prime Minister Mikhail Kasyanov has complained in this regard that, "Nothing has been done to move felling away from cities and villages." As a result, Russia, which contains 25 percent of the world's timber reserves, accounts for just 3 percent of world timber trade and even imports 35 percent of its paper products.[141]

From this point of view, it is perhaps not entirely coincidental that the initial "development" costs for coal, gold, silver, diamonds, and so on, in such locales as Vorkuta, Magadan, Yakutia, and elsewhere in the Russian North were assumed by slave labor under the economic jurisdiction of the NKVD. According to the 1941 "State Plan of the Development of the National Economy of the USSR," a copy of which landed in the famous Smolensk Archive, now housed in the Hoover Institution at Stanford University, 18 percent of Soviet capital investment that year, apart from transportation and the armed forces (for which no data was given), fell within the responsibility of the NKVD (that is, 6.81 billion rubles out of 37.65 billion rubles in all). According to Gosplan chief Nikolay

*[handwritten marginalia: small profit for remote resource recovery]*

---

[139] Parshev, *Pochemu Rossiya ne Amerika*, p. 77.
[140] Ruge, *Sibirisches Tagebuch*, pp. 78, 115.
[141] www.pravda.ru, at *JRL*, #6316, June 19, 2002, item no. 9, at www.cdi.org.

Voznesensky (who himself fell victim to a purge later in the decade), the
NKVD's capital investment responsibilities came to 12 percent of a total
national investment pool of 57 billion rubles. In the field of construction,
the NKVD was responsible for 17 percent of all production, exploiting
over 1.17 million forced laborers for that purpose. In lumber, the NKVD's
share of total national production was 12 percent, although, importantly
for our purposes, in northern regions the percentage was much higher:
in Arkhangelsk oblast, 26 percent; in Khabarovsk krai and the Karelo-
Finnish republic, each more than 33 percent; in Murmansk oblast, more
than 40 percent; and in the Komi Autonomous Oblast, more than 50 percent. Virtually all of Soviet gold production was administered by the
NKVD, which governed huge territories such as Kolyma toward that
end. Likewise, the NKVD was to produce 150,000 tons of chrome out
of a total Soviet production of 370,000 tons, 5.3 million tons of coal,
250,000 tons of oil, and 82 million bricks in the Khabarovsk and
Maritime oblasts alone.[142] In the end, it remains unclear "whether or not
this pool of forced labor – civilians, prisoner of war or simply criminal–
ever really contributed to the national economy more than it cost to su-
pervise and support. . . ."[143] In fact, the virtually blanket amnesty that the
post-Stalin government issued to Gulag prisoners soon after the dictator's
death in 1953 threw the mining industry in the Far North into crisis, as
many of the establishments could not be maintained apart from the slave
labor and low overhead costs made possible by KGB administration.[144]

Long after the death of Stalin and the end of the mass terror, Siberian
economic development was mainly subsidized by the Soviet government,
that is, by other, economically more viable regions of Russia. For example, in the mid-1970s, Vladimir Putin, now president of Russia, earned
1,000 rubles for one-and-a-half month's work in the Komi Republic, north

---

[142] Merle Fainsod, *How Russia Is Ruled* (Cambridge, MA: Harvard University Press, 1963),
pp. 459–60; see also Anne Applebaum, *Gulag: A History* (New York: Doubleday, 2003),
pp. 450, 460–75; Stanislaw Staniewicz, "The Main Features of Soviet Forced Labor," in
William L. Blackwell, ed., *Russian Economic Development from Peter the Great to Stalin*
(New York: New Viewpoints, 1974), pp. 276–91.

[143] Bater, *The Soviet Scene*, pp. 218–20. Similarly, Ryszard Kapuscinski wonders at the
distortions to the Soviet steel industry, and to the economy at large, created by the
omnipresence of barbed wire along the vast border, around the camps, around closed
installations, and so on. *Imperium*, pp. 94–5. See also Michael Thumann, *Das Lied von
der russischen Erde: Russlands Ring um Groesse und Einheit* [The Song of the Russian
Earth: Russia's Struggle for Greatness and Unity] (Stuttgart: Deutsche-Verlags Anstalt,
2002), p. 231.

[144] Ruge, *Sibirisches Tagebuch*, p. 130.

of the Urals. By contrast, the average doctor or teacher could expect to earn 180 rubles in the same period of time, a discrepancy of more than 5:1.[145] Large-scale urban settlement in much of Siberia was made possible by a generous package of subsidies made available by the Soviet government. This package typically included double and triple pay, paid vacations home or to the Black Sea resort area, a rich network of cultural and athletic establishments, low rents, and no heating bills. Industrial as well as "consumer" fuel and energy were subsidized, as were the necessary trucks and machinery, which were simply incorporated into the Five-Year Plan and delivered to the region.[146] In effect, the rest of Russia paid the price for Siberian development.

Market economics and Arctic development simply do not mesh well, as Canada's Arctic North (as well as Alaska), with a population density one-fifteenth that of late-Soviet Russia, testifies.[147] In fact, the first post-Soviet decade has had a dramatic impact on Russia's "territorial demography": The population of the Chukotka peninsula opposite Alaska has fallen by 50–60 percent; that of Magadan, once home to the notorious penal colony, by 50 percent; 15 percent of the population of the strategic northern city of Murmansk has left for good; the Russian population in the gold mining province of Sakha (Yakutia) has declined by 20 percent; while at least 1 million Russians, or 12 percent of the total, have left the Russian Far East for European Russia. Twenty percent of the population of Russia's most remote settlements in the Far North have had to be evacuated; in Siberia and the Far East, three hundred settlements have become ghost towns.[148] No longer can gold mines be run to support entire cities, as was true in the late-Soviet period. The impact of market economics on Siberian settlement, if not development, may be gauged in a comparison of a typical diamond operation in Sakha province (Yakutia), which in 1997 employed thirty-three hundred workers in a permanent settlement, to a comparable operation in Australia, which employs three hundred to four hundred workers who are flown in to work in shifts for several weeks at a time. The costs of production are thus incomparably cheaper in Australia, making Russian gold production on the traditional model uncompetitive under market conditions. (Indicatively,

---

[145] Pierre Lorrain, *La mystérieuse ascension de Vladimir Poutine* (Monaco: Editions de Rocher, 2000), p. 121.
[146] Ruge, *Sibirisches Tagebuch*, pp. 43, 78, 94.
[147] Gladkin et al., *Sotsial'no Ekonomicheskaya Geografiya Rossii'*, p. 109.
[148] Thumann, *Das Lied von der russischen Erde*, pp. 223–38; Traynor, "For Siberia, a Return to Wasteland."

more recent oil fields east of the Urals are now employing the Australian method.[149] Under market conditions, parts of Siberia may be developed, but they will not be peopled as during the Soviet period.) The liberal Russian economist German Gref – a key Putin minister – has correctly noted in this regard that Siberia, from a liberal market point of view, has become a drain on limited Russian resources.[150] What then is to become of Russia?

## IX. Conclusions

What conclusions may be drawn from the preceding analysis? First, on strictly liberal market grounds, most of the Russian economy should be declared bankrupt. As Columbia University economist Richard Ericson has observed, "A large proportion of [Russian] firms in any industry, and all firms in some basic processing industries, are nonviable in the most basic sense – they can never produce goods that could sell for more than the cost of production."[151] By 1998, nearly 49 percent of Russian enterprises were operating in the red (under admittedly opaque Russian accounting practices).[152] One indication of the impact of market logic on the Russian economy may be seen in the fact that, while using nonmarket (largely physical) indicators the Soviet economy of the mid-1980s is now estimated to have been about one-fourth that of the United States, application of market (that is, value-based) criteria placed the Russian gross domestic product at just 2.5 percent that of the United States just two years after Soviet collapse in 1993.[153] Swedish economist Stefan Hedlund has written in this regard:

No mental transformations conceivable would have solved the problems of what to do with derelict, value destroying industries; with resource extraction in places where nature precludes all sense of profitability; or with urban concentrations north of the Arctic Circle, which under any remotely economically rational regime would never have been put there in the first place.[154]

---

[149] Ruge, *Sibirisches Tagebuch*, p. 247.

[150] Traynor, "For Siberia, a Return to Wasteland."

[151] Richard Ericson, "Economists and the Russian Transition," *Slavic Review*, vol. 57, no. 3 (Fall 1998), p. 622.

[152] Bard, *Investitsionnye Problemy Rossiyskoy Ekonomike*, p. 212; Radvanyi, *La Nouvelle Russie*, p. 146. Bard notes that another 30 percent of firms are on the verge of the red whereas just 20 percent of firms are significantly profitable, even in the face of widespread tax evasion.

[153] Andrianov, *Rossiya v mirovoy ekonomike*, pp. 6–7; Igor Birman, *Ya–Ekonomist* [I am an Economist] (Moscow: Vremya, 2001), p. 380.

[154] Hedlund, *Russia's "Market" Economy*, p. 13.

Second, taking geography seriously underscores that there is an enormous difference between geologically existing resources and economically available resources.[155] It is the huge initial costs of development associated with Siberian investment in the context of the political and legal uncertainties that have deterred foreign and Russian investors from paying for new systems of production rather than depleting the stocks of Soviet-era investment (and investing their money elsewhere). As a team of Russian economic geographers recently concluded:

> It is clear today that, under market conditions, many of the gigantic Soviet-era construction, production, and mining projects, which were undertaken, literally, "at the end of the world," could never have been carried out at all in light of the enormous capital investment requirements as well as their unprofitability.[156]

And even then, the physical inaccessibility of much of Russia's oil and gas reserves means that it is, in the words of one Russian economist, "no more accessible than methane from Jupiter."[157] Where massive, outdoor infrastructure is not concerned, as for example in the computer and especially the software industry, climatic-geographical factors clearly apply much less if at all. There is no intrinsic reason that Russia should not be a worldwide software leader. But here institutional considerations prevail: that is, rampant software piracy, while of obvious short-term benefit to the impoverished Russian consumer (who can pay $1 but not $20 for a CD), raises impossible economic obstacles to the development of a legitimate, native Russian software industry. The inability of the Russian state to contain software piracy places Russia at a clear competitive disadvantage compared to India, which has even lower labor costs, more widespread use of English, placement of myriad Indian executives in U.S. companies, the aid of the government, and a reasonably effective legal system for the protection of intellectual property rights. As a result, India's software industry generates revenues of more than $60 billion per year, compared to $1–2 billion for its Russian counterpart. In such cases, the barrier of legal and administrative uncertainty remains, whatever the degree of climatic-geographical influence upon the costs of production.[158]

---

[155] Gladkin et al., *Sotsial'no Ekonomicheskaya Geografiya Rossii'*, p. 118, passim.
[156] Ibid., p. 114. See also Bard, *Investitsionnye Problemy Rossiyskoye Ekonomike*, p. 281.
[157] Parshev, *Pochemu Rossiya ne Amerika*, p. 62.
[158] John Baroli, "Russia Takes Advantage of Brain Power at Home," *International Herald Tribune*, May 28, 2001, p. 12. Russian computer programming outsourcing totaled $110 million in 2000 compared to $6 billion for India in 2001; Ashlee Vance, "From Russia with Code," *Infoworld*, March 16, 2001, at www.bisnis.doc.gov.

It was thus not surprising that in 1998, when the Russian government decided that the state would own all patents, patent applications dropped to zero.[159] Neither does it help when companies such as Exxon/Mobil and Chevron/Texaco stand to lose $60 million in exploration and research capital because the Russian government – under pressure from the state-controlled oil group Rosneft – reneged on a ten-year old tender for the exploration rights to the Sakhalin 3 oilfield, as happened in late January 2004.[160]

Third, under these circumstances, it is clear that liberal economic premises have much less applicability to Russia's circumstances than the famous "Washington consensus" of the 1990s presumed. Russia as a whole cannot be developed economically without the state. This is not to say that there is no place for the market in the Russian economy. But in a liberal world economic order, why should capital automatically flow to a Russia whose costs of development are typically two to three times higher, even with cheap and relatively skilled labor, than almost anywhere else in the world? It is hard enough to envisage how Russia can develop with its existing "quasimarket" and in the presence of the corrupt and criminalized state that prevails today.[161] As Thane Gustafson has observed, "The quasi-stabilization we see in Russia today, founded on what remains of the Soviet inheritance, is not viable over the longer run, because it cannot generate growth and prosperity."[162] But I find it implausible to imagine how even an efficient and incorruptible Russian economy and public sector can thrive under strictly liberal auspices, without a state structure and state policies designed to compensate for the many inherent disadvantages that Russia faces as a result of its economic geography. This now includes the massive investment required to reconfigure Russia's urban-industrial infrastructure away from large-scale Siberian settlement toward a more Eurocentric Russian political economy. As in Western Europe in the first decades after 1945, only the state can assume the costs of raising the public infrastructure that is the prerequisite for broad-based, self-sustaining economic development. The nexus between politics and economics thus remains; the only serious question is, under which auspices and for which purposes?

---

[159] CNETnews.com, January 29, 2004.

[160] *Financial Times*, January 30, 2004, at www.ft.com.

[161] Aleksandr Nekipelov, "Kvazirynok kak rezul'tat rossiyskikh reform" [The Quasi-Market as the Result of Russian Reforms], *Pro et Contra* (Moscow), Spring 1999, pp. 5–27.

[162] Gustafson, *Capitalism Russian Style*, p. 9.

Russia's biggest "entrepreneurs" have been acting, albeit often in legally dubious fashion, in ways that reflect this logic. Political protection is understood to be critical not only in acquiring valuable assets (often at a fraction of their true market value) but in protecting those assets from real market competition, whether Russian or foreign. "Political influence is still very crucial," notes Mikhail Fridman, oil tycoon and chair of Moscow's Alfa financial group. Aluminum magnate Oleg Deripaska – who by mid-2002 controlled 70 percent of Russian aluminum production – concurs, conceding that, "If we don't have a strong [monopoly] position in the market, we will lose." Correspondingly, Deripaska has been vigorously lobbying the Russian government to raise tariffs on the import of secondhand cars, which he views as crucial to the survival of his automobile business.[163] Truly free trade and open access to Russia's investment market, which is implicit in Russia's eventual adhesion to the World Trade Organization, would likely wipe out the preponderance of what remains of Russia's declining industrial base.[164]

There is plenty of room to debate the kinds of state policies and their relationship to the market economy – for example, the degree of tariff protection; the most beneficial currency valuation[165]; industrial policy and the inevitable subsidy as well as investor guarantees that the policy implies[166]; redistribution across classes, sectors, and regions; the degree of free movement of goods in relationship to the free movement of capital (that is, open versus closed capital accounts); the relative importance of ownership (state or private) versus competition among enterprises[167];

[163] "Russia's New Wealth," *Business Week*, August 5–12, 2002, pp. 28–34.
[164] A study conducted by the Russian Academy of Sciences and the National Investment Council in July 2002 concluded that just twenty-three of Russia's eighty-nine regions stood to gain from admission into the World Trade Organization. These were mainly (southern) border regions, Moscow, and raw materials export regions. In early 2003, spokespersons for the Russian machine-building and arms sectors, respectively, stated that early WTO admission would destroy 90 percent of their enterprises. Keith Bush, "Russland und die WTO–Stand der Verhandlungen," in Lueke and Weber, *So Kommen Sie nach*, p. 372. Industrial production made up just 26.5 percent of Russian GDP in 2002, continuing a progressive decline even while the energy industries increased their share of Russian GDP. See www.imf.org.
[165] A point emphasized by Tabata, "The Great Russian Depression of the 1990's," p. 397.
[166] For an analysis of the prospects of such arrangements in Russia, see "Oil Change," *Economist*, September 21, 2001, at www.economist.com; for President Putin's endorsement of the concept, see Interfax News Agency (Moscow), in English, 0756 gmt, September 3, 2000.
[167] Gustafson, *Capitalism Russian Style*, pp. 50–1.

special economic zones, and so on.[168] At a minimum, some combination of a weak ruble, targeted protectionism, production-sharing agreements for foreign investors, and a legal basis for trading in land that could collateralize Russian land holdings to stimulate domestic mortgage, loan, and insurance markets would seem necessary to encourage substantial direct investment – including foreign direct investment – in Russia and the prospects of a sustained, broad-based recovery going beyond the fuels sector. Here there is little distinction between Russian and non-Russian capital: Holders of capital, whatever their nationality, can no longer be coerced into financing Russian development. Instead, they must be persuaded to do so. Tools of persuasion, in addition to those just mentioned, must include clear, stable, and enforceable property rights and transparent corporate governance.

Yet two questions remain: in an increasingly liberal world economic order, characterized not only by free movement of goods but free movement of capital, is it possible for the Russian state (a) to offer the massive (and essentially neocolonial) concessions needed to induce large-scale capital investment in Russia's decaying economic infrastructure, and (b) to enforce (as does the Chinese government) essentially mercantilistic controls on the movement of capital? If the answer to either of these questions is no, then two final questions arise: (1) To what extent does a liberal world need Russia at all? (2) Indeed, to what extent can historical Russia exist in a predominantly liberal world order? That such questions must be seriously entertained suggests that the burden of proof now lies on those arguing against the centrality of the state for Russia's prospects.

---

[168] See Bard, *Investitsionnye Problemy Rossiyskoy Ekonomike*, pp. 142–53, 327–37, for an essentially Keynesian analysis and model of Russia's economic challenges.

# ⟨ Conclusions ⟩

> Foreigners are unwilling to invest money in those areas of the Russian economy 'which we want them to invest in [that is, national infrastructure and science-intensive industries]; [and] we do not let foreign companies invest in those areas they want to invest in [that is, natural resources].
>
> – Aleksandr Livshits, Deputy General Director of the Russian Aluminum Company.[1]

## I. Summing Up

It is with justifiable trepidation that one attempts projections as to what may happen in Russia over the coming years. We could have an amusing time solely devoted to reviewing previous such attempts and comparing the forecasts with the outcomes. To save time, let us just recall Franklin D. Roosevelt's words to a joint session of Congress upon his return from the Yalta Conference in February 1945: "We are going to get along with the Russians just fine!"[2]

The memorable failures in speaking of the future derive more from failures of imagination than failures of analysis of existing factors. It is the intervention of discontinuous change that tends to falsify the linear projection of existing trends into the future, however ably such a projection might be-made. Meteorology rather than calculus seems to be the right metaphor. All of us have 1989 (the collapse of communism in Eastern

---

[1] Rosbalt (Moscow), January 27, 2004, in *Johnson's Russia List* (hereafter *JRL*), #8035, January 27, 2004, item no. 4, at www.cdi.org.
[2] *New York Times*, March 1, 1945, p. 1.

Europe), 1990 (the unification of Germany), and 1991 (the peaceful dis-integration of the USSR) in mind, of course.

Just to give one instance of how the best-laid plans are themselves waylaid by a failure to imagine the unimaginable, let us recount a now forgotten Group of Seven (G-7) summit meeting, held in Houston in July 1990 and detailed in Chapter 3. At that summit, the G-7 leaders tasked the world's leading international economic institutions to compile a re-port with recommendations on how the USSR and the West might best proceed to reform the Soviet economy. In December of that year, they presented their report, which in effect recommended a program of long-term, progressive, highly structured and regulated evolutionary reform of the Soviet economy.[3] Whatever chances such a program had to be imple-mented were probably eliminated by the unexpected Soviet collapse of 1991, which completed the destruction of institutions that were required for the development of such a complex and comprehensive reform. Yet note that it was not just the Soviet collapse that changed the equation but the behavior of the G-7 states themselves, above all the United States, as they now faced a Russian setting that was receptive to Western influence in ways that were without precedent, save perhaps for the fateful spring and summer of 1917, when liberal Russia plunged herself headlong into military defeat and then political collapse for the sake of its Western al-lies. Think also of the fate of the verbal promise made by George Bush and Helmut Kohl in 1990 not to expand NATO eastward, once Mikhail Gorbachev (as well as Bush) were no longer in office. Whatever else one may say for the 1990s in American–Russian relations, that decade – punctuated by significant US involvement in Russia's domestic affairs, political as well as economic, as well as by the continual expansion of NATO – ended with the first mass-based wave of anti-American senti-ment in Russian history, unseen at any time during the cold war.

So, a prudent self-skepticism is in order when speaking of the future, as is self-consciousness about the assumptions underlying our projections and the conditions that might falsify, or even magnify, them. What, then, does the preceding analysis in the book imply for Russia's prospects and the position of the outside world toward Russia?

Let us review the relevant findings of the book. Most importantly, 1991 witnessed the disintegration of a centuries-old political order in Russia, one characterized by a patrimonial, autocratic, imperial state. This

---

[3] Stefan Hedlund, *Russia's "Market" Economy: A Bad Case of Predatory Capitalism* (UK: UCL Press, 1999), pp. 114–15.

distinctive fusion of wealth and sovereignty, of despotic and colonial rule, permitted Russia's rulers to defend and extend Russia's territorial and political jurisdiction in the hostile, Eurocentric international order that persisted throughout modern Russian history and that continued in different form in the cold war confrontation between Soviet Russia and the United States. Interestingly, the reduction in international tensions at the end of the 1980s both reflected internal Soviet reforms and propelled the disintegration of the distinctive Russian regime type. Fortunately for the Russians, and in this they owe an eternal debt of gratitude to Gorbachev, the collapse of Russia's historical political chrysalis found Russia facing the most benign interstate environment in its history. Other equally remarkable consequences followed the end of Soviet rule, *inter alia*:

- Political power and economic wealth in Russia are further removed from each other than they have been since before Ivan IV's ("the Terrible") reduction of the boyars in the late-sixteenth century, with the partial exception of the turn of the twentieth century. While we may speak of neopatrimonial tendencies under Putin, the historically tight fusion of state and property has been dissolved, likely for good.
- Democratic forms have replaced autocratic ones in defining the terms of establishing and replacing governments. While the state has been able to engineer significant constraints on substantive democratic accountability, no substitute for the holding of nominally competitive elections has been found credible. The forms of governance thus retain the potential to constrain rulers' preferences.
- Russia in the form of the Russian Federation is more Russian than at any time in recent memory: Ethnic Russians constitute more than 80 percent of Russia's population, compared to 40–4 percent of the late Russian Empire and 50 percent and declining in the late USSR. Ethnic tensions are thus unlikely to destroy the Russian Federation in the manner of the USSR, Yugoslavia, and Czechoslovakia. Russia, in effect, will have to be destroyed by the Russians themselves, and they appear to have ample incentive to avoid this scenario.[4]
- As noted, Russia's international environment, or at least its interstate environment, remains unthreatening even amid a decade-long quagmire war in the province of Chechnya, which might have been thought to invite unwelcome foreign attentions in an earlier period of history.

[4] Reneo Lukic and Allen C. Lynch, *Europe from the Balkans to the Urals: The Disintegration of Yugoslavia and the USSR and International Politics* (Oxford, UK: Oxford University Press, 1996), pp. 385–93.

- With Soviet disintegration, the economic and demographic center of gravity of Russia has moved farther northward, underscoring the influence of economic geography on the costs of production and thus on Russia's prospects for integration along liberal lines into the international economy.
- In spite of five years of impressive economic growth between 1999–2003, Russia remains starved for capital investment, especially foreign direct investment, which remains miniscule by any standard of comparison.
- Russia has in fact tried (albeit briefly in its pure form) and rejected economic reform along liberal lines, a view that was given electoral sanction in the December 2003 parliamentary elections and the overwhelming reelection of Vladimir Putin as Russian president in March 2004. Yet neither does the old statist model provide obvious answers to Russia's economic challenges, which entail adaptation to high-productivity models of intensive economic growth instead of the extensive patterns of growth more typical of Russian history and for which the patrimonial state had some relevance. Absent a convincing answer, Russia risks sinking, even if slowly due to its residual natural resource base, into a ghetto of the world political economy. Dramatic political consequences could then follow, as is suggested by a juxtaposition of Russian and Chinese economic growth rates since 1980.
- The rise to power and genuine popularity of Putin reflects a deep-seated reaction throughout Russia to the failure of a perceived liberal experiment. Putin has exploited a charismatic legitimacy, reinforced by the instrumentalities of elections, to consolidate the superpresidentialist political system bequeathed to him by Boris Yeltsin. At the same time, it remained unclear as of the time of writing, and for reasons as stated previous, what Putin can make of his extraordinary formal powers to encourage the regeneration of Russia. For instance, no primarily raw materials exporting economy has sustained high levels of growth for a long period of time in the past half century.[5] Yet as we have seen (in Chapter 6), Russia faces massive capital requirements to replace and restructure Soviet-era infrastructure as well as significant obstacles in attracting the scale of investment requisite to the task. All the while, the fiscal stability of the Russian state and the macroeconomic health of the country continue to hinge on a relatively

[5] Economist Intelligence Unit, "Russia's Long-Term Growth Prospects: Is Foreign Direct Investment the Key?" *Country Forecast: Russia* (July 2003), at www.amcham.ru.

high global price of oil. As Russia is the highest cost producer of oil in the world, it is especially sensitive to fluctuations in this commodity market that twice in the recent past ruined the policies of Russian heads of state, that is, Gorbachev in the late 1980s and Yeltsin in the late 1990s. The worldwide experience of countries dependent on the export of oil and minerals suggests a powerful debilitating long-term effect of resource dependency upon both growth rates in the economy and the integrity of national political, legal, and administrative institutions. The temptations of "rent seeking" – to exploit privileged institutional access to "extractive" export revenue – gravely weaken incentives to build rule-governed institutional regimes. This is above all true in those countries, such as post-Soviet Russia and postcolonial Nigeria, that inherited already devastated institutional landscapes upon the end of the previous regime, that is, communist and colonial, respectively.[6]

Two implications follow from these findings: First, the Russian state will continue to be preoccupied with system maintenance over the foreseeable future. Second, the outside world should be preoccupied with this as well. Such are the considerations that frame the following analysis of the influence of domestic factors on Russia's world position over the coming decade.

## II. Twelve Theses on the Influence of Domestic Factors on Russia's World Role

### Point 1. *The Continuing Preeminence of Security*
My initial and basic premise is that the security of Russia's numerous archipelagoes of nuclear, chemical, and biological materials, as well as of the weapons systems themselves, represents the number one problem of international security. This problem has multiple dimensions:

- Traditional proliferation issues, reflecting mainly economic pressures, such as the Russian nuclear sales to Iran
- The operational safety of Russia's system of nuclear power reactors
- The integrity of civilian and military waste sites (For example, the submarines at Murmansk)

---

[6] Xavier Sala-i-Martin and Arvind Subramanian, "Addressing the Natural Resource Curse: An Illustration from Nigeria," National Bureau of Economic Research, Working Paper 9804, June 2003, at www.nber.org/papers/w9804. Thanks to Paul B. Stephan III for bringing this article to my attention.

- Pressures that could lead to an accidental launch due to maintaining a nuclear force and command and control structure that strives to be competitive with the United States (see the Kursk accident for an object lesson, *inter alia*)[7]
- Terrorist attacks on weapons of mass destruction (WMD) or civilian waste materials sites
- Leakage of material abroad

Most of the world's poorly guarded storage facilities are in Russia. These facilities house more than 20,000 nuclear warheads in 120 facilities. The tactical nuclear devices are not equipped with electronic locks; just 20 percent of Russian nuclear materials have security systems that meet U.S. standards (most of these have been funded by the United States through the Cooperative Threat Reduction program, otherwise known as the Nunn-Lugar program); whereas 15 percent of Russian uranium stockpiles have been rendered unusable for weapons, at current rates, completion of the process will take more than twenty years. Moreover, the CIA estimates the number of Russian tactical nuclear warheads with a margin of error in the hundreds.[8] A recent Center for Strategic and International Studies (CSIS) panel convened in London concluded that these WMD facilities pose a far more serious threat to the world than did, and probably could, Iraq.[9] In this light, it is remarkable that the U.S.–Russian Cooperative Threat Reduction program is funded at just $1 billion per year, compared to $41 billion per year for the Department of Homeland Security and $79 billion for the costs associated with the invasion and initial occupation of Iraq, a country whose potential to threaten vital U.S. interests seems epiphenomenal in comparison to the consequences of the breakdown of public order in Russia.[10]

## Point 2. The Continuing Centrality of the State in Russian Political Development

To the extent that this is true, then it is the viability of the Russian state rather than the political or economic coloration of the government of the

---

[7] Bruce G. Blair, "Hair-Trigger Missiles Risk Catastrophic Terrorism," at www.cdi.org, April 29, 2003 (contact bblair@cdi.org); Walter Pincus, "Nunn Urges U.S., Russia To Ease Hair-Trigger Nuclear Alerts," *Washington Post*, May 22, 2003, p. A23.

[8] For information on the public record, see the article by Seymour Hersh, "The Wild East: Organized Crime Has Russia Even More Firmly in Its Grip Than Has Been Reported," *Atlantic Monthly*, vol. 273, no. 6 (June 1994), at www.theatlantic.com.

[9] *Novye Izvestiya*, February 4, 2003, in *JRL*, #7047, February 4, 3003, item #5.

[10] *Chicago Tribune*, May 4, 2003, at www.chicagotribune.com ; see also www.nti.org/cnwm.

day that should be the focus of international efforts to engage Russia. This should be as plain to liberals as to realists, since democratic government itself is unimaginable without a market-based economy and rule of law that presuppose the existence of a competent system of state administration.

### Point 3. The Persistence of Russian Weakness

Under the most favorable assumptions, Russia will remain a large country rather than a great power, although it may not be politic for political leaders to say so. Russia will strain to attain the capabilities simply to defend its own borders, as the wars in Chechnya demonstrate. A policy of "military Keynesianism" in the manner of Nazi Germany is excluded. Yet while Russian power will remain weak and fragile, Russian cooperation is still essential to establishing a workable system of international security. One should be wary, then, of conflating power with influence. Russia will remain weak in traditional power terms for the foreseeable future; yet Russian cooperation – barring extreme scenarios – cannot simply be coerced.

### Point 4. Russia as an Enclave Economy

Again, under the most favorable assumptions, Russia will remain an enclave economy in which both macroeconomic equilibrium and the fiscal health of the federal government remain disproportionately and dangerously dependent on the price of oil on international markets. Energy-related revenues accounted for 38 percent of the central government's budget in 2002 and nearly half in 2004; that budget currently balances at $21.50 per barrel of oil on the world market.[11] Oil and gas together account for 56 percent of Russian export revenues whereas all raw materials and semifinished materials make up 80 percent of all export revenues, in contrast to 60 percent in the Soviet period.[12] The Russian economy and thus the Russian government are more dependent on the energy and raw

---

[11] Chris Weafer, "Too Much Oil Could Be Bad for Russia's Health," *Financial Times*, April 29, 2003 at www.ft.com.

[12] A Yu. Skopin, *Ekonomicheskaya Geografiya Rossii* [Russian Economic Geography] (Moscow: Prospekt, 2003), p. 35. See also Grigory Yavlinsky, "Demodernization," at www.eng.yabloko.ru, at *JRL*, #7057, February 11, 2003, item #8; for George Tenet's statement, see "CIA, Tenet Testimony on Russia," *JRL*, #7059, February 12, 2003, item #7.

materials sector than ever before, a telling sign that structural reform of the economy has yet to take place.[13]

### Point 5. Russia's Remains a Dependent Economy

Consequently, Russia remains in a state of tension between the temptations of high oil prices, which mitigate the urgency of structural reforms and the danger of low oil prices, which threaten the viabililty of the state itself, as they did after 1986 and in 1998, when the world price of oil sank to $10 per barrel. This is, of course, the fate of petrostates around the world. Russian President Putin seems to understand this situation perfectly, as his remarks in the 2003 annual State of the Nation address reveal: "Our economic foundation is ... unreliable and very weak. ... Russia will [prosper] only when it is not dependent on ... unpredictable changes in external markets."[14] To take just one additional indicator of dependence, Russia's ratio of net debts to current account receipts stood at 78 percent in mid-2003, compared to a median of 32 percent for a group of twelve investment-grade economies outside of those of North America, Western Europe, and Japan.[15]

### Point 6. The Fragility of Russian Stability

Therefore, both the Russian economy, which has been improving in the past four years, and the Russian state, which has been consolidated (or *gleichgeschaltet*) to an extent under Putin in the same period, remain fragile accomplishments. Linear extrapolation from current economic and political trends ten years down the road seems tenuous. This is especially so since the primary impulses for Russia's recent spurt of economic growth derive from two factors, one of which was a one-time event with diminishing returns, that is, the 75 percent devaluation of the ruble in August 1998 and the spur this gave to domestic manufacturing; the other was an external shift in the terms of trade over which Russia has no real influence, that is, the near quadrupling of the price of oil between 1999 and early 2003.[16] Most direct investment in that time has been targeted

---

[13] For reliable data and projections on the Russian economy, see the periodic forecasts published by the U.S.–Russia Business Council, at www.usrbc.org.
[14] Transcript of President's State of the Nation address, *BBC Monitoring*, May 16, 2003, at *JRL*, #7186, May 18, 2003, item no. 1.
[15] Andrew Hurst, "Russia Has Hill To Climb To Win Investment Grade," Reuters (Moscow), February 7, 2003, at *JRL*, #7051, February 7, 2003, item no. 19.
[16] Jacques Sapir, "Russia's Economic Growth and European Integration," paper presented to conference of the Norwegian Foreign Policy Institute, Oslo, October 11, 2002, and

to areas that have been directly favored by these two factors, consumer perishables and oil. Given expanding global supplies and normal fluctuations in the global oil market, especially after the stupefying American victory in Iraq and the securing of the oil fields there, a third collapse of oil prices to the vicinity of $10–15 per barrel in three decades cannot be realistically excluded over the course of the next ten years. Even if the average price of oil over this period remains relatively high, a single, prolonged collapse of world oil prices could have devastating effects on Russia's economic and political stability.[17] Even barring such a scenario, Russia's macroeconomic and fiscal health are highly sensitive to oil price and exchange rate fluctuations; a 10 percent change in the price of oil corresponds to a 0.8 percent change in GDP, whereas a 10 percent change in the value of the ruble corresponds to a 1.4 percent change in GDP.[18]

### Point 7. The Priority of Domestic Affairs in Foreign Policy

Because of the magnitude and mutually reinforcing character of Russia's multiple domestic challenges – social, demographic, political, military, as well as economic – Russia will remain utterly absorbed by its domestic problems. Domestic needs are unlikely to be sacrificed to foreign policy ambitions. Indeed, the primary purpose of foreign policy will be to sustain the enclave economy and the international access without which Russia would sink altogether. While foreign adventures may safely be excluded, the ease and price of cooperation with Russia can be affected by the tenor of Russia's relations with the G-7 states, above all with the United States; this point becomes all the more pertinent if Russia develops a more truly accountable political system. Ironically, to date, an ultimately pliant Russian diplomacy has rested upon a presidential authority that is safely insulated from normal political accountability and thus from the anti-Americanism of Russia's national security elites and increasingly of the Russian population itself.[19]

---

idem, "Is Russian Growth Bound To Disappear?" *Russian and Eurasian Review*, vol. 2, issue 2, January 21, 2003, at www.jamestown.org.

[17] Robert E. Ebel, "Russian Energy and the Power of Oil," paper presented to the CSIS/NDU Seminar on the Sources and Limits of Russian Power, December 17, 2002, p. 10.

[18] Laza Kekic, "How Dependent Is Growth on the Oil Price?" *St. Petersburg Times*, February 3, 2004, p. 9.

[19] For a careful study of Russian elite and mass opinion on foreign policy during the 1990s, see William Zimmerman, *The Russian People and Foreign Policy* (Princeton, NJ: Princeton University Press, 2002).

### Point 8. Political Effects of Fluctuations in World Oil Prices

A prolonged decline of global oil prices below $15 per barrel could precipitate the third collapse of the Russian political economy in as many decades, a view shared by World Bank economists.[20] In spite of claims by Yukos to pump oil for less than $2 per barrel, factoring in actual investment costs would place most new Russian production in the $14–15 per barrel range, making it relatively costly oil to produce. To give one current example, Exxon, which is heavily involved in the exploitation of the new Sakhalin I oil fields, is projecting a profit margin of 14 percent assuming that it can sell oil for $19 per barrel; this would make Exxon's production costs approximately $16.60 per barrel.[21] As noted, today, at $21.50 per barrel, the Russian government's federal budget is in balance. At $18, reserves will have been exhausted and the budget will have to be redone. A price below $15 for a prolonged period of time will tend to undermine the government's capacity to fund its various domestic obligations, including military reform, pensions, and state wages, not to mention the government's ability to raise wages for the "civil service" and provide for the massive infrastructure needs to replace the disintegrating Soviet-era facilities. In any prolonged period in which oil prices stayed below $20 per barrel, "stagnation would gradually set in in the absence of significant improvements in other growth generators, that is, the overall business environment."[22] While the Russian system seems viable in providing only a quarter of its citizens with a chance for a reasonable life, one wonders if this viability can be sustained if that figure is cut in half or more (and this after having exhausted many of the reserves bequeathed by the Soviet years)?

### Point 9. Russia Might Not Recover

Even if such a calamity is avoided, it is far from axiomatic that a self-sustaining Russian recovery is inevitable. Factors affecting such a recovery include the following:

- Even greater economic crises in much of what should be Russia's economic hinterland within the CIS.
- The integration of Russia's most developed historical peripheries into non-Russian metropoles, that is, the economic and political gravitation

---

[20] Ebel, "Russian Energy and the Power of Oil."
[21] "Energy Giants Begin Tapping Sakhalin's Vast Oil and Gas Reserves," Agence France Presse, May 6, 2003. See also Ebel, "Russian Energy and the Power of Oil," passim.
[22] Kekic, "How Dependent is Growth on the Oil Price?"

of the Baltic region as well as East-Central Europe into the European Union and NATO (while the Caucasus and Central Asia are open to Western economic influence and the Russian Far East ponders the choice between a Moscow-centric stagnation or a risky economic integration into the Pacific Rim).

- The lack of adequate investment in Russia's human as well as physical infrastructure, which over time tends to deprive Russia of what had been thought to be one of the country's comparative advantages, that is, a labor force that is not only cheap but relatively well skilled. (For example, the average age of a scientist in the Russian Academy of Sciences now exceeds the figure for male life expectancy, at 59 compared to 58.9).[23]

Here are a few instances:

- Half of Russia's scientists are thought to be employed outside of their profession while the ranks of Russian science are simply not being replenished.
- Russia has been spending less than one-quarter of the G-7 norm on research and development as a percentage of GDP over the past decade.[24]
- By the end of the 1990s, Russia's capital stock was rapidly disappearing; capital investment was approaching 20 percent of 1990 levels, and although investment has increased 30 percent since 2000, it is still low by Russian historical standards and relevant international comparisons, at about 18 percent of GDP.[25] Prospects thus remain bleak for any broad-based Russian recovery, a view echoed by Russian President Putin in his 2003 State of the Nation speech.[26]
- The stock of foreign direct investment (FDI) in Russia since 1989 is just $30 billion, compared to $390 billion for China (the PRC excluding Hong Kong) and $185 billion for Brazil[27]; this stock of FDI is just over half the flow of FDI into China in any given year (at $53.5 billion for

---

[23] See the testimony of Russian Nobel Laureate Zhores Alferov in *JRL*, #7042, January 31, 2003, item #7.

[24] Oleg Kuzin, "Russian Society in Critical Condition," *Rosbalt*, April 25, 2003, at *JRL*, #7155, April 26, 2003, item #1.

[25] Hurst, "Russia Still Has a Hill To Climb To Win Investment Grade."

[26] Transcript of President's State of the Nation address.

[27] Julien Vercueil, "Opening Russia? Contemporary Foreign Trade," *Russia and Eurasian Review*, vol. 2, issue 4, February 18, 2003, at www.jamestown.org. The Russian State Statistics Committee places the figure for FDI stock in Russia as low as $19.594 billion, although the baseline year for measurement is not clear. Interfax (Moscow), May 19, 2003.

2003, although including Hong Kong would add more than $12 billion in the same year).[28]

- The several billion dollars per year in direct investment – Russian as well as foreign – has gone mainly into areas that are especially vulnerable to external variables (that is, world prices and exchange rates), for example, accelerating recovery of oil and consumer perishables, such as food, tobacco, and beer production, and hardly any investment in Russian industrial manufacturing.[29] Much less appears to have gone into intensive new oil exploration – indeed, paradoxically, the aggressive recovery operations from existing fields, while increasing production in the short term, actually shorten the life of the field itself.[30] Moreover, investment in consumer perishables is a fragile thing in light of the secular appreciation of the ruble against the dollar and Euro; gradually, foreign food imports are becoming cheaper compared to Russian items.

- Finally, when considered against the magnitude of investment requirements, the current flow of domestic as well as foreign investment may be adequate to prevent an utter collapse in the enclave economy but insufficient to generate a broad-based recovery that could move Russia away from energy dependence. Estimates for the oil and gas sectors are for a minimum of $10 billion per year in direct investment over the next twenty years (compared to a fraction of that today); in the electricity sector, the figure is $6 billion per year over the next ten years (compared to the current $2 billion). Similar sums and ratios apply to other key infrastructure items such as telecommunications, roads, railroads, ports, and education.[31]

The cumulative effects of these massive investment deficits are that even under the most favorable circumstances, Russia's return to world power status is a matter of decades while Russia's effective collapse as a

[28] *Wall Street Journal*, January 15, 2004, at www.wsj.com.
[29] Stanislav Menshikov, "Oil on the Move," *Moscow Tribune*, February 14, 2003, at www.tribune.ru.
[30] Rosbalt (Moscow), February 17, 2004, in *JRL*, #8071, February 17, 2004, item no. 9, at www.cdi.org; Jeanne Whalen, "New Force in Energy Markets: Russian Oil Tycoon's Ambitions," *Wall Street Journal*, May 16, 2003, p. A6.
[31] "Education in Russia Needs USD 1.5 Billion by 2004 To Avert Degradation," Rosbalt, April 26, 2003, at *JRL*, #7053, February 8, 2003, item no. 17; Guy Chazan, "Russia Is Likely To Start Liberalizing Its Electricity Sector This Week," *Wall Street Journal*, February 13, 2003, p. A10.; Sarah Karush, "Russia's Heating System Is in Collapse," Associated Press (Sudogda, Russia), February 10, 2003, at *JRL*, #7056, February 11, 2003, item no. 1.

functioning state could happen at virtually any time within the next ten years. The level of investment growth even since 1999 is simply inadequate for an economy in which the average age of industrial equipment and major infrastructure – including nuclear weapons infrastructure – now approaches thirty years.[32]

WTO accession is unlikely to improve this situation, as Russian manufacturing stands to lose the most from Russian adherence to WTO rules, if in fact they can be enforced in the Russian setting.[33] Nor do prospects for Russian arms exports look quite as bright after the recent war in Iraq (these bring in revenues of $4.5–5 billion per year).

### Point 10. A Narrow Foundation of State Authority

The Russian political system remains narrowly and superficially institutionalized, without the advantages of the old mobilizational party-state or the organizational efficiencies of accountable and therefore legitimate democracies. A neopatrimonial state within the framework of façade democracy is being consolidated, as in Romania and Serbia under Ion Iliescu and Slobodan Milosevic, respectively. The latent fragility of the Russian political system renders the federal center vulnerable should the terms of trade on the global oil market suddenly turn for the worse. We could then see a return to the situation immediately after the August 1998 crash, when most state power, including control over substantial parts of the armed forces, was wrested from the federal center by regional barons who, unlike the center, were able to pay state officials. Putin's ability to maneuver among the "oligarchs," such as it is, depends on a steady stream of oil and gas revenues into state coffers. Russia's rich cannot plausibly threaten to bring the government down by their financial decisions – as they frequently did under Yelstin – when world oil prices are high and the government is relatively flush with cash.[34] A steady decline in world

---

[32] According to former Prime Minister Yevgeny Primakov, at *JRL*, #7060, February 13, 2003, item #11.

[33] Harry G. Broadman and David Tarr, "Russia's Path to WTO Accession: Prospects and Impacts," paper delivered to the joint Center for Strategic and International Studies (CSIS) / National Defense University (NDU) Seminar on Sources and Limits of Russian Power, March 26, 2003.

[34] This point was underscored by Vladimir Mau, rector of the Russian Institute of the National Economy, at a conference on Russia and Europe organized by the Norwegian Institute of International Affairs, Oslo, October 11, 2002. For a plausible Russian political analysis, see Vyacheslav Nikonov, "Putinizm" [Putinism], in idem, *Sovremennaya Rossiyskaya Politika* [Contemporary Russian Politics] (Moscow: OLMA-PRESS, 2003), pp. 29–43.

oil prices could well change the balance between state and finance chiefs, to the distinct disadvantage of the former. On the other hand, high commodity prices in export-dependent states such as Russia have tended to work against the development of rule-based institutional regimes that are a prerequisite for any broad-based and sustained Russian economic recovery.[35]

### Point 11. A Pragmatic Nationalist Consensus in Foreign Policy

Russia retains a "pragmatic nationalist" consensus about the nature of its foreign policy, even while almost all of the presumptive sympathy for the United States has evaporated from among Russian foreign and security policy elites and part of the population. A profound suspicion – at best, incomprehension – of U.S. motives has sunk in, leaving many to wonder whether the United States does not in fact desire to see a weak Russia as the best guarantee of U.S. interests being served. While Russian elites understand that the bulk – and it is a growing bulk, both absolutely and relatively – of Russia's foreign economic activity will remain within the framework of Russian-EU trade,[36] they also seem to understand that there is no substitute for a working relationship with the United States in respect to Russia's broad international security interests. While many may not like this, they understand that it has an "objective" dimension that they cannot wish away.[37]

Population trends probably support this view, in that, while a declining Russian population is becoming increasingly non-Russian (the Muslim and Chinese population will increase significantly in coming decades), the ethnic Russian population is becoming more European, both territorially as Russians out-migrate from Siberia and as they become more entwined

---

[35] Martin and Subramanian, "Addressing the Natural Resource Curse."

[36] The EU accounted for fully 44 percent of Russian trade outside the Commonwealth of Independent States (CIS) area. Bilateral Russian trade with Germany alone amounted to $14.6 billion, compared to $7 billion for the United States. Russian–Chinese trade amounted to $9.2 billion. See the letter of Roland Nash, Head of Research at Renaissance Capital, Moscow, in *Wall Street Journal*, April 2, 2003, p. A15. See also Philip Hanson, "Joining in But Not Signing Up? Russia's Economic 'Integration' Into Europe," *Russia and Eurasia Review*, vol. 2, issue 6, March 18, 2003, at www.jamestown.org.

[37] Sergei Karaganov, "Novye vyzovy bezopasnosti i rossiyskaya politika" [New security challenges and Russian policy], in Yvacheslav Nikonov, ed., *Sovremennaya Rossiyskaya Politika* [Contemporary Russian politics] (Moscow: OLMA-PRESS, 2003), pp. 185–97; Fyodor Burlatskiy, "Mirovoye Pravitel'stvo" [World governance], in IMEMO, ed., *God Planety: 2003* [World annual: 2003] (Moscow: Ekonomika, 2003), pp. 24–8.

with European economic forces.[38] At the same time, these trends increase the financial pressure on the Russian government in that emigrants tend to be among the best-educated and highly skilled whereas immigrants, Russians included, tend to be at the lower end of the educational and skills spectrum.[39] In any event, a declining population in deteriorating health underscores the unavailability of extensive labor resources for future growth, declining domestic demand and a corresponding increase in the importance of foreign trade, and the unviability of a mass-based draft army.

**Point 12. A Russian Implosion Is Not Inevitable But Cannot Be Excluded**
In this light, the most important projection from Russian domestic forces on Russia's world position ten years' hence is that a destabilizing implosion of the Russian state cannot be excluded as a possible, and not merely imaginable, outcome. To the extent that this is so, the primary task of international security is (a) to address the structural economic conditions that continue to make this outcome possible, that is, the fragility of Russia's dependence on volatile world oil markets; and (b) to prepare for the worst if economic insurance fails, by reinforcing the insulation between Russia's multiple WMD archipelagoes and the latent fragility of the Russian state. Specifically, this entails the following:

- Addressing the structural economic conditions that continue to make this outcome possible. Elements of such an approach could include, at a minimum, a focused international diplomacy to maintain world oil prices at a level no less than about $20 per barrel. Such a floor would establish a reasonable price for producers and consumers and buy time for the Russian state to develop a more stable longer-term economic and political foundation. More ambitiously, the G-8 states (now including Russia) might develop more institutionalized measures, such as (a) a negotiated price range for the sale of Russian oil; (b) forgiveness of the bulk of Soviet-era debt in exchange for the accelerated repayment of post-Soviet era obligations; (c) a special fund, like Norway's, that would accumulate energy surpluses to be allocated to indispensable infrastructure and developmental needs and not simply, as is the case

---

[38] "Russian Society in Critical Condition," Rosbalt, April 25, 2003, at *JRL*, #7155, April 26, 2003, item #1.
[39] Harley Balzer, "Demography and Democracy in Russia: Human Capital Challenges to Democratic Consolidation," *Demokratizatsiya*, vol. 11, item #1, Winter 2003, at www.undp.sk/files/HIV%20AIDS%20Annex%202.pdf.

with the government's current fund, to cover unanticipated expenses.[40]
To work properly, given reasonable skepticism about the integrity of
likely Russian supervisors, such an arrangement would have to be mul-
tilateralized, perhaps within a Russia-EU management framework.

- Preparing for the worst if economic insurance fails, by reinforcing the
  insulation between Russia's multiple WMD archipelagoes and the latent fragility of the Russian state. At heart, this means building on
  the Nunn-Lugar approach to Cooperative Threat Reduction to mul-
  tilateralize effective control over nuclear and other weapons of mass
  destruction, as well as the related production cycles that make them
  possible. Such an approach would involve several steps:
  - Reviewing policies that reinforce Russian reliance on nuclear
    weapons (inclusion of former Soviet republics in NATO, degrees of
    alert status, separation of warheads from weapons, and so on).
  - Reinforcing Nunn-Lugar measures to maximize short-term security.
    This would be sufficient so long as world oil prices remain relatively
    high or the Russian economy diversifies dramatically. Note that this
    approach implies the continued integrity of the Russian state.
  - Beginning to recast the nuclear arms control regime in the direction of
    the original Baruch Plan so as to address the problem of nuclear (and
    WMD) control when national stability cannot be taken for granted.
    In other words, the Russian reminder that nuclear powers may not
    be stable polities calls for the effective internationalization of control
    over nuclear energy in its military as well as civilian applications. This
    could be accomplished within the framework of the new Russia–
    NATO relationship and could make Russia a true partner of NATO.
    For this approach to be politically palatable, the United States would
    have to submit to the same range of control measures.

While such proposals may now seem far-fetched, are the premises upon
which they are based equally so? If not, then the question becomes, do
we wish to invest in prevention now, when there is time and space to do
so, or rather to risk paying a much higher price should political authority
decompose in what remains a nuclear superpower? Such a decomposition
is of course not inevitable; it is merely possible, and not as a fantasy
of the imagination but as one logical outcome of currently recognizable
factors and trends. Political calendars being what they are, we should be

[40] The current fund equals about 2 percent of Russian GDP. Andrius Vilkancas, "Russia
To Run Budget Surplus, Reserve Fund in 2004–5," Reuters (Moscow), April 29, 2003.

surprised if leaders invest significant resources now to prevent an indirect threat from possibly emerging within the decade. Yet given the resources already invested in preventive military operations in Iraq, where the threat was by any measure much less worrisome, failure to invest relatively cheap economic and political resources to prevent a possible Russian meltdown suggests a willingness to tolerate risk that would seem to render the Iraqi operation itself inexplicable.

# Select Bibliography

## I. Internet Sources

American Chamber of Commerce in Russia, at www.amcham.ru.
Carnegie Endowment for International Peace, Russia Program, at www.carnegie.ru.
Goskomstat [Russian State Statistical Committee], at www.goskomstat.ru.
International Monetary Fund, at www.imf.org.
Johnson's Russia List, at www.cdi.org.
Prime-Tass business news agency, at www.prime-tass.ru.
Radio Free Europe/Radio Liberty Research Institute, at www.refrl.org.
Rosbalt news agency, at www.rosbalt.ru.
Russian and Eurasian Review, at www.jamestown.org.
Russian Ministry of Finance, at www.minfin.ru.
United Nations Conference on Trade and Development, at www.unctad.org.
U.S. Central Intelligence Agency, at www.cia.gov/cia/publications/factbook.
U.S. Department of State, at www.state.gov.
U.S.–Russia Business Council, at www.usrbc.org.
World Bank, at www.worldbank.org.
World Press Service, at www.wps.ru.
www.strana.ru (web-based Russian news service).

## II. Newspapers

*Economist* (London, weekly)
*Financial Times* (London)
*Finansovaya Izvestiya* (Moscow)
*Frankfurter Allgemeine Zeitung*
*International Herald Tribune* (Paris)
*Izvestiya* (Moscow)
*Le Monde* (Paris)
*Moscow Times*

*Moscow Tribune*
*Neue Zuercher Zeitung* (Zurich)
*New York Times*
*Nezavisimaya Gazeta* (Moscow)
*Rossiya* (Moscow)
*Rossiyskaya Gazeta* (Moscow)
*Segodnya* (Moscow)
*St. Petersburg Times*
*Sueddeutsche Zeitung* (Munich)
*Wall Street Journal*
*Washington Post*


### III. Serial Publications: Reference

*Country Forecast for Russia* (London: Economist Intelligence Unit, annual in July).
*Country Reports on Human Rights Practices* (Washington, DC: U.S. Department of
   State, annual).
*Financial Times Annual Survey: Russia* (London: annual in April).
*God Planety* [World Annual] (Moscow: IMEMO, annual).
*Handbook of World Statistics* (Geneva: UNCTAD, annual).
*The Military Balance* (London: IISS, annual).
*Nations in Transit* (New York: Freedom House, annual).
*Russian Economic Report* (Washington, DC: World Bank, annual in August).
SIPRI Yearbook (Stockholm: Stockholm International Peace Research Institute,
   (SIPRI) annual).
*Sotsial'noye Polozheniye i Uroven' Zhizni Naseleniya Rossii* [The social condition and
   standard of living of the Russian population] (Moscow: Goskomstat, annual).
*Studien der Bundesinstitut fuer ostwissenschaftliche und internationale Studien* [Studies
   of the Federal Institute for East European and International Studies] (Berlin:
   weekly).


### IV. Serial Publications: Scholarly Journals

*ACE: Analysis of Current Events*
*Archives Europeenes de Sociologie*
*Demokratizatsiya*
*Ekonomika i Zhizn'*
*Europe-Asia Studies*
*Finance and Development*
*Foreign Affairs*
*Foreign Policy*
*Gosudartsvo i Pravo*
*Herodote* (Lyons)
*International Affairs* (Moscow)
*Internationale Politik*
*International Security*
*Mezhdunarodnaya Zhizn'*

*Ost und West: Politik und Wirtschaft in GUS und Baltikum*
*Petroleum Review*
*Post-Soviet Affairs*
*Post-Soviet Geography and Economics*
*Pro et Contra*
*RFE-RL Research Report*, at www.rferl.org
*Russian Review*
*Slavic Review*
*Sotsiologicheskiye Issledovaniya*
*Svobodnaya Mysl'*
*Transitions Online* (Prague), at www.tol.cz
*Voprosy Ekonomiki*
*Voprosy Istorii*


## V. Literature: Books, and Such

Adelman, Johnathan. *Torrents of Spring*. New York: McGraw-Hill, 1994.

Andrianov, A. D. *Rossiya v mirovoy ekonomike* [Russia in the world economy]. Moscow: Vlados, 1999.

Applebaum, Anne. *Gulag: A History*. New York: Doubleday, 2003.

Arbatov, Alexei, Kaiser, Karl, and Legvold, Robert, eds. *Russia and the West: The 21st Century Security Environment*. Armonk, NY: M. E. Sharpe, 1999.

Aslund, Anders. *How Russia Became a Market Economy*. Washington, DC: Brookings Institution, 1995.

Balzer, Harley, ed. *Russia's Missing Middle Class*. Armonk, NY: M. E. Sharpe, 1996.

Bard, V. S. *Investitsionnye problemy rossiyskoy ekonomiki* [Investment problems in the Russian economy]. Moscow: Ekzamen, 2000.

Bater, James. *The Soviet Scene: A Geographical Perspective*. London: Edward Arnold, 1989.

Beissinger, Mark. *Nationalist Mobilization and the Collapse of the Soviet State*. Cambridge, UK: Cambridge University Press, 2002.

Beissinger, Mark and Young, Crawford, eds. *Beyond State Crisis? Post-Colonial Africa and Central Eurasia in Comparative Perspective*. Washington, DC: Woodrow Wilson Center Press, 2002.

Besancon, Alain. *Present sovietique et passé russe* [Soviet present and Russian past]. Paris: Le Livre de Poche, 1980.

Bettleheim, Charles. *Class Struggles in the USSR*. Two volumes (1917–23, 1924–30). London: Harvester Press, 1977, 1979, resp.

Birman, Igor. *Ya – Ekonomist* [I am an economist]. Moscow: Vremya, 2001.

Birman, Igor and Piyasheva, Larisa. *Statistics of the Level of Living of the Russian Population*. Washington, DC: U.S. Department of the Treasury, Office of Technical Assistance, 1997.

Blackwell, William. *The Beginnings of Russian Industrialization*. Princeton, NJ: Princeton University Press, 1968.

———, ed. *Russian Economic Development from Peter the Great to Stalin*. New York: New Viewpoints, 1974.

Brown, Archie and Shevtsova, Lilia, eds. *Gorbachev, Yeltsin, Putin: Political Leadership in Russia's Transition*. Washington, DC: Carnegie Endowment for International Peace, 2001.

Brucan, Silviu. *Social Change in Russia and Eastern Europe: From Party Hacks to Nouveaux Riches*. Westport, CT: Praeger, 1998.

Bunce, Valerie. *Subversive Institutions: The Design and Destruction of Socialism and the State*. Cambridge, UK: Cambridge University Press, 1999.

Carrere d'Encausse, Helene. *La Russie inachevée* [The unfinished Russia]. Paris: Fayard, 2000.

Chua, Amy. *World on Fire: How Exporting Free Market Democracy Spreads Ethnic Hatred and Global Instability*. New York: Doubleday, 2003.

Cohen, Stephen. *Failed Crusade: America and the Tragedy of Post-Communist Russia*. New York: W. W. Norton, 2000.

Colton, Timothy. *Transitional Citizens: Voters and What Influences Them in the New Russia*. Cambridge, MA: Harvard University Press, 2000.

Conquest, Robert. *Harvest of Sorrow*. New York: Oxford University Press, 1986.
———. *The Great Terror: A Reassessment*. London: Hutchinson, 1990.

Corvisier, Andre. *Armées et societés en Europe de 1494 à 1789* [Militaries and societies in Europe from 1494 to 1789]. Paris: Presses Universitaires de Paris, 1976.

Courtois, Stephane, ed. *Le Livre Noir du Communisme* [The black book of Communism]. Paris: Robert Laffont, 1997.

Dallinn, David and Nicolaevsky, Boris J. *Forced Labor in Soviet Russia*. London: Hollis and Carter, 1948.

Desai, Padma and Idson, Todd. *Work without Wages: Russia's Non-Payment Crisis*. New York: Columbia University Press, 2000.

Eckstein, Harry, Fleron, Frederic J., Jr., Hoffmann, Erik P., and Reisinger, William M. *Can Democracy Take Root in Post-Soviet Russia?* Lanham, MD: Rowman and Littlefield, 1998.

*Ekonomicheskaya Geografiya* [Economic geography]. Moscow: Ekzamen, 2003.

Ertman, Thomas. *Birth of the Leviathan: Building States and Regimes in Medieval and Early Modern Europe*. Cambridge, UK: Cambridge University Press, 1997.

Fainsod, Merle. *How Russia Is Ruled*. Cambridge, MA: Harvard University Press, 1953.

Figes, Orlando. *A People's Tragedy: A History of the Russian Revolution*. New York: Viking, 1997.

Finker, Kurt. *Stauffenberg und der 20 Juli 1944* [Stauffenberg and the Conspiracy of July 20, 1944]. Berlin: UnionVerlag, 1971.

Fogel, Robert William and Engerman, Stanley L. *Time on the Cross: The Economics of American Negro Slavery*. Boston: Little, Brown, 1974.

Fuller, William. *Strategy and Power in Russia, 1600–1914*. New York: Free Press, 1992.

Furet, Francois. *Le passé d'une illusion: Essai sur l'idée communiste au xx-e siecle* [The passing of an illusion: An essay on the communist idea in the twentieth century]. Paris: Robert Laffont/Calmann Levy, 1995.

Gambetta, Diego. *La mafia siciliana* [The Sicilian Mafia]. Turin: Einaudi, 1993.

Gellner, Ernst. *Conditions of Liberty: Civil Society and Its Rivals*. New York: Allen Lane/Penguin Press, 1994.

Gerschenkron, Alexander. *Economic Backwardness in Historical Perspective*. Cambridge, MA: Harvard University Press, 1962.

Gladkin, Yu. N., Dobrosok, V. A., Semenyonov, S. P. *Sotsial'no-ekonomicheskaya geografiya Rossii* [A social-economic geography of Russia]. Moscow: Gardariki, 2000.

Goldgeier, James and McFaul, Michael. *Power and Purpose: U.S. Policy toward Russia after the Cold War*. Washington, DC: Brookings Institution Press, 2003.

Goldhagen, Daniel. *Hitler's Willing Executioners*. New York: Alfred A. Knopf, 1996.

Goldman, Marshall I. *The Piratization of Russia: Russian Reform Goes Awry*. London: Routledge, 2003.

Greenfield, Leah. *Nationalism: Five Roads to Modernity*. Cambridge, MA: Harvard University Press, 1992.

Grinevskiy, Oleg. *Tysyachya dnei s Nikita Sergeyevichim* [One thousand days with Nikita Khrushchev]. Moscow: VAGRIUS, 1998.

Gustafson, Thane. *Capitalism Russian Style*. Cambridge, UK: Cambridge University Press, 1999.

Hardt, John, ed. *Russia's Uncertain Economic Future: Compendium of Papers Submitted by the Joint Economic Committee of the U.S. Congress*. Washington, DC: U.S. Government Printing Office, 2002.

Hauner, Milan. *What Is Asia to Us? Russia's Asia Heartland Yesterday and Today*. Boston: Unwin Hyman, 1990.

Hedlund, Stefan. *Russia's "Market" Economy: A Bad Case of Predatory Capitalism*. London: UCL Press, 1999.

Hellbeck, Jochen, ed. *Tagebuch aus Moskau, 1931–1939* [Moscow Diary, 1931–1989]. Munich: DTV Dokumente, 1996.

Heller, Michel. *Histoire de la Russie et de son empire* [A history of Russia and its empire]. Paris: Plon, 1997.

Hill, Fiona and Gaddy, Clifford. *The Siberian Curse: How Communist Planners Left Russia out in the Cold*. Washington, DC: Brookings Institution Press, 2003.

Holloway, David. *Stalin and the Bomb*. New Haven, CT: Yale University Press, 1994.

Hough, Jerry. *The Logic of Economic Reform in Russia*. Washington, DC: Brookings Institution Press, 2001.

Huntington, Samuel P. *Political Order in Changing Societies*. New Haven, CT: Yale University Press, 1968.

———. *The Third Wave: Democratization in the Late Twentieth Century*. Norman, OK: University of Oklahoma Press, 1991.

Inozemtsev, V. L. *Za desyat' let: k kontseptsii postekonomicheskogo obshchestva* [Ten years later: toward the concept of posteconomic society]. Moscow: Academia, 1998.

*Investitsii v Rossii, 2003* [Investments in Russia, 2003]. Moscow: Goskomstat, 2003.

Kapuscinski, Ryszard. *Imperium*. Paris: Feux Croises/Plon, 1994.

Kennedy, Paul. *The Rise and Fall of the Great Powers*. New York: Random House, 1987.

Klyamkin, Ilya and Shevtsova, Lilia. *The Omnipotent and Impotent Government: The Evolution of the Political System in Post-Communist Russia*. Moscow: Carnegie Moscow Center, 1999.

Knight, Amy. *Spies without Cloaks*. Princeton, NJ: Princeton University Press, 1996.

Kogon, Eugen, Langbein, Hermann, and Rueckerl, Adalbert. *Les chambers à gaz: secrets d'état* [The gas chambers: A state secret]. Paris: Editions de Minuit, 1984.

Kollman, Nancy Shields. *Kinship and Politics: The Making of the Muscovite Political System, 1345–1547*. Stanford, CA: Stanford University Press, 1987.

Kotkin, Stephen. *Magnetic Mountain: Stalinism as a Civilization*. Berkeley, CA: University of California Press, 1995.

———. *Armageddon Averted*. Oxford, UK: Oxford University Press, 2001.

Kurys, N. V. *Inostrannye Investitsii: Rossiyskaya Istoriya* [Foreign investment in Russian history]. St. Petersburg: Yuridicheskiy Tsentr, 2003.

Lane, David and Ross, Cameron. *The Transition from Communism to Capitalism: Ruling Elites from Gorbachev to Yeltsin*. New York: St. Martin's, Press 1999.

LeDonne, John. *The Russian Empire and the World, 1700–1914*. New York: Oxford University Press, 1997.

Levi, Margaret. *Of Rule and Revenue*. Berkeley, CA: University of California Press, 1988.

Lewin, Moshe. *The Gorbachev Phenomenon: A Historical Interpretation*. London: Radius, 1988.

Lieven, Anatol. *Chechnya: Tombstone of Russian Power*. New Haven, CT: Yale University Press, 1998.

Lorrain, Pierre. *La mystérieuse ascension de Vladimir Poutine* [The mysterious rise of Vladimir Putin]. Monaco: Editions de Roche, 2000.

Lueke, Gabriele and Weber, Gustav. *So kommen Sie nach...Russland: Der Wirtschaftswegweiser fuer den Mittelstand* [Come to Russia: A Guide to the Russian Economy for the Small and Medium Businessperson]. Munich: PrimeVerlag, 2003.

Lukic, Reneo and Lynch, Allen C. *Europe from the Balkans to the Urals: The Disintegration of Yugoslavia and the USSR and International Politics*. New York: Oxford University Press, 1996.

Lynch, Allen C. *The Soviet Study of International Relations*. Cambridge, UK: Cambridge University Press, 1987.

———. *Does Russia Have a Democratic Future?* New York: Foreign Policy Association, 1997.

MacIver, R. M. *The Modern State*. London: Oxford University Press, 1926.

Malia, Martin. *Comprendre la revolution russe* [Understanding the Russian Revolution]. Paris: Editions du Seuil, 1980.

———. *The Soviet Tragedy: A History of Socialism in Russia, 1917–1991*. New York: Free Press, 1994.

———. *Russia under Western Eyes: From the Bronze Horseman to the Lenin Mausoleum*. Cambridge, MA: The Belknap Press of Harvard University Press, 1999.

Margolina, Sonia. *Die Fesseln der Vergangenheit* [The Chains of the Past]. Frankfurt am Main, 1993.

———. *Russland. Die nichtzivile Gesellschaft* [Russia: The Uncivil Society]. Hamburg: Rowohr, 1994.

Matlock, Jack F., Jr. *Autopsy of an Empire: The Ambassador's Account of the Collapse of the Soviet Union.* New York: Random House, 1995.

Mayer, Arno. *The Persistence of the Old Regime: Europe to the Great War.* London: Croom Helm, 1980.

McFaul, Michael and Petrov, Nikolai. "The Changing Function of Elections in Russian Politics," in *Russia after Communism.* Anders Aslund and Martha Brill Olcott, eds. Washington, DC: Carnegie Endowment for International Peace.

Migdal, Joel. *Strong States, Weak Societies: State–Society Relations and State Capabilities in the Third World.* Princeton, NJ: Princeton University Press, 1988.

———. *State in Society: Studying How States and Societies Transform and Constitute One Another.* Cambridge, UK: Cambridge University Press, 2001.

Mizelle, Peter Christopher. *"Battle with Famine": Soviet Relief and the Tatar Republic, 1921–1922.* Ph.D. dissertation, University of Virginia: Department of History, 2002.

Moore, Barrington. *Social Origins of Dictatorship and Democracy: Lord and Peasant in the Making of the Modern World.* Boston: Beacon Press, 1966.

Motyl, Alexander J. *Dilemmas of Independence: Ukraine after Totalitarianism.* New York: Council on Foreign Relations, 1993.

Mrktchyan, M. T. et al. *Sostoyaniye i protivorechiya ekonomicheskoy reformy* [The condition and tensions within economic reform]. Moscow: Ekonomika, 1998.

Nikonov, Vyacheslav, ed. *Sovremennaya rossiyskaya politika* [Contemporary Russian politics]. Moscow: OLMA-PRESS, 2003.

Nolte, Ernst. *La Guerre Civile Européene, 1917–1945* [The European Civil War, 1917–1945]. Paris: Editions des Syrtes, 2000.

Nolte, Hans-Heinrich. *Kleine Geschichte Russlands* [A Short History of Russia]. Stuttgart: Philipp Reclam jun., 1998.

North, Douglass C. *Institutions, Institutional Change and Economic Reform.* Cambridge, UK: Cambridge University Press, 1990.

Orlova, E. P. *Investitsii* [Investments]. Moscow: OMEGA-L, 2003.

Orwell, George. *Collected Essays.* London: Secker and Warburg, 1961.

Paar, Hans. *Dilettanten gegen Hitler: Offiziere in Widerstand: ihre Worten, ihre Taten* [Amateurs against Hitler: Officers in Resistance: Their Words and Deeds]. Preussische Oldendorf: K. W. Schultz, 1985.

Parshev, A. N. *Pochemu Rossiya ne Amerika* [Why Russia is not America]. Moscow: Krymskiy Most, 1999.

Petro, Nicolai. *The Rebirth of Russian Democracy.* Cambridge, MA: Harvard University Press, 1995.

Pipes, Richard. *The Formation of the Soviet Union.* Cambridge, MA: Harvard University Press, 1954.

———. *Russia under the Old Regime.* Second edition. London: Penguin Books, 1995.

Poe, Marshall. *The Russian Moment in World History.* Princeton, NJ: Princeton University Press, 2003.

Pokrovskiy, Mikhail. *Russkaya Istoriya* [Russian history]. Two volumes. St. Petersburg: Poligon, 2002.

Polyakov, Yu. A. *Lyudskiye poteri v period vtoroy mirovoy voyny* [Human losses in the Second World War]. St. Petersburg: Institut Rossiyskoy Akademii Istorii RAN, 1995.

Primakov, Yevgeniy. *Gody v bol'shoy politike* [Years in national politics]. Moscow, 2000.

Pryce-Jones, David. *The Strange Death of the Soviet Empire*. New York: Henry Holt, 1995.

Przeworski, Adam. *Democracy and the Market: Political and Economic Reform in Eastern Europe and Latin America*. Cambridge, UK: Cambridge University Press, 1991.

Putin, Vladimir. *Ot pervogo litsa: Razgovory s Vladimirom Putinom* [First person: conversations with Vladimir Putin]. Moscow: Vagrius, 2000.

Putnam, Robert. *Making Democracy Work*. Cambridge, MA: Harvard University Press, 1993.

Radvanyi, Jean. *La nouvelle Russie* [The new Russia]. Paris: Armand Colin, 2000.

Ragsdale, Hugh. *The Russian Tragedy: The Burden of History*. Armonk, NY: M. E. Sharpe, 1996.

Rahr, Alexander. *Wladimir Putin: Der "Deutsche" im Kreml* [Vladimir Putin: The "German" in the Kremlin]. Germany: Universitas, 2000.

Reddaway, Peter and Glinsky, Dmitri. *The Tragedy of Russian Reform: Market Bolshevism versus Democracy*. Washington, DC: U.S. Institute of Peace, 2001.

Riess, Curt. *The Berlin Story*. New York: Dial Press, 1952.

Rose, Richard and Munro, Ross. *Elections without Order: Russia's Challenge to Vladimir Putin*. Cambridge, UK: Cambridge University Press, 2001.

Rossman, Jeffrey. *Worker Resistance under Stalin: Class and Gender in the Textile Mills of the Ivanovo Industrial Region, 1928–1932*. Ph.D. dissertation, University of California, Berkeley: Department of History, 1997.

Ruge, Gerd. *Sibirisches Tagebuch* [Siberian Diary]. Munich: Knaur, 2000.

Samuylov, S. M., ed. *Rossiyskaya tsivilizatsiya: cherez ternii k zvyozdam* [Russian civilization: from the depths to the stars]. Moscow: Veche, 2000.

Satter, David. *Darkness at Dawn: The Rise of the Russian Criminal State*. New Haven, CT: Yale University Press, 2003.

Schneider, Eberhard. *Das politische System der russischen Foederation* [The political system of the Russian Federation]. Wiesbaden: Westdeutscher Verlag, 1999.

Scott, James C. *Seeing Like a State: How Certain Schemes to Improve the Human Condition Have Failed*. New Haven, CT: Yale University Press, 1998.

Shamberg, Vladimir. *Soviet Defense Industries: History and Implications after the Collapse of the Soviet Union*. Colorado Springs, CO: U.S. Air Force Academy, June 2000.

Shevtsova, Lilia. *Putin's Russia*. Washington, DC: Carnegie Endowment for International Peace, 2003.

Silverman, Bertram and Yanowitch, Murray. *New Rich, New Poor: Winners and Losers on the Russian Road to Capitalism*. Armonk, NY: M. E. Sharpe, 1997.

Simes, Dmitri. *After the Collapse: Russia Seeks its Place as a Great Power*. New York: Simon and Schuster, 1999.

Skocpol, Theda. *States and Social Revolutions*. Cambridge, UK: Cambridge University Press, 1979.

Skopin, Yu. A. *Ekonomicheskaya Geografiya Rossii* [An economic geography of Russia]. Moscow: Prospekt, 2003.

Smirnov, Pavel S. *Russia's National Security: Trade Policy Issues*. Moscow: Consultbanker Publishing, 2002.

Solnick, Steven. *Stealing the State: Control and Collapse in Soviet Institutions*. Cambridge: Harvard University Press, 1998.

Solonevich, Ivan. *Rossiya v kontslagere* [Russia in a concentration camp]. Washington, DC, 1958.

Solzhenitsyn, Aleksandr I. *Pismo k vozhdyam Sovetskogo Soyuza* [Letter to the Soviet Leaders]. Paris: YMCA Press, 1973.

———. *Iz pod glyb* [From under the rubble]. Paris: YMCA Press, 1974.

Soto, Hernando de. *The Other Path: The Economic Answer to Terrorism*. New York: Harper and Row, 1999.

———. *The Mystery of Capital: Why Capitalism Triumphs in the West and Fails Everywhere Else*. New York: Basic Books, 2000.

Speer, Albert. *Errinerungen* [Memoirs]. Berlin: Propylaen Verlag, 1969.

Sperling, Valerie, ed. *Building the Russian State*. Boulder, CO: Westview Press, 2000.

Stiglitz, Joseph. *Globalization and Its Discontents*. New York: W. W. Norton, 2002.

Talbott, Strobe. *The Russia Hand: A Memoir of Presidential Diplomacy*. New York: Random House, 1992.

Taubman, William. *Khrushchev: The Man and His Era*. New York: W. W. Norton, 2003.

Thumann, Michael. *Das Lied von der russischen Erde: Moskaus Ringen um Einheit und Groesse* [The Song of the Russian Earth: Moscow's Struggle for Unity and Greatness]. Stuttgart: Deutsche-Verlags Anstalt, 2002.

Tilly, Charles. *Coercion, Capital and European States, AD 990–1992*. Cambridge, UK: Blackwell, 1992.

Tilly, Charles and Blockmans, Wim P., eds. *Cities and the Rise of States in Europe, AD 1000–1800*. Boulder, CO: Westview Press, 1989.

Tompson, William. *Khrushchev: A Political Life*. New York: St. Martin's Press, 1995.

Trotsky, Leon. *The Revolution Betrayed: What Is the Soviet Union and Where Is It Heading?* New York: Pioneer, 1945.

Tumarkin, Nina. *The Living and the Dead: The Rise and Fall of the Cult of World War II in Russia*. Armonk, NY: Basic Books, 1992.

Ulam, Adam B. *Russia's Failed Revolutions: From the Decembrists to the Dissidents*. New York: Basic Books, 1981.

United Nations Development Program. *2000 Human Development Program for the Russian Federation*. March 2000, at *www.undp.ru*.

Vassiltchikov, Marie. *The Berlin Diaries, 1940–1945*. London: Chatto and Windus, 1985.

Vernadsky, George. *Political and Diplomatic History of Russia*. Boston: Little, Brown, 1936.

Voskressenski, Alexei. *Russia and China: A Theory of Interstate Relations.* London: RoutledgeCurzon, 2003.

Wedel, Janine. *Collison and Collusion: Western Aid to Eastern Europe.* New York: St. Martin's Press, 1998.

Wesson, Robert. *The Russian Dilemma: A Political and Geopolitical View.* New York: Praeger, 1986.

White, Stephen P. *Russia's New Politics: The Management of Post-Communist Society,* Cambridge UK: Cambridge University Press, 2000.

White, Stephen, McAllister, Ian, and Rose, Richard. *How Russia Votes.* Chatham Press, 1997.

Yakovlev, Aleksandr N. *Krestosev* [Sowers of graves]. Moscow: Vagrius, 2000.

———. *Omut pamyati* [Vortex of memory]. Moscow: Vagrius, 2000.

———. *A Century of Violence in Soviet Russia.* New Haven, CT: Yale University Press, 2002.

Yaney, George L. *The Systematization of Russian Government: Social Evolution in the Administration of Imperial Russia, 1711–1905.* Urbana, IL: University of Illinois Press, 1973.

Yergin, Daniel and Gustafson, Thane. *Russia 2010: And What It Means for the World – The CERA Report.* New York: Random House, 1993.

Zimmerman, William. *The Russian People and Foreign Policy.* Princeton, NJ: Princeton University Press, 2002.

## VI. Literature: Selected Articles and Book Chapters

Aslund, Anders. "Russia's Collapse," *Foreign Affairs,* September/October 1998, www.foreignaffairs.org.

———. "Social Problems and Policy in Postcommunist Russia," in *Sustaining the Transition: The Social Safety Net in Postcommunist Europe.* Ethan Kapstein and Michael Mandelbaum, eds. New York: Council on Foreign Relations, 1998, pp. 124–46.

Aslund, Anders and Dmitriev, Mikhail, "Economic Reform versus Rent Seeking," in *Russia after Communism.* Anders Aslund and Martha Brill Olcott, eds. Washington, DC: Carnegie Endowment for International Peace, 1999, www.ceip.org/people/as/russiaaftercom.html.

Bahry, Donna. "Rethinking the Social Roots of Perestroika," *Slavic Review,* Fall 1993, pp. 525–39.

Balzer, Harley. "Russia's Middle Classes," *Post-Soviet Affairs,* vol. 14, no. 2 (1998), pp. 165–85.

Cottrell, Robert. "Putin's Trap," *New York Review of Books,* December 4, 2003, www.nybooks.com/archives.

Ellman, Michael. "Soviet Repression Statistics: Some Comments," *Europe-Asia Studies,* vol. 54, no. 7 (November 2002), pp. 1151–72.

Ericson, Richard. "Economists and the Russian Transition," *Slavic Review,* vol. 57, no. 3 (Fall 1998), pp. 609–25.

Fainsod, Merle. "Bureaucracy and Modernization: The Russian and Soviet Case," in *Bureaucracy and Political Development.* Joseph LaPalombara, ed. Princeton, NJ: Princeton University Press, 1967, pp. 223–65.

Field, Mark G. "Health in Russia: the Regional and National Dimensions," in *Beyond the Monolith: The Emergence of Regionalism in Post-Soviet Russia.* Peter J. Stavrakis, ed. Washington, DC: Woodrow Wilson Center Press, 1997, pp. 165–80.

Frisby, Tanya. "The Rise of Organized Crime in Russia: Its Roots and Social Significance," *Europe-Asia Studies*, vol. 50, no. 1 (January 1998), pp. 27–49.

Hanson, Stephen and Kopstein, Jeffrey. "The Weimar/Russia Comparison," *Post-Soviet Affairs*, vol. 13, no. 3 (1997), pp. 252–83.

Kryshtanovskaya, Olga and White, Stephen. "Putin's Militocracy," *Post-Soviet Affairs*, vol. 19, no. 4 (October–December 2003), pp. 289–306.

Lynch, Allen C. "The Crisis of the State in Russia," *International Spectator*, April–June 1995, pp. 21–34.

———. "The Realism of Russian Foreign Policy," *Europe-Asia Studies*, vol. 53, no. 1 (January 2001), pp. 7–31.

———. "Dilemmas of Russian Economic Reform: Liberal Economics versus Illiberal Geography," *Europe-Asia Studies*, vol. 54, no. 1 (January 2002), pp. 31–49.

Mackinder, Halford J. "The Geographical Pivot of History," *The Geographial Journal*, vol. 23, no. 4 (1904), pp. 421–44.

Mastepanov, Alexei. "Main Points of Russia's Energy Strategy," *International Affairs* (Moscow), vol. 47, no. 2 (2001), www.in.mid.ru/bl.nsf/mnsdocmg.

Maurself, Per Botolf. "Divergence and Dispersion in the Russian Economy," *Europe-Asia Studies*, vol. 55, no. 8 (December 2003), pp. 1165–86.

Medvedev, Sergei. "Power, Space and Russian Foreign Policy," in *Understandings of Russian Foreign Policy.* Ted Hopf, ed. University Park, PA: State University Press, 1999, pp. 15–55

Mendelsohn, Sarah. "Democratic Assistance and Political Transition in Russia: Between Success and Failure," *International Security*, vol. 25, no. 4 (Spring 2001), pp. 68–106.

Millar, James. "The Little Deal: Brezhnev's Contribution to Acquisitive Socialism," *Slavic Review*, vol. 44, no. 4 (Winter 1985), pp. 694–706.

Milov, L. V. "Prirodno-klimaticheskiy factor i osobennosti rossiyskogo istoricheskogo protsessa" [The natural-climatic factor and particularities of the Russian historical process]. *Voprosy Istorii*, no. 4–5 (1992), pp. 37–56.

Naim, Moises. "Russia's Oily Future," *Foreign Policy*, January/February 2004, pp. 96–7.

North, Douglass C. "Economic Performance through Time," *American Economic Review*, vol. 84, no. 3 (1995), pp. 359–68.

Pavlova, I. V. "1937: Vybory kak mistifikatsiya, terror kak real'nost'" [1937: Elections as illusion, terror as reality], *Voprosy Istorii*, no. 10 (2003), pp. 19–37.

Remington, Thomas F. and Smith, Steven S. "The Development of Political Parties in Russia," *Legislative Studies Quarterly*, vol. 20, no. 4 (November 1995), pp. 457–89.

Rowney, Don K. "Center–Periphery Relations in Historical Perspective: State Administration in Russia," in *Beyond the Monolith: The Emergence of Regionalism in Post-Soviet Russia.* Peter J. Stavrakis, ed. Washington, DC: Woodrow Wilson Center Press, 1997, pp. 11–31

Rutland, Peter. "Russia in 2003," *Transitions Online*, at www.tol.cz.

Sala-i-Martin, Xavier and Subramanian, Arvind. "Addressing the Natural Resource Curse: An Illustration from Nigeria," National Bureau of Economic
Research, Working Paper 9804, June 2003, at www.nber.org/papers/w9804.

Scherrer, Jutta. "'Lasst die Toten ihre Toten begraben': Warum Russland von den
sowjetischen Massenverbrechen nichts wissen will [Let the Dead Bury Their
Dead: Why Russia Does Not Want to Know About Soviet Crimes Against
Humanity]," in *Der Rote Holocaust und die Deutschen: Die Debatte um das
"Schwarzbuch des Kommunismus"* [The Red Holocaust and the Germans: The
Debate over the "Black Book of Communism"] Horst Mueller, ed. Munich:
Piper Verlag, 1999, pp. 80–5.

Selyunin, Vasiliy and Khanin, Grigory. "Lukavaya tsifry" [Lies, damn lies, and
statistics], *Noviy Mir*, no. 2 (1987), pp. 181–201.

Shlapentokh, Vladimir. "Hobbes and Locke at Odds over Putin," *Europe-Asia
Studies*, vol. 55, no. 4 (November 2003), pp. 981–1008.

Stephan, Paul B. "Toward a Positive Theory of Privatization: Lessons from Soviet-
Type Economies," *International Review of Law and Economics*, vol. 16 (1996),
pp. 181–9.

Tabata, Shinichero. "The Great Russian Depression of the 1990's: Observations
on Causes and Implications," *Post-Soviet Geography and Economics*, vol. 41,
no. 6 (2000), pp. 389–98.

Tilly, Charles. "War Making and State Making as Organized Crime," in *Bringing the State Back In*. Peter B. Evans et al., eds. Cambridge, UK: Cambridge
University Press, 1985, pp. 169–91.

Ullman, Richard. "The United States and the World: An Interview with George
F. Kennan," *New York Review of Books*, August 12, 1999, www.nybooks.
com/archives.

Varese, Federico. "Is Sicily the Future of Russia?" *Archives Europeenes de Sociologie*, vol. 35 (1994), pp. 224–58.

Vernadsky, George. "The Mongol Impact on Russia," in *Readings in Russian Civilization*, volume I. Thomas Riha, ed. Chicago: University of Chicago Press,
1969, pp. 173–93.

# Index

abortion, Russian attitudes, 107
absolutism, 19, 86
    European compared to Russian, 31
Adamov, Yevgeny, 123
Adelman, Jonathan, 188
Afghanistan, 6
Africa, Russia compared to, 192–4
Agrarian Party, 145
agriculture, 168
    comparative productivity, 44, 224,
        227–8
Aksyonenko, Nikolai, 123
Aleksandr II, reforms, 23
Alfa financial group, 237
Alstom co., 216
Altai region, 231
anti-Americanism in Russia, 87, 240,
    247
Arbatov, Georgy, 62
arbitrage transactions, 79, 97
Arctic, Russian, 234–5
    compared to Canadian, 233
Aristotle, 170
Artem town, 217
Ash, Timothy Garton, 60
Aslund, Anders, 79
Auditing Commission, 110
Austro-Hungarian Empire, 24, 30
autocracy
    constrained, 7, 20, 34
    Russian, 25
Aven, Pyotr, 166

Baltic states, 52, 249
banking sector, 91, 218
Bater, James, 225, 230
Baturin, Yuri, 116
bauxite, costs, 231
Berezovsky, Boris, 73, 154–5, 162
Beria, Lavrenty, 62
Bettleheim, Charles, 77
Bolsheviks, 7, 9, 11, 28, 30, 48
Borodin, Pavel, 156
British Petroleum (BP), 80, 97
Brucan, Silviu, 72–3
Brzezinski, Zbigniew, 61
Buchanan, Sir George, 129
budget
    federal Russian, 14–15, 164, 196–7,
        199, 207, 217, 248
    Imperial Russian, 42
bureaucratization, 89, 98, 152
Bush, George H. W., 240
business: see small and medium-sized

Camessus, Michel, 82
Canada, Russia compared to, 224–5,
    233
capital
    controls, 238–9
    external transfers to Russia, 193
    flight, 90, 127, 218–20
    stock, comparative, 204
    stock, depreciation of 201, 203,
        249–50

269

*Index*